AGAINST THE GRAIN

THE HISTORY OF BUFFALO'S FIRST WARD

TIMOTHY BOHEN

To Tom,
I hope you enjoy the book!
Tim Bohen
9/15/12

Published August 2012 by Bohane Books, LLC

Designed by: Kristopher Miller
Editor: Phil Nyhuis
Author Photo: Amy Doyle
Photo on front cover: Collection of Buffalo and Erie County Historical Society, used by permission.

ISBN: 978-0-615-62052-7

For more information please visit: www.oldfirstward.com

Printed in Buffalo, New York by Petit Printing

To Timothy Bohane (1850-1915) and all the immigrants who settled in the First Ward, toiled in the hulls of grain ships and on the docks, and endured countless hardships in order to give us a better life.

TIMELINE OF EVENTS

1841   St. Patrick's Church Dedicated

1842   Joseph Dart Invents Steam Grain Elevator / Senecas Leave Buffalo Creek

1844   Tidal Wave Hits the Ward

1847   Bishop Timon Arrives

1856   Irish Migration Convention

1858   Sisters of Mercy Arrive

1859   St. Bridget's Church Founded

1862   155th Union Regiment Formed from First Ward

1866   Fenian Invasion of Canada

1880   Land League Convention in Buffalo

1892   William Sheehan Elected Lt. Governor of New York

1895   John Sheehan Becomes Tammany Hall Boss in New York City

1897   Seneca Streetcar Opens Migration to South Buffalo

1899   Strike of 1899 / First Ward Shuts Down Great Lakes Shipping

1900   William "Fingy" Conners Forms the Buffalo *Courier-Express*

1907   Our Lady of Perpetual Help Church Founded

1907   Great Storm of 1907

1918   Colonel William Donovan is the Most Decorated Soldier in U.S. History

1923   Algie McGuire Wins National Sculling Championship

1926   Michael Shea Opens "Shea's Buffalo"

1927   Jimmy Slattery Wins National Light Heavyweight Boxing Championship

1940   Opening of Commodore Perry Projects

1959   Opening of the St. Lawrence Seaway

1978   Jimmy Griffin Elected Mayor of Buffalo

2003   Grain Scoopers Unload Last Freighter

CONTENTS

INTRODUCTION

It was a rather innocent curiosity about the proper spelling of my Bohen family name that landed me in this unfamiliar place—the First Ward of Buffalo, New York. It proved to be fertile ground. As a rich history of this hidden away community, located just south of downtown Buffalo, began to reveal itself to me, the elusive spelling of my family name became less and less important.

I came to realize that this was a story that had to be told. Although there are already numerous books that include a chapter or essay on some aspect of Buffalo's First Ward, no one had devoted an entire nonfiction book to this important subject. I assumed the role of amateur historian and set out to tell the untold story of a small group of predominantly Irish, but also German, Italian and Polish immigrants, who had landed in a city which, at the turn of the 20th century, would become one of the most prosperous cities in America.

Many of us wonder about our ancestors. What did they look like? How did they earn a living? Were they famous or infamous? In reading of the places and the events of the Ward, I hope that the reader can—if only for a moment—be transported back in time to the way of life of our ancestors. Far from being distant relatives of a different time and place, we come to realize that who we are is tied up in the lives and stories of our families before us. Buffalo's First Ward is not just another American neighborhood. Its residential housing wedged in next to industrial and commercial constructions gave rise to disasters such as towering grain elevators set aflame and violent labor-management confrontations. Its proximity to Lake Erie meant that the Ward was subjected to violent weather and natural disasters that destroyed lives and property.

At the same time, its geographical isolation gave rise to an insular community within a city. Families remained tied to the Ward for generations. The neighborhood geography included a powerful river, canals, a massive water basin, lift-bridges, railroad tracks, and majestic architectural wonders: the grain elevators. Even in spite of limited material and monetary resources, the First Ward's unique intersection with history—events such as the Fenian Raid into Canada and the Great Strike of 1899—produced the various characters and notable figures who shaped this history: the Sheehan Brothers, William "Fingy" Conners, General William Donovan, Michael Shea, Jack O'Brian, Jimmy Slattery and Jimmy Griffin. Both ordinary and extraordinary people knew the streets of the First Ward in Buffalo. This is their story.

PART I

FIGHTING FOR SURVIVAL

To every man his little cross. Till he dies. And is forgotten.
— Samuel Beckett, *Waiting for Godot*

CHAPTER ONE

THE FIRST WARD IS BORN

Irishmen's backs are the cheapest elevators ever built.
– Mahlon Kingman's claim to Joseph Dart, the inventor of the steam grain elevator

On an autumn day in 1842 in Buffalo, New York, along the banks of the Buffalo Creek, Mahlon Kingman, a forwarding merchant, confronted a fellow merchant, Joseph Dart. Dart was supervising the construction of his wooden-framed contraption that he hoped would revolutionize the transportation of grain, or, at least make it more efficient than the current system of using the shoulders of Irish laborers. Dart theorized that he could use steam to transport grain up to a storage bin using a conveyor and bucket system referred to as an elevator. Kingman, who had failed at his own attempt at such an endeavor using horsepower, tapped Dart's shoulder and told him that he was wasting his time. "Dart, I am sorry for you; I have been through that mill: it won't do; remember what I say; Irishmen's backs are the cheapest elevators ever built."[1] Dart was not deterred, however, and with the help of an innovative engineer, Robert Dunbar, he finished his project in time for the opening of the 1843 spring shipping season.

Dart's unique bucket-conveyor system could be placed inside the hull of a ship and, when powered by steam, it transported bulk grain out of the ship and into a warehouse storage area. The iron buckets held two quarts of grain and were placed twenty-eight inches apart on a canvas conveyor, which allowed for a transfer of about 1,000 bushels of grain an hour. Three years before Dart's invention, in 1839, a bulk shipment of grain arrived in Buffalo consisting of 1,678 bushels of grain stored in barrels; it required seven days to unload it by hand.[2] With Dart's new elevator, this same task could be accomplished in less than two hours. A transportation revolution had begun. One Buffalonian described Dart's elevator this way:

> It has done away with the old methods of handling it in bags or by rope, pulley and bucket, by man or horse-power. Now the huge elevator by the use of steam runs its trunk into the holds of vessels, swallows up the grain without stopping to take breath and discharges it in one continuous process through its conductors and spouts into large storage bins, canal boats, or cars, without effort except trifling puffs of steam.[3]

Dart's design and implementation of the first steam grain elevator on the waterfront in Buffalo, New York had monumental implications for Buffalo and the settlers in an area called the First Ward. Far from needing fewer laborers, as some first thought, these goliath-sized elevators that sprang up along the banks of the Buffalo River required thousands more. Immigrant laborers—mostly Irish— would be integral in Buffalo's role in the transferring and milling of millions of bushels of grain from the Midwestern states to the burgeoning East Coast cities. Within eighteen months of Joseph Dart's invention, ten more steam grain elevators were built along the banks of the Buffalo River. The First Ward as an industrial center was born. As more elevators were constructed, Buffalo solidified its competitive advantage over other Great Lakes cities with an almost limitless capacity to store, process, and ship grain. Along the way, Buffalo's moniker became "The Grain Capital of the World."

After the construction of the Erie Canal was completed in 1825, Buffalo grew steadily. The fact that Buffalo was on the eastern end of Lake Erie meant that it was a strategically important port for trade between the Great Lakes and the eastern United States. Goods that previously traveled over mountains and difficult terrain could now travel more quickly over water. At the dawn of the grain trade in Buffalo, around 1827, the grain and flour on the lake ships had to be unloaded in Buffalo, divided into smaller lots and placed on canal vessels and, in later years, onto railroad cars. Buffalo became a "chokepoint" because the large Great Lakes ships filled with goods from states like Michigan and Illinois were too large to travel down the canal, so they had to be unloaded in Buffalo.[4] During the 1850s and 1860s, farmers in the eastern United States grew less of their own grain and consequently they relied even more on Midwestern grain. As grain production shifted to the Midwest, Buffalo's port business exploded; Buffalo eventually became the largest grain storage and milling center in the world.

While the initial growth of the First Ward stemmed from the grain trade, as time went on, laborers were needed to unload other goods from the massive trading arrangement between cities on the Great Lakes. Warehouses and factories sprang up downtown and south of the city to handle this booming business. Buffalo not only transferred goods, but also people. It became "America's Crossroads" not just because most traded goods between the East Coast and the Midwest had to traverse through Buffalo, but also because thousands of immigrants passed through on their way to settle in the Midwest.[5] All of this servicing of goods and people required laborers and the newly arrived immigrants were eager to assist.

Ward Boundaries and Geography

The city of Buffalo was divided into political divisions called wards, and initially there were only five of them. The First Ward was the area of the city just south of downtown along the banks of the Buffalo River. In 1832, at Buffalo's inception as a city, the First Ward's boundaries were: Exchange Street for its northern boundary, the Buffalo Creek Indian Reservation as its eastern boundary, the Buffalo River as its southern border and the canal district near Main Street as its western border. Over the years the boundaries of the First Ward changed as the city grew and the number of wards increased, but it was generally the area east of Michigan Avenue, west of Hamburg Street, south of Exchange Street and north of the Buffalo River. The Ward was distinguished by the fact that many of its streets were named after U.S. states and cities: Louisiana, Michigan, Tennessee, Kentucky, Mississippi, Illinois, Ohio, Alabama, Sandusky, Baltimore, St. Clair, Vincennes, Mackinaw, and Chicago. In terms of its physical geography, the First Ward is situated in one of the lowest lying parts of Buffalo, with a swampy terrain that made it undesirable for housing and prone to periodic flooding. In fact, it was so swampy that some people joked that the First Ward was where even "the geese wear rubber boots."[6] Most people with ample financial resources chose to settle on higher ground away from the Ward.

Elk Street—the main east-west corridor in the Ward—and the area just north of it was the land most desirable for housing. When Joseph Ellicott, the surveyor

and planner of Buffalo, developed his layout of Buffalo in 1804, Elk Street was
one of only a handful of streets that he planned in the First Ward. It is quite
possible that after surveying the land he did not foresee residents inhabiting the
swampy land south of Elk Street. The other Ward streets in Ellicott's original
plan included: Beaver, which was later renamed Perry Street after the naval hero
from the War of 1812; Crow Street, which became Exchange Street; Marvin
Street, which stayed the same; Willink, which was later renamed Main Street;
Lake Street along Lake Erie near the present Fuhrman Boulevard; Buffalo Street
on the south side of the Buffalo Creek; and Water Street on the north side of
Buffalo Creek (see photo page 8).

One Buffalonian remembered how in the 1840s there was a sizeable community of "thrifty citizens" located on and around Elk Street.[7] There were even
a few stately homes on Elk Street. Perry Street, another east-west artery north
of Elk Street, was also home to some good housing stock, as was Fulton Street,
which was originally called Maria Street until 1835. Jacob W. Banta, a wealthy
shipbuilder, lived in a 1820 classical-revival home at the corner of Hayward and
Perry Streets, and it was considered the oldest home in the area.[8] But the flood-
prone area south of Elk Street, prior to the 1840s, consisted of primitive cottages
and was suited only for those with limited financial resources. At the time of
Dart's invention there was a fair mix of ethnic groups represented in the Ward
including New England transplants, Irish, English, Scottish, and Canadian immigrants, and even a small community of Portuguese. The demographics of the
Ward, however, changed very quickly due to the devastating Irish Famine of
1845-1850. The Irish streamed into the First Ward, conquered it, and changed
it forever.

The first settlers of the First Ward, like the rest of the United States, were
Native Americans—specifically the Seneca Tribe. The first permanent settlement
of the Senecas in Erie County, New York occurred in 1780 just four miles from
the mouth of the Buffalo Creek, and thus a few miles from the Ward, at a place
called Martin's Corner. The Senecas were not interested in the land near the
mouth of the Buffalo Creek where it met Lake Erie, so they gave this land to
their friend Lieutenant William Johnston who around 1800 deeded it to Joseph
Ellicott for his new town.[9] By 1790 various members of the Seneca tribe built
huts along the banks of the Buffalo Creek towards the mouth of the Creek, near
modern-day downtown Buffalo, and into the boundaries of the First Ward.[10]
One of the legendary Seneca Indian chieftains, Farmer's Brother, famed for
leading the Battle of Devil's Hole—also known as Devil's Hole Massacre—
against British troops in 1763, built his cabin along the Buffalo Creek at the
end of Katherine Street.[11] Perhaps this legendary Seneca warrior was the first
permanent settler in the First Ward.

The roughly two thousand Senecas on the Reservation would not, however, remain in the area for very long. Farmer's Brother and the other Senecas were forced by the Buffalo Creek Treaty to abandon their reservation lands just south of Buffalo. On May 20, 1842, in the same year Dart invented his revolutionary grain elevator, the Senecas gave up their rights to the land along the Buffalo River and began their migration to Allegany and Cattaraugus, New York. In 1843 and 1844 the Senecas moved *en masse* south to their new reservation. This migration opened up more land for commercial and residential growth south of the Buffalo River.

The First Ward's main geographical feature was the Buffalo Creek, later dredged and widened, and renamed the Buffalo River. There does not seem to be a precise date as to when the name was officially changed to the Buffalo River, and there are even maps from the 1890s that refer to it as the Buffalo River and then subsequent maps in the early 20th century that refer to it as the Buffalo Creek. In the early part of the 19th century, the mouth of the Buffalo Creek, which joined Lake Erie, was filled with so much sediment in some spots that people could actually walk across it waist high.[12] Areas of the creek further upstream were just as sediment filled, and there were parts that were best navigated by canoe because of the silt buildup. But some of the early leaders and industrialists of Buffalo envisioned a bustling port if the mouth of the Buffalo Creek could be properly dredged. Around 1821, leaders of the new city like Samuel Wilkeson were able to create a sufficient harbor, which allowed the mouth of the Buffalo Creek to become the western terminus of the Erie Canal instead of the town of Black Rock. It is doubtful, however, that the visionary Wilkeson could have ever imagined that Buffalo would eventually become one of the busiest ports in the world.

Although many of the former New England industrialists made fortunes in businesses along the Buffalo River, they had little desire to live near the river. One English biographer of the famous First Warder William Donovan harshly described the First Ward as "a raucous, damp, watery place of shanties where the arctic winds came straight down from Canada, gathering speed and cold from Lake Erie".[13] It was these harsh conditions that made this land desirable only to those who had such little resources that desire was second to necessity. Due to the limited demand to live in the area, rents were inexpensive. The immigrant laborers also desired to settle in the area near the Buffalo River because they did not have access to transportation, so they had to live in close proximity to their jobs. Some people also theorize that many of the Irish immigrants came from areas of Ireland near the Shannon River and the Lee River, and living along the Buffalo River was desirable because it was familiar to them.[14] Perhaps living near the river made some Irishman feel at home, but most of these former rural farmers would have felt terribly disconnected in this bustling industrial hub.

Within just five years of Dart's invention, waterfront access along the river became a precious commodity. In 1848, the city announced a major development in the Ward that would affect the geography of the Ward and its commercial prospects for years to come. By the early 1840s, the countless canal boats occupied so much surface space on the Buffalo River that there was not enough area to unload and load goods.[15] Consequently, the city decided to build more inland canals and basins to accommodate the armada of boats. In 1848, plans were announced to build a massive ten-acre basin in the First Ward between Louisiana Street and Chicago Street which would serve two purposes: first, to connect the Buffalo River to the city canal system; and second, to allow lake vessels an easy turnaround in the basin to go back up the river after they unloaded their goods. During the summer of 1848, there was great hope for an economic uplift from the Ohio Basin and the Ohio Slip, which ran northward to connect the Buffalo River to the Main and Hamburg Canal.

Also in 1848, the Buffalo Board of Trade lobbied for a canal to be built from the mouth of the Buffalo River southeast between the shore of Lake Erie and the south bank of the Buffalo River.[16] The two-mile Blackwell Canal, as it was initially named, was completed in 1852. It was later renamed the City Ship Canal. Once slips were dug to connect it to the Buffalo River, which ran parallel to it, it provided even more opportunities for grain storage facilities, as well as more space for the flotilla of Great Lakes ships that needed to load and unload their goods. The building of this canal created a small strip of land between it and the Buffalo River, and the locals called this new geographical feature: The Island.

By 1851, the Ohio Basin was operational and goods were smoothly moving from Lake Erie up the Buffalo River to the Basin and then onto the city canal system. The benefits from the basin project were short-lived, however, because railroads made most of the canals and basins obsolete within a few years of their completion. By 1855, there were pleas to close the Main and Hamburg Canal because there was such a limited flow of water that the water stagnated and became a public nuisance. After many attempts to rectify the problems, and thousands of dollars wasted in this effort, the city of Buffalo abandoned the Hamburg Canal and converted it into a city sewer. Unfortunately, this had some deleterious effects for the Ohio Basin, which received some run-off from the crude sewer system. In fact, some speculate that this sewer runoff into the Ohio Basin may have contributed to the frequent cholera outbreaks of the 1850s in the First Ward. Within a few years of completing the Ohio Basin in the heart of the Ward, there were frequent calls to fill it in because of sanitation issues. But the industrialists controlled the city decision-making, so it remained open. In the meantime, more industries opened up along the banks of this newly created waterfront access. This introduced even more employment opportunities for the steady stream of immigrants.

Invasion of the Irish

Scotch-Irish Protestant immigrants lived in Buffalo as early as 1804, but the first Irish Catholic settler arrived closer to 1815 when Patrick O'Rourke and his family settled in Buffalo.[17] Within two years, there was a small Irish community living south of Exchange Street in the "Flats" consisting of the O'Rourkes, the Bowens, the Daughtrys and the Mooneys.[18] There are other reports that around the same time, in 1818, there was a small settlement of Irish living along Lake Erie near the present Fuhrmann Boulevard in an area called "The Beach."[19] The first Bishop of Buffalo, John Timon, estimated that there were only about 400 Irish residents— many left over from the building of the Erie Canal—residing in Buffalo in the 1830s.[20] Many of the first settlers resided in the Third Ward near the downtown area and west along Niagara Street, but as the masses of famine Irish arrived in Buffalo they settled in the more sparsely populated First Ward. Many of these early Irish settlers came via New York City or Philadelphia and then worked their way to Buffalo; others first settled in Canada and then later moved to Buffalo. These included such well-known First Warders as the William J. Conners family, Michael Shea's family, Father James Lanigan, Thomas V. O'Connor's family, and Bishop James Quigley's family.

As the Irish outgrew their settlement in the "Flats" they migrated into the boundaries of the Ward. By the late 1840s, these settlers built wooden shanties and cottages along Ohio Street. The demographic and census data from this period reveals much about employment and living conditions. In 1845, there were a total of 7,107 people living in the First Ward—which had much larger boundaries than it did at the end of the 19th century—with a good mix of Anglo Americans and Irish at this time.[21] However, as the famine immigrants streamed into Buffalo the demographics quickly changed. Residents of Buffalo witnessed an explosion of the city's population from 1845 to 1855 as the number of residents increased from 30,000 to 70,000; so many immigrants poured into Buffalo that by 1855, seventy-five percent of the family heads of household were foreign-born.[22] Not surprisingly, the largest Irish migration to Buffalo happened during the five year period, 1847-1852, as a result of the Famine.[23]

Interestingly, according to the 1855 New York State census, only 1% of the Buffalo Irish residents at that time had been around since 1830, so the notion that there was a large Irish settlement in Buffalo left over from the building of the Erie Canal is not accurate.[24] By 1850 there were close to 6,400 native-born Irish living in Buffalo and almost 50% of them lived in the First Ward, with others scattered in the Eighth Ward on the West Side of Buffalo.[25] Five years later, in 1855, of the approximately 10,000 Irish in Buffalo, 57% of them resided in the lakeshore and canal corridor slums of Buffalo in overcrowded wooden frame houses in and around the First and Eighth Ward.[26] The demographics of the head of households from the First Ward in 1855 shows how quickly the Irish seized control of this area of Buffalo: 966 Irish, 239 native-born Americans, 161 English, 119 Germans, 82 Canadians, 68 Scots, 11 Poles, 9 Welsh, and 6 African Americans.[27] Despite this enormous migration of Irish immigrants to the Ward, the Irish still only made up 18% of Buffalo's population in contrast to the Germans who comprised 44%.[28] In fact, Buffalo was a German city for much of its first century of existence.

Resources to purchase or build housing were so scarce that the Irish crowded into primitive houses and cottages. To save money, the First Ward Irish subdivided their homes with an average of ten residents per house compared to only two residents per house in the German Sixth Ward of Buffalo.[29] The area in the heart of the Ward, near the modern-day Our Lady of Perpetual Help parish, was still sparsely populated. During this period there was still a heavy settlement on streets like Ohio, Fulton, Elk, and Chicago, but only a scattering of residents on streets like Kentucky and Tennessee.[30] In terms of occupations, in 1855 only 17% of Irishmen were in skilled or semi-skilled occupations with the rest in unsteady laborer positions.[31] In fact, nearly half of the Buffalo Irish in the 1855 census did not have a regular place of employment. Ten years later, in 1865, employment prospects improved slightly, but the Irish were still stuck in manual labor roles with only 24% as semi-skilled or skilled workers.[32] Many of the men worked in physically demanding jobs as longshoremen where they unloaded ships filled with goods such as grain, dry goods, lumber, hides, corn, and livestock. Irish families in the First Ward even supplemented their income by raising cows to produce milk, which they would sell in the market.[33] Life for the first wave of Irish in the Ward was generally characterized by an epic struggle for survival.

Buffalo historian Mark Goldman, in his book *High Hopes*, describes the Irish in the Ward like this:

> Isolated in the First Ward as much by choice as by prejudice, Buffalo's Irish—very much like the Senecas earlier in the century—were separate and, as far as the rest of the city was concerned, largely invisible.[34]

Goldman also contrasted the physical landscape differences between the First Ward and the German East Side. In the First Ward, "schools, churches, and homes shared the limited land area with breweries, grain elevators, railroad yards and market places."[35] The Germans meanwhile lived in a more traditional residential setting.

Pre-Famine Irish

There were differences between the Irish who came before the Great Famine and those who came after. The first ones came to the United States to build the Erie Canal, and author Peter Quinn described them "as the advanced guard...whose spadework dug the country's canals and put in place the foundations of America's industrial transformation."[36] One such Irish immigrant was John Brinkworth, an example of the pre-Famine immigrants who arrived in the Ward. Brinkworth, the son of a British soldier stationed in Ireland and an Irish Catholic mother, was born in Tipperary and came to America in 1834 at the age of twenty-two. Not much is known about his first fifteen years in America, but he eventually settled in Buffalo around 1849 just six years after Dart's elevator was operational. As part of the first wave of immigrants, he had the advantage over the Famine immigrants who followed him of being more established with American customs and way of life.

John initially lived at "Geltson's Boat Yard" along the waterfront near the ship canal close to the First Ward; it is unclear if he lived in a cottage or some other type of primitive housing in this boatyard. John's first occupation was "working on the Lake," which either meant working on the docks as a longshoreman or on the lake boats. John Brinkworth must have had access to some primary education because the U.S. Census claimed he could both read and write, which would have given him a significant advantage in commercial enterprises over the vast majority of Irish immigrants who were illiterate. It is also interesting to note that when John later opened up two businesses, he possessed entrepreneurial skills that were not generally characteristic of other Irish Catholic immigrants who were mainly farmers in their native land. Buffalo was booming during the 1850s as evidenced by the fact that its native son, Millard Fillmore, was sworn into office as the thirteenth president of the United States. In John's first five years, Buffalo's population exploded, almost doubling from 42,261 to 74,214. John was taking advantage of this explosive growth by adding to his skills and capitalizing on the need for semi-skilled workers. Within a few years, John learned the skill of nail making, eventually owning his own shop.

In 1855, Brinkworth was living on Chicago Street near Fulton Street in the First Ward working as a "horse nail maker," a business in which he prospered. By 1868, three years after the end of the Civil War, John had saved enough money to open up a saloon to service the crush of thirsty Irish laborers in the Ward. Saloon ownership was difficult because you had to have money for the down payment and most of the immigrants lived from hand to mouth. One First Ward expert claimed that, "Ownership of a saloon was viewed as a key avenue of upward mobility within the community..."[37] Saloons were not just places for drinking alcohol, but they were vitally important places for employment networking and politics. Saloon owners quickly became powerful community figures who could dole out jobs and provide votes for eager candidates.

Brinkworth settled in the slightly more affluent area north of Elk Street. The location of Brinkworth's First Ward saloon at 297 Perry, near Chicago Street, was also advantageous for its strategic location near a thriving manufacturing district. By 1874, the Brinkworth saloon and family residence, located just on the northern edge of a residential neighborhood, was nestled in an area that comprised the Gowans & Stover Soap Manufacturing, the J. Wheeler Malt House, the Delaney Forge & Iron Company, and the Bush & Howard Leather manufacturing company. The Brinkworth saloon certainly benefited from this prime location filled with laborers and residents alike.

John Brinkworth's situation was not the typical First Ward Irish story. He came from Tipperary and not County Cork or County Kerry where many others had lived. In addition, he came in the first wave of immigrants and benefited by being established before the new influx of immigrants streamed into Buffalo. Brinkworth could read and write and he possessed skills that enabled him to start two businesses. For the most part, the Famine immigrants that arrived after Brinkworth were a less fortunate bunch. Few of them had the means to establish their own businesses, and many lacked the skills that would enable them to rise above manual labor.

Famine Immigrants

Much has been written about the Irish Famine of 1845-1850 and it is not necessary to repeat all of the details here. However, since many of the Irish who settled in the First Ward of Buffalo were from the regions of Ireland that were the most adversely affected by the Famine—County Cork, County Kerry and County Clare—it is important to mention some of the relevant facts. The Famine certainly left an indelible mark on the psyche of immigrants in the Ward. The Archbishop of New York, John Hughes, a fellow Irishmen, wrote about the Irish in New York as "the poorest and most wretched population that can be found— the scattered debris of the Irish nation."[38] For many from the First Ward, we are the descendants of this "debris."

There was a sizable population of the First Ward Irish from the southwestern part of County Cork, which comprised towns like Goleen, Skibbereen, Schull, Clonakilty, and Baltimore. Prominent Ward families like those of General William Donovan, William "Fingy" Conners, Mike Regan, Jack White, and the Sheehans all originated from Cork. This area of Ireland was utterly devastated by the Famine. Within County Cork some areas were impacted more than others. One of the most devastated areas of County Cork—the Skibbereen

Poor Law Union—consisted of parishes like Goleen, Schull, Kilcoe, Caheragh, Drimoleague and Drinagh, which had a combined population of 43,266 prior to the Famine. By the middle of the famine, it is estimated that two-thirds of them were in distress as a result of the potato blight. In the year between September 1846 and September 1847, 7,332 residents of the six aforementioned parishes in the Skibbereen Union (17% of the total population) died from symptoms of hunger.[39] The demographic breakdown of the 7,332 people who died that year shows that it didn't spare gender or age: 2,396 men, 1,800 women and 3,136 children. The causes of death were 3,191 (44%) of fever, 2515 (34%) of starvation, and 1626 (22%) of dysentery.[40] Observers at the time of the Famine recount the biblical devastation in southwest Cork with entire families, emaciated from lack of food, piled on each other in their thatched cottages, dead.

Most victims of the Famine were tenants of wealthy English or Anglo-Irish landholders who held short term, verbal contracts with their masters. The potato farmers were singularly focused on growing potatoes in order to sustain themselves and pay the landholders for use of the land. If anything happened to their crop they would be unable to survive. Unfortunately, that is exactly what happened when the potato blight surfaced in the 1845 harvest. The English public and politicians were at first sympathetic regarding the suffering of their fellow countrymen in Ireland, but they quickly turned callous. Within a few years of the start of the famine, many English felt that they had paid enough for relief efforts and reasoned that the Irish deserved this because they were lazy and unproductive. Laissez-faire economics was the guiding principle for economic policy at the time, and this led to more apathy by the decision makers at the plight of those struggling. In 1847, the worst year of the Famine, the *Times of London* callously noted, "The Celt is less energetic, less independent, less industrious than the Saxon. This is the archaic condition of his race."[41] The Irish Poor Laws of 1847 exacerbated the problem by declaring that anyone holding more than a quarter-acre of land could not receive aid. This forced thousands of Irish farmers to give up their land rather than starve to death.

For those lucky enough to survive the hunger, and for those who had enough money for passage to the United States, Canada, or Australia, they then had to endure the seven-week trip at sea where people were packed into ships like livestock. Diseases spread rampantly, and a sizable percentage did not survive the voyage. Thus the term "coffin ship" was used to describe their journey.

It is difficult to imagine the emotional suffering endured by the Famine immigrants when they decided that there were no other options but emigration to the United States and other foreign lands. We can try to imagine their sense of loss and disconnectedness of arriving in this new and strange land, but we will never truly know what they felt. It has been said that before an emigrant left

Ireland they held a wake, which had as much sadness and merriment as one for a corpse because once you left Ireland your family would never see you again.[42] As a result of the famine, one of the values that were indelibly printed into the minds of the Irish immigrants, and later their children, was thrift. One of the characters in Eugene O'Neill's "Long Day's Journey into Night" sums up the value of thrift. After Edmund Tyrone accuses his father, James, of being a miser, James responds to his son, "I learned the value of a dollar and a fear of the poorhouse." The elder Tyrone later explains, "My mother was left a stranger in a strange land with four small children. There was no damn romance in our poverty."[43] The famine shaped many aspects of the survivors including their insular nature, their indefatigable support for the Irish independence movement, their distrust of the laissez-faire market economy, and the persistent problems with alcoholism that some suffered. Many of these consequences of the Famine surface throughout the life of the first- and second-generation Ward residents.

Neighborhoods

As the Irish moved into the Ward they settled into distinct neighborhoods based on two factors: their economic circumstances, and the county or region in Ireland from which they originated. People from County Cork and Kerry predominantly inhabited the area south of Elk Street down to the railroad tracks at Republic Street—an area sometimes called the Flats. Residents north of Elk Street, from more prosperous counties such as Wexford and Tipperary, often looked down on their fellow Irishmen south of Elk Street.[44] The northern streets of Elk, Perry, and Fulton generally had better housing stock than the cottages that were available in the Flats, and the residents of these streets tended to be the skilled or semi-skilled Irish immigrants like John Brinkworth.[45] These initial divisions based on county origin, however, quickly dissolved and other factors divided the Ward.

The Flats overlapped with an area that was once referred to as Hakertown. The boundaries of Hakertown are debatable with some saying it was the area from Miami to Republic Streets, but others claiming a larger area bounded by Elk and South Streets. Both groups agree that the east-west boundaries are roughly from Louisiana Street to Hamburg Street. This area, which developed shortly before the Civil War, was populated by thousands of first, second, and third generation Irish. Congressman Richard Max McCarthy claimed that his great-grandfather, Cornelius Sullivan, built his homestead at 141 Kentucky Street in 1861,which was the beginning of the major migration into the heart of the Ward. Legend has it that the name of the area was derived from the fact that so many residents were from County Cork and were known for their abundant consumption of hake-fish in Ireland.[46]

Republic Street was a further division within Hakertown or the Flats neighborhood. Before it was a street, Republic Street was originally the Tecumseh and Ottawa Canal from about 1850 to about 1872. Around 1872 the canal was filled in and transferred over to the railroads, which proceeded to build tracks down the middle of this residential neighborhood, continuing the division in the community. There was a friendly debate between both the north and south side of this dividing line as to who lived on the "wrong side of the tracks."[47] Those who lived north of the tracks, near O'Connell Avenue, were sometimes referred to as "dough-boys" because many of the men worked in the flourmills such as Washburn-Crosby (later General Mills), Pillsbury Flour Mill, Russell Flour Mill, Agway, and Cargill.[48] The area south of Republic Street to the Buffalo River comprised the neighborhood where residents were called "creek-rats" or "rubber-neckers;" this area was prone to flooding.[49] Residents along South Street enjoyed picturesque views of what some call "Elevator Alley" because of the high concentration of elevators along the Buffalo River including the Standard and the Lake and Rail. Rogues' Hollow was the appellation given to the area of the Ward south of Ohio Street; "scamps and hooligans" purportedly populated it.[50] Congressman McCarthy jokingly recalled how his father said it was the area where "all the thieves lived long ago."[51]

One of the most interesting areas of the Ward was a community literally built on the seawall located on land adjacent to Lake Erie. In 1838, the city of Buffalo constructed a seawall to prevent surges in lake water that could flood the area known as the Flats. As a result of the improved conditions, by about the 1850s, poor Irish and Portuguese residents of Buffalo built dwellings on this no-man's land along the waterfront. This area had several names: the Beach, the Sea Wall Strip, Buffalo's Bohemia, Wall Street, and Squatter's Row.[52] It was one of the earliest settlements in the First Ward, and was located near the modern-day Fuhrmann Boulevard at the foot of Michigan Avenue, on a peninsula. One of Jim Shine's distant relatives, Eugene Newman, a ship's captain, had been at the Beach as early as the 1830s.[53] The "Beachers," as they were known, lived in their cottages on city-owned land with no land deeds—consequently they benefited from not having to pay taxes.[54] Technically they were not even part of a political ward because it wasn't zoned for residential housing, but it was adopted by the First Ward. Because of the geography of the area, water and docks on one side, and grain elevators and the railroads on the other, they were cut off from the rest of the Ward and the city. In a sense, they were invisible to their fellow citizens in Buffalo. Even their fellow Irishmen from the more upscale sections of the Ward looked at them as lower-class Irish and gave them names like "squatters" and "shanty Irish."[55] One Ward memoir detailed how many Ward children went down to the Beach to swim in the summer, despite the fact that the residents had a "rough and ready reputation" and it was a place where many fights broke out.[56]

While Irish immigrants dominated the area, it is purported that there was a small Portuguese clan that lived in this area and intermarried with the Irish residents.[57] Families from the Beach with surnames such as Freitus, Joseph, Silvey, Grande, and Clouden claimed Portuguese ancestry.[58] These working-class citizens, many of whom worked as scoopers at nearby elevators, were sustained by a yearlong diet of Lake Erie fish, which they could catch out their front doors.[59] By the 1880s, the Beach, which had previously been associated with extreme poverty, had actually become a place of respectability.[60]

One news reporter who wrote about the Beachers in 1903 described their homes as being simple and lacking in paint, wallpaper, and parlor furniture.[61] The squatter's homes were located between the Blackwell Canal (later called the City Ship Canal) and Lake Erie, and starting at the Coast Guard station, extended one mile down the shore of the lake. One reporter claimed that almost one thousand people lived on this strip of the "Island", but this number seems high based on the number of dwellings.[62] Most of the homes were built to face the canal in order to escape the harsh weather off Lake Erie, but then they traded waterfront views for a view of railcars and grain elevators. The reporter described the Beachers, most of whom were commercial fishermen, as a hardy people who lived outdoors year round during all of the stormy Lake Erie weather. Another reporter claimed, "They were squatters – tough people who could persevere against the odds."[63]

Many lost their homes in a powerful hurricane in 1884, but that didn't stop these resilient people from rebuilding and starting over again. Fishing vessels and nets were littered around their modest homes, and many kept large dogs such as Newfoundlands and mastiffs, which accompanied them during their fishing expeditions and carried their sleds in the winter when they went ice fishing from dawn to dusk. In 1903, a reporter interviewed the oldest Beacher, John Foley, who had been a resident on the beach since the early 1850s when there were only two or three squatters living there. Over the years a very tight community developed where everyone knew each other and socials like dances were held in a home and the entire community was invited.[64] The area mostly consisted of the resident's cottages, but there were also some commercial and social structures such as Foley's Fish House, Barrett's Buffett, and the Celtic and Lighthouse Rowing Clubs.

Uniontown, located at the foot of Katherine Street and bounded by the Buffalo River to the south and Hamburgh Street to the west, was yet another neighborhood within the Ward boundaries that was formed around the Civil War years.[65] In 1860, the Palmer, Wadsworth, Thompson & Company Buffalo Union Iron Works, later shortened to Union Iron Works, established an iron-ore factory at the foot of Hamburgh Street near the Buffalo River. The company was founded because an abundant supply of iron was discovered near Lake Superior, and this could be easily shipped to Buffalo, converted into iron goods, and then shipped around the country. The company prospered throughout the Civil War years, providing needed iron for the Northern war effort; and, by 1863, through innovative manufacturing techniques, they were producing the longest rails for the railroad industry: 50 feet long versus the then-standard 21 feet.[66] The plant also produced iron beams used in bridges and buildings across the country.

Around the 53-acre factory grounds, a self-contained small village sprang up. In addition to three blast furnaces and a rolling mill, there were also blacksmith shops, machine shops, boat yards, and stables. Wooden-sided houses on stilts were built on dirt streets with names like Excelsior, Pioneer, and Monitor. Saloons, grocery stores, and even a barbershop also sprang up along Hamburgh Street (later spelled Hamburg Street) to accommodate the hundreds of workers and their families at the Union Iron Works; popular saloons in the neighborhood included Louis Heilback, Jack Tripole's, and the Hole-in-the-Wall.[67] Interestingly, the housing and factory were surrounded by a large wooden wall, which had a dual purpose: to protect the factory assets and keep the workers inside the compound.

The families that lived in Uniontown were originally almost all Irish and they worked as puddlers of iron ore. These men, about 500 at the peak of the factory's existence, worked long shifts using heavy machinery to pump out iron ingots. There were some negative environmental consequences as result of living next to the factory including a pungent smell that wafted throughout the area and an acrid smoke, laced with particles of silicone, which coated houses and probably damaged lungs. In fact, to smelt the ore, the company consumed 45,000 tons of anthracite coal each year, which probably contributed to the poor air quality in the Ward. Some of the names of the families from this neighborhood included Patton, Byrnes, Kane, Hayden, Hughes, Trimmins, Oldman, Sullivan, Gorman, Connors, Dray, Lucy, O'Neill, Reagan, Teal, McMahon, McClusky, Mullen, Spenser, Griffin, Murphy, Carden, Clancy, Bannister, Lewis, McGrath, Conrad, Sheehan, Mahon, McBride, Boyle, Mahoney, Esford, and Reardon.[68]

The Island—a strip of land nestled between the City Ship Canal and the Buffalo River—was another area of the Ward that was developed around the Civil War years. This area became the milling center of Buffalo and contained the shortest railroad line in the world, the Buffalo Creek Road. Trains coming into the Island would drop off machinery and raw materials and leave with tons of cereal, which would be shipped all over the United States. The main thoroughfare of the Island was Ganson Street—originally Coatsworth Street—named after John Ganson, the Democratic Buffalo Congressman who voted for all of Lincoln's War measures including slave emancipation. Other than elevators and grain mills, Ganson Street was mostly barren with the exception of a few taverns, a dry dock, and a handful of homes. In later years, the *W.S. Grattan* fireboat with its 18 hoses was docked in the water near Michigan Avenue. The well-known marine laundry boat, whose crew collected the bundles of dirty clothing from the incoming sailors, was also parked nearby.[69]

Not all of the Irish immigrants settled into neighborhoods in the First Ward. Some settled in the West Side of Buffalo, which was originally the Third Ward and then later carved into the Eighth and Ninth Wards. There was somewhat of a rivalry between the Irish immigrants of this area and of those in the First Ward. Chronologically both areas were settled around the same time. The West Side's mother church, Holy Angels, opened in 1858, the same year as the Ward's mother church, St. Bridget's. The Irish from the West Side were mostly semi-skilled or skilled workers and because of their additional financial resources, they could afford to live away from the industrial sprawl in the First Ward. From the Irish arrival in Buffalo and through the 1860s, the Irish from the West Side held leadership positions in the Catholic Church, military, and Irish independence movements in Buffalo. For instance, in 1860, in the numerous leadership positions of organizations such as the Friendly Sons of St. Patrick, the Conference of St. Vincent de Paul, and the Young Men's Catholic Association, there was only one representative from the First Ward: Charles McCarthy. The rest of the leaders resided in the West Side or in the downtown district. But as time went on the men from the First Ward would increasingly vie for these leadership positions, often settling for, at best, a shared arrangement with their fellow Irishmen from the West Side. As men in the Ward gained fame or financial resources, the natural choice was to leave the Ward and migrate to the West Side. But it was a choice reserved for only a few.

Within just twenty years of Dart's elevator, the Ward had been transformed from a swampy, forested area into an industrial-residential community. It was a microcosm of the dramatic growth that was occurring as immigrants streamed across the United States. While these immigrants did find work and homes to live in, America wasn't the Promised Land that many had envisioned. A biographer of First Ward native General William Donovan declared that life in the First Ward during the early years was a lot like Ireland: "Life was an unrelenting struggle with floods, unemployment, disease, drains, crime, the police."[70] As to why the residents did not leave, the author continues, "They were cooped up in the First Ward with little or no prospect of breaking away from the laboring classes, unless they were wholly exceptional individuals-usually pugilists, priests, performers or politicians."[71] While this view may seem cynical it was fairly accurate for the early settlers in the Ward. But these were not the only problems the Irish encountered in their new land. Similar to their experience in Ireland, their Protestant masters disliked Celts and distrusted Catholics. Things were bound to explode.

CHAPTER TWO

IRISH FARMERS THRUST INTO
THE INDUSTRIAL AGE

*On the way home I noticed the elevators—they looked like tall grim and sinister
prisons of some sort.* – Charles Burchfield, Buffalo artist

*They [the elevators] do have an almost Egyptian monumentality in many cases, and in
abandonment and death they evoke the majesties of a departed civilization. Or so it
used to seem to me, looking downstream on the Buffalo River from the angle of South
Street. On either side of the water, like an avenue of mighty tombs, were structures
representing almost the whole history of the grain elevator, certainly no other city in
the world possessed so concentrated a set of historically valuable elevators as Buffalo
then did, along that half mile of river down to the Ohio Street Bridge.*

– Reyner Banham from *Concrete Atlantis*

Throughout the mid-nineteenth century, Buffalo was awash in grain. Wheat was the most abundant grain stored and transshipped in Buffalo, but workers also handled massive quantities of corn, oats, barley, and rye. In 1831, grain shipments to Buffalo comprised a modest 173,000 bushels of wheat and 57,000 barrels of flour. By 1855, less than 25 years later, Buffalo laborers were handling a staggering 25 million bushels of grain—more than a hundredfold increase.[1] By 1850 Buffalo was the largest grain market in the country—a designation that would remain until 1880 when Chicago surpassed it.[2] Around 1860 merchants in Buffalo shipped and stored about half of the grain coming from America's Midwest.[3]

Businesses needed more and more laborers to accommodate the rapid expansion of the grain trade. Laborers were needed to dry, sort, and weigh the grain in the elevators as well as run the machinery. But grain scooping is the job that is most closely associated with the laborers who lived in the First Ward, and it was often the first job many Irish immigrants took when they arrived in Buffalo. Grain scoopers used shovels to scoop up the loose grain in the hull of ships into buckets on a steam-powered pulley system, which then transported the grain up into a storage bin or warehouse. Even though equipment and techniques improved over the years, men were always needed to move the grain from the hulls of ships to a storage facility. After working as a scooper for a few years, laborers would have saved enough of their meager wages to send for their brothers and cousins to come to Buffalo to scoop grain.[4] During the peak years, close to 1,600 men were employed as scoopers—almost all of Irish descent. Even as late as 1940, the Irish dominated this industry, holding on to almost 90% of jobs. Thousands of other Ward residents in the 19th and 20th centuries worked in other industries such as lumber, iron-ore, railroads, barrel making, or shipbuilding. Although these were also important and thriving industries, it was the grain industry that defined the First Ward from the time of Dart's invention in 1842 until the St. Lawrence Seaway opened in 1959.

Prior to Dart's elevator, the banks of the Buffalo River were densely forested with trees: elms, sycamores, black walnut, basswoods, and oaks.[5] After 1843, tree-lined riverbanks gave way to grain elevators, docks, warehouses, and railroad beds. By 1855, ten major grain elevators lined the Buffalo River with names such as Brown, Hatch, Evans & Dunbar; Fish Seymour & Wells; Dart, Sterling Hollister, Richmond; and Holley & Johnson.[6] As the Civil War was under way in 1861, demand for grain spiked and shipments of grain to Buffalo rose to 60 million bushels. To keep up with this new demand, grain merchants built four more grain elevators in Buffalo, and hired more workers to staff them. By 1887, there were a total of thirty-nine elevators in Buffalo, which could transfer 3.5 million bushels a day.[7] Buffalo not only transported Midwestern grain, but it also became one of the largest milling towns in America. By 1846, two steam-powered flourmills were built in Buffalo, and this increased the demand for more grain to be shipped to the Queen City.[8] Most flourmills were initially centered in the Black Rock area of Buffalo, but by 1860 the First Ward was home to Buffalo City Flour Mills at Chicago and Miami Streets, Wadsworth Mills at 60 Ohio Street, and E & B Holmes on Michigan Street.

The intimacy of its industrial and residential areas is one of the unique features of the Ward. Outside of the Ward, few Americans have ever lived so close to train depots, towering grain elevators, dusty lumber mills, giant sand mounds, and massive lake freighters. The Irish, German, and Alsatian farmers who settled in the Ward were accustomed to the rolling hills, rivers, and small towns of their homeland. These former rural farmers and fishermen were newly living alongside ten-story grain elevators and soot-spewing manufacturing plants; they were forced to contend with canals, the congested and polluted Ohio Basin, as well as an extensive railroad system. At least four major railroad companies laid tracks through the residential neighborhoods in order to gain access to the banks of the Buffalo River: the New York Lake Erie and Western Railroad; the Lake Shore and Michigan Southern Railroad Company; the Lehigh Valley Railroad; and the Delaware, Lackawanna and Western Railroad. Some of these tracks were located only a few feet from the corner of First Ward homes.

Marine towers were another architectural wonder found along the banks of the Buffalo River. These grain storage towers moved on rails that would allow a docked freighter to remain stationary. The tower would then move back and forth in order to unload the grain in the ship's hull. A marine leg with buckets was connected to each tower that moved into the hull of the ship; men would then shovel grain onto the marine leg that would transport it to the elevator. The sight of massive buildings moving on rails must have been stunning for new immigrants coming to the Ward from rural European towns. But not all onlookers were favorably impressed. On a visit to Buffalo, English novelist Anthony Trollope wrote of the elevators: "As ugly a monster as yet produced."[9]

Profile of a Grain Scooper

My own ancestor Timothy Bohane was a typical Irish immigrant grain scooper who lived most of his life in the Ward. Timothy was born into a family of hake fishermen who most likely managed a potato plot as well. Timothy and his twin brother, Patrick, were both baptized on December 24, 1850 in a small town in Ireland, Skibbereen, located in the southwest of County Cork. Although he was born at the end of the Great Famine, the fact that he was raised in Skibbereen— one of the most devastated areas in Ireland—surely had a profound influence on him as a young man. This eighteen-year-old fisherman arrived in the United States in 1868, three years after the conclusion of the Civil War.

Timothy had little or no education in Ireland as evidenced by the fact that the 1900 New York State Census claimed that he could neither read nor write. In fact, Timothy fit the common profile of many First Ward grain scoopers of his time: an illiterate farmer or fisherman from the south or west of Ireland. In 1873, Timothy lived at 181 Kentucky Street and in the *Buffalo City Directory* he was simply listed as a laborer. In the following year, he moved around the block to 45 Sandusky Street (later renamed O'Connell Avenue) where he lived for the next forty years. For his first 25 years in Buffalo, his last name was shortened to Bohan, which is how it was listed in the city directory. Then around 1900, it was changed to Bohen, perhaps as the result of a simple clerical error or Timothy's illiteracy. As a laborer on the docks, Timothy acquired the nickname Strong Man or Strong Bohen. As there was no retirement in this era, he worked as a laborer up until his death in 1915. Despite the common perception of a universal affiliation of Irish immigrants with the Catholic Church, Timothy only attended Catholic Mass once a year on Passion Sunday.[10]   This may have been because there was not a strong institutional church in rural Southwest Ireland where he was raised.

Within a few years of arriving in Buffalo, Timothy met and fell in love with another County Cork native, Mary Elizabeth Driscoll. Mary was born in 1851 in Ireland to Daniel Driscoll and Julie (O'Brien) Driscoll. She most likely arrived in the United States in the late 1860s and became a citizen in 1871. Unlike her husband, Mary could both read and write, which may have been the result of her living in Liverpool, England where educational opportunities would have been more abundant than in her native Cork. Her Cork-born father, Daniel, was arrested in Ireland for alleged political activities in support of Ireland, and was thrown into an English prison, most likely during the Fenian uprisings during the 1860s. Mary's mother, Julie, born in Ireland in 1819, was forced to move the family from Ireland to Liverpool—incidentally the largest community of Fenians and Fenian sympathizers in England—in order to be closer to her imprisoned husband. After settling in an Irish neighborhood in Liverpool, Julie was forced to find work to support her family. Unfortunately, Daniel died in prison sometime in the 1860s, and Julie and her daughter Mary Elizabeth emigrated to Buffalo's First Ward to be close to Daniel Driscoll's cousin Timothy Driscoll, the undertaker for many First Warders buried in Holy Cross Cemetery.

Timothy Bohane and Mary Driscoll married around 1874 at St. Patrick's Church just north of the Ward. The marriage between these two families was not unusual and was evidence of the clannish nature of the Irish. Many first-generation Irish immigrants married others from the same counties or regions in Ireland. The Bohane and Driscoll families were—and still are today—heavily concentrated in the Skibbereen/Baltimore section of County Cork, Ireland, and intermarried for many centuries. In fact, Timothy Bohane's mother was a Driscoll, and the name Bohane is an agnomen (a nickname used to distinguish people from the same clan) for the name Driscoll. Today, in Skibbereen's Famine Memorial, there is a plaque dedicated to the "members of the Bohane/Driscoll clan" who perished in the Famine.

After their wedding, Timothy and Mary quickly grew their family—giving birth to ten children. Unfortunately, the family suffered great personal loss as they fell victim to the high infant mortality rate of their day. Only three of their children—Mary, Daniel, and Rose—survived past early childhood. This survival rate was typical—especially for families in the Ward—and was due to a lack of proper sanitary conditions and medical treatment. The cause of death for their deceased children—Julia, Brigid, Anne, Elizabeth, Margaret, and two boys who were not named—was scarlet fever and diphtheria. The emotional toll of burying seven children must have been overwhelming for Timothy and Mary. As we will find out later in this chapter, these tragedies would not be the only ones they suffered.

Railroads, Shipbuilding, Lumber, and Other Industries

The Erie Canal's monopoly on transportation from Lake Erie to the East Coast lasted roughly twenty years from its inception in 1825, until the railroads emerged in Buffalo in the early 1840s. At first, local government officials tried to suppress railroad service in order to protect the canal system, but within a few years of the laying of the first tracks, railroads were allowed to compete on equal terms. Before the consolidation of railroads in the 1860s and 1870s, most railroad companies typically ran short distances between two strategic points. By the early 1840s, the Attica and Buffalo Railroad laid tracks along Exchange Street (known then as Old Crow Street) on the northern boundary of the First Ward. By 1853, there were at least three railroads that had laid tracks in a circular pattern around the First Ward: the Buffalo & Rochester, Buffalo & State Line, and the Buffalo & New York City.[11] Two of the railroads terminated at the strategically important Ohio Basin in order to gain access to goods arriving from the Buffalo River. The race for access to the lucrative waterfront industries was on. By the mid-1850s, the New York Central Railroad erected the world's largest railroad depot on Ohio Street along the Buffalo River to receive grain and other goods from lake vessels.[12] Grain boats were able to pull right up to the depot and unload their goods onto railcars, which would then transport their cargo to destinations throughout the United States. Rail transportation was so much more efficient and cost effective than canal transport that by 1855 the railroads were carrying twice the amount of flour to Buffalo as canal boats.

This railroad expansion created jobs for the newly arrived immigrants in the Ward. Not only were men hired to lay new railroad tracks, but permanent positions were created for engineers, conductors, switchmen, and yard managers. These year-round jobs were more desirable than grain scooping because they were not limited to the short shipping season, and employees could count on steady income throughout the year. By 1877, even more railroad tracks were laid in the Ward for companies such as the New York Central, the Buffalo & Jamestown, the Lake Shore & Michigan Southern, the Buffalo Creek, and the Erie.[13] Unfortunately, these new rail tracks fragmented the existing residential neighborhoods and provided hazards to the residents who lived there.

In 1864, a serious threat to the monopoly of lake-vessel shipments of grain to Buffalo occurred when the first, all-rail shipment of grain from Chicago arrived in Buffalo.[14] Rail travel of goods had two significant benefits over lake travel: railroads did not shut down in the winter when Lake Erie was frozen, and they transported goods faster. The shift from lake shipments of goods to the railroads became increasingly common during the Civil War years; the exception was bulk goods like wheat, which was still cheaper to ship by lake freighters.[15] The lower cost of shipping wheat by ships preserved hundreds of grain scooper jobs in the First Ward during these years. But shipments of other goods increasingly shifted to rail, which jeopardized the Ward's strategic position because transshipment and storage of goods could bypass the area. In 1874, shipments of goods by rail surpassed those carried over the lake and canal.[16] Buffalo's rail importance continued after the Civil War, and by the 1870s and 1880s Buffalo had become the second largest railroad center in the nation—second only to Chicago. The area around the Ward was a vital hub in this network. But not all was well in terms of job prospects along the waterfront.

The decade between 1875 and 1885 was a particularly dark period for waterfront laborers because Midwestern farmers increasingly shipped their goods from Chicago via rail to points outside of Buffalo. Lake shipments to Buffalo fell significantly during this period and demand for unskilled labor along the waterfront also dropped. Fortunately, for workers in the Ward, grain production in 1885 shifted further west of the traditional grain belt into states like Minnesota and North and South Dakota. Now Duluth, located on the western edge of Lake Superior, emerged as a major grain transshipment point; this meant that it once again became more economical to ship goods across the Great Lakes in lake vessels rather than from Duluth via the railroads to points east. In 1886, another development assisted the prospects of the Ward when steel-hulled vessels started to replace wooden-hulled boats. These new steel freighters could handle more freight, which added to the financial competitiveness of lake shipping.[17] As a result of these two developments, the First Ward was back in business. At the approach of the 20th century, grain shipments to Buffalo continued their explosive growth. In 1891, 128 million bushels passed through Buffalo; in 1898, that number almost doubled to a staggering 221 million bushels.

In 1882, the Lehigh Valley Railroad—a railroad that primarily shipped anthracite coal—created a ship canal and rail terminal on the old Tifft Farm, just south of the Ward, which added two miles of dock space on the waterfront and created more jobs.[18] Despite this new capacity, rail traffic in Buffalo was still congested. In the 1890s, there were sometimes 1,000 rail cars loaded with grain waiting to be unloaded; and it might take two months to unload a car because of the logistical logjam.[19] Similar to unloading a lake freighter, railroad companies employed grain scoopers to unload the boxcars using a large shovel powered by steam.[20] Numerous railroads operated in and around the Ward, and the names changed as a result of consolidation and bankruptcies, but two railroads were critically important for waterfront shipments of goods. In the latter part of the nineteenth century, the Lake Shore and Michigan Southern line controlled the critically important route between Buffalo and Chicago. The New York Central was established to run from Buffalo to Albany, and because of the incredible volume of traffic, it was the first long distance railroad in the world to have a four-track line. In 1914, the New York Central bought the Lake Shore and Michigan Southern Railway to form a powerhouse railroad from New York City to Chicago with Buffalo as a critical intermediary hub. Throughout these years, the railroads provided steady employment for thousands of First Ward men, and helped propel some of them into the middle class. By the early 1900s, Buffalo had roughly seventeen rail terminals, and it ranked as one of the largest rail centers in the country.[21]

As early as the 1830s, businesses not directly associated with the grain industry started moving into the Ward because of its inexpensive land and its proximity to the Buffalo River. Marine-related businesses were naturally attracted to the Ward's proximity to the river. As early as 1836, Carrick & Bidwell built and repaired boats at the dry docks at the foot of Ohio and Elk Streets. This was the beginning of one of the most important industries in the Ward. In 1839, after Jacob W. Banta took over for John Carrick and the firm changed its name to Bidwell & Banta, the company became one of the most prosperous shipbuilding businesses on the Great Lakes. In the late 1840s, the company moved its shipbuilding enterprise further into the Ward, opposite the foot of Chicago Street on the Buffalo River.

Bidwell & Banta specialized in palace steamers, which were described as "some of the largest and most luxurious wooden side-wheel steamboats in the world."[22] These paddle-wheel steamboats rivaled the ocean-going vessels in the Atlantic in terms of size and luxury; some measured more than 300 feet long. The steamboats carried passengers, often immigrants, across the Great Lakes to cities like Toledo and Detroit. One expert on these steamboats described them as such: "The interiors were as ornate as any ocean liner of the time. They had mirrored grand salons and staircases, stained glass windows, exotic polished woodwork, crystal chandeliers and ornamental fountains."[23] He went on to describe, "The lavish interiors were embellished with sculpture and oil paintings. It was said to be as good as a visit to a fine art gallery to tour the cabins of the first-class steamers."[24]

These massive ships required hundreds of shipbuilders, and many of these workers came from the First and Eighth Wards.[25] These skilled laborers produced grand lake steamboats such as the *Western Metropolis*, the *Chicago*, the *City of Buffalo*, the *Western World*, the *Crescent City*, the *Queen City*, the *Queen of the West*, and the *Plymouth Rock*. Some of these ships could hold as many as 2,000 passengers and could accommodate 250 people in their palatial dining halls. When the boats were completed and ready to sail the Great Lakes, large crowds gathered in the First Ward at their launch ceremonies, during which bands played and bells rung throughout the harbor.[26] Interestingly, Jacob W. Banta, the co-owner of Bidwell & Banta, was one of the very few industrialists in the nineteenth century who actually resided in the First Ward; he lived at the corner of Perry and Hayward Streets.

The financial panic of 1857 crippled the palace steamboat industry, and in 1858, Benjamin Bidwell and Jacob Banta both retired from shipbuilding. As a result of the financial collapse, many of the local laborers who worked as shipbuilders were laid off. As the economy recovered, the business reopened and was renamed Mason & Bidwell. The new owners transformed the business to build propeller driven iron-hulled steamboats instead of the ornate wooden paddle-wheel steamboats.[27] As continuous rail service operated along the Great Lakes, the need for luxurious passenger travel subsided. Throughout the rest of the 19th century and much of the 20th, skilled laborers were engaged in the shipbuilding business along the dry docks opposite Chicago Street, although the company name and construction techniques changed over time.

Iron manufacturing also sprouted up in the Ward environs to meet the demand for machines and machine parts for the growing waterfront industries including shipbuilding. Shepard Iron Works on Ohio Street was one firm that made steam engines and boilers for the growing flour and saw mill industries. They also built steam engines for shipbuilders like Mason & Bidwell. During the middle of the 19th century, there was also Globe Foundry at the corner of Chicago and Carroll Streets and J. & N.C. Scoville's Car Wheel Foundry on Louisiana Street. Farrar & Trefts, located at 47-61 Perry Street, manufactured steam engines, boilers, and propeller wheels; by the early part of the twentieth century, it employed 600 men. Lake Erie Boiler Works at Chicago and Perry Streets, as well as King Iron Works at 226 Ohio Street, also made marine boilers, marine engines, and propellers. Coal storage and distribution was also a critical industry in the Ward because as businesses grew so too did their demand for fuel. Cadwaller Bull built a coal yard at the corner of Ohio and Chicago Streets. Spencer Kellogg built a company named for himself located at Ganson and South Michigan Streets which was the largest manufacturer of linseed oil—used for paint, putty and wood varnish—in the United States. Kellogg's first linseed mill was opened in 1879, and by the early part of the 20th century the company managed two large elevators at the foot of Michigan Street (Kellogg "A" and Kellogg "B"). The Ward was bustling with diverse industries.

Buffalo also became one of the largest processors of lumber in the country, much of which was processed in the Ward. Edward and Britain Holmes formed a large planing mill and lumberyard on Michigan Street in 1852. These two successful entrepreneurs capitalized on the building boom in Buffalo by manufacturing in-demand products such as flooring, siding, ceiling, panel stuff, brackets, molding, sash, doors, and blinds. It was the company's invention of an automated process to manufacture barrels, however, which propelled it to prominence. The firm eventually became one of the largest employers in the Ward. Around 1859, the E & B Holmes Company opened up a new factory at 59 Chicago Street, closer to the heart of the Ward. Specializing in manufacturing barrel-making equipment for the oil, pork, liquor, and flour industries, the firm began making and selling their machinery all over the world. The planing yard and lumberyard continued to employ hundreds of laborers until it went bankrupt in 1890. E & B Holmes competed with other planing and lumberyards, like the Dart Planing Mill, alongside the Ohio Basin in the Ward, and in later years the Buffalo City Planing Mills that also operated along the Basin.

Workplace Injuries and Child Labor

Throughout much of the 19th century, railroad workers, longshoremen, and grain scoopers often worked twelve-hour days, and seven days a week during the peak-shipping season. Thomas Evans, an Irish immigrant who lived in the First Ward in the late 1880s, succinctly summed up the life of a grain scooper: "Long hours for little pay."[28] At the Union Iron Works, iron-ore puddlers worked twelve-hour days from Monday to Friday, and six hours on Saturday—Sunday was the only day of rest.[29] Congressman Richard Max McCarthy recalled the backbreaking job his paternal grandfather had unloading iron-ore ships with a shovel; to numb the pain Grandfather McCarthy and his fellow laborers purportedly consumed two quarts of whiskey each day.[30] McCarthy claimed that even in the 20th century, his father worked twelve-hour days, seven days a week at the railroads. Compensation for these long backbreaking days was meager, for there was an overabundant supply of workers and a lack of organized labor. Moreover, various macroeconomic forces, such as changing technological advances as well as frequent periods of unemployment due to the shortened shipping season in Buffalo, made it difficult for workers to budget their income.

Prior to OSHA regulations, working conditions in the Ward could be perilous. Joe Marren, whose family resided in the Valley and the Ward for several generations, described three tragedies that struck his family. Both his great-grandfather and grandfather worked on the railroads. On September 26, 1888, Joe's great-grandfather, Thomas Marren, a section hand for the Western New York and Pennsylvania Railroad, stepped between two railcars and was struck by the engine. At 34 years of age, he was immediately crushed to death. It was only four months earlier that Thomas came from Ireland where he worked as a farmer to live with his brother-in-law at 612 Exchange Street, hoping to save up enough money to eventually bring his wife and his five children to Buffalo. Thomas Marren's family eventually did make it to Buffalo. But a second tragedy struck the family, when his son John died in a similar manner as Thomas. On January 31, 1906, at 19 years of age, John Marren was struck by a train at Exchange and Alabama Streets at the cross-over switch of the Nickel Plate, Erie, and New York Central tracks. He too died instantly. A final tragic incident occurred around 1910, when Joe Marren's grandfather Jim, a switchman for the Nickel Plate yards, lost his leg in an accident while attempting to switch the tracks.[31]

Mike Catanzaro, a former First Ward resident, relates a similar story of how his grandfather, Michael J. Catanzaro, also lost his leg working as a signalman for Leigh Valley Railroad. Likewise, in the Evans' family manuscript, the author describes two workplace accidents suffered by members of her First Ward family. The author's great uncle, William Evans, was lost overboard while working on a Lake Erie boat at the age of twenty-five, and in another accident her great uncle, Tim Evans, lost his leg working at a railroad crossing.[32] Mary Dyczek remembers how her uncle Mike Comerford, who had survived fighting the Germans in World War I, came home to Buffalo to work as a watchman at one of the grain elevators. Within one year of his return from the war, a brick fell from an elevator, shattered his skull, and killed him.

My own ancestors suffered a similar loss from perilous work conditions. Timothy Bohen's son-in-law, Edward Johnson, who was married to Timothy's daughter Mary, was an ironworker of Norwegian and Irish heritage. After Edward and Mary were married at Our Lady of Perpetual Help on July 2, 1903, they lived in the Ward at 45 Sandusky Street in Timothy's rear cottage. Edward was a business agent for his ironworker union. Occasionally, laborers in the Ward had to travel out of the area for work. Johnson accepted an offer to work on the massive Quebec Bridge project in Quebec, Canada, which was to span the St. Lawrence River from Quebec City to Levis, Quebec. Edward's wife Mary temporarily moved herself and their two children to Quebec to be near her husband at his jobsite. During this time, one of the engineering teams associated with the project was complaining of flaws in the design of the bridge.

They noticed that iron beams were starting to bend and buckle, which the head engineering firm claimed were minor issues. On the late summer day of August 29, 1907, Mary, who was pregnant with her daughter Mary Alma, brought her two other children to meet Edward at quitting time in the late afternoon. Shortly after the work stoppage whistle blew, the bridge—which was nearing completion after four years of construction—buckled and collapsed in just 15 seconds as Mary and her children watched in horror. The crash killed 75 workers including Mary's husband, Edward Johnson. The Quebec Bridge disaster is still one of the worst disasters in Canada's history. Edward Johnson's body was never recovered from the wreckage in the St. Lawrence River, but a memorial marker in his honor can be found in Holy Cross Cemetery in Lackawanna, New York.

Injuries and death from grain scooping were just as common as they were for railroad workers and ironworkers. A random review of the 1913 medical records of one Ward grain scoopers, Dan Driscoll, reveals that in a fifteen-year period he was seriously injured on the job at least six times. The injuries he suffered ranged from broken ribs resulting from a beam striking him, to abrasions on his legs, to a knee contusion, which required time off from work. Working well past the modern retirement age, Driscoll was seventy-one years old when he suffered his knee contusion.[33] Grain elevators were also the sites of horrific fires, usually sparked by grain dust. The author of the Evans' manuscript describes how all six of her uncles witnessed elevator fires during their lives as scoopers. On August 25, 1882, Buffalo experienced a devastating explosion at the Erie Elevator, most likely caused by a gas explosion. Five men who were blowing and screening a cargo of wheat were killed—four of them burned to death and one, Timothy Driscoll, was blown out of the elevator and later died of his injuries. In addition to the loss of life, there was a $450,000 loss of property including the loss of the stored wheat, corn, and oats.[34] Deadly grain elevator fires were almost a yearly occurrence until advancements in elevator construction were instituted. In addition to explosions and fires, tuberculosis, asphyxiation and asthma were widespread among the scoopers. Working conditions in the factories could be just as dangerous as in the elevators. Accidents from heavy machinery killed and injured many workers in factories such as the Union Iron Works.[35]

Prior to the 1870s, child labor was common and expected for children of the Ward. Throughout the late 1870s and 1880s, New York State enacted labor laws that increased the protection of children. Prior to these laws, however, it was possible for young men to start working manual jobs as early as age ten. In 1874, the age of compulsory education was extended to fourteen,[36] however children as young as twelve could work if they had the proper paperwork showing school attendance. These laws required that students attend school for at least fourteen weeks a year. But even this could be modified in cases in which the family needed the support of the wages from their children. This may have been the case with Mary Kane, age 14, and Minnie Connors, age 12, both of whom lived in Union-town and worked for the Fruit Factory in 1880.[37] William J. "Fingy" Conners reportedly started working on lake ships at age thirteen.

An 1873 photo of workers at the Dart Planing Mill, a lumber mill on the Ohio Basin, shows a row of boys dressed in work clothes who look no older than ten to twelve years old. Laws were also passed that capped how long children could work: no more than 10 hours a day, and no more than 60 hours a week—still quite onerous from our modern perspective. Unfortunately, some of the laws were issued too late for a group of Irish First Ward children who worked in the Birge Wallpaper Factory on Perry Street near Washington Street. On December 17, 1880 a raging fire broke out in the factory. As the young workers rushed higher up in the building to escape the fire, ten of them were either burned to death or jumped to their deaths. Most of the victims were burned beyond recognition and were buried in a mass grave at Holy Cross Cemetery.

If a boy was lucky, he could avoid factory work by ferrying men around on the Buffalo River and other places in the harbor. Some laborers were ferried in small boats around the waterways to their places of employment, while others took a ferry to get from a ship to shore. All of the workers at the Bidwell & Banta shipyard needed to be ferried across the Buffalo River from Chicago Street to the dry-dock on the other side. There is even a report that Father Nelson Baker was ferried from the shore near St. Joseph's Cathedral over to the Beach in the Ward to say Mass on certain Sundays. These unique water taxis, which were roughly sixteen to twenty feet long, were shaped like wide-bodied punts rather than the slim gondolas that are common in Venice. The oarsman had only one oar, and stood in the back of the boat rather than rowing with two oars in the middle of the boat, which allowed more space for cargo and more passengers. The young boys propelled the boats by manipulating the oar in a figure eight pattern similar to the motion of a fish tail. In a Buffalo newspaper article in 1869, the young oarsmen were described as shrewd, intelligent, and dexterous.[38]

The captains of these small boats were mostly sons of Irish grain scoopers and stevedores who lived in the Ward. The parents of the boys usually owned the boat and lent it to them to make some money to contribute to the family coffers. Two of the most famous politicians to come from the Ward, John C. and William F. Sheehan, earned money by working as oarsmen for the water ferries on the Buffalo River. In 1869, the fare charged to transport someone across the river was about two cents, and by 1883 the fares ranged from five to ten cents.[39] Another famous First Warder who operated a ferry service was T. V. O'Connor who charged ten cents in the 1880s to transport workers along the Buffalo River. In the 1870s there was a fleet of about sixty of these boats and each followed a designated route with a flexible timetable based on the needs of the passengers.[40]   Irish influence was apparent in the names of their crafts: "Wild Irish Girl," "Fenian Girl," and "Dandy Pat."[41]   By the 1930s, with the advent of outboard motor boats, the need for these wooden oar-propelled boats had dried up.

In later years in the Ward, children worked less onerous jobs such as bringing milk and lunch to workers at the elevators.[42]   Another common child occupation in the 20th century was known as "rushin' the growler"—children would stop at the saloon for a 15-cent pail of beer and bring it to their fathers at work.[43]   Even in the 20th century, after state and national laws were passed, it was not uncommon for boys to leave school at eighth grade in order to go to work along the waterfront.

Harsh Conditions in an Industrial Neighborhood

In the early years, residents of the Ward experienced many calamities such as family dissolution, crime, alcoholism, poverty, and disease. Crime statistics from this period are revealing. The Irish were overly represented in the Erie County prison: in 1857 the Irish incarceration rate was as high as 42.5% even though the Irish only made up a fraction of the city population.[44] The typical profile of an incarcerated citizen was a twenty to thirty-year-old laborer arrested for vagrancy, intoxication, or disorderly conduct.[45] These incarceration statistics did not specify which ward they resided in, and it is most probable that the typical First Ward married male would not have been imprisoned. But some of the sailors and un-married laborers living in boardinghouses might have spent some time in prison. Intoxication was one of the leading causes of arrests. This fact contributed to the negative perceptions of the Irish held by other non-Irish Buffalonians, and alien-ated them from these other ethnic groups.[46] One sad story of an intoxicated Irish immigrant laborer who lived near the docks was that of Michael Kelly. One night in April 1835 Kelly had too much to drink, came home, and plunged a butcher knife into his wife, killing her. Scores of people from all over Western New York came to witness Kelly's execution.[47] He was the first person to be executed since Buffalo was incorporated as a city.

Living in an industrial area without access to good medical care also led to a high mortality rate. In addition to the workplace deaths and injuries previously mentioned, Ward residents also had to contend with a prevalence of disease, accidents, and even deadly storms. The infant mortality rate of my ancestors Timothy and Mary Bohen was very typical in the First Ward. Not only did Timothy have to bury seven of this ten children and his son-in-law, Edward Johnson, but he also lost his two eldest grandchildren. His widowed daughter Mary was left with three children after her husband died in the Quebec Bridge accident in 1907: Catherine, Edward (Eddie), and Mary Alma. In 1908, Eddie died at age two of scarlet fever, and on September 18, 1910, one week after her first week of school, six-year-old Catherine died of diphtheria. Timothy and Anna Donovan, the parents of the famous William J. Donovan, suffered a similarly high mortality rate with the first four of their children dying from meningitis and only two of their children living to an old age.

The Evans' family history reveals that their family was cursed with numerous cases of tuberculosis. Tom Evans' first wife, Nora Fitzgerald Evans, who was described as lovely but frail, died of tuberculosis; their son and daughter died of the dreaded disease as well.[48] After Nora's death, Tom Evans married Nell Carey and together they lost three more children to tuberculosis: Nelly, Annie, and Johnny "Bucko" Evans.[49] Our family's Patrick Bohen, a cousin of Timothy, lost his twelve-year-old son Patrick to pneumonia. As the Bohen parents were busy attending to Patrick's needs on the day of his death, their eight-year-old son William snuck out of the house and accidentally drowned in a nearby body of water giving that family the tragic distinction of losing two sons in one day.[50] Other tragedies such as house fires stole lives of Ward residents as well. "Fingy" Conners' only sister perished when she rushed back into a blazing fire at the Conners' cottage in order to retrieve her sewing machine.[51]

One Buffalo writer and former congressman explained how the perception of a happy-go-lucky attitude among the First Ward Irish really was just a coping mechanism for their hard lot in life. Richard McCarthy observes the following:

> Many people think that those old Buffalo Irishmen were simply a fighting, rollicking lot of merry characters who went happily through life with infectious grins and lilting songs. But the fact is, that despite their wit, they led pretty hard and grim existences. Much of their humor, in fact, came from an effort to find a lighter side in their burdensome lives. At heart they were deeply complex and mystical people with centuries of suffering behind them who worked for long hours at exhausting jobs.[52]

Many of the first generation of immigrants who suffered in Ireland, and then struggled to establish themselves in America wanted to forget the past and start anew. From my own family's oral history, Timothy Bohen apparently refused to speak about his family or experiences in Ireland. When one of his enthusiastic grandchildren once asked him about Ireland, Timothy's response was, "Forget Ireland! You are living in the best country in the world." Peter Quinn, in a book on the story of the Irish in America, adds a further explanation:

> For their part, the poor have traditionally not only lacked the education and time to record their lives, they have also lacked the interest. The stories the poor carried with them were rarely about their own particular travails and

tragedies. These events weren't remarkable or exceptional, but the everyday context of life itself. For people steeped in rural existence, or only recently in transition from it, the storytelling they were familiar with was communal rather than individual. It offered mythic explanations of evil, death, failed crops, cures, curses, the feared or welcomed interventions of heroes, fairies, angels, saints, or God himself.[53]

Quinn quotes the historian Robert James Scally who suggests that the Irish immigration bears "more resemblance to the slave trade or the boxcars of the Holocaust than to the routine crossings of a later age."[54] Quinn also believes that the less we know about our relatives, the more likely they came over during the famine. The process of piecing together the puzzle will always be incomplete. "Silence is among the greatest legacies of the Great Famine."[55]

Residents of the Ward also had to contend with devastating storms off of Lake Erie. Powerful Atlantic Ocean storms in Ireland were rare, so very few Irish immigrants would have been prepared for the devastating storms that they would face in Buffalo. One of the worst storms occurred on October 18, 1844. As residents along the waterfront were trying to sleep after a long day's work, they were kept awake by unusually high winds howling outside their homes. Storms accompanied by strong winds were common in Buffalo. But on this particular night, the residents were in for a once-in-a-lifetime experience. On rare occasions, a peculiar phenomenon can occur on the Great Lakes when a storm with high winds literally pushes water from one side of the lake—in this case Lake Erie—to the other. Later the winds recede and the water comes rushing back to the other side of the lake. This phenomenon—called a seiche—creates a lake tidal wave with devastating effects. On the night of October 18th, at 11 p.m., one of these events occurred and a tidal wave close to thirty feet high crested over the fourteen-foot seawall. Within just thirty minutes, most of the lower part of the city was under two to eight feet of water. The area closest to the waterfront was the most devastated in terms of life and property.

The losses from the storm varied: the First Ward offices of shipbuilders Banta & Bidwell were literally moved from one side of the Buffalo Creek to the other side; Joseph Dart, inventor of the grain elevator, lost one of his warehouses, and Mahlon Kingman lost three of his brick stores; almost all warehouses along the waterfront suffered losses of their stored goods; the steamboat *Robert Fulton* was completely destroyed, and five other steamboats such as the *Commodore Perry*, the *St. Louis*, the *Great Western*, the *Chautauqua* and the *Indian Queen* were all severely damaged and suffered a large loss of life of crew members on these vessels. At least two hundred small buildings along the waterfront were completely destroyed.

There was not a building on Elk Street in the Ward that was not damaged, nor a building on the "other side of the Buffalo Creek" that was left standing.[56] The steamer ship *G. Dole* was lifted and dropped onto Ohio Street in the Ward, and the steamer *Columbus* met the same fate on Michigan Street. The storm surge even pushed canal boats all the way up to Seneca Street near Michigan Street. Samuel Welch, a witness to the storm, described the debris from the storm as a mass of "lumber, boxes, hogshead, dead cattle, swine, wrecked houses, and the vestiges of human creation generally."[57] In terms of loss of life, many of those killed were in the First Ward environs. Areas near Ohio Street and Elk Street, and the south side of the Buffalo Creek were the locations for many of the dead. The names of the dead are proof that the storm did not favor one ethnic group over another. These names also serve as evidence that the Ward at this time was not exclusively Irish: O'Brien, Smith, Redding, Nelson, Bowen, Chase, Havens, Blanchard, Wheeler, Malay, and Stolicker are the family names of some who were lost in the devastating storm. There are several stories about families that were trapped in their houses as the floodwaters raged. As the water levels quickly rose, they tried in vain to reach higher ground in their houses, until eventually they had to cut holes in their roofs to escape. Wealthy shipbuilder Jacob Banta, who lived at Perry and Hayward Streets, risked his life to rescue neighbors who were tossed about in the raging waters. When the storm subsided, 78 people had drowned. This still remains the largest loss of life from a natural disaster in Buffalo's history. This would not, however, be the last natural disaster to visit the First Ward.

CHAPTER THREE

BISHOP JOHN TIMON:
SAVIOR OF THE IRISH

John Timon's nature was like a torrent rushing down the mountain crushing every obstacle that impeded its course. – Father Patrick Cronin[1]

Fierce debates about immigration raged throughout the nineteenth century in the United States, and Buffalo was one of the cities at the forefront of the debate. One of the central arguments at the time—similar to the debate at the turn of the twenty-first century—centered on whether or not native citizens should have to pay for the social services needed to care for the recently landed immigrants. In Buffalo, during the mid-nineteenth century, the Irish immigrants consumed more city services than they paid for and as a result, some native-born Buffalonians used the label of "civic parasitism" to characterize them.[2] The debate also centered on the issue of political power, which the Irish and German immigrants in Buffalo were quickly wresting from the Protestant establishment. The culmination of these factors led some of the Protestant establishment to form the Know-Nothing Party, which at its core had a strong distrust of Catholic immigrants. The Know-Nothing Party, officially known as the American Party, started in 1839, but the apex of its power was 1856. The members of this nativist party were bound "not to vote for any man for office unless he were [sic] an American citizen, born of Protestant parents and not united in marriage to a Roman Catholic."[3]

At the peak of its popularity, Millard Fillmore, a former Buffalo lawyer and recent president of the United States, led the American Party. Fillmore abhorred the political and the demographic changes occurring in East Coast and Midwestern cities like Boston and Buffalo. His perception and that of others in his party was that masses of Irish immigrants were streaming into the cities, using precious city resources and then gaining control of the Democratic Party to the detriment of the native Protestants. The nativists also worried that with the ascendancy of Irish Catholics, the influence of Rome would play a greater role in U.S. politics. Interestingly, Fillmore had less disdain for Irish Catholics than other members of his party did. In fact, the former President contributed money to the construction of St. Joseph's Cathedral, and he even sent his daughter to a Roman Catholic school operated by the Sisters of the Sacred Heart.

During the 1856 election, members of the Buffalo branch of the Know-Nothing Party employed campaign slogans such as, "Pure American common school system," "Hostility to all Papal influence in whatever form," and "Protection of the Protestant interests."[4] These discriminatory messages were clearly directed at the masses of the poor Irish immigrants along the waterfront and especially to those in the First Ward. The *Commercial Advertiser*, a Buffalo newspaper with a bias toward the Protestant establishment, openly voiced the message of the nativists. In one editorial, the editor's contempt for those in the First Ward was displayed when he described them this way:

> Verrest tag-rag and bot-tail who ever go drunk at a wake, men who infallibly chose a location in a swamp, and live in a shanty with pigs under the bed and

chickens roosting on the headboard... these fellows are hewers of wood and drawers of water...simply because they are drunken wretches, without the ambition or the brains to better their conditions.[5]

Hostility to the Irish in the Buffalo press was not confined to the *Commercial Advertiser*. Even the editors at Buffalo newspapers like the *Courier* and the *Republic*, which were loyal to the Democratic Party, were unsympathetic to the plight of the Irish. There are even reports that Almon Clapp, the editor of the *Express* newspaper in Buffalo, hired thugs to prevent the Irish from voting.[6] According to local historian David Gerber, "Irish poverty, crude peasant ways, hard drinking, violence and single-minded unity in pursuing group interests troubled Americans across partisan lines."[7] Another local historian, Mark Goldman, describes the effects of this hostility from the Know-Nothings to the Catholics this way:

> Forced to explain themselves, their behavior, and their customs to the outside Protestant world, they became far more aware of their ethnic and religious identity. Mostly it was the Irish who were the target of this campaign of hate. Less often it was the Germans. But always it was the Catholics.[8]

The nativists stirred up enough animosity with their rhetoric that it actually led to violence in several parts of the country. For instance, riots broke out for three days in Philadelphia as the nativists burned down two Catholic churches, the local Catholic seminary, and a theological library. Irish Americans were physically assaulted in Louisville, Kentucky and in Baltimore. Even in Buffalo a riot broke out on Main Street across from the American House on July 14, 1854 between the nativists and the Irish, who were protesting a nativist preacher who had come to speak in Buffalo. According to a report in the *New York Times*, "seven or eight Irishmen's heads were broken, but no one was killed. Five Irishmen were arrested and fined $25 each."[9]

Defenders of the Irish: Bishop Timon and Thomas D'Arcy McGee

Not only were the Irish being provoked by the nativists and mocked in local newspapers, but they were also exploited by the Protestant elite in Buffalo who owned the factories, controlled the capital, and made the laws. The Irish immigrants were paid meager wages, worked long hours, and most lived in deplorable conditions compared to their fellow Buffalonians. Adding to their troubles, these poor immigrants were more vulnerable to diseases like cholera because of poor sanitation, and they lacked adequate services to address these calamities. At this time they were also shut out of the political process in Buffalo, so they were without legislative protection. Quite simply the Irish in Buffalo needed a savior, and they found one in a fifty-one-year-old priest and fellow Irish American, John Timon.

On April 23, 1847, the Vatican created the Catholic Diocese of Buffalo in order to minister to the growing number of its members in Western New York. Later that year, on October 17th, Bishop John Timon, Vincentian missionary priest, and son of Irish immigrants from Cavan County in Northern Ireland, was jubilantly welcomed as the first Bishop of Buffalo by 12,000 of the faithful in a pouring rainstorm.[10] A fine carriage was waiting to pick him up, but Bishop Timon—setting a tone of solidarity with his poor flock—decided to walk with his carpetbag and umbrella in hand.[11] At the time, the center of the Buffalo Roman Catholic Church, and the presumed home for the new bishop, was the stately St. Louis Church on Main Street, a French and German parish. However, Bishop Timon, born of humble beginnings, had a strong affinity for the struggling Irish, and desired to live with those who were most in need.

On November 23, 1847, only four weeks after arriving in Buffalo, he packed up his few belongings at St. Louis Church and set up residence several blocks away in a rented apartment across from St. Patrick's Church on Ellicott Street and Batavia Street (now Broadway Street), to more closely look after his Irish flock. While St. Patrick's was north of the First Ward by several blocks, it was the closest church and considered the Ward's home parish. At this time there were roughly 6,300 Irish people living in Buffalo and many of them lived close to St. Patrick's Church.[12] There were, however, only 300 registered families in St. Patrick's Parish when Bishop Timon arrived, so clearly thousands of the Irish were not being ministered to.[13] The first Bishop of Buffalo didn't waste time and confirmed a staggering 4,167 people in Buffalo in his first year—proof that Buffalo was mission territory. When Timon wasn't performing his ecclesiastical duties, he was putting plans together to create an institutional church that would help lift its downtrodden members out of poverty.

Before Timon arrived, there was already a divide between the German, French, and Irish Catholics in Buffalo, and his initial actions involving a property dispute at St. Louis Church further exacerbated these tensions. The lay leadership of St. Louis Church argued that the trustees owned St. Louis Church, not the new Bishop of Buffalo. However, this view contrasted with Timon's understanding of the property deed and more broadly his vision for the church in Buffalo: a highly centralized and institutional Church. The Bishop threatened the trustees of St. Louis with excommunication and eliminated all services at the church for several months. This not only irked the German and French Catholics, but it also fed the growing anti-Catholicism of the Protestant establishment in Buffalo who now feared an erosion of separation of church and state with Timon's arrival. But the feisty Timon did not back down and it wouldn't be the last time that he would be obstinate when dealing with the Buffalo establishment.

Catholic immigrants were desperate for spiritual and material resources and Bishop Timon worked tirelessly toward meeting their needs. These needs ranged from services for orphans and the aged to hospitals, schools and even basic food supplies. In the 1850s most of the city poorhouses were filled with Irish men, women, and children and many city-run institutions were overtly biased against Catholics.[14] One such problem existed at the Buffalo Orphan Asylum, which was hostile to Catholic spiritual needs even though many of the residents were Catholic.[15] After Bishop Timon unsuccessfully fought some of these policies at established Protestant institutions, he decided he had to create his own institutions to guarantee that Catholics would be taken care of physically and spiritually.

Timon knew that the problems were too numerous for him to fix by himself, so in 1848, he invited the Sisters of Charity to come to Buffalo to run an orphan asylum as well as establish a new hospital at Pearl and Virginia Streets.[16] On June 3, 1848, six Sisters of Charity arrived in Buffalo from their convent house in Baltimore and immediately went to work. Interestingly, although the Protestant establishment of Buffalo had discussed establishing a hospital, it was the Sisters of Charity, in 1848, who opened the first hospital in the Queen City. This 100-bed institution was open to all Buffalo residents regardless of religious denomination. Within one year, the hospital treated over 1,500 patients and half of these were charity cases. Many First Ward residents were also taken care of by Sisters of Charity at the only hospital in Buffalo at that time.

The following year, in 1849, the sisters opened St. Vincent's Orphanage, located at Ellicott Street and Broadway adjoining St. Patrick's Church. Timon's timing in creating both institutions was opportune because in the summer of 1849 a terrible cholera epidemic swept through the poorest areas of Buffalo, especially the First Ward, and there were 2,535 reported cases of this deadly disease. Almost ninety percent of the 877 who died from this cholera epidemic in Buffalo were foreign-born laborers, mostly Irish.[17] This devastating disease, caused from bacteria found in untreated water, resulted in severe diarrhea, and many patients would die a painful death from dehydration. Fortunately, the Sisters of Charity assisted in saving many lives and even the Buffalo *Medical Journal* commended the Sisters of Charity for achieving a much lower mortality rate among cholera victims than the established city institution.[18]

The need for the orphan asylum grew quickly because cholera epidemics struck Buffalo again in 1851, 1852, and 1854. These epidemics continued to disproportionately impact the immigrant communities, especially the Irish along the waterfront. Since there was no treatment for it, and since sometimes both parents ingested the contaminated water, children could be left parentless. Dire economic circumstances and an early death of a mother or father also caused an abundance of orphans. In 1857, the need for the orphanage was strong as evidenced by an editorial in the *Catholic Sentinel* urging an expansion of the facility because "the almost unprecedented severity of the times has thrown upon our hands a large number of destitute children whom widowed mothers are no longer able to provide with common necessities of life who must perish if we do not come to their relief."[19] Due to dire poverty, young Irish women who weren't in stable families were often exploited, so the sisters also took care of wayward and homeless young women.[20] In addition to providing shelter, the sisters also educated them to become self-supporting and provided them with technical skills such as dressmaking and cooking.[21] The sisters were very successful in keeping many women from falling into prostitution or other denigrating activities.

Anti-Catholic bias in the school system was another issue on Timon's agenda. The first bishop of Buffalo knew the ultimate way to improve the conditions of the Irish was education, but Timon didn't want his flock losing their Catholic faith in the public schools. The Buffalo city schools were typical of their day in that, "they read the King James Version of the Bible, sang Protestant hymns, and read nativistic textbooks."[22] The Bishop vociferously condemned the fact that Catholics paid high taxes so that the public schools could secretly proselytize Catholics, purchase anti-Catholic books for their libraries and hire only non-Catholics as teachers.[23] So Timon once again took matters into his own hands and recruited a vibrant community of sisters from Ireland and set them up in the heart of the Ward.

The Sisters of Mercy, a Catholic community of nuns founded in Ireland, is dedicated to educating children and serving the needs of the poor. By 1843, the group sent its first group of sisters from Ireland to Pittsburgh, Pennsylvania to administer to the needs of the Irish immigrants. As their community grew, they established foundations all over the Northeast. It was from their foundation in Providence, Rhode Island that Bishop Timon requested a few sisters for a convent in Rochester, New York, which was then part of the Buffalo diocese. At this time, Timon already had a small school in the First Ward, which was staffed by the Sisters of St. Bridget or "Brigidine Sisters" who taught First Ward kids at St. Bridget's Parish from 1854 to 1858. However, this community lacked enough sisters to sustain their mission so they disbanded in 1858. Perhaps Timon had foreseen the Brigidine Sisters impending disbandment and this prompted him to actively recruit the Sisters of Mercy to come to Buffalo. Regardless, his timing was perfect for as the Sisters of St. Bridget folded, the Sisters of Mercy arrived in Buffalo.

On a cold February day in 1858, three sisters and a postulant arrived in Buffalo from Rochester: Mother Mary Teresa Austin Carroll, Sister Mary Raymond O'Reilly, Sister Mary Regis Madden and Mary Ann McGarr, a postulant. The enthusiastic sisters had a rather unwelcoming arrival to the Ward because their dwelling on Fulton Street—which was previously ravaged by a fire—was completely lacking in staples like beds, bedding, and other essential supplies. Bishop Timon assisted them in gathering the necessary supplies and even borrowed a candle from a neighbor to illuminate their dwelling.[24]   In a history of the Mercy Sisters the author claims that Bishop Timon watched over the Mercy Sisters in the Ward "like a vigilant father."[25]   The Irish residents of the Ward, who were familiar with the "walking sisters" from the old country, were thankful for their arrival.[26] No one then knew how much of an impact the sisters would have in the Ward over the next hundred years.

The day after their arrival the Bishop gave them money to set up a soup and bread kitchen for the poor in the Ward as well as to establish a pharmacy.[27] All of these services were needed because the immigrants in the Ward were disproportionately affected by the Panic of 1857—a financial crisis involving the banks and railroads—which led to mass layoffs in Northern urban areas. A notice in a local newspaper in 1858, during the height of the financial crisis, announced that "the Sisters of Mercy on Fulton Street have begun distributing soup and bread daily to poor persons. The thinly clad and famishing poor have not far to go for nourishing food."[28] In these days, the sisters went two by two with brown baskets that contained food and medicine to the homes of the sick and poor in the Ward.[29] They were also forced to beg for resources to assist the poor.

Aside from their charity mission, the sisters also managed in their first year to establish St. Joseph's Academy with 30 pupils and Our Lady of Mercy School, a parochial school with 200 pupils, both run by Sister Mary Regis Madden. Their original school at St. Bridget's parish was in a horse barn while they waited for a more permanent building to be constructed.[30] The community of sisters grew in numbers and just five years after their arrival, on July 19, 1863, Bishop Timon laid the cornerstone for a convent for the Sisters of Mercy in the Ward adjacent to St. Bridget's parish. By 1871, the sisters opened a new school, which was bursting with over twelve hundred students.[31] Timon had a vision of how to elevate the Irish out of their current conditions through education, but it was the Sisters of Mercy who did the work.

St. Patrick's, St. Joseph's, and St. Bridget's

While schools, orphanages and hospitals were important in addressing the material needs of the poor immigrants, it was the churches that provided for their spiritual needs. Churches also provided a social and communal bond for these displaced immigrants. For the Irish Catholics that lived in Buffalo in the late 1830s and early '40s, participation in church rituals and sacraments was limited. Prior to 1837, the only Catholic Church for the Irish or any other Catholic from the First Ward was St. Louis Church on Main Street, several miles from the Ward. The Irish didn't feel welcome at this church because of the French and German influence, and the distance was considerable from their homes near the waterfront, so many chose not to attend church services. Others rented a building near Niagara Street— closer to where the English-speaking Catholics lived—and periodically Father Charles Smith, a traveling priest from Schenectady, New York, roughly 275 miles from Buffalo, performed Catholic Mass there. Fr. Smith had to administer to the needs of other Catholics throughout Western New York so he only presided over mass once a month at this church in Buffalo. At the urging of Father Smith and New York City Bishop John Hughes, a few laymen investigated building their own church in 1839. Bank credit to build a new church was difficult to obtain and the terms of the deed to purchase the land were onerous; the terms stated that the church needed to be erected in four years and the entire loan had to paid off in ten years. Of the original eight signers of the deed, four backed out and those remaining were Patrick Milton, Maurice Vaughn, Patrick Cannon and Patrick Connolly.[32]

St. Patrick's was the appropriate name given to this new church—located at the corner of Ellicott and Broadway Streets, just north of the First Ward boundaries—that catered to the growing Irish immigrant community near the waterfront. Most of the labor to build the church came from the parishioners themselves because resources were too scarce to hire professional builders. The roof was put on before the winter of 1840, and after two years of construction, this simple brick structure was dedicated on St. Patrick's Day in 1841; however, it did not open until May of that year. After Father Smith was transferred to Brooklyn, Father William Whelan was named the pastor of this new church. Not much is known about the early years of the parish except for the fact that Father Whelan was known for his preaching on temperance and encouraged hundreds of parishioners to take the pledge against alcohol. At the time many parishioners were involved with building the new rail lines for the Boston & Buffalo Railroad, and they were paid in money and whisky: 50 cents a day and three to five cups of whiskey; the new pastor knew that this arrangement only encouraged alcoholism. Father Whelan also started a school in the basement of the church to teach the children and he hired Mr. McNicoll, Mr. Kelly and Mr. Garrigan to teach the children secular and religious subjects.[33]

The church became the hub of spiritual activities for the Irish who lived in the area of the "Flats" as well as those along the waterfront. The sacramental needs of the Irish parishioners at St. Patrick's were neglected for so many years that at a retreat Bishop Timon preached on December 19, 1847 at St. Patrick's he confirmed 234 parishioners. The congregants had so little in the form of religious instruction that the Bishop had to explain the ceremonies of Holy Week to both the congregants and the priests.[34] Bishop Timon also established the first Buffalo seminary across the street from St. Patrick's which initially had two or three seminarians enrolled who were taught by three professors: the pastor of St. Patrick's Church, the pastor of St. Louis Church, and the bishop himself. The most famous parishioner of this church is Father Nelson Baker, the candidate for sainthood, who was baptized there on November 29, 1851. The influence of the parish began to wane when Timon moved his residence in 1852 to Franklin and Erie Streets, and then in 1853 and 1855, he directed that two new parishes be created to minister to the Irish immigrants. St. Patrick's closed in 1855 and was turned over to the Sisters of Charity who converted it into an orphanage. Timon had other plans for a new place of worship for the Irish in the Ward—as well as Catholics in the downtown district—one that they would be proud of.

Bishop Timon had numerous conflicts with the Protestant establishment who tried to thwart his initiatives at every turn, but in 1851 he had a significant surprise for them. Two years earlier, the tireless first bishop of Buffalo had traveled to Europe to meet with the pope and during his journey he toured the great cathedrals of Europe. Timon was confident that Buffalo was going to be a great city and great cities need impressive cathedrals. Throughout the late 1840s until the early 1850s, he also traveled extensively through North America, Mexico, and Europe secretly raising funds for a new cathedral. The Pope gave him $2,000 to start his efforts and he then met "with the Kings of Bavaria and Naples, Prince Metternich, Austrian archdukes and Italian princesses, French nobles and English peers" to secure more funds.[35] Timon even convinced the King of Bavaria to donate some award-winning stained glass windows for this endeavor.

The Irish bishop of Buffalo originally planned to put the Catholic cathedral on Washington Street where St. Michael's Church is currently located, but an opportunity arose to be in the heart of downtown Buffalo and the bishop changed his mind. The Catholic diocese was able to purchase the beautiful Webster Garden Estate, located in Buffalo's "loveliest district with a beautiful park and rolling terraces stretching down to the shores of Lake Erie."[36] Apparently, once the Protestants discovered the plans for the site, they quickly tried to repurchase the land from him, but it was too late.[37] Bishop Timon chose the Irish-American architect Patrick Keeley from New York City to design his monumental project. Keeley designed a Gothic church similar to the prominent ones in Europe with dimensions that were 200 feet long, 100 feet wide and 75 feet high.

The cornerstone of St. Joseph's Cathedral was laid on February 6, 1851, and Irish laborers from the West Side of Buffalo and the Ward did most of the work during the four years of construction.[38] Many of the laborers were so poor that they could not contribute anything monetarily, so they provided their labor. After grueling hours at their day job, the laborers would come after work to haul stones or provide the masonry work for the project.[39] Obtaining finances for the cathedral was difficult, so Timon continually begged parishioners, foreign dignitaries, and his fellow priests for assistance. Finally, on July 1, 1855, St. Joseph's Cathedral was dedicated in front of an overflowing crowd of 3,000—including many prominent ecclesiastical figures from around the United States—who came to witness the magnificent cathedral. The cost of the project was $150,000 and Bishop Timon had it paid off by 1863.

There are some interesting stories regarding the cathedral and the First Ward. While the cathedral was being built in 1853, there was a punishing storm that hit the houses along the waterfront. As a result, numerous families were left homeless, so Bishop Timon instructed them to set up tents in the half-completed cathedral grounds where they could gain some protection from the elements. Another interesting fact involved Father Nelson Baker, who was stationed for a time at St. Joseph's Cathedral as Vicar General for the diocese. Fr. Baker would row a boat from the banks near the cathedral over to a rustic Catholic chapel at the "Beach" called Our Lady of Mercy; at the chapel he would administer the sacraments to the poor Irish and Portuguese (the Beachers) and teach them their prayers and elementary Christian doctrine.[40]

While some First Warders journeyed to the majestic St. Joseph's Cathedral for mass, for many it still didn't feel like their native church. Even though almost all of the pastors and priests for decades were Irish—Frs. Peter Bede, Francis O'Farrell, William Gleason, John McEvoy, Edward Kelly, James Quigley, James A. Lanigan, John Biden, Thomas Walsh, Henry Mooney, John J. Sheehy and Edward Britt—and the lay trustees and organizations were almost all staffed by Irish natives, the residents in the Ward needed their own church. Timon had created a branch of the Society of St. Vincent de Paul on Fulton Street in 1850, which was run by lay members and was supervised by Fr. Martin Corbett. This organization administered relief to the impoverished Irish in that neighborhood, and lay members taught Sunday catechism classes for First Ward children in a rented room in a frame house on Fulton Street.[41] As the First Ward continued to expand, Bishop Timon decided to create a parish, which would be the first one located inside the Ward boundaries. The Rev. Charles D. McMullen was named the first pastor of St. Bridget's Church, and he quickly began work on the construction of a 100 by 40-foot small frame church on Fulton Street at Louisiana Street in 1853; the first baptism was recorded on February 13, 1853.[42] Unfortunately, the $3,000 church, which was built primarily by the immigrants themselves, was not constructed up to city codes and was condemned as unsafe.

In 1858, the Bishop chose the experienced church-builder Fr. Martin O'Connor to replace Fr. McMullen. The new brick church, designed in the Romanesque style, filled the corner of Louisiana and Fulton Streets. In June 1859, Bishop Timon laid the cornerstone for the new church, which was designed to be larger and more imposing than the first one.[43] Unfortunately, on October 18, 1859, hurricane winds destroyed the newly built roof and walls and the frustrated workers and parishioners had to begin again. The dedication of the new church, which cost $16,000 to construct, finally occurred in December 1860 and it was well worth the wait.[44] There was one other minor structural setback, which occurred during Christmas midnight mass in 1866 when the floor in the church collapsed with a packed congregation on it; fortunately there were no reported injuries.

There aren't many written details about Father O'Connor, the pastor of St. Bridget's Parish from its inception until 1870, except that he was described as having an 'energetic, nervous temperament.' In contrast, his successor, Fr. William Gleason, was described as 'genial and gentle' as well as 'cheery [and] faithful.'[45] Despite their different dispositions, both of these men helped guide and develop the growing parish and each left a mark on hundreds of Irish First Ward families. In fact, it is claimed that Fr. William Gleason baptized, confirmed, married and buried thousands of First Ward residents during his twenty-four-year tenure from 1871 to 1895.[46] Fr. Gleason was also remembered for his sound judgment, which led Bishop Stephen Ryan, the second bishop of Buffalo, to chose him to be his "right hand" man.[47] In addition to the spiritual and sacramental assistance, these priests also provided for the material well being of their flock.

There is an interesting debate regarding the spelling of the name of this important church. For most of the 19th century, the church and school were spelled St. Bridget's, in honor of the famous female Irish saint. At the dawn of the 20th century, however, the names (St. Bridget's and St. Brigid's) were used interchangeably in print. For instance, in the March 4, 1909 issue of the *Catholic Union and Times*, there was a reference to both spellings in the same edition of the newspaper. An issue of the 1909 *Buffalo Express* newspaper contained one of the first instances of the new spelling: St. Brigid's. The formal diocesan newspaper preferred St. Bridget's during the early 20th century years, but in 1923, the *Buffalo City Directory* officially switched the spelling to St. Brigid's. Even during the next two decades, the name switched back and forth until around 1943 when all official documents used the St. Brigid's spelling.

A representative from the Catholic Diocese of Buffalo claims that the name changed officially in 1920 in order to distinguish it from a different saint from Sweden: St. Bridget.[48] St. Brigid is the spelling more common in Ireland. Most likely the Irish in the First Ward desired a more authentic spelling—especially during the Irish independence years around 1916-1922 when there was a movement in Ireland to return to using the Irish spellings for people and places. If you ask First Warders who grew up in the latter part of the 20th century for the correct spelling they will invariably respond: St. Brigid's.

While Bishop Timon spent most of his energy defending his flock from those he considered enemies of the Church, there were times when he disciplined or exhorted better behavior from his beloved constituents, the Irish. In the 1856 election, with the Know-Nothing Party at its peak, he issued a pastoral letter urging his flock to vote and then leave the polling places immediately rather than risk any physical confrontations with the nativists. He also urged them to refrain from intoxicating drinks and to conduct themselves like "well behaved (sic) and Christian people."[49] He then added that he was not endorsing any candidates, but if the Catholic voters cast their vote for a party with anti-Catholic views—a reference to Millard Fillmore, the Know-Nothing candidate—then they would have that on their conscience. Taken together, this was a clear command to get out and vote; don't linger at the polling places and provoke confrontations; and refrain from being drunk at the polling places, which the Irish were sometimes known to do. He believed that these behaviors would only encourage the Know-Nothing supporters of Millard Fillmore in propagating their stereotypes about Irish immigrants. Interestingly, in a letter to another ecclesiastical figure, Bishop Timon expressed more concern with the hidden anti-Catholicism in the Republican Party than the outward expression of it in Fillmore's Know-Nothing Party.[50]

A year later, in 1857, Timon wrote another pastoral letter urging Catholics not to engage in any activities that were a desecration of religious rites and ceremonies, especially at wakes and funerals. The penalty of excommunication was used to prevent "drunkenness, debauchery and other crimes" at funerals and wakes.[51] This must have been a difficult letter to write because imbibing in spirits was a long tradition at Irish wakes dating back centuries in Ireland. Bishop Timon also realized that he needed to provide some direction to his fellow countrymen regarding alcohol abuse. Earlier, in 1851, Timon's concern about alcoholism led him to invite Fr. Mathew, a charismatic abstinence preacher, to St. Patrick's Church to administer the pledge of abstinence; over 6,000 men took the pledge.[52] Timon also continually urged his fellow Irish to be respectful on St. Patrick's Day, March 17th, and to control their alcohol consumption, so as to not add to the nativists' stereotypes.

Modern Buffalo historians have positive comments about Timon's tenure as the first Bishop of Buffalo. His advocacy for the most vulnerable Catholics, mostly Irish laborers, was indisputable. Mark Goldman, in his book *High Hopes*, sums up the impact of Bishop Timon and the Church that he established:

> While the Irish had been in Buffalo for over twenty years prior to the arrival of Bishop Timon in 1847, it was not until he came that the rest of the people of Buffalo became daily and seriously aware of them. Strikes by Irish workers along the canal had been regular but easy dealt with occurrences. The Irish

churches and religious societies were highly ethnocentric and invisible, and the periodic Irish newspapers had no circulation beyond the confines of the First Ward. Timon's arrival changed all of this. Now, for the first time, Buffalo's Irish working-class population had a brash and bold spokesman who rallied and inspired the Irish and in the process frightened the older German and WASP community.[53]

David Gerber, another local historian, emphasized the importance of Bishop Timon's charitable activities, not just to the Irish, but to all Buffalonians:

Furthermore, because the American Protestant response to poverty and other local welfare needs was, besides the poorhouse, largely non-existent before 1847 and inadequate after it, Timon simultaneously, almost single-handedly, created the institutional foundations of much of local charity.[54]

Timon was remembered for more than his charity. A Sisters of Mercy historian claimed that those who knew the first bishop of Buffalo compared him to St. Paul; he was relentless in his travels through the cold and fatigue to preach and to administer the sacraments to his flock.[55] Archbishop Hughes from New York, a contemporary of Timon, considered him to be the most humble man he ever met: "He [Timon] had no ostentation or outward ceremony but [was] always plain, simple and unassuming in his manners and habits."[56] If anyone could point to a fault of Bishop Timon it would be that he wasn't good at compromising with those whose opinion differed from his, and that he may have been too focused on his Irish flock to the detriment of the German and French Catholics.

If it had not been for Timon's efforts, thousands of immigrants would possibly have suffered from hunger, sickness, and homelessness. On April 16, 1867, two days after preaching the Palm Sunday Mass in St. Joseph's Cathedral, the indefatigable Bishop Timon passed away and finally was at rest. There were enormous gatherings to commemorate this man in Buffalo and Rochester, and in other cities throughout Western New York. It was estimated that close to 100,000 people in Buffalo turned up to view his body; many thousands lined the streets of downtown Buffalo, including the children from the asylums and schools that Timon built, to view his casket led by six gray horses. Archbishop McCloskey from New York and Archbishop Kenrick from St. Louis did the eulogy at the funeral mass. Bishop Timon was laid to rest beneath his beloved St. Joseph's Cathedral.

Fortunately for Buffalo this tireless pastor gave every ounce of himself so that his flock might flourish spiritually and materially. The Irish, and particularly the First Ward Irish, greatly benefited from the fact that their Bishop, a fellow Irishman, had a special place in his heart for these downtrodden people. He used to joke to friends that even though he was born in America he was conceived in Ireland.[57] Other subsequent bishops would face difficult conditions and situations during their tenure. However, no one would face more obstacles and opposition with so few resources, and still accomplish as much as Bishop Timon did. It can be argued that Timon, a diminutive figure who stood at just over 5 feet tall, accomplished more for the Catholic Church in Buffalo during his tenure than any subsequent ecclesiastical figure. Along the way he planted the seeds that would uplift the Irish both economically and spiritually. All descendants of the Ward should be thankful for his efforts.

In addition to ecclesiastical advocates like Bishop John Timon, there were also lay advocates who endeavored to improve the lot of the Irish in Buffalo. Buffalo was fortunate, if only for a short while, to have one of the major Irish-American journalists and former Irish Nationalist living and writing in Buffalo. This man was Thomas D'Arcy McGee. While this Catholic journalist lived in a Protestant enclave of Buffalo, at Virginia and Franklin Streets, his writings and his vision were directed at the working-class Irish like those in the First Ward. McGee's ideas had an impact in his home country of Ireland, in the United States and ultimately in Canada where he is considered one of the founding fathers of that country.

In the 1850s, there was a fierce debate on both sides of the Atlantic Ocean about the racial superiority of the Anglo-Saxon race over the Celts; specifically the Celts were viewed as less industrious and lazy by nature. In Ireland, a radical group named Young Ireland would fight these claims in their newspaper, the *Nation*, and on speaking tours throughout Ireland. The basis for their formation was to urge for repeal of the Union between Ireland and England. This movement climaxed in a failed uprising in 1848 in Ireland, but several of its leaders fled to the U.S. and Canada and had a great influence on the Irish in North America.

In 1852, Bishop Timon recruited Thomas D'Arcy McGee to come to Buffalo to edit a national Irish-American newspaper, the *American Celt* and *Catholic Citizen*. From his office on Washington Street in downtown Buffalo, McGee vigorously counter-attacked the political and editorial claims in British and U.S. newspapers, such as Buffalo's *Commercial Advertiser*, which often disparaged the Irish. After the defeat of the Young Ireland uprising in 1848, and still in the midst of the Famine, the Irish on both sides of the Atlantic were deeply demoralized. McGee, after escaping British authorities, immigrated to America and was immediately shocked to see the state of the Irish people in this prosperous land. He inquired how people from this once proud Celtic race would be relegated to "waiters at Hotels… shovellers of earth-works, carriers of mortar-spades and axes, tools and tackle, for other mens [sic] uses."[58] McGee, like Timon, prescribed education as a way for the Irish to rise out of their poverty and his rallying cry was "Educate! Educate!"[59] McGee's newspaper was going to be one of the vehicles used to educate the Irish.

Timon wanted McGee to help stimulate an Irish intellectual life, which up until this point was largely absent in Buffalo. Timon and McGee, along with other lay leaders and clergy, established the Buffalo Catholic Institute, which hosted lectures and lent books to help educate local Catholics. The institute even had an America-Celtic Society to encourage the study of Irish history and culture with the purpose of countering the bigoted claims of the Protestant majority.[60]

In 1853, Thomas D'Arcy McGee left Buffalo for New York City to be closer to the action on the East Coast as well as the more timely arrival of European news, which was necessary for the success of his paper.[61] But he would not forget about Buffalo. On Tuesday, February 12, 1856, McGee organized a convention in his former hometown of Buffalo, which advocated for establishing colonies for Irish Americans in the United States and Canada. This convention centered around a scheme that advocated for the Irish to finally own their own land, and to get away from their back-breaking life in industrial slums. This weeklong event was another example of the intersection of Irish-American history in Buffalo, New York. Over one hundred delegates came to wintry Buffalo from all over Canada (Toronto, Hamilton, Ottawa, Quebec, London, Brantford) and the United States (New York, Boston, Detroit, Dubuque, Albany, Jersey City, Cleveland, Chicago, and New Haven, CT) for this purpose. The priests from St. Patrick's and St. Bridget's in the First Ward were in attendance.[62] As their mission statement exclaims:

> We are agreed that the social condition of many of the Irish landed in America in our time is somewhat beneath that of emigrants from other countries of equal opportunity, and much below that of natives of no great industry and intelligence. It is a fact…of the existence of a large and steadily increasing class, to whom the acquisition of land is absolutely impossible and who have no hopes of permanently improving the condition of themselves or their posterity. We have the land; there exist the means by which that land may be made accessible to the poorest of our population; to apply these means to that end is the great object of our Convention.[63]

The delegates came not just from all over the country but also from all sectors of society: judges, military officers, priests, and merchants. Information was shared about where land could be obtained (Missouri, Illinois, Michigan, Wisconsin and the Ottawa Valley in Canada); and how much it would cost to acquire the land (25 cents to $1.25 an acre). The estimates at the time were that it would cost $12,500 to buy a township, which would include 40 acres for a church, school, and a priest farm.[64] The leaders proposed that joint stock companies were the best arrangement to accomplish this task. These joint stock companies would be able to make loans to Irish Americans at low interest rates or even defer interest.[65]

As early as the spring of 1856 plans were in place to start one of these townships in Nebraska with the name of St. Patrick; however, for various reasons the plan failed and so too did the idea of a mass colonization of Irish immigrants into the American West or into Canada and away from the urban slums where McGee felt they were destined for misery and failure.[66]   Some of the reasons for the failure of the colonization plan were actually positive developments: the influence of the Know-Nothing Party started to decline; demand for Irish labor increased in the urban areas; and the Irish were already moving West on their own.[67] While the Irish were progressing in the areas of education and land ownership, McGee was still disturbed with the individualism and materialism that were part of the American experience. Ultimately, he realized that the economic system in Canada was closer to his ideal—where the majority of Irish Catholics were engaged in farming and living in rural areas.[68] Failure of the convention to mobilize the Irish as well as frustration with events in the United States led McGee to abandon the United States for Montreal, Canada one year later.

As a young man, Thomas McGee advocated violent methods to improve the welfare of the Irish in Ireland, but the middle-aged McGee advocated for peaceful means in North America. However, many of his fellow Irish Americans were not convinced that a peaceful approach would work. McGee pushed forward in Canada and is recognized as one of the founding fathers of the nation. A decade after his move to Canada, a faction of the Fenians—an Irish independence group—condemned McGee's pacifist views and even declared him a traitor to his people. Sadly, in 1868, Patrick James Whelan, a Fenian sympathizer, who at one time lived in Buffalo, NY, assassinated him.

Bishop John Timon, the Sisters of Mercy, Thomas D'Arcy McGee, and countless other religious and lay citizens built the foundations for the Irish in the Ward to become self-sufficient and productive citizens. While the immigrants' situation improved somewhat during this period, the bias against the Irish Catholics by the Protestant establishment didn't disappear overnight. But the fight against bigoted Protestants wasn't the biggest worry for the Irish. With the attack on Fort Sumter on April 12, 1861, many of the Irish would quit their jobs and pack up to fight in the South. There their efforts would bring some of the respectability they desired from the Protestant establishment.

CHAPTER FOUR

THE FIRST WARD AT WAR WITH CONFEDERATES, CANADIANS, AND THE BRITISH

There wasn't a family in the Ward that didn't house and feed 'the boys.'
– Evans family manuscript on the Ward's efforts during the Fenian Raid

In 1860, the grain transshipment, grain milling, and lumber industries were thriving in and around the First Ward, but the election of Abraham Lincoln raised questions about whether the southern states would secede, and if so, what would happen to the local economy. As the months went by after Lincoln's election, it became clear that the southern states would actually follow through on their threat; by December 20th South Carolina seceded. At the time, no one knew how this conflict would be resolved or the extent of the devastation that would result. Some thought the war would be over quickly and others, such as factory and railroad owners, thought the war might even be good for business. In fact, by 1861 industries in Buffalo were thriving once the war mobilization was in full swing.

With the Northern loss at the Battle of Bull Run and losses in the Shenandoah Campaign, it was clear that the Confederacy was not going to be easily defeated. Few First Ward men signed up for service at the start of the war, and those that did were put into Buffalo regiments of mixed ethnicity. One man who did enlist early in the war effort was Irish-born John Sullivan, a laborer from Louisiana Street. Sullivan was married to Mary McGrady and enlisted in the 49th Infantry Division, Company E on August 20, 1861. Just a year later, he fell with a gunshot wound to his arm at the Second Battle of Bull Run, and while he was recuperating at Harewood Hospital in Washington, D.C., he contracted typhoid and died.[1] John Sullivan left behind a widow and two sons, one of whom, John P. Sullivan, would become a successful First Ward politician and businessman a few decades later.

As the military campaigns of the Union Army continued to fail, it became clear that many of the Irish laborers in Buffalo would be called on to fight on behalf of their new country. In the summer of 1862, the Irish in Buffalo desired a regiment of their own—an idea even supported by Bishop John Timon. There was genuine enthusiasm to enlist among many of the Irish immigrants in and around the Ward. Some enlisted for a sense of adventure, some to show their patriotism for their new country, some for the money, and others to gain military experience with future plans to fight the British in order to free their homeland. Most, however, would not have been motivated to liberate the thousands of black slaves who they feared would compete with them for jobs. Regardless of the reasons, enthusiastic recruits, who had no idea of the carnage that they would witness or inflict on their fellow countrymen, answered the call.

The Buffalo Irish regiment, the 155th, was organized in the summer of 1862 and it went into service on November 18th of that year. John E. McMahon, an Irish immigrant and lawyer from Pearl Street, received orders to recruit four companies of men from Buffalo for this new regiment. The 155th was to combine with other forces in New York State to fight in Corcoran's Irish Legion, also known as the Fighting 69th, led by Brigadier General Michael Corcoran. These Irish regiments across New York were also known as "Green Flag Regiments" and they were composed almost entirely of Irish immigrants or their immediate descendants.[2] A recruiting office was established near the waterfront in Buffalo and roughly 570 men were recruited in just three weeks time.

Unfortunately, due to desertions—the Buffalo Irish regiment dropped from 570 to 400 in a short time—and poor recruiting in some parts of New York State, Corcoran had to reorganize his brigade, so he kept companies "I" and "K" with the 155th and moved Buffalo's "C" and "D" into the 164th. Apparently, this move disturbed the Irish from Buffalo who desired to fight as one unit and led to some desertions from men who felt they were deceived.[3] Furthermore, Corcoran moved Colonel John McMahon and his brother, Lt. Colonel James McMahon, into the 164th, which further angered the Buffalo recruits. The two regiments, the 155th and 164th, fought side by side in many battles throughout the last years of the war, but it wasn't the same being separated.

The 155th regiment was divided into two companies with Irish leaders from the West Side of Buffalo as well as from the First Ward: Company "I" was led by Captain John Byrne from Ellicott Street, Lieutenant James Worthington, and Second Lieutenant Hugh Mooney from Elk Street in the Ward; Company "K", was led by Captain James McConvey from North Division Street, First Lieutenant John McNally from Seneca Street, and Second Lieutenant John Ternan. This unit recruited heavily from the working class Irish along the waterfront as well as the First Ward. The 155th only had to wait two months for their first engagement, which came in January 30, 1863 in Virginia at the Battle of Deserted House. The unit fought in several bloody engagements in the Virginia campaign such as the Siege of Suffolk, and the battles of Spotsylvania, North Anna, and Cold Harbor; their greatest number of casualties occurred toward the end of the war at Cold Harbor.[4]

They also fought in the Battle and Siege of Petersburg and some made it to the surrender of the Confederate troops at Appomattox Court House. By the end of the war in 1865, the 155th suffered a 60% casualty rate with 189 deaths and 280 injured out of the 820 enlisted men; three years after the formation of the regiment only 130 men were present at Lee's surrender at Appomattox.[6] Even the captain of the unit, John Byrne, had his eye shot out at Spotsylvania and was captured and sent to Libby's Prison in Richmond until the end of the war.[202] In a history of the city of Buffalo the authors commented that this band of Irish soldiers "sustained the reputation for impetuous valor borne by those of that nationality [Irish]."[7]

Two First Ward brothers, Patrick and John Donohue from Louisiana Street, joined the 155th and were in Company I. Patrick Donohue was slightly injured in one battle and then was one of 1,700 Union men captured in August 1864 during the Battle of Ream Stations during the Siege of Petersburg. He was sent to Salisbury Prison in North Carolina where he attempted escape twice— the first time unsuccessfully and successfully the second. His brother John was injured at the Battle of Spotsylvania Courthouse and returned to his unit. Their experiences were typical of this unit that suffered such a high casualty rate. The Donohues eventually returned to the First Ward where they worked as laborers on the waterfront.

Meanwhile, McMahon's 164th regiment included two Buffalo companies: "C" was led by Captain Timothy W. Kelly and Company "D" was led by Christopher Graham. Most of the recruits were young laborers who worked along the waterfront, but others were tavern owners, blacksmiths—even a medical student enlisted. After two months of training, the companies of the 164th regiment marched out of Buffalo with their green silk flag which had an image of a harp with wreaths of shamrocks, and the expression "Corcoran Guards: We Strike for the Union and Constitution." Interestingly, the 164th was the only Irish Zouave unit in the Union army and they were dressed in the North African French colonial uniforms.[8]

McMahon's 164th regiment also fought in the critical Virginia campaign from 1863 to 1865. This Irish unit from Buffalo played a significant role at the battles of Cold Harbor, Spotsylvania, Strawberry Plains and Petersburg; some of the men were also at the surrender of General Robert E. Lee at Appomattox. The commanding officer and the recruiter of the regiment, John E. McMahon, died of tuberculosis on March 11, 1863, and his younger brother, James McMahon, a twenty-nine-year-old lawyer, replaced him as the regimental colonel twelve days later. At the savage Battle of Cold Harbor, James P. McMahon, with a green flag in his left hand and a sword in his right, tried to rally his men up the enemies' entrenchment; only a handful of men, however, followed him. Colonel McMahon turned and exclaimed "Now boys we got 'em." At that same moment, he was struck with a hail of Confederate bullets; at least seven bullets pierced him. One historian poetically described the scene this way, "For an instant he [James McMahon] was there outlined, against the sky of the summer morning, the beau ideal of the Irish warrior. Then he was down and done and the Green Flag fallen across his body."[9]

All told, ten officers and over a hundred men from this Buffalo regiment were killed in conflicts throughout the Virginia campaign. Of the 766 men recruited into this regiment, 490 of them were lost to death, injury, or capture. In 1864, at Sangster's Station, Virginia, eight men, all Irish soldiers from Buffalo, were captured and sent to the infamous Andersonville Prison in Georgia. The prisoners' fate, like many others at this prison, was death.[10] The leaders of the 164th, John and James McMahon, were both buried in Holy Cross Cemetery in Lackawanna, but their bodies were moved in 1905 to a cemetery in Utica, New York to be closer to John's widow.[11]

Interestingly, as the "Buffalo Irish Regiment" was away fighting in Virginia in 1863, Irish dockworkers in Buffalo went on strike for higher wages. The business owners responded by hiring African-American replacements in an attempt to end the strike. The Irish—already upset about the unfairness of the military draft, which they felt disproportionately burdened them—witnessed the disappearance of their jobs to African Americans, which caused an explosive atmosphere. On the steamy day of July 6, 1863, Irish dockworkers rioted against the African Americans working along the waterfront. Much like the Draft Riots in New York City, these riots turned deadly, but not as destructive. By the end of the day, two blacks were reportedly chased into the water and drowned, and a large number of African-American laborers were horribly beaten.[12] In late July and in early August of 1863, Bishop Timon urged his followers not to take any actions involving lawlessness or mob rule regarding the tensions with the African Americans. Unfortunately, tempers were boiling and the message by John Timon was not heeded by all; about 100 men marched from the waterfront to a small enclave of blacks on the east side of Buffalo with intent to enact bodily harm.[13] Unfortunately, one African-American man was killed by the angry mob of Irishmen and several homes and businesses were destroyed, but the mob was dispersed when two local militia regiments, local police, and a posse of concerned citizens confronted them. No more violence occurred. This event, however, was not the last confrontation between the Irish and the African Americans.

Fenians

One of the most interesting intersections between the First Ward and international affairs occurred in the year following the end of the Civil War; an event which is better known in Ireland and Canada than in Buffalo, where it started. Throughout the Civil War, many men in the 155th and 164th regiments from Buffalo, as well as most Irish regiments in the Union Army, were also secretly involved in an Irish independence movement called the Fenians or the Irish Republican Brotherhood. In general, loyalty to the cause of Ireland's freedom was almost an obsession for both first- and second-generation Irish Americans, and those from the First Ward were no exception. The Fenian movement, based both in the United States and Ireland, was officially created on St. Patrick's Day in 1858 in Dublin; its secretive mission was to secure Ireland's independence by the use of military force. Michael Corcoran, the leader of the 69th Irish Regiment, was one of the founders of the Fenians in the United States. Before the start of the Civil War he, like other Irish leaders in the U.S., created "Phoenix Brigades" which were composed of Irish militia members with secret plans to organize an attack on England. At the start of the war, Corcoran didn't want the men in these Irish militia to waste themselves in a fight with Confederates and thought that there were plenty of other Irishmen who would be interested in that fight. Corcoran's views changed and as we know he did sign up to fight the Southerners, but he never forgot the real enemy: the British.

The Fenians initial plan was to raise funds and recruit men willing to return from America to Ireland to fight the British and secure Ireland's independence; there were tens of thousands of Irish Americans who willingly joined the group and money and men flowed freely back to Ireland. In fact, by 1865 there were 300,000 members of the Fenians in 30 states and about 25,000 of these were willing to fight in the Irish Republican Army.[14] By the early 1860s, the U.S. leadership of the Fenians felt the timing for a military conflict to free Ireland was imminent, and the invaluable training their members were gaining in the American Civil War encouraged them. While some Fenian leaders still dreamed of sending these battle hardened veterans back to Ireland to fight the British, others thought of a different idea: plans were drawn up to capture British North America—now Canada—and hold it ransom for the freedom of Ireland. While this idea seems preposterous from a modern sensibility, Canada did not have a standing army or even a strong central government to defend itself, so if the plan was executed properly it had a chance of success. Furthermore, the Irish leaders were counting on the tacit support of the U.S. government because of unresolved issues surrounding England's support of the Confederacy during the Civil War. While many men from the First Ward in 1866 would have been anxious to partake in such a plan, none had any idea that Buffalo would be the central launching spot for the greatest Fenian battle on either side of the Atlantic.

The multi-pronged attack was to take place around several towns along the Canadian-U.S. border; Buffalo was just one component of a much larger plan. Interest in the Fenians was so strong in Western New York that they had their own regiment in the Irish Republican Army, the 7th Regiment. In contrast, other regiments of the I.R.A. needed men from several states to staff a single regiment like the 18th, which was formed from soldiers in Tennessee, North Carolina, South Carolina, Georgia and Alabama. Interestingly, a year after the Civil War, Irish veterans from the North and South who bloodily fought against each other just one year prior were now united to fight in a cause they deemed worthier: freedom for their native Ireland.

While the leadership of the Buffalo Irish brigades in the Civil War was composed primarily of wealthier Irish from the West Side of Buffalo and the downtown district, the leadership of the Buffalo 7th regiment of the Fenian Army, or Irish Republican Army, was composed primarily of men from the First Ward. The 7th regiment was led by Colonel John Hoy, from Ohio and Illinois Streets in the Ward; Captain James McConvey from one block north of the Ward; Captain Hugh Mooney from Elk Street in the Ward; Captain Michael Lynch from Abbott and Elk; Lieutenant Edward Lonergan, a ship carpenter from the Ward; and Assistant Lieutenant Matthew O'Gorman from Elk and Chicago Streets.[15]The rank and file of the 7th Regiment drew heavily from the Ward as well. Men like Patrick Donohue, who had fought in the 155th, secretly joined the Fenians during the war. After Donohue returned to Buffalo, he participated in the Fenian invasion into Canada.[16]

Fenian soldiers, disguised as railroad laborers, began to steadily stream into Buffalo during the last few days of May 1866, arriving in earnest on May 30th from as far away as Kentucky, Tennessee, Indiana and Ohio. In order to avoid the authorities who were waiting for them at the Exchange Street rail station, the enthusiastic soldiers jumped off trains a mile earlier near the Union Ironworks in the Ward.[17] Several accounts say they were welcomed throughout the First Ward and other parts of South Buffalo where they were housed in warehouses, halls, and the homes of sympathetic Irish residents. In one Ward manuscript, the author claims there "wasn't a family in the Ward that didn't house and feed 'the boys.'"[18] There is even evidence that the grandfather of General William Donovan, who lived at Fulton and Chicago Streets at the time, housed the Fenians during their movements between Canada and the United States.[19] According to another memoir, the Fenians stored their guns in the basement of St. Bridget's Church in the First Ward as well as in taverns and saloons. Another memoir claimed, "wagonloads of arms and ammunition were assembled in the First Ward."[20] In fact Buffalo was one of the seven cities designated by the Fenians as an arms depot for their military campaign. While the primary headquarters for the Fenians in Buffalo was on lower Pearl Street at Patrick O'Day's Auction House, the backup headquarters was in the Ward at Hugh Mooney's saloon on Ohio Street.

On the night of May 31st, the Fenians, who were now dressed in military uniforms, marched to Black Rock, near Pratt Rolling Mill at Ferry Street, and in the dark of night at 3:15 a.m. on June 1st, the first wave of soldiers was ferried across the Niagara River to Canada on canal boats pulled by tugs. The Fenians were described as young men ranging in age from twenty to twenty-seven years old; many wore green jackets and most had black hats—with a few even sporting the stovepipe style. It is claimed that some wore "I.R.A." pins on their jackets and this may have been one of the first uses of the acronym. Some were veterans of the Union forces and others had fought for the Confederacy, but all were united in their effort to free Ireland.

Their mission was to take Fort Erie and then take control of the Welland Canal to disrupt British troop movements between Eastern and Western Canada. As word spread about the attack, citizens of Buffalo rushed to the banks of the river to see this once-in-a-lifetime military mobilization. As the highest-ranking commander on the battlefield, Colonel John O'Neill, thirty-five years old, with a medium build, a sturdy physique, and battle-hardened from the Civil War, led the campaign. By 4:00 a.m., the Irish flag was proudly planted on Canadian soil—an event that apparently led to loud cheers from the men, which could be heard across the Niagara River in Buffalo.[21] Orders were given to cut telegraph lines, destroy a railroad bridge, and take the Old Fort Erie ruins. The situation looked fairly promising for the I.R.A., but British and Canadian volunteers were streaming in from Toronto and Hamilton, and it was becoming clear that a major battle was imminent.

By some accounts, O'Neill had as few as 500 active men, as he lost some to desertion. With the combined British and Canadian troops the Irish commander was outnumbered almost ten to one. Therefore, he realized he must strike the smaller Canadian force led by Lieutenant Colonel Booker, who commanded the Queen's Own, the 13th Battalion of Hamilton Volunteers, and the York and Caledonia Rifles before they could unite with the larger force under Colonel Peacocke in St. Catharines.[22] On June 2, 1866, O'Neill's men engaged Booker's men at a place west of Fort Erie called Ridgeway or Lime Ridge. Despite difficult terrain, and fewer soldiers, the Fenians had the advantage because they were battle-hardened and more experienced than their enemy. When gaps in the British and Canadian forces lines opened up, the Fenians pounced with a charge and drove their opponents back. The Canadian defenders suffered as many as twelve dead and two times as many injured as a result of the Fenian assault; the Fenians had won the battle, but events that were out of O'Neill's control were about to change the course of their campaign.

O'Neill ordered his men to retreat to Old Fort Erie while he waited for reinforcements and supplies. The passionate commander exclaimed that he was willing to make the old fort a slaughter pen because he was not going to surrender.[23] However, Fenian reinforcements from Buffalo were not imminent, and in fact they were never going to arrive. The USS *Michigan* gunboat was now patrolling the Niagara River and Buffalo Harbor with a mission to prevent Fenian reinforcements and supplies from crossing the river.

In fact, the USS *Michigan* wasn't even supposed to be in Buffalo at the time of the invasion, but luckily for the Canadians it was being repaired and overhauled on the dry docks in the First Ward since earlier that spring. Due to rumors of a possible summer invasion of Canada, the U.S. military commanders in Washington, D.C. had decided to keep it in Buffalo even after the repairs were finished. On the night of May 31st, U.S. District Attorney Dart alerted the commander of the USS *Michigan*, Commander Andrew Bryson, that a Fenian launch on the Niagara River was imminent, so Bryson readied the vessel with steam and loaded his guns. However, much to the commander's consternation, the pilot of the vessel, Patrick Murphy, was missing as well as James P. Kelley, the ship's second assistant engineer. It has been theorized that James Kelley was either a Fenian or a Fenian sympathizer, and it turns out he played an integral role in the invasion.

Kelley's secret mission was to put the *Michigan* out of action and he realized that without pilot Patrick Murphy the vessel would be stranded. Using age-old methods, Kelley delayed the usually prompt Murphy by enticing him with alcohol, cigars, and a certain "lady friend."[24] Both Murphy and Kelley arrived at the boat around 5:00 a.m., which was several hours too late to stop O'Neill and his men. Commander Bryson had them both arrested, but he was still forced to use Murphy to pilot the vessel up to Black Rock. At the end of the Fenian conflict, Commander Bryson admitted that Kelley's tactics in delaying the *Michigan* were ingenious.[25] The efforts of this naval ship in preventing Fenian reinforcements and men singlehandedly ended the Fenian Raid into Canada. By June 3rd, despite a victory at the Battle of Ridgeway, the Fenians, with no new reinforcements, were forced to retreat to Fort Erie and then across to Buffalo; the war was lost less than 72 hours after it began.

Many leaders in the U.S. Federal government, including several Congressmen, were sympathetic to the Fenians and desirous of the Irish vote, so they delayed any intervention into the Fenian activities in Canada. In fact, even the sitting President Andrew Johnson, a reported Fenian sympathizer, waited several days before acting in an effort to allow the Fenians enough time to accomplish their task.[26] However, with pressure from the British diplomats Johnson was forced to act or else risk the possibility of a war with Great Britain. The President ordered General Ulysses Grant to halt the movement of Fenians and their weapons across the border into Canada. On June 3rd, Grant sent the Irish Catholic General George G. Meade, who led the Army of the Potomac at the Battle of Gettysburg, to Buffalo to take control of the situation before it escalated even further. Meade immediately banned Fenian meetings and stationed troops along the shore; by June 15 he had successfully dispersed the Fenian threat.[27] On that day it is claimed that there were 5,166 Fenians paroled in Buffalo.[28]

When the sound of gunfire ceased at the Battle of Ridgeway and when the other skirmishes near Fort Erie fizzled out, the British and Canadian forces suffered a total of 16 dead and 74 wounded while the Fenians had five dead and 17 wounded. One of the Fenian dead was a First Ward ship carpenter, Edward K. Lonergan. Lonergan, born on June 2nd 1845, was a typical Buffalo Fenian, a single laborer under the age of thirty. Not much is known about the personal life of Lonergan, but we know he worked as a carpenter at the Jones Ship Yard and lived at Ohio and Chicago Streets in the First Ward. Lonergan's sacrifice was not forgotten and the Fenian leadership erected a large monument for him in Holy Cross Cemetery in 1867. One hundred and thirty years later, in 1997, the Police Emerald Society and the Ancient Order of Hibernians refurbished his monument in Holy Cross Cemetery in Lackawanna, New York. The inscription on his monument declares, "Edward Lonergan: Who fell gallantly fighting Ireland's enemies on the Famous Field of Ridgeway on June 2, 1866."

The attempt of the Fenians to control Canada ultimately failed. At the time, many newspaper reports of the invasion mocked the invasion as inconceivable, ill-planned, and outrageous, but this was partially inaccurate; even today there is a perception among some that this was just a group of drunk, feisty Irishmen dreaming of nonsense. The Fenians, however, were well organized, well funded and had strong leaders. The organization had an executive mansion in New York City, a chief executive, an elected Senate, and a lower assembly of representatives, as well as the ability to raise funds by issuing bonds; they also received significant assistance from officers in the U.S. Army such as Brigadier General Thomas Sweeney.

During the Ridgeway Raid, the Canadians took several Fenians prisoner, and in October 1866 a few were even sentenced to death. One of those taken prisoner was Buffalonian William Duggan, who was forced to spend eight months in a Toronto prison. The Fenians in Buffalo readied a brigade to try to rescue the prisoners, but members of President Andrew Johnson's administration were able to work out a compromise with the Canadians for the prisoners' release.[29] In 1867, Buffalo had the largest Fenian arms depot in the country with 4,000 Springfield rifles and 500,000 cartridges on hand. The Fenians were quiet in the Buffalo area until they staged a mass rally on January 22, 1868 in Buffalo; in fact, there was more talk of attacking Canada again—which actually happened in 1870 when they launched an attack from Vermont with results equally disastrous as 1866. Around this same time, the Fenians withered away and less militaristic movements like the Land League and the Irish National League replaced the violent aims of the Fenians.

While the Irish Republican Army failed in their efforts to free Ireland from England's rule, fifty years later in Dublin, the IRA engaged in a new armed struggle that ultimately lead to Ireland's freedom. Few of the Fenians that engaged the British and Canadians at Ridgeway lived to see that day in 1916, but their efforts, while seemingly fruitless at the time, were part of the 800-year continuum that was needed to finally give birth to the Irish nation.

There are a few memoirs that claim that some of the Fenians settled in Buffalo after their incursion into Canada, however there is no supportive documentation of these claims. It is true that the First Ward was a destination for Fenians, and IRA members later, as a place that was safe to settle in; perhaps it is related to the fact that because the Irish in the First Ward were isolated, they could conceal people more easily. We know that the family of Daniel Driscoll, a Fenian, emigrated and were welcomed into the Ward.

In the 20th century, this tradition would continue. Jack O'Brian, the famous columnist from the First Ward, recalled how his grandfather, John Kelleher, who was from County Cork, was 'on the run' from the hated British and that he even had the honor of having 'a price on his head.'[30] Also, in the Evans' family history we learn that one of the several George Evanses that lived in the Ward was a member of the IRA before he immigrated to Buffalo in 1924. George Evans was hiding in the mountains in Ireland, and because of an informer in a nearby village, he was captured and tortured by the Black and Tans.[31] After arriving in the Ward, George Evans worked for the Great Lakes Corporation and then the Buffalo Post Office. Patrick Cleary—known in the boxing ring as Paddie Lavin—was a champion boxer from Ireland in the early 1900s and was forced out of Ireland for his activities on behalf of Sinn Fein and his involvement with the Easter Rebellion. Over the years the Ward was filled with Irish rebels and with even more Irish independence sympathizers.

The Irish Independence Movement

After the failed Fenian invasion, the Irish in Buffalo did not lose hope for a dream of an independent Ireland. Historian David Gerber noted that the Irish in Buffalo were good at balancing Ireland's struggle for freedom and maintaining their patriotism to their new homeland in America.[32] In fact, this dual allegiance was especially true during the mid-to-late 19th century as was evidenced by their participation in the Fenian movement as well as their efforts in the Civil War. One historian aptly described the dual allegiance of many Irish immigrants in familial terms; they had a mother image of Ireland and a daughter image of the United States.[33] This intense interest in the political situation in Ireland would continue until the mid-1920s when Irish Americans either became disillusioned with the Irish civil war or felt that Ireland was on its way toward self-government.

Military attempts at liberation were shelved in favor of freedom by peaceful means and once again men and women in the First Ward provided assistance. Two figures in Ireland, Charles Stewart Parnell and Michael Davitt, spearheaded the issues of land reform and then Home Rule. The issue of tenant farmers' rights in Ireland was an important one for Irish Americans, many of whom still held vivid memories of the tenant evictions during the Famine. As a result of poor harvests in Ireland in 1877 and 1878 there were worries on both sides of the Atlantic that a new famine might occur with possible devastating effects in rural Ireland. In 1879, Irish leaders like Parnell and Davitt formed an organization called the Land League in an attempt to rectify centuries-old issues surrounding land ownership. Specifically, the organization fought to end "Landlordism" and worked to transfer land from the absentee landlords to the tenant farmers who worked it. The organization also vociferously argued against English rule and claimed England was continuing to subjugate the Irish people with evictions and arbitrary arrests.

Buffalo's Irish community—one of the largest in the country at the time—was often a destination for fundraising and rallying support for the cause of freedom.

In fact, as early as 1852, Thomas Meagher, one of the Young Ireland leaders and future Brigadier General in the Civil War, came to Buffalo in 1852 to raise funds and awareness of the Irish cause. While New York City was considered the American center for Irish political agitation, Buffalo was in the top five with Boston, Philadelphia and Chicago. Charles Stewart Parnell, the "Uncrowned King of Ireland," visited Buffalo during his tour of America in 1880.[34] On January 25, 1880, Parnell—described as "lithe, active and wiry with a frame of steel," by the local Catholic newspaper—and John Dillon, his companion, were greeted at the Exchange Street rail depot in Buffalo by a crowd of several thousand people.[35] Their stop in Buffalo was planned by Buffalo Irishmen from the West Side and the First Ward: men like James Mooney, John C. Sheehan, Patrick Short, and William Naughton. In James Mooney's welcoming address for the two Irish visitors he proclaimed, "Irish hearts in Buffalo still burn with love for the old land, still beat with hope to see her rise from her sorrows and misfortunes."[36] Parnell and Dillon stayed at the Tifft House before their sold-out address at the Academy of Music at Main and Seneca Streets. Their visit to Buffalo netted $7,000 for the cause—equivalent to $154,000 in 2010—and Parnell described his visit to Buffalo—which followed Philadelphia, New York and Boston—as "by far the most respectable, best organized, and I believe financially, the most successful of any reception we have had yet."[37]

After their visit, the First Ward also became a hotbed of activity and fundraising for the Irish Land League. At Stephen's Hall, at Franklin and Swan Streets, the local Parnell Branch of the Land League was formed on October 3, 1880, ten months after Parnell's visit to Buffalo. While many of the local leaders of this group were West Side Irish, many of the rank-and-file members were from the First Ward. In fact, there were two Land League branches in Buffalo with one of them headquartered in the First Ward at St. Bridget's Church. The purpose of this organization was to assist in agitating for Ireland's freedom and to redistribute the land from the Anglo-Irish landlords to the tenant farmers. The Buffalo chapter was remembered as being one of the most vociferous and aggressive in the nation according to a local newspaper.[38] Local leaders of this nascent organization included Anselm J. Smith, T. J. O'Brien from Perry Street, William Forsythe, Dr. William C. Callanan, and Edward C. Callanan.[39]

Interestingly, the causes of land reform and Irish independence were not an all-male affair. In 1880, Fanny Parnell, a sister of Charles Stewart Parnell, called on Irish-American women across the country to organize on behalf of the Irish nationalist movement. Tens of thousands of women responded in forming the Ladies' Land League. One such group of Irish-American women was formed in Buffalo on December 16, 1880. While women had been active in parish fundraising prior to this time, this was one of the first mass movements in which Irish-American women banded together to assist those suffering in their native land.[40] Some in the Church hierarchy were disapproving of their activities, including Bishop Steven V. Ryan, C.M. of Buffalo, who denounced the activities of the group as "not befitting of women." Others like Bishop Gilmour of Cleveland had this to say about the group:

> If there are women who will turn themselves into brawling politicians, then they shall not be Catholic women, and if here-to-fore they have so-called themselves, then the public shall know they are no longer. The Catholic woman must live within modesty of the home; she must be the ornament of the family circle, and her womanly delicacy and gentle nature shall not be tainted with the noisy brawl of virago.[41]

However, the women in Buffalo, some from the First Ward, did not relent and they continued in their efforts in raising funds and awareness for those suffering in Ireland. As a result of the Bishop's proclamation, the Ladies Land League held a mass meeting in Buffalo on June 4, 1882 to respond to his statement.

Enthusiasm for both the men's and ladies' branches of the Land League were building, and it intensified when Buffalo hosted the Land League national convention. On January 12th and 13th 1881, Buffalo had the privilege of hosting the first Land League convention in the United States with 120 delegates from around the country.[42] An unofficial convention took place in New York City the prior year, but the Buffalo convention was the first official one, followed by Washington, D.C., Philadelphia, and Chicago. Furthermore, in 1882, two Buffalonians were named to the national leadership of the Land League of America. James Mooney, who introduced Parnell on his visit to Buffalo, was named President and John J. Hynes, from 169 Fulton Street in the Ward, was elected Secretary.[43] Mooney and Hynes would be instrumental in leading this national organization with tens of thousands of members from their headquarters in the Arcade Building in Buffalo.

John Hynes's rise to a prominent national post with the League was somewhat unlikely. His parents, both famine immigrants, arrived in the United States in 1847 and settled in Buffalo sometime after. His father, Michael Hynes, settled at Elk and Marvin Streets and his wife gave birth to John in 1855. John Hynes attended public school until he was fourteen and because of his strong intellectual gifts he attended Bryant and Stratton College the following year. At age fifteen, he worked as a clerk and accountant until 1877 when he entered law school. Two years later, he won election to the Board of Supervisors representing the First Ward; he won as a Republican in an overwhelmingly Democratic ward. John was described as "possessing notable organizing abilities, and having an immense capacity for serious and intelligent work."[44] These gifts served him well both in politics and as one of the organizers of the "McMahon Corps," which was an Irish-American unit of the National Guard of New York; he served as its commander for two years. He was also one of the charter members of the Catholic Mutual Beneficial Association and the one-time Supreme National leader of that organization.[45] As the son of famine immigrants, one of John's main causes was Ireland's independence. As a lawyer, Hynes also served his fellow Irish railroad workers in the deadly 1892 Switchmen Strike.

Hynes started out as the secretary for the two Buffalo Land League branches, including the one at St. Bridget's. Even though Hynes was not from the wealthier West Side of Buffalo—where many of the local leaders for this organization lived—his indefatigable quest for Ireland's freedom and his great organizational skills were two of the reasons that he was eventually elevated to the national post of secretary. Regardless, he served admirably in his capacity of corresponding with the five hundred active branches of the Land League and collecting money for the cause; it is estimated that Irish Americans eventually donated over $1 million to the Land League movement. As the third highest-ranking member of this national organization, Hynes met and corresponded with Irish leaders such as Charles Stewart Parnell, Michael Davitt, Patrick Egan, William Redmond, and John Dillon. Hynes is a relatively unknown First Ward hero of the Irish cause of freedom.

The Land League dealt with two crises while Mooney and Hynes were at the helm. First, in 1882, the Phoenix Park murders of Lord Frederick Cavendish and Under Secretary Burke in Dublin almost caused the disintegration of the organization in the United States. U.S. branches dissolved in protest of the violence in Phoenix Park and demanded an apology from the central leadership of the Land League. Mooney and Hynes disagreed with this sentiment and refused to apologize because the Land League wasn't responsible for the murders. Rather than retreat, they went on a successful recruitment campaign to grow the organization as well as donations to it. The second crisis was another famine in the West and North of Ireland during the winter of 1882 and 1883, which led to an increase in evicted tenants.[46] Mooney and Hynes hatched a plan where every Irish-American citizen would send one dollar to the group and this money would be transferred to relieve those who were suffering. While it is unclear exactly how many Americans contributed, the campaign was a success and many of the 25,000 evicted tenants were assisted.

The organization in the United States, including the leadership in Buffalo, received a morale boost in the summer of 1882. On the night of June 29, the legendary founder of the Irish Land League and former Fenian leader, Michael Davitt, visited Buffalo for a rally. Davitt spoke at St. James Hall to a packed crowd and spoke of the accomplishments of the Land League and outlined its future endeavors. Most importantly, the Irish leader vehemently denied any

Land League involvement with the Phoenix Park murders. It was reported that Davitt received a tremendous reception and ovation from the crowd in Buffalo.[47]

Other Irish dignitaries came to Buffalo during these years of the Land League and Home Rule movement. For instance, Fr. Eugene Sheehy from Limerick came to speak at Buffalo following his release from Kilmainham Jail in Dublin after his arrest by the British. Father Sheehy spoke on December 5, 1881 at St. Stephen's Hall where the Mayor of Buffalo, Grover Cleveland, introduced him. Cleveland was sympathetic to the Irish cause of freedom, and exclaimed that the Irish are entitled to have their "just and natural rights."[48] He went on to say that these rights should be obtained peacefully and within the limits of the law.[49] Father Sheehy passionately explained the evils of the landlord-tenant system in Ireland in which, after paying the rent and expenses, most tenant farmers barely had enough to subsist on. Buffalonians of Irish heritage greeted Sheehy with remarkable demonstrations of support and he was able to solicit $28,000 for the Irish Land League cause.[50] Another meeting was held on April 9, 1882 in St. James Hall to protest the arrest in Ireland of Irish Americans by security forces loyal to England. This mass meeting was presided over once again by Mayor Grover Cleveland and the Irish demanded the release of the prisoners and advocated fair rights for Irish-American citizens living abroad.

In the spring of 1883, twelve hundred Irish-American delegates from various Irish organizations in the United States, Canada, and Australia met in Philadelphia in an effort to broaden the mission of the Irish Land League in America—along the way they changed the name of the group to the Irish National League. In Ireland, Charles Stewart Parnell, the leader of the Irish National League, had changed the Land League's mission from redistribution of land to Home Rule for Ireland; the U.S. organization did the same thing. Once again First Warder John Hynes was selected to be one of its national leaders: Secretary of the Irish National League of America. Incidentally, out of all the prominent Irish-American leaders across the country, two of the four permanent officers of the Philadelphia Convention were from the First Ward: John Hynes and William F. Sheehan—future Lieutenant Governor of New York State.[51] In the same year, Patrick Egan, the former treasurer of both the Irish Republican Brotherhood and the Irish Land League, came to Buffalo on March 22, 1883 and spoke to a packed crowd at St. Stephen's Hall; his mission was to obtain more funds and support for the new Home Rule movement founded by Charles Stewart Parnell.

By 1890, Parnell and his group had made significant progress in terms of tenant rights—the number of absentee landlords plummeted—and he was building a coalition with opposition members with the possibility of self-government for Ireland. Things had never looked brighter for the Irish people. But then, as has been the case for centuries regarding Ireland's independence, an unexpected crisis developed: credible allegations that Parnell was having an affair with Katharine O'Shea, the wife of another member of Parliament, surfaced. Parnell's seemingly innocuous affair with Kitty O'Shea brought Ireland's dream of freedom to an abrupt halt. Irish Americans were particularly split on whether or not Parnell was still fit to lead the movement, and without American financial support he was doomed.

A *New York Times* article in 1890 captured the sentiment in the United States with the sub headline: "His [Parnell's] greatest strength seems to be in New York, but in Buffalo and other cities and Canada opposition to him is strong." A breakdown of Parnell's local supporters and detractors was revealing with Bishop Steven V. Ryan of Buffalo strongly opposed to Parnell but with his flock of priests in favor of him. Fr. Patrick Cronin, the editor of the powerful *Catholic Times*, was in favor of Parnell as were most of the officers of the various Irish-American associations; however, many of the rank-and-file members of these organizations— including Parnell's own Irish National League—were opposed to him.[52]   Charles Stewart Parnell, the "Uncrowned King of Ireland," was effectively removed from his leadership post and within a year he died a broken man at the age of forty-five. Ireland's independence, which seemed so close, would have to wait for almost three more decades.

Irish Americans, however, were not deterred for long. In 1908, organizers of the Sinn Fein Society started a branch in Buffalo. This organization—an offshoot of Arthur Griffith's organization in Ireland—advocated for an independent Irish state free of any British control. First Ward-born William Shaddock spearheaded the Sinn Fein Society in Buffalo.[53] Shaddock, a plumber with a shop on Elk Street, was president of the Friendly Sons of St. Patrick and helped with the 1913 revival of the St. Patrick's Day Parade. It is unclear what activities—other than fundraising—the Sinn Fein Society of Buffalo contributed to the group in Ireland. Even the mother church of the Ward was indirectly involved with the organization. On March 4, 1909, a local newspaper described how St. Bridget's choir, under the leadership of Miss Cecilia Lanigan, performed at a Sinn Fein meeting.

The same month that the 70 boys and men from the St. Bridget's choir were playing for Sinn Fein, the Irish rebel leader and former Fenian organizer, John Devoy, spoke at a commemoration ceremony for the Irish martyr Robert Emmet to a capacity crowd at the Lyric Theatre on Washington Street. After Devoy's speech on Emmet and his accomplishments, a declaration of principles was read to the crowd. The statement declared that the citizens of Buffalo of Irish birth or descent pledge themselves to the cause of Ireland's freedom and to the Sinn Fein movement; they also thanked their fellow German-American citizens for helping to defeat the proposed military alliance between the United States and England; and they congratulated the efforts of the new national university in Dublin to preserve Irish language, literature, and history.[54]

On December 22, 1919, Buffalo was once again on the top of the list for a fundraising stop for the top leader of Ireland: Eamon de Valera. The Irish rebel leader spoke in Irish hot spots like Chicago, New York, Boston, San Francisco, Philadelphia, and even Los Angeles, so it was a great honor for Buffalo to be included on his itinerary. De Valera arrived in Buffalo a few days before Christmas and spoke in front of 8,000 supporters at the Broadway Auditorium—including Bishop William Turner who introduced the Irish leader and denounced the pro-British faction in the United States.[55]

For over seventy years many First Warders provided financial resources, leadership, support and even their lives for the cause of Ireland's freedom. Buffalo hosted the Irish Colonization Convention in 1856 with the First Ward pastors assisting in the leadership of the event. Then ten years later, the most significant Fenian battle was launched from Buffalo with considerable assistance from First Warders. Many in the Ward sheltered and fed the Fenians, others fought in the 7th Regiment, and some like Edward Lonergan even gave their lives for the cause. Buffalo hosted the first Irish Land League Convention; and First Warders John Hynes and William F. Sheehan played significant roles in the national leadership for the Land League. Rank-and-file First Warders were active in the Sons of Ireland, the Ancient Order of Hibernians and the Sinn Fein Society—started by First Warder William Shaddock. Buffalo generously supported and hosted Irish independence leaders like Meagher, Davitt, Parnell, Sheehy, Egan, Dillon, Devoy, and de Valera in an effort to raise funds to assist the Irish cause. The First Warders never forgot those who were left behind in Ireland. While the struggle for freedom in Ireland dragged on, in Buffalo many First Warders found a way to improve their condition in their new homeland: politics.

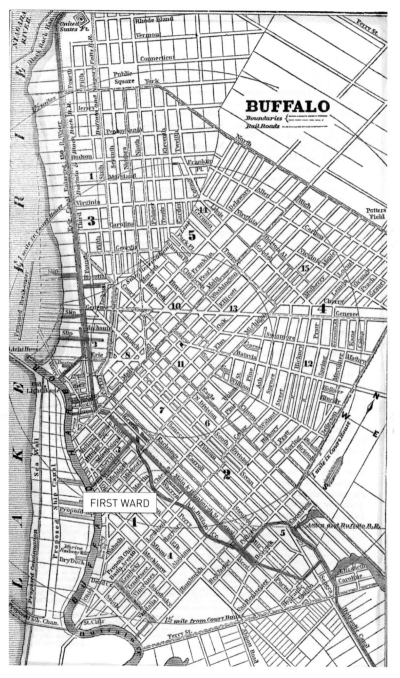

The First Ward of Buffalo comprised the area south of downtown along Lake Erie and the Buffalo River (the area near the large number 1).

A rare snapshot of the homes along the shore of Lake Erie in an area called the Beach or Sea Wall. Close to 1,000 residents lived in this community until Mayor Louis Fuhrmann evicted them in 1917. (From the coll. of Lower Lakes Marine Historical Society)

A bathhouse along the Beach in the Ward.

The Simmons' family house located in the Beach neighborhood was typical of the cottage style found there. Railroad tracks were laid just one foot from the edge of the family home.

The Beach community included restaurants, fish markets, and a rowing club.

After Joseph Dart's invention, wooden grain elevators, like the one in the right side of the picture, sprang up along the Buffalo River into the First Ward. (From the coll. of Lower Lakes Marine Historical Society)

The Michigan Street Bridge crossing the bustling Buffalo River in 1888. For many former Irish farmers this was their new reality. (Collection of Buffalo and Erie County Historical Society, used by permission)

The Ohio Basin with the Barcalo Manufacturing in the background. The basin was a source of pollution, disease, and drownings for local residents. Still powerful business interests kept it open for over 100 years. (From the coll. of Lower Lakes Marine Historical Society)

The Ohio Basin with a giant crane and canal boats. The basin was located in the midst of the Ward's residential area.

(From the coll. of Lower Lakes Marine Historical Society)

Shipbuilders at the dry docks across from Chicago Street. From its inception until the 1960s, shipbuilding was one of the largest First Ward industries.

(From the coll. of Lower Lakes Marine Historical Society)

Workers building and repairing parts for boats at the Buffalo Dry Dock Company on the Buffalo River. (From the coll. of Lower Lakes Marine Historical Society)

Large crowds like this one turned out to see the launch of new vessels built in the Ward.
(From the coll. of Lower Lakes Marine Historical Society)

Dart's Planing Mill on the Ohio Basin, 1873. The lumber industry was another bustling industry in the Ward. Notice the young age of the boys in the front row.

Bishop John Timon focused on improving the material and spiritual welfare of his fellow Irishmen.

The convent of the Sisters of Mercy in the Ward. The Mercy nuns significantly improved the welfare of the Irish immigrants.

Colonel James McMahon led
one of the regiments in the Civil
War staffed with First Ward
men. He was killed at the Battle
of Cold Harbor.

First Warder John Hynes was
one of the national leaders for
the Land League.

New York Lt. Governor William "Blue-Eyed Billy" Sheehan ran a version of Buffalo's Tammany Hall from the First Ward.

John Sheehan, Billy's older brother, ran Tammany Hall in New York City for several years.

Congressman William H. Ryan was one of
many successful First Ward politicians.

William Love was the first Catholic
Superintendent of the Buffalo Public Schools.

J.P. Sullivan was one of the most powerful
Democratic leaders in the city of Buffalo.

Joseph E. Gavin was comptroller of Buffalo.

Daniel Kenefick was the first NY State Supreme Court Judge from the First Ward.

William J. "Fingy" Conners cut workers' wages which led to the Great Strike of 1899.

Bishop James Quigley rallied the workers to fight Conners' efforts.

First Ward's Timothy
Donovan was Bishop Quigley's
representative during the Great
Strike. He was also father to
General William Donovan.

28

Strikers gather in front of St. Bridget's church during the Strike of 1899.

In the Buffalo River with fans cheering him on, Algie McGuire, the 1923 National Sculling Champion.

Bill Aman won the World Champion Single Scull in 1907 and 1908.

Cornelius and Earl Coughlin at the corner of O'Connell Avenue and Hamburg Street. Both former Ward boys died in World War I.

The iconic white horses at Engine 8 firehouse on Chicago Street.

Civil service jobs allowed fireman Daniel Bohen and hundreds of First Warders financial security and a ticket to the middle class.

Police officer Michael Regan was one of five First Warders who eventually became Buffalo Police Chief.

Patrons gathered in front of the Ganson House saloon on Ganson Street.

(Collection of Buffalo and Erie County Historical Society, used by permission)

PART II

MAKING HISTORY

CHAPTER FIVE

POLITICS AS A WAY FORWARD

The political life seemed to come naturally to the Irish. They seemed to have a built-in faculty for shaking hands, speech-making and for rallying people to a cause.
– U.S. Congressman Richard "Max" McCarthy

The period from 1880 until 1910 was a sort of golden age in the history of the First Ward. In fact, in an eight-year period, from 1857 to 1865, the seeds of this remarkable generation were sown. Men who dominated in politics, government, entertainment, and commerce were born including William J. "Fingy" Conners (born 1857), Michael Shea (b. 1859), William Sheehan (b. 1859), Michael Regan (b.1859), William H. Ryan (b. 1860), John P. Sullivan (b. 1860), Daniel Kenefick (b. 1863), Rowland Mahany (b. 1864), William Love (b. 1864), and John Nash (b. 1865).[1] One would be hard pressed to find any Buffalo neighborhood—especially one as disadvantaged as the Ward—which produced as many accomplished men in such a short period of time. It was in politics, however, where this generation left its greatest legacy.

The first epoch in the Ward was characterized by struggle, strife, and strikes with the established Protestant political and business leaders taking advantage of the newly arrived Irish immigrants. By the 1880s, however, First Warders saw a slight improvement in their welfare. The Irish, more than any previous immigrant group, mastered the political system and used politics to improve their condition. Irish-American historian Peter Quinn explained that although the transition from rural farm communities to urban areas was difficult, the Irish were remarkably quick to reorganize themselves:

> Within little more than a generation they translated their numbers into control of the Democratic Party in the major cities and turned municipal patronage into an immediate and pragmatic method for softening the ravages of boom-and-bust capitalism. Barred from the privileged circle of high finance, equipped with few entrepreneurial skills, suspicious through experience of theories that made capital accumulation the supreme good, the Irish spearheaded the rise of organized labor.[2]

Quinn continued, "They [Irish Americans] used the Democratic Party the way they used the Catholic Church, as a rallying point and redoubt, a place in which they gained the resources and discipline to recover from the shattering dislocation endured in their mass exodus from the ancient, familiar patterns of rural life to the freewheeling, winner-take-all environment of urban America."[3] Theodore Kenefick, the son of a former First Warder, Supreme Court Judge Daniel J. Kenefick, claimed, "politics was their way to acceptance—they had no entrée."[4] By the 1890s they were very good at the political game and they controlled most of the Democratic Party organizations in Northern and Midwestern cities.[5] The list of party bosses in 1894 included: John Kelly and Richard Crocker in New York City, Hugh McLaughlin in Brooklyn, Mike McDonald in Chicago, Pat Maguire in Boston, Christopher Buckley in San Francisco and William Sheehan in Buffalo.[6] Unlike other ethnic groups who were content being members of the Democratic Party, the Irish grabbed hold of the party leadership and never let go. This power grab was the impetus that enabled many Irish to move up from their former circumstances.

The Irish not only understood the utility of politics, but they were also innately good at it. U.S. Congressman Richard "Max" McCarthy, whose family lived in the First Ward for at least three generations, exclaimed that "the political life seemed to come naturally to the Irish. They seemed to have a built-in faculty for shaking hands, speech-making and for rallying people to a cause."[7] The former congressman added that even though the Irish in the Ward could be puritanical in many ways when it came to morality, when it came to a little political graft, they didn't have much of a problem with it.[8] Edward Levine argues that the Irish were "given to politics" and that no other ethnic group made the same contribution to the building of urban machines.[9]

In Buffalo, the Democratic Party doled out civil service jobs so if you were Irish, and not independently wealthy, you stayed loyal to the Democratic Party. But the clever Irish in the Ward built political machines for both major political parties. The First Warders were practical and by playing both sides they were ready to grab patronage jobs and monies when the Republicans were elected to city office as well. Obviously the Democratic Party held the most sway in the Ward, but the Ward also was home to a small Republican minority, led by Jack White. It was the "First Ward first and the party later with both Republican and Democratic leaders."[10]

A list of the aldermen representing the First Ward shows that from the city's inception in1832 until 1850 it was mostly Anglo-Protestant men—such as Smith, Brown, Prince, Goodrich, Mack, Kimball, Pierce, Lamb, Atkins, Banta and Bidwell—who ran the Ward. In 1850, the desperate Irish seized control of this elected office and dominated it for the next century.[11] In that same year,

John Walsh was the first alderman from the Ward of Irish heritage, and he was succeeded by others such as Hagan, Walsh, Fitzgerald, Whalen, Ryan, Byrns, Doyle, and Cotter. The same is true of the Ward supervisor position, which was held by men with Anglo surnames such as Milton and Edmunds. However, by 1859, the Irish were firmly in control of this elected office with men such as Michael Collins, John O'Donnell, James Fleeharty, Dennis McNamara, Austin Hanrahan, Maurice Courtney, Edward Mullihan, James McCarthy, Jeremiah Higgins, John Hynes, Joseph McCarthy, and Dennis Corbett.[12] While residents of the Ward were now firmly in control of elected offices in their district, it would take another generation before they would start to make their influence at the state and national level. First Ward men like John Sheehan, William Sheehan, William J. Conners, and William Donovan were eager to lead the way.

The Sheehan Boys and Buffalo's Tammany Hall

William Sheehan Sr. and his wife Hanora, both from County Cork, Ireland, settled at 422 Elk Street near Alabama Street, where they raised their large family. Their sons John, born in 1848, and William, born in 1859, became two of the most influential New York State politicians of their time. Their father William was a railroad contractor and engineer who lost a considerable amount of money at the time of the Civil War and was forced to become a day laborer. As a result of the Sheehans' compromised financial situation, William Sr. put his young boys to work as ferrymen on the Buffalo River to supplement the family income.[13] The boys ferried longshoreman across the Buffalo River to their places of work at the elevators and docks. This experience of hard work along the waterfront, coupled with the boys' extraordinary ambition and charisma, provided both of them with the tools needed to achieve political success.

After working as a ferryman, John C. Sheehan worked on the waterfront at a marble dock owned by Charles A. Sweet on Illinois Street. One day, a block of marble slipped off a nearby crane, crushing Sheehan's foot and necessitating the amputation of his leg.[14] Manual labor jobs became impossible for him so he was forced to obtain a clerical position at a local railroad office. Later, after working as a telegraph operator, John studied law and opened a practice on Franklin Street. But politics—and the power that came with it—was his real ambition. With the help of his younger brother they would shape Democratic politics across New York State for several decades.

John was described as tall, rather slender and having grey eyes. Descriptions of his character varied. He was described as having a "gentlemanly character, which readily disarms opponents and wins him hosts of friends."[15] A *New York Times* writer, in an article detailing a financial scandal that Sheehan initiated, explained Sheehan's success in a more sinister manner: "It is no surprise to well-informed persons in Buffalo that he [John C. Sheehan] has exhibited rare abilities to combine office holding with the most scientific and advanced wire pulling, for Buffalo never produced his equal in these regards."[16] In the autumn of 1877, at age 29, John was elected comptroller for the city of Buffalo. He held this influential position for four years and was expected to run again; that was until a neophyte politician named Grover Cleveland refused to run on the Democratic ticket with him.

In 1881, Cleveland was a successful lawyer in Buffalo with no interest in running for mayor, but powerful men in the city relentlessly urged him to run. At first Cleveland hesitated, but then he decided he wanted to make a difference by fighting corruption, which was rampant in city politics. A majority of Buffalonians at the time were registered Republicans, while Cleveland was a registered Democrat.[17] Cleveland's biographer explained the situation this way:

> After an intense barrage that he reconsider, Cleveland sent word that he might—not definitely, just might—run if the devious and corrupt Democratic "boss" John C. Sheehan, who was seeking the second-spot office of comptroller, was bounced from the ticket. This posed a problem: Sheehan was the boss of the voter-heavy First Ward, a mostly working-class Irish constituency. Besides he was ringmaster of that year's nominating circus.[18]

Cleveland knew one of the keys to winning was to carry the Democratic stronghold of the First Ward. He campaigned in the First Ward in saloons night after night in order to win the Irish vote. As a young man, Daniel J. Kenefick, a future state Supreme Court judge, remembered Grover Cleveland campaigning at Charles Diebold's saloon at 336 Ohio Street near Chicago Street. The portly Cleveland stood on a beer table at Diebold's and urged those in the First Ward to work with him for municipal reform.[19] During his mayoral campaign he was testing slogans such as "public officials are trustees of the people" which resonated with folks from the Ward even though many would have benefited from the corrupt graft that flowed from the likes of the Sheehan brothers.

Meanwhile, John Sheehan was so confident that Cleveland would lose, and that the reform movement would fail, that Sheehan removed himself from the ticket per Cleveland's ultimatum.[20] The Sheehan machine encouraged their loyal friend Timothy J. Mahoney to run for comptroller in place of John Sheehan on the Cleveland ticket. In fact, John Sheehan and his brother William, fellow Democrats with Cleveland, were quietly trying to derail Cleveland's candidacy by encouraging the Irish to vote for his competitor, Milton Beebe. Despite the efforts of the Sheehan machine at derailing the Cleveland candidacy, the First Ward Irish voted for Cleveland and he defeated the favored Republican candidate.

Interestingly, if the Irish in the Ward had listened to the Sheehan brothers and not voted for Cleveland, then perhaps he would not have been elected mayor of Buffalo or later governor of New York and president of the United States.

Timothy Mahoney won the comptroller job and he quickly discovered the shocking surprise that his friend John Sheehan had left office with $5,900 of city money missing.[21] After a series of missteps to cover up his embezzlement of city monies, and with efforts to repay it more complicated, it was increasingly clear that John Sheehan needed a fresh start. So in 1885, he moved to New York City and immediately immersed himself in Tammany Hall politics, which was the primary engine for political advancement for Irishmen in that city.[22] This former First Warder quickly rose up in the Tammany leadership and was selected as Police Commissioner of New York City in 1892; despite the fact that he was an outsider and many were aware of his financial scandal in Buffalo because of stories in the *New York Times*.

In 1895, after only ten years in New York City politics, Sheehan rose to the all-powerful position as the leader of Tammany Hall, a title that he shared with powerful men like William Tweed, John Kelly, and Charles F. Murphy. He served in this capacity for two years until Richard Crocker, the previous leader, returned from Ireland to retake control of Tammany Hall.[23] Even though Sheehan's reign only lasted for two years, it was an unlikely feat for an outsider from the First Ward of Buffalo to gain the top position of this infamous political machine. In 1899, John Sheehan, longing for the previous control he had over New York City politics, engaged in a power struggle to pry the reigns of Tammany back from Richard Crocker; but he was ultimately defeated.[24] He kept his hands in politics running his district for many years and rejoined Tammany Hall in 1905. With the help of his younger, more astute brother William he continued to shape New York State politics for years to come.

John's younger brother, William "Blue-Eyed Billy" Sheehan, was born on Elk Street on November 6, 1859, and his political fortunes eventually eclipsed John's. William had learned the art of politics from his older brother and because of his tutelage he achieved fame even more quickly than his able brother. As a young boy, Billy supplemented the family income working as a newsboy on the busy streets of Buffalo and also as a ferryman on the Buffalo River. After clerking at his brother's law firm, Tabor and Sheehan at 83 Franklin Street in Buffalo, William was elected to the New York State Assembly as a representative of the First Ward at the unusually young age of twenty-six. "Blue-Eyed Billy" served in the assembly from 1885 to 1891and as the leader of the Democratic Party for five of those years. Then, in 1891, he was elected to the powerful position of speaker of the New York State Assembly, which would not have been an easy task due to the powerful influence of New York City politicians compared to those from the rest of the state. In a *Harper's Weekly* article during the 1891 election, the writer credited Sheehan's success with the fact that he "was a born parliamentarian, a well-equipped debater, an earnest and vigorous speaker, and an uncompromising partisan."[25] Throughout his tenure, William Sheehan continued to secure funds for Buffalo's harbor, as well as patronage jobs, and this endeared him to his constituents.

In 1892, at only age 33, he was the youngest lieutenant governor of New York in history. Sheehan was twice considered for the position of U.S. senator from New York, a position appointed by the state legislature at that time. On November 11, 1892, in an article profiling the various candidates, the *New York Times* described William Sheehan as "young, ambitious, aggressive, and [he is] proud of the victory the party won under his management."[26] Although he was an exciting candidate, it wasn't his time and the legislature chose someone else. Throughout the years, Sheehan's prestige across the state increased. In 1911, when a new opportunity came up to select a U.S. senator from New York, "Blue-Eyed Billy" Sheehan had positioned himself as the inevitable candidate. Sheehan was the leading candidate in the caucuses, but, more importantly, he was the choice of the presiding Tammany boss, Charles F. Murphy. On December 30, 1910, the *New York Times* claimed that because of Sheehan's work getting the Democratic majority elected in the New York State legislature, many legislators felt Sheehan's reward was the open senate seat. The writer claimed that, "the consensus of opinion expressed at the Capitol is that Mr. Sheehan has a better chance than any other candidate now in the field."[27] Indeed, it was finally Sheehan's time. However, a young and feisty New York state legislator, desiring a reform of the Democratic Party, successfully blocked "Blue-Eyed Billy" Sheehan's seemingly inevitable candidacy.[28] That state legislator was Franklin Delano Roosevelt.

The twenty-nine-year-old Roosevelt objected to the fact that William Sheehan was the candidate endorsed by the corrupt Tammany Hall faction of the Democratic Party; Roosevelt demanded a reform candidate. Conrad Black, one of Roosevelt's biographers, described Sheehan in the way Roosevelt would have viewed him: as "a smooth but corrupt political roué."[29] After Roosevelt rallied twenty-one Democratic legislators to oppose Sheehan, including Buffalo's Frank Loomis, the seemingly inevitable candidate resorted to threats and political rallies in an attempt to silence Roosevelt and the rest of the opposition. Roosevelt, however, was not intimidated and he was able to hold the opposition together; Sheehan's candidacy was now on life-support.

On February 14, 1911, on a stormy night with near-blizzard conditions, Sheehan staged a lackluster hometown rally in Buffalo in front of 2,000 attendees at Convention Hall. The desperate Sheehan was trying to appeal to two of the local legislators who had joined the Roosevelt camp in opposing his candidacy.

William passionately exclaimed to the crowd: "Thirty-five years of my life were spent with you. You saw me enter political life with everything a young man desires except money. You saw me leave it ten years later with nothing but political scars."[30] But his message didn't create much excitement and some of the only enthusiasm from the rally occurred before he even spoke when cheers of "First Ward, First Ward" were heard throughout the hall.[31] The lackluster rally in his hometown was symbolic of the unraveling enthusiasm for his candidacy across the state. Eventually he was forced to capitulate and withdraw his name from consideration. Roosevelt had won.

Sheehan returned to his prosperous law career in New York City and enjoyed a purported multi-million dollar fortune which was primarily earned from his law practice and perhaps a little graft. Another Buffalo lawyer, John Lord O'Brian, explained that "[Sheehan] was looked upon as a man who made a fortune as a lawyer out of his political connections."[32] Sheehan represented the large corporate interests in New York such as utility companies and profited from the contacts he made in his earlier years in government.

Grover Cleveland

While Grover Cleveland detested the Sheehans, his interactions with other Irish Americans from the Ward and the rest of Buffalo was more mixed. In 1870, before his mayoral run, Cleveland was urged by his friends to run for Erie County sheriff. One of the main themes of his campaign for sheriff was to improve the crime-ridden waterfront of Buffalo, which was mostly in the Canal District, just northwest of the First Ward, and mostly inhabited by Irish immigrants. His time as Erie County sheriff was short but memorable. During his tenure, two Irish Americans were sentenced to hang for committing gruesome crimes, and Cleveland insisted that he personally pull the lever for the doomed men. As a result, Cleveland earned the moniker "The Buffalo Hangman" and is remembered as the only U.S. President to personally execute someone. It is unclear how the Irish in the Ward reacted to these public executions of two of their own. However, due to the nature of the cases, it is fair to say that they probably accepted the penalty—although they would not have liked the publicity that furthered the negative stereotypes of the Irish in Buffalo.

The most famous case involved Patrick Morrissey, the twenty-nine-year-old native of County Tipperary, a laborer who lived just outside the Ward. Patrick's troubles with the law started early and at age 11, after breaking the law he was sent to a reform institution. At age 14, like many boys his age, he went to work as a sailor on the Great Lakes. In his twenties, after being convicted of larceny, he was sentenced to Auburn State Prison and returned to Buffalo after his time served. Patrick's mother, Ann Haley, owned a boarding house and saloon on the waterfront at 7 Packet Dock near the Commercial Street Bridge. Ann had a reputation for frequent inebriation and being physically abusive to her four children. On June 23, 1872, Patrick, who was under the influence of alcohol himself, engaged in a fight with his mother and plunged a seven-inch knife into his mother's chest, killing her almost immediately. Before his death at the hands of Cleveland, Morrissey was contrite and made a speech warning of the dangers of intoxication and urging others to "shun evil associates."[33] After meeting with his spiritual director, Father Mallony, and three Sisters of Charity, Patrick dropped seven feet to his death at the hands of Sheriff Cleveland.

Another Irish American, John Gaffney from Terrace Street, did not help the stereotype of the Irish as being unruly, drunk, and violent. John was raised and lived in the Canal District his entire life and was representative of the hard life some of the Irish endured. This area on the western edge of the First Ward was notorious for lawlessness and uncivilized behavior. In the 1880s, there were over 100 saloons along the waterfront and many houses of prostitution.[34] It was an easy place to get in trouble. Gaffney was raised by his mother, a "woman of the town," and he never knew his father.[35] His violent life included numerous assaults and attempted murders. One night Gaffney had a run-in with another Irishmen at a saloon and shot him three times. Gaffney was convicted and sentenced to hang and on February 14, 1873, Cleveland once again pulled the lever. It is said that there was "much local sympathy" for Gaffney, so Cleveland probably damaged some goodwill he had with the Irish residents of Buffalo.[36]

As Buffalo's mayor, Cleveland had several interactions with the Ward and most of them positive. As previously mentioned, he was sympathetic to the Irish Land League movement and introduced Irish rebel leaders at local rallies. Cleveland was also concerned with improving the water quality and sewer system of Buffalo which was an issue that disproportionately affected the Irish in the Ward. Cleveland recognized that poor water quality was costing too many lives in Buffalo. The mayor reminded his fellow citizens that 36% of all deaths in the city were from diseases that were based on poor sanitary conditions—a fact many in the Ward would have been familiar with.[37] In campaign speeches in the Ward he also committed to cleaning up the Ohio Basin. This reform-minded mayor successfully convinced the aldermen of the city to go along with his plans to improve the water quality and sewers, which was also beneficial for Ward residents

Another point of intersection with the Ward occurred when Martin Flanagan, a grain scooper, was sentenced to death for the murder of his foreman, John Kairns. Cleveland felt Flanagan was not adequately defended at his trial and appealed his case to state authorities in Albany.[38] Fortunately for Flanagan, Cleveland prevailed and Flanagan's death sentence was reduced. This incident was also important in building Cleveland's reputation across New York State as someone concerned with those who were disadvantaged. Another incident, and one of Grover Cleveland's last acts as governor of New York, was when he commuted the sentence of a First Ward man, Jim Kelly. Kelly, a longshoreman, was celebrating in a saloon at the corner of Ohio and Michigan Streets one night when he stabbed a total stranger, killing him.[39] As sheriff of Erie County, Cleveland took Kelly to the state prison in Auburn for the offense, but as governor he agreed that it was not an intentional act, so he released him. As the reform movement in New York gained traction, this upstate mayor built a reputation that propelled him into the New York governor's office and eventually to the presidency of the United States. However, if Cleveland hadn't gained the trust of the Irish in their saloons in the First Ward years earlier in his mayoral run, history may have turned out differently.

Before Cleveland's career ended, he had one more confrontation with the Sheehans. Even though Cleveland was elected president of the United States in two non-consecutive terms—in 1884 and then again in 1892—he was mentioned as a potential challenger in 1904 to the popular Theodore Roosevelt. In fact, a wealthy railroad owner, James J. Hill of the Great Northern Railroad, desired to see Cleveland back in the White House. Hill was willing to put up $10 million of his own money for such a chance, so he summoned U.S. Congressman William H. Ryan, who was from 236 Hamburg Street in the Ward, to act as an intermediary with William F. Sheehan.[40] Sheehan, however, was set on nominating his friend Alton B. Parker, chief judge of the New York State Court of Appeals, as the Democratic candidate for president of the United States and refused to entertain a Cleveland run. Even though twenty-five years had passed since the clash between Cleveland and John Sheehan, the younger Sheehan didn't forget. Teddy Roosevelt eventually trounced Parker, the Sheehan candidate, in the 1904 presidential election. If Sheehan hadn't held a long grudge with well-known Grover Cleveland, he may have been the nominee and possibly beaten Roosevelt. Also worth recognizing is the power that William "Blue-Eyed Billy" Sheehan still had that he could shape the dynamics of a U.S. presidential election. The defeated Democratic candidate, Alton B. Parker, later joined the law practice of his friend William F. Sheehan in New York City.

Jack White

As a registered Republican, John "Jack" White, a former ship carpenter from Perry Street, was an exception to the Democratic homogeneity in the Ward. There were certainly other Republican Irishmen in Buffalo, but they were scattered in the downtown area and the West Side. Jack's motivation to become a Republican is uncertain. He may have been supportive of the Republican platform, but more than likely he was just practical. The Republicans and Democrats equally ruled Buffalo politics for much of the late 19th and early 20th century and the Cork-born White was clever enough to realize that if he was the Republican leader of the Ward, then he would benefit when the Republicans ruled the city. By aligning with the Republicans, he could dole out patronage jobs, which increased his power in his neighborhood. When it came to patronage jobs, White desired quantity over quality. A *New York Times* article claimed that White preferred to trade his vote for twenty bridge tender jobs at $2 a day compared to one $1,500 yearly canal section boss.[41] Jack was also friends with owners of railroad companies, steamboats, and grain elevators, and in exchange for his vote in the Common Council, he was able to place people in private sector jobs as well. Sometimes legislation in the Buffalo Common Council would end in a tie and Jack White's vote was the tiebreaker—a fact that gave him even more power. White's success is so much more remarkable considering he was a Republican in a heavily Democratic ward.

In one Ward manuscript, the author claimed, "Jack White put more Irish policemen and schoolteachers to work than anyone in the history of the city."[42] In an 1880 Buffalo *Morning Express* article, the author claimed that Jack, by colluding with the Democrats, had a gift for getting his way when it came to municipal committee appointments. By appointing these key figures, he could then obtain steady employment for his constituents in departments like sewers, streets, schools, and fire.[43] The writer of the newspaper article complained that White had appointed four Irish members to the streets committee and even made one of them chairman. What made this so unusual was that the First Ward '[had] scarcely a paved street on it,' while representatives from other Wards with paved streets were not appointed to the committee.[44] White's reign as Republican alderman from the Ward, which started in 1877, lasted almost a quarter-century.

Throughout his reign, Jack White fought fiercely with the ruling William Sheehan machine. Despite both coming from the Ward, there was no love between the two politicians. As was often the case, political alliances changed quickly in the Ward, and, in 1892, Sheehan and White had a major falling out. The tensions boiled over the next year during Jack White's re-election campaign for First Ward alderman; William Sheehan decided it was time for White to be defeated, so he ran his cousin, John Sheehan (not to be confused with his brother John), to oppose him. "Blue-Eyed Billy" Sheehan was the lieutenant governor at the time, but his web of control over Buffalo's politics was still extensive. Sheehan loyalists William J. "Fingy" Conners and James Kennedy were put in charge of the election campaign in the First Ward's second and fourth districts respectively. Sheehan also controlled the loyalties of the police department and the comptroller's and assessor's offices of Buffalo, which allowed him free reign to employ his dirty tactics to elect his cousin John.

Sheehan's multi-pronged attack on White's campaign started in July of 1893, when his government cronies held up issuing liquor licenses to saloonkeepers allied with Jack White. Without a liquor license, saloonkeepers could not serve alcohol and consequently would lose any influence they had over their customers' voting preferences; it was a clever way to control votes for the fall election.[45] The most flagrant abuses, however, came on Election Day. Jack White suspected voter fraud, but it wasn't until several months after the election that a formal investigation exposed the vastness of Sheehan's plot.

In the fourth district of the Ward, Sheehan's man James Kennedy established a temporary residence in the Ward—even though he lived in the Eighth Ward—to run the campaign. He immediately hired three thugs—Charley Marks, Reddy Strause, and Billy Baker, all former boxers—to intimidate voters at the polling places. In the meantime, Charles McDonnough, the Division Superintendent of Canals, a Sheehan loyalist from Chicago Street, handpicked deputy sheriffs to "keep order" at the polling places. McDonnough, with the help of Kennedy and Fingy Conners, recruited more thugs loyal to Sheehan —who were to act as deputy sheriffs—from the Ward's "Island" area. Desiring even more loyal deputies, James Kennedy boldly went to the *Buffalo Times* printing house and had hundreds of fake deputy badges produced and then distributed them to even more Sheehan loyalists.

The police force was also actively engaged in the Sheehan campaign. The night before the election, Captain Michael Regan from the Ward escorted John Sheehan to various saloons in the Ward, further proof that the police force was playing favorites. On election day, there were even allegations that Captain Regan looked the other way as the Sheehan thugs started throwing White's poll watchers out of the polling area; apparently they even threw some of the voters into puddles of mud in the middle of the street.[46] James Kennedy threw out Wallace Thayer, the pro-Jack White poll watcher, from his polling place. After an arrest warrant for Kennedy was initiated because of his actions, a police detective tipped him off that he was going to be arrested; Kennedy escaped the grasp of the law with the help of a law enforcer. At the Perry Street polling place, fifty-four Italians lined up at 3 a.m. in order to vote for Jack White when the polls officially opened at 6:40 a.m. However, James Kennedy and his entourage of prize-fighters, fake deputies, and Captain Regan dispersed the Italians and forced them to line up to vote behind the Sheehan crowd which had arrived much later that morning. Even after the polling booth opened, Kennedy and the Sheehan supporters prevented some of the Jack White voters from entering the polling place and even threw out others that had been allowed in. Meanwhile, Sheehan supporters were allowed to hang out in the voting compartments and were responsible for folding the ballots after they were marked; this obviously opened up the opportunity for a massive fraud.[47]

There were also very suspicious voting patterns in the second and fourth districts of the First Ward. In 1892, there were 2,400 people registered to vote and based on previous elections 1,200 would cast votes. For the 1893 election, however, 2,000 people voted or over 90% of the eligible voters in the Ward, which would have been highly unlikely. Not only was the turnout high, but there was a spike in year-over-year voter registration. In the fourth district in 1892 there were 452 people registered to vote, but one year later it surprisingly jumped to 889 registered voters. Similar increases in registration occurred in the second district of the Ward as well. The adage to "vote early and often" seemed to be true in the First Ward. William F. Sheehan's masterful plan worked and his cousin John was elected against the favorite Jack White. Jack White contested the election, and after the investigation, White's fraud claims were proven correct.[48] However, John Sheehan remained in office for the next several years. These were the sort of tricks that the Sheehans had been famous for over the years, but by the 1890s they were being exposed by the press and foes alike. In 1894, a year after the fraudulent election, the New York State Constitutional Convention committee extensively detailed this First Ward election and put in controls to prevent such a thing from happening again.

Grover Cleveland certainly disdained the Sheehan brothers and their brand of politics, which he successfully squashed when he was in Buffalo; but Cleveland equally detested Jack White. Throughout his term as mayor of Buffalo, Cleveland consistently clashed with Jack White in Buffalo's Common Council.[49] Four months after arriving in Washington as president of the United States, Cleveland still couldn't forget about Jack White. In fact, in a letter to another Buffalonian, President Cleveland wrote the following:

> We find that Jack White has, through some kind of political manipulation and influence, been receiving $1150 for work for which $600 is usually paid. I don't want that thieving scoundrel to draw another month's salary after this nor any part of it. This is a special point with me.[50]

One week later, a jubilant President Cleveland wrote his same friend and exclaimed:

> I told Vilas (the Postmaster General) to cut off Jack White's head today... and I received word that it was done. And so I have the satisfaction of ridding the public service of one scoundrel today.[51]

It is remarkable that the President of the United States, who was so obviously occupied with national and international affairs, still had an ax to grind in the First Ward of Buffalo. However, despite Cleveland's glee, Jack White's political influence in the Ward and Buffalo extended for many years after the president passed away. Jack White, who had probably amassed a nice sum of money from all of the favors owed to him over the years, continued to live in the Ward at 141 Fulton Street until his death.

So what eventually happened to the Sheehan brothers? On February 9, 1916, at the age of sixty-seven, John C. Sheehan, who was leading the prosperous life of a lawyer, collapsed in his office at 253 Broadway in New York City and later died.[52] He was survived by his wife and four children and was buried outside of New York City. On March 14, 1917, only a year after the death of his older brother John, William "Blue-Eyed Billy" Sheehan succumbed to kidney disease while living in Manhattan. Sheehan's body, unlike his brother's, was brought back to Buffalo for burial in Holy Cross Cemetery in Lackawanna, New York just a few miles from where he grew up. Interestingly, both men were thwarted from higher political office by two future U.S. presidents: Grover Cleveland ended John Sheehan's promising future in Buffalo; and Franklin Roosevelt prevented William from obtaining his coveted U.S. Senate seat. Cleveland and Roosevelt were both reformers and neither liked the brand of politics that the Sheehan boys had perfected in the First Ward. For three decades, the two charismatic Sheehan brothers from Elk Street left an indelible mark on Democratic politics in Buffalo, New York City, and across New York State.

Other Prominent Politicians

Other politicians emerged during the latter part of the 19th century. In 1860, John Patrick Sullivan or J.P. was born in the First Ward to John and Mary Sullivan. The younger John never knew his father, who was killed from wounds suffered at the Battle of Bull Run during the Civil War. At age 16, Sullivan completed his education at the public schools and went to work on the docks like so many other men of his time.[53] As a dock laborer, he joined the first scoopers' association and continued working as a longshoreman until the strike of 1884. The enterprising Sullivan started a business harvesting, storing, and selling ice—an endeavor which made him a prosperous man for the rest of his life. During the winter ice harvest on Lake Erie, John employed hundreds of men who broke the ice into blocks and then pushed them to shore along a melted channel in the lake. Sullivan's ice was used in packinghouses and other commercial operations all around the city. His company quickly grew and he had a large ice-making plant on the Hamburg Turnpike within a few years. But like the Sheehan brothers, Sullivan's real passion was politics.

During the latter part of the 1880s until the early 1890s, there was a fierce battle between Jack White, William and John C. Sheehan, William J. Conners, and John P. Sullivan to control both First Ward and Buffalo politics. Even though all of them were Irish Catholics, former waterfront laborers, and from the same neighborhood, they were ruthless in their quest to gain control. The *Buffalo News* reported that Sullivan "learned his politics in the rough school of the Buffalo waterfront, where strong arm methods occasionally had to be employed if one remained on top."[54] With the Sheehan brothers involved in Albany and New York City politics and Fingy Conners involved with his business interests, Sullivan ultimately prevailed in controlling Democratic politics in the Ward. His ability to gain control was related to the fact that Sullivan had political gifts of wit, charm, and unflappability as well as a keen sense of which way the political winds were shifting.[55] J.P.'s political career started in 1890 when he was elected alderman for the First Ward and lasted an incredible twenty-five years.[56] The power that came with this political office was coveted by many of his political opponents, but no one could figure out a way to defeat John P. Sullivan.

The main players in Ward politics constantly changed their allegiances to suit their interests. The relationship between William Conners and J.P. Sullivan was a typical example of the shifting allegiances of political leaders in the Ward. For instance, in a 1908 article about Conners, the writer claimed that Sullivan and Fingy Conners had mutual hate for each.[57] But this description of their relationship wasn't always accurate. In fact, throughout most of their lives they socialized together: Fingy Conners and John P. Sullivan were founding members and the leaders of the Mutual Rowing Club; both men served together as representatives from the 42nd District at the 1924 Democratic National Convention; and Sullivan even sold his ice business to Fingy Conners.[58] But as was often the case, some days the leaders from the Ward could be friends, and the next day fierce enemies; Sullivan was a master of this art. In his obituary, a *Buffalo News* reporter captured the political acumen of Sullivan when he wrote, "He [Sullivan] found himself battling with, and again against every Democrat who has attained any prominence in Erie County Democratic politics," and "there were times when he made a quick shift of sides and others when his exact status was a matter of some doubt to everybody but Sullivan himself."[59] The reporter added, "More often his strategy was to beguile his opponents, a role in which his talent was widely recognized."[60] First Ward politics at the end of the 19th century was indeed a very messy business.

In the end, Sullivan was able to outmuscle the wealthy and powerful Conners when it came to local politics. He had an incredible knack for connecting with people, a fact that eluded the abrasive and temperamental Fingy, who ruled by fear. Aside from his affability Sullivan was known as an excellent debater and speaker, which were two characteristics that improved his electability. Over time he was recognized as the Democratic boss of the Ward, but his influence stretched much further.[61] John P. also served in the powerful position of Democratic County Chairman during the 1920s, and was influential in New York state politics as well. Sullivan was friends with Charles F. Murphy, the leader of Tammany Hall, and Governor Alfred E. Smith, and was asked several times to heal political divisions in the New York State Democratic Party.

As a result of his earlier career on the docks, J.P. Sullivan was an ally of organized labor throughout his elected office. As a resident of the Ward, living on Hamburg Street, he stood up against the powerful railroad companies, which wanted to lay more railroad tracks in the neighborhood, on the grounds that they degraded the quality of life of the residents.[62] Toward the end of his life, the wealthy Sullivan moved out of the Ward to Depew Avenue in tonier North Buffalo, but he still remained connected to the Ward until his last days. After his retirement as Democratic County Chairman in 1926, Sullivan was often asked for his advice and wisdom on local political matters. In his obituary, the *Buffalo News* summed up his political career rather well:

> A hard-pounding, sometimes shifty fighter in the political arena, he asked no quarter and at times gave none; yet, the battle over, he held no resentments. The enemies of yesterday were his friends today and tomorrow. He would go to the limit for a friend and, by the same token, for an enemy. Of these latter he had few; if any. It isn't in human nature to long nourish a grudge against John P. Sullivan. He was that kind of man.[63]

There were other successful Ward politicians during this era. One was Joseph E. Gavin, born in 1855 to Michael and Rosana (Flannigan) Gavin from 435 Perry Street. Gavin was educated in a public elementary school, attended St. Joseph's College for high school, and then graduated with honors from St. Michael's College in Toronto. University graduation was a rare accomplishment for men of his era, especially one from this working-class waterfront neighborhood. After graduation, he entered his father's coal and wood business; however, politics and political service was his passion. He impressed Grover Cleveland, the former mayor of Buffalo, and was made deputy customs inspector during the president's first term in office. In 1891, during the heyday for Ward men in politics, he was elected comptroller of the city, which was one of the most powerful positions after mayor. Gavin earned praise as "an astute financier" from both Democrats and Republicans alike.[64] In one case he saved the city over $100,000 after discovering that fines collected from criminals should have been placed in the city treasury instead of the county treasury. Vastly different from John Sheehan's tenure, which was filled with graft and embezzlement, Gavin was honored by the Common Council of Buffalo at the end of his term and by all of the major newspapers in Buffalo. In 1894, during the Republican surge to power, Joe Gavin lost a

Democratic bid for U.S. Congress. After his years as comptroller, he entered the municipal bond business where he had great success.

William H. Ryan was born in Massachusetts in 1860—the same year as John P. Sullivan—to Patrick and Jane Ryan. At the age of six, his father moved the family to Buffalo and settled in the First Ward where they were members of St. Bridget's parish. After attending high school, he learned the trade of boot and shoe making, which he worked at for twelve years until he entered politics in 1894.[65] In 1897, he married Ellen T. Cosgrove from the Ward. After serving on the Board of Supervisors for Erie County, William Ryan was elected to the U.S. Congress in 1899, which was the first of five consecutive two-year terms. Ryan, a friend of William Sheehan, was the man who acted as a go-between with James J. Hill and Sheehan in an attempt to nominate Grover Cleveland in 1904 for the U.S. Presidency. He also served on the Democratic National Committee and was successful in the insurance business after his political career ended. Despite his political and business success, Ryan was a member of St. Bridget's parish for over 40 years, and resided in the Ward at 236 Hamburg Street.

In the 20th century, the tradition of an affinity for politics among residents of the Ward continued. Between 1910-1913, three important figures were born: Peter Crotty, Andrew Morrisey, and B. John Tutuska. Peter Crotty was born in 1910, the son of an Irish immigrant father who worked as a longshoreman on the waterfront, and an Irish mother. The Crotty family originally lived on Fitzgerald Street and then later moved to Abbott Road and then Pries Avenue in the Valley. Young Peter Crotty was educated by the Sisters of Mercy at St. Stephen's School. Years later, in a letter to the Sisters of Mercy he recounted his childhood in the 1920s at St. Stephen's Parish and the impact that the sisters had on him.

> Our parish in the first quarter of the [20th] century was made up predominantly of wage earners and their families. Its residents were, for the most part, employed in the feed mills, railroad, and other industries in the vicinity. It was a poor parish and the good Sisters experienced their share of sorrow and heartache which sometimes characterizes life in an industrial community. But, when I look back upon the problems which they faced so courageously, I marvel at their accomplishments.[66]

After graduating from Canisius College and University of Buffalo Law School, Crotty worked for the National Labor Relations Board under the administration of Franklin D. Roosevelt. In 1947, the ambitious Crotty was elected president of the Buffalo City Council, with aspirations for even higher political office; however, this would never materialize. He served as the chairman of the Democratic Party in Erie County from 1954 to 1965, and along the way he was an unsuccessful candidate for both mayor of Buffalo and attorney general of New York State.

One writer said that he was better at getting others elected than he was at getting himself elected.[67] Peter J. Crotty was the unofficial boss of Democratic politics in New York State during John F. Kennedy's presidency; and he was remembered as the man who bridged the old boss rule and the new reform movement that was emerging in the 1960s.[68] Crotty was instrumental in swinging the New York delegation to John F. Kennedy in 1960, and in 1964 he successfully paved the way for Robert F. Kennedy in his Senate run. In fact, Ted Kennedy fondly remembered how Peter Crotty was the first Democratic leader in the nation to support John F. Kennedy's presidential campaign.[69] In 1965, Crotty relinquished his Erie County Democratic chairmanship to his rival Joseph F. Crangle, with whom he often feuded. Peter Crotty was remembered in a *New York Times* obituary as the "erudite king-maker who dominated western N.Y. politics."[70] Ray Hill, the *Buffalo News* columnist, claimed that Peter Crotty elevated power in politics to an art form.[71] Crotty is remembered with his name adorning the pavilion in Cazenovia Park in South Buffalo.

Andrew J. Morrisey, a long-standing local Democratic politician who represented the Ward, was born in 1913. After attending Our Lady of Perpetual Help School and then South Park High School, at age 21 he launched his political career in Tut's Tavern, later called Frank Hahn's.[72] Morrisey, who lived at 151 Kentucky Street, won election as the Erie County supervisor representing the First Ward. He held this county supervisor position for eight two-year terms until he ran for the office of South District city councilman. In 1956 he became the councilman-at-large which he held until 1972. Morrisey's political career included an impressive thirteen election victories and he left an indelible mark on the Ward and South Buffalo.

Following the lead of Jack White, Republican politicians emerged from the First Ward and challenged the Democrats' tight grip on political power. Their successes, however, were not in their local neighborhood where the Democratic majority dominated, but rather at the county and state level. Ray Lawley, a one-time amateur boxer from the Ward, was eventually selected to chair the Republican Party in Erie County—an incredible accomplishment for an Irishman from the Democratic south side of Buffalo. The 6'1" Lawley, son of a fireman whose family roots went back to County Cork, grew up at 228 Hamburg Street and attended St. Bridget's school. In 1925, he worked as a clerk for the firm Kenefick, Cooke, Mitchell and Bass, and even dabbled in Wall Street, eventually losing everything in the Depression.[73] While his family members and neighbors were all Democrats, Lawley realized that if he wanted to enter into politics his way forward would have to be as a Republican as there were too many other Democrats in front of him. His son Bill Lawley explained that in those days the country was not as polarized and the philosophical differences between the two parties were not as great as they are today, so it was easier to switch political parties.[74] After all, Lawley's best friend was Peter Crotty, the Democratic Party Chairman with whom he played cards every week, despite being on opposite ends of the political spectrum.

Lawley dominated Republican politics in South Buffalo for many years. An affable man, Lawley worked full-time as one of the two Erie County election commissioners, and also worked as secretary for Ed Jaeckle, the longtime ruling Erie County Republican Chairman. From Jaeckle, Lawley learned the art of politics. But he also possessed the natural gifts needed to be successful. His son Bill claimed that his father was quite a character and always entertained those he met with a good story or a sharp one-liner. He would also treat a parking lot attendant with the same respect he would a U.S. Senator.[75] During this time when no one had much money, they took care of each other regardless of political affiliation—Lawley often granted favors in helping people get jobs. It was these traits that helped him when he eventually became Erie County Republican Chairman. Later in his life, in 1945, Ray and his wife Edna, a German American from the Fruit Belt, started an insurance business to supplement the family's finances. As of 2012, this firm is still thriving.

Another prominent local Republican politician from the Ward was B. John Tutuska. Tutuska was born in the Ward in 1911 to a father who ran a tavern and a barbershop at Sidway and Katherine Streets. One Ward resident remembers him as more "well-off" than his neighbors due to the fact that his family owned the tavern.[76] Tutuska served as Erie County sheriff from 1959-1969, and was then elected Erie County executive. He was the second county executive in the history of Erie County, but he only served for a short period due to a heart attack. Stanley Bauer, a St. Valentine's parishioner from Fulton Street, was another notable Republican politician. Bauer worked for the Local 36 union, which represented the Polish millers, and later served in the New York State Senate from 1951 to 1958.

Without question, the efforts of the Irish to control local politics—although ruthless and underhanded at times—was an important element in stabilizing the second and third generation of First Ward residents. Other Buffalonians abhorred this political "gangsterism" in the Ward—it even led some newspapermen to refer to it as the "Bloody First."[77] The importance of politics for First Ward men continued throughout the latter part of the 20th century, culminating in the mayoral election of one of the most colorful Ward politicians, Jimmy Griffin.

CHAPTER SIX

THE LABOR MOVEMENT AND THE GREAT STRIKE OF 1899

The diamonds he wears are the crystallized tears of your women.
– Father Patrick Cronin on William "Fingy" Conners

FREIGHT-CAR FIRES, LEHIGH VALLEY R. R. YARDS. SWITCHMEN'S STRIKE, AUGUST, 1892.

Since there was little in the way of a legal system to protect workers' rights, the owners of industry had the upper hand when disputes arose with their employees. Prior to the 20th century, strikes often became violent because local and state governments—which often looked at them as rebellions or riots rather than peaceful acts of resolving labor disputes—reacted forcefully when they arose. In contrast to strikes today, which often focus on achieving better benefits for workers, the strikes in the early to mid-nineteenth century were more consequential; a significant cut in wages might mean not being able to provide food for one's family, or even worse, a visit to the poorhouse.

One of the first strikes in Buffalo involving Irish laborers occurred in January 1849. The strike, called the "Tow-Path Rebellion," occurred when 600 Irish laborers, some from the Ward, wanted to increase their wages from 62.5 cents a day to 75 cents a day. At the time of the strike, the workers and their families were suffering immensely and some were close to starving.[1] The contractor of the project ignored their demands and hired scabs. The Irish responded by rioting and only quieted down when the state militia arrived.[2] The Irish laborers and their supporters lined the path along the canal towpath with pitchforks and a few rifles to intimidate the scabs, but little violence occurred.[3] While the politicians and ruling class of Buffalo were alarmed by the actions of the Irish workers, the strikers had the support of their fellow laborers, the wealthier Irish residents, and the Catholic newspaper: the *Sentinel*.[4]

It only took eight years for another labor flare-up. In the spring of 1857, the Irish laborers from the First and Eighth Wards formed the "Workingmen's Movement." This association, which was supported by the local Catholic newspaper and local Irish politicians, urged the workers to use political elections to obtain restitution for economic grievances.[5] Little did the Irish laborers or anyone else know that later in 1857 the country would fall into a severe economic depression. As a result of this depression, the Irish laborers, who were disproportionately affected by the economic collapse, demanded that the city of Buffalo use tax revenues to create jobs and ease the suffering of the unemployed.[6] This "Workingmen's Movement" in 1857 was one of the first labor organizations in Buffalo, but it still did not have the power that unions would possess later in the century. Another one of the nascent labor movements was called "Work or Bread," and the leaders of this group organized demonstrations during the continued economic downturn of 1858. Irish laborers from the First and Eighth Wards protested in front of the mayor's office demanding that the city create jobs for them.[7] Four years later, in August 1862, the first of many strikes occurred on the waterfront as the longshoremen sought 25 cents an hour instead of the current 20 cents.[8] The military was called in and the riot was squelched but this was not the last time the Irish laborers from the Ward would demand greater rights.

During the Civil War, the disparity between the capitalists and the laborers increased significantly because wages didn't keep up with the increased wartime inflation. Immediately following the onset of the Civil War, trade unions mushroomed throughout the Northeastern United States, but it would take several decades before the well-organized unions would emerge. The railroad industry, which increasingly played a significant part of the First Ward's economy, was the first testing ground for organized strikes.

Strike of 1877

The First Ward played a significant role in a nationwide strike which occurred when railroad companies cut workers' wages. In 1873, the United States suffered a severe financial collapse prompted by the bursting of a bubble in railroad securities held by Wall Street banks; banks had lent too much money to railroad companies, which built too many railroad tracks. Consequently, railroad companies started going bankrupt—by 1876 half of all railroads were out of business—and massive employee layoffs resulted. In the winter of 1873 to 1874 these laid off workers held mass demonstrations throughout the country. Tens of thousands of workers were out of work with no safety net during what was one of the longest and most painful economic depressions in American history.[9] The stage was set for an ugly confrontation.

Four years after the collapse the railroads were still stagnating, so they instituted employee wage cuts. In July of 1877, railroad workers with the Baltimore & Ohio Railroad suffered a 10% cut in their wages, the second cut they received that year. In response, railroad workers in Martinsburg, West Virginia walked off the job and prevented scab workers and soldiers from operating the trains; violence ensued and the strike then spread to Baltimore and Pittsburgh. Buffalo railroad workers, also affected by wage cuts, were sympathetic to the plight of their fellow workers across the country and decided to join the effort. Many of these workers lived hand-to-mouth so any cut in wages—especially two in one year—had a devastating effect on their finances.

The troubles in Buffalo started on Saturday July 21st and much of the mayhem occurred in the First Ward or just north and east of it. At first only the brakemen and railroad firemen struck, but eventually conductors and engineers joined in. When the strikers stopped a train in East Buffalo, the strike was on. Later that night, the mob took over the roundhouse of the Lake Shore and Michigan Southern Railroad, which was just north of the Ward bounded by Red Jacket, Scott, and Heath Streets. The activities of the strikers did not seem to be coordinated but rather spontaneous mobs springing up south and east of the city. Another mob gathered at the Buffalo Creek Bridge and stopped trains from coming into the First Ward. Soon almost all train traffic, except for mail service, was prevented from entering or leaving Buffalo.

Police from the two local precincts, Precinct 7 at Louisiana and South Streets and Precinct 2 at Louisiana and Seneca Streets, were called in to control the strikers, but there was little they could do to subdue the crowds. Police Captain John M. Flanagan and his men had no idea of the violence that was about to commence. On Sunday July 22nd, a mob gathered at the Lake Shore & Michigan Southern yard at Perry and Van Rensselaer Streets and prevented police and militia efforts to move the freight trains. Later that night, one of the strikers was arrested and taken to Precinct 2 and a mob ensued demanding the prisoner's release.[10] The mob started throwing stones at the police outside of the station and four patrolmen—Dennis Maloney, Patrick Gilroy, Michael Roach, and Sergeant John H. Conley—were injured. By Monday morning the 23rd, ordinary citizens throughout the city of Buffalo were seriously worried about the possibility of mob rule. Many of the citizens were sympathetic to the railroad strikers, but they despised the violence of the tramps and toughs that had joined the strikers.[11]

On Monday morning, a large mob armed with clubs and stones gathered at the L.S.&M.S. roundhouse just north of Perry Street and forced employees to stop working; about 200 workers walked off the job.[12] Later, 400 to 500 strikers gathered at the Hamburgh Street railroad crossing where several rail lines converged, making it an ideal place to disrupt train traffic.[13] Two hours later, another mob stopped a passenger train in the Ward on Louisiana Street. On Monday evening, armed strikers stopped a train carrying a company of militia at the Buffalo Creek Bridge. The conflict was about to get deadly. The strikers demanded that the militia disarm before they went further; the commander of the militia refused and the strikers replied by shooting into the train. The militia shot back through the train windows and then lined up outside of the rail car and fired a round. When the skirmish was over seven militiamen were wounded, two seriously, and the militia fled on foot to a house in present day Lackawanna. The rioters suffered one fatality, eighteen-year-old Michael Lyons from Michigan Avenue, and seven seriously wounded including John Cleary, Patrick Brahon, James Hickey and Michael Murphy.[14] The roughly 500 strikers set the militia train car on fire and refused to let the firemen put out the flames. The strikers became more emboldened by their victories and the momentum was in their favor. More units of the militia, however, were on their way to Buffalo to smother the rebellion.

By the fourth day of the strike, ordinary citizens in Buffalo were increasingly worried about the continued violence, but it was the residents of the First Ward and East Side of Buffalo who had a close-up view of the violence, fires, and chaos occurring in and around their neighborhood. The strikers decided to change tactics. Now their efforts were centered on convincing workers in other industries to join the strike. They implored the scoopers and stevedores at the Niagara Grain Elevator and the City Elevator in the Ward to join, but they didn't find many takers. The strikers then focused on workers at lumber mills and other industries like the Boler and Rechtenwalt's Planing Mill at Chicago and Carroll; Farrar and Treft, a steam engine plant on Perry Street; and J.C.& N. Scoville on Louisiana Street, where the strikers actually forced the workers to go home.[15] Now the strike was directly impacting ordinary First Ward workers and their families.

On Tuesday July 24th, hundreds of soldiers arrived in Buffalo to quell the rebellion that was spreading throughout the eastern and southern part of the city. Militia units came in from Warsaw, Lockport, Batavia, Westfield, and even Auburn, New York; even retired Civil War veterans were called up. Ordinary citizens were deputized into the police force: 300 from the West Side of Buffalo became deputized sheriffs with batons and badges and 500 men were sworn in as police officers.[16] With the increased numbers of police and militia, the momentum now swung against the strikers. On Wednesday, a mob gathered on Elk Street and two of the ringleaders, Hugh O'Melia and Michael Dorlan, were arrested by Sergeants Edward G. Burns and Conley. The strikers did find success persuading seventy-five workers at Dakin's coal-yard at Louisiana and Ohio Streets to join them. But the mob at Dakin's turned violent against Police Captain John M. Flanagan of the 7th Police Precinct at Louisiana Street and three of his officers—Gorman, Collins, and Sweeney—were injured.[17]

As of Wednesday the 25th, passenger train traffic still could only get as far as Tifft Street, which meant that travelers were prevented from arriving in Buffalo for four days. By Thursday, events were turning in favor of the police and security forces. At the Hamburg Street railroad crossing, three ringleaders—Daniel O'Leary, from 408 Fulton Street, C. O'Leary, and Louis Primo—were arrested. John "Reddie Jack" Clary, a switchman, and one of the most prominent organizers of the violent skirmishes—including the militia assault at Buffalo Creek Bridge—was arrested at his girlfriend's house on Perry Street.[18] As the leaders of the strike were apprehended, the mobs started to dissipate and train traffic started to come in and out of Buffalo unmolested. Striking railroad workers were now worried about losing their jobs so many quickly returned to work.

By Friday, the strike was basically over. Sadly, the workers received almost no concessions from the railroad management as a result of the strike. The first major nationwide strike was a colossal disaster from the workers' standpoint. The strike caused so much devastation and violence, created animosity between ordinary citizens of Buffalo and the railroad workers, and resulted in no improvements. For most First Warders, many of whom were employed by the railroads or were related to someone who was, this strike was particularly painful. Fortunately, later in the fall of 1877, the owners of the New York Central Railroad restored half of the wage cut incurred by workers, but it took three more years before the workers had their wages fully restored.[19] Both sides of this strike, however, learned valuable lessons that shaped the famous Switchmen's Strike of 1892 fifteen years later.

The Switchmen's Strike of 1892

On Friday August 12, 1892, at Gammel's Hall on Seneca Street, the Switchmen Association voted overwhelming, 80 to 15, to strike against the Leigh Valley, Erie, and Buffalo Creek Railroads. Unlike the Strike of 1877, this strike was not part of a nationwide effort, but rather a localized strike. Barney J. Donohue, who was the head of the switchmen's union, was the leader of the strikers and he faced off against John McMahon, who served on the grievance committee for the railroad. Railroad brakemen were paid $60 per month to work a 26-day month—they only received one day off a week—and they worked twelve-hour shifts. On May 20, 1892, New York State enacted a ten-hour work law, which stated that any work after a ten-hour shift would be paid with extra compensation above what was received at the previous twelve-hour rate. Even after this law went into effect, the railroad workers complained that they often worked shifts as long as fifteen hours with no extra compensation and little or no time to eat.[20]

On Saturday, the day after the strike was declared, violence began without delay. One of the strikers, John Gibson from 538 Elk Street, assaulted a railroad yardmaster on Ohio Street in the Ward, and was promptly arrested. Police reserves were called up to the Police Precinct 7 at Louisiana Street. In the early hours of Sunday morning, at Dingens and South Ogden Streets, the strikers released a series of interconnected railcars with the result that fifteen cars were destroyed after they crashed—the strikers then torched twelve of them. More railcars were destroyed later that day and the police quickly deputized 150 new police officers. Dozens of sheriffs were also sworn in but many of these new security forces later resigned because of intimidation by the strikers. New York State authorities ordered the militia to Buffalo. By Tuesday morning, the government called up 200 more soldiers armed with bullets not blanks, but this was just the start of what turned out to be a massive scale-up. A day later, General Peter C. Doyle called up fourteen companies of infantry—2,000 men—from all over central and western New York; the leadership of the militia had learned from 1877 that they needed overwhelming strength to properly control the situation.

The strikers, however, were also scaling up. On Tuesday, the New York Central switchmen joined the strike, which doubled the number of strikers. As a result of the New York Central workers joining the strike, shipping on Lake Erie practically came to a halt. Grain elevators, already filled to capacity, couldn't be unloaded and coal boats stopped coming to Buffalo because there was no way to transport coal once it arrived.[21] John Hanlon from 126 Fulton Street and Philip Saltier were arrested for assaulting Officer John Patten and were locked up at Precinct 7. An angry mob of 200 people, many of them women, charged a militia line demanding their release. At a meeting between city and railroad officials at the Buffalo Club, it was decided that the situation was deteriorating; a call was made to the Governor of New York to send in the National Guard. Regiments of the Guard were activated from New York City, Brooklyn, Albany, Yonkers, and Troy and eventually 7,000 guardsmen and militia were sent to Buffalo. By Thursday August 18, the ranks of the strikers grew as well with the addition of strikers from the L.S.&M.S. and New York West Shore & Buffalo Railroads. By Friday, the first full week of the strike had ended and workers were desperate from forfeiting a week of pay. Furthermore, public sentiment, newspaper editorialists, judges, and law enforcement all seemed to be united against the strikers. Just as it seemed like the strike might be winding down, violence flared up once again. Henry Duggan, a striker from 248 Fulton Street, snuck by the militia lines on Perry Street and assaulted one of the strikebreakers. At the Ohio Basin, strikers threw coal, stones, and coupling pins at strikebreakers and Martin Hanlon and Thomas Mills were arrested for assault.

By 4 p.m. on Friday, the Ward's own William "Blue-Eyed Billy" Sheehan, the Lieutenant Governor of New York, arrived with a delegation that complained about the overwhelming presence and cost of the militia in Buffalo: there was a ratio of 30 soldiers for every striker.[22] Other members of the delegation included Michael Martin, an engineer from the L.S.&M.S. who lived at 799 Elk Street, Dr. Thomas M. Crowe from 777 Elk Street, and George Mackintosh. Opponents of the strikers responded that this strike was different from 1877 because of the vast increase in railroad infrastructure that had to be protected, so an increase in law enforcement presence was justified. The militia set up camps throughout the southern and east sections of Buffalo; two camps were set up in the Ward with one at Louisiana and Ohio Streets and the other at Ganson Street and Michigan Avenue. At first, the residents in the First Ward were respectful of the militia in their neighborhood, with some even bringing them dinner, but events soon changed.

The disruption of train service in and around Buffalo started to raise the prices of goods on the East Coast: prices of chicken, eggs, and meat started to increase in New York City.[23] Grain merchants were losing thousands of dollars every day. As a result, the railroads recruited strikebreakers with reports of as many as 2,500 coming to Buffalo. By Tuesday, August 23, switchmen from the two remaining railroad companies—the D.L.&W. and B.R.&P.—joined the strike, bringing most train service to and from Buffalo to a halt. Much to the dismay of the strikers, however, the strike did not spread beyond the vicinity of Buffalo; union leaders in other parts of the country did not feel that this was a fight they wanted to join. Violence continued on Ganson Street when two strikers attacked two strikebreakers and the militia responded by firing bullets and wounding Thomas Monaher. The mob fled to O'Brien's Saloon on Ganson Street but the militia caught up to them and arrested Thomas O'Laughlin from 193 Hamburgh Street, Bernard Dunn, Patrick Madigan from Ganson Street, and William Cotter from 176 Chicago Street and charged them with rioting.[24] The militia tried to close Dennis Collins' saloon at 114 Michigan Avenue and the strikers pelted them with stones.

Finally, on Wednesday, August 24th both sides agreed to allow the Board of Mediation and Arbitration to mediate the strike. First Ward native John J. Hynes represented the strikers in the dispute. At the hearing, witnesses for the strikers detailed numerous abuses by the railroad managers. George Dalton from 94 Hamburgh Street claimed that he worked a 36-hour shift without a break to go home to sleep or eat; another worker complained he regularly worked 19-hour shifts; and John Scanell complained that he often worked five or six hours after his twelve-hour shift with no extra pay.[25] Two of the railroad yardmasters, Mr. McGowan from 203 Smith Street and Bernard Mulvaney, were publicly accused of cheating their workers during the hearing.

As these hearings were held, tragedy struck in the First Ward on Wednesday August 24th. A seventeen-year-old boy, William Broderick—who had emigrated from Ireland five months earlier—and a few of his friends started throwing stones at a train and at the militia at the corner of South and Louisiana Streets. Broderick, who was standing one block from his house, started to flee with the others as the militia chased them with bayonets. After the militia ordered the boys to halt, all of them complied except Broderick who was climbing over a fence when the militia opened fire. The young Broderick was struck three times and died later that night of his wounds. His friends, Michael Clifford, James Murphy and John Kelly were all arrested. Residents in the Ward were incensed. Further accusations of abuse by the militia were reported. One Ward resident claimed that the troops ransacked her house and others claimed that the militia regularly insulted women in the neighborhood. William Dray from South Michigan Avenue and Patrick Burns, two residents from the Beach, complained to Police Captain Mike Reagan that the militia had indiscriminately fired shots into their homes; these claims were later verified as true. Militiamen retorted that their camp in the First Ward was the worst in the city because "the population is denser and almost to a soul sympathizes with the strikers and their friends."[26] With 450 strikers versus 7,000 soldiers, the odds were against the strikers. The leader of the strike, who was not from Buffalo, stepped down and Michael J. Moriarity from 234 Peabody Street was named the new leader.

Many of the strikers were Irish from the Ward and the surrounding area, but there was a minority of Germans from the East Side of Buffalo. Newspapers in the city of Buffalo differed in their editorials as to whom to blame for the violence and damage. The *Catholic Union and Times*, the Catholic diocesan paper, as well as the *Buffalo Courier* wrote favorably of the strikers noting that of the 30 people arrested only six were switchmen and the rest were sympathizers or thugs.[27] The other local papers, however, were less sympathetic. The strikers were becoming increasingly isolated and the strike was winding down.

By Friday August 26th, two weeks after the strike commenced, most of the militia started to depart from Buffalo. Sporadic violence still occurred, with the area around Precinct 7 on Louisiana Street in the Ward considered the last trouble spot in the city. Daniel J. Delaney from 69 Fulton Street and Owen Kief were arrested for throwing stones at trains at both Fulton and Perry Streets. Even the police added to the violence when Sergeant Florence Driscoll and his men accidentally clubbed some non-strikers at the L.S.&M.S. roundhouse in the Ward. These were the last incidents of violence, however, and the strike was over the next day.

In the end, the railroad owners and management had won again. After the strike, the strikers received no concessions, some lost their jobs, and many went without pay for at least a week or more. The railroads lost tens of thousands of dollars in revenue and damages. The Catholic Church leadership was supportive of the strikers but relatively silent; seven years later during the grain scoopers strike they would come to life. Support for the strikers was relatively isolated to their fellow residents in communities like the First Ward and the East Side of Buffalo. Other than these few supporters it was the strikers against everyone else. The switchmen's strike in Buffalo in 1892 set the stage for the much more massive, deadly and widespread Pullman Strike in Chicago two years later. However, when the Pullman Strike organizers, specifically Eugene Debs, asked for the Buffalo railroad workers to join his strike, the head of the Buffalo union, James Malican from 854 Exchange Street, declined. No one had come to Buffalo's assistance in 1892 and the Irish strikers had not forgotten.

William "Fingy" Conners, Bishop James Quigley, and the Great Strike of 1899

One of the most significant employers in the history of Great Lakes commerce hailed from an unlikely place: the First Ward of Buffalo. On January 3, 1857 William J. Conners was born to a pair of Canadian-Irish immigrants, descended from County Cork, who lived on Louisiana Street. The family later moved to Ohio Street and then to 51 Sandusky Street. Peter Conners, William's father, progressed from a lake sailor to the more skilled position of a stonecutter, which enabled him to save enough money to buy a saloon. Young William, also known as "Jimmy," dropped out of school at age eleven or twelve to become a porter on steamboats on the Great Lakes, and later worked stacking cords of wood for the railroads.[28] At age seventeen, the blue-eyed, muscular Conners became a longshoreman on the docks and because of his toughness and fighting ability he became a leader of a small gang.[29] The charismatic "Fingy" was a natural leader, but he exhibited a characteristic that differentiated him from other natural leaders in the Ward: ruthlessness. This trait would guide him, for better and for worse, throughout his future commercial and political endeavors.

There is an interesting story that exemplifies William's fearlessness and explains how he acquired his nickname. Conners claims that when he was a young boy, one of his friends questioned whether or not he had the nerve to have "one of his fingys" cut off by the friend. William retorted that it was his friend that did not have the nerve to actually perform the operation; William, however, underestimated his friend's psychological state and the friend did indeed cut off one of Conners' fingers on his left hand. As the legend goes, after the unfortunate event Jimmy Conners ran down the street with a bloody stump yelling "he cut off my fingy" and from that moment until his death he was known as Fingy Conners.[30]

Unfortunately, sadness would strike Fingy in his late teens when his only sister died in a house fire in the Ward. At about age 19 he lost his mother from the grief of his sister's death, and his father died the following year. These events led to an abrupt end to his youth; Fingy was now a man dependent on himself for survival. However, out of these numerous tragedies his fortunes would change as well. He inherited his father's saloon and rooming house at 193 Louisiana Street near the Ohio Basin, and he used the insurance money from his parents' and sister's deaths to expand his saloon operation. Fingy's saloon gave him a taste for making money, but he wasn't adequately satisfied from the modest profits of a saloon. By the 1880s he expanded the saloon to include a boarding house at 444 and 446 Ohio Street near South Street. Using his gift of leadership, the inheritance money and his keen sense for business, Fingy calculated how to profit even further from the burgeoning commerce on the waterfront.

Success for many people is intricately tied to being at the right place at the right time and this was one of the keys to Conners' success. As the need for dockworkers exploded in the late 19th century, shipping companies lacked the resources to hire dockworkers directly, so they handed this task off to saloon owners, who would then control the task of hiring workers to unload packaged goods from the boats. For instance, the captain of the ship would go to a saloon owner and ask for ten workers; the saloon owner, or "boss" as they were called, would then pick his ten favorite customers. If you weren't a regular at the saloon you were out of luck. Saloon bosses like Conners obviously preferred to hire the single men who would also be boarders at their saloon and their most loyal bar patrons. The workers pay was even paid out as a tab at the saloon, which further lined the pockets of the saloon boss owners. If you have ever seen the movie "On the Waterfront" and remember the longshoremen's union boss, Johnny Friendly, you get a sense of the power that a saloon boss wielded.

There were several saloon owners who profited from this system, but it was Fingy who envisioned monopolizing this fragmented system of bosses with him as the premier boss—a task he accomplished with ruthless precision. In 1885, as a reward for keeping costs low and running his operation efficiently, he was awarded a contract for all of the shipments on the Great Lakes for the Union Steamboat Company.[32] Fingy now controlled the operations of unloading goods from the lake vessels to the docks, but the unsatisfied Conners desired ownership of the remaining operations: from the dock-to-the-warehouse and from the warehouse-to-the-railcars. Fingy eventually controlled both of these pieces as well. At the young age of thirty-eight, he was reportedly the largest freight contractor in the United States, a newspaper publisher, the president of a local brewery, and a successful building contractor.[32]

However, while his system was extremely profitable for himself and his cronies and efficient for the shipping companies, it was vehemently opposed by the workers, by the neighborhood priests, and by some in the press. Their public criticism, however, could not derail Fingy Conners and it may have further emboldened him. Within a decade after Fingy consolidated his freight handling of dry goods, he set his sights on controlling the lucrative grain handling business. Fingy eventually monopolized this business as he had the others; he always got what he desired. But as Fingy was rising, so too was another Irishmen from Buffalo who was ready to challenge "The Uncrowned King of the Docks."

A proud moment for the Irish First Warders came on February 24, 1897 when the pastor of St. Bridget's, Father James E. Quigley, was consecrated as the third Bishop of Buffalo at the young age of forty-one. James Quigley was born in Oshawa, Canada on October 15, 1855 to poor Irish immigrants who moved to Rochester, New York a few years after he was born. In 1865, the ten-year-old Jimmy Quigley was sent by his mother and father to live with his uncle, Father Edward Quigley, the rector of Immaculate Conception Church in downtown Buffalo. The wavy-haired, handsome Jimmy was the favorite student in his class and the star pitcher on the baseball team at St. Joseph's Collegiate—a local Catholic high school.[33] One of his high school language teachers, Dr. Doyle, once commented to a fellow teacher on what a special student Jimmy was.

> That boy is a marvel at acquiring learning. He picks it up without any apparent effort. I've taught school in a good many countries, but that is the brightest boy I ever knew. He's full of life and vivacity, doesn't study any longer than he has to, but absorbs knowledge surprisingly. Watch him.[34]

After graduating at the top of his high school class he planned on attending West Point Military Academy where he was accepted. Instead, the charismatic Quigley decided to become a Catholic priest. As a seminarian he was sent to Europe for studies and was ordained at Innsbruck, Austria. A rising star in the Buffalo diocese, Quigley was a noted pulpit speaker whose charisma endeared people to him.[35] After serving at the mother church of the diocese, St. Joseph's Cathedral, Quigley asked Bishop Ryan permission to become rector of St. Bridget's in the Ward in 1896.[36] His exact motive is unclear, but perhaps as the son of working-class Irish parents, he may have wanted to assist the families of the Irish laborers in the Ward.

While his tenure at St. Bridget's was short and mostly free of any major events, a connection was made with the workers and their families that would impact his tenure as Bishop of Buffalo. Specifically, his policy on Church involvement with labor unions started to evolve. Quigley was also praised for transforming the rectory, the church and the surrounding area of the parish in less than a year. In addition, he inspired a young man, William Donovan, the future World War I hero and founder of the OSS. Donovan later claimed that Father Quigley was his boyhood idol.[37] He had become a champion of the working-class Irish and was much loved by those in the Ward. On December 12, 1896 James Quigley was named Bishop of Buffalo and ordinary Catholics were excited with his appointment. Even the non-Catholic press wrote favorably about him describing him as popular, intelligent, progressive and inclined toward the liberal wing of the Catholic Church.[38] These qualities would serve him well in his clash with Fingy Conners.

In the winter of 1898-1899, the Lake Carrier's Association, a trade association representing vessels on the Great Lakes, awarded Fingy Conners control over all of the loading and unloading of the grain boats including the lucrative task of hiring the grain scoopers.[39] Up to this point he only controlled the freight-handling business on the waterfront. Conners immediately set up a network of cronies at saloons in the Ward and on the waterfront who devised a scheme to profit from this new operation. Basically, the saloon-bosses started to add fake names to the roster of workers on a particular job and then collect the pay themselves for these fictional characters. For instance, if thirty scoopers worked a job, the saloon bosses would say there were forty and keep the pay of the ten fictional workers. The grain scoopers immediately realized this resulted in a reduction of their pay and threatened to strike. Not wanting any disruptions in his business, Fingy Conners immediately put an end to these shenanigans.

The year before Conners was granted his contract, a grain scooper averaged $4.90 a day and his pay was based on how many bushels he unloaded. Fingy thought he could squeeze some more of the workers' wages so he hatched another scheme. He created a new compensation plan with a fixed rate of 28 cents an hour of work versus the previous wage system based on bushels unloaded.[40] Almost overnight this resulted in a 50% decline in pay. This new system was even worse for the workers than the previous one where the bosses were just skimming some profits. To make matters worse, the bosses continued to give hiring preference to workers who spent money in their saloons. Saturday evening was payday and the workers had to go to the saloon to receive their wages over the counter at the bar.

The workers' wages were the net of their earnings less any alcohol and boarding fees, and from the saloon bosses perspective, if your check was too large that meant you were not spending enough at his establishment; consequently your future prospects of employment were limited. This system obviously favored young, single workers who boarded at the saloons and who enjoyed frequent libations over married men with families.

To further profit from this system, Fingy directed his saloon-boss cronies to purchase the saloon's alcohol from a local brewery where he was the director: Magnus Brewery.[41] In addition, whenever there were any hints that the workers wanted to strike, Fingy would insert his cronies into the local union leadership at Local 51 to ensure that any reforms would be stifled. The leadership of Local 51 decided to accept Conners' change in the pay structure, and this infuriated the majority of grain scoopers. Finally, in late April of 1899, the grain scoopers, furious with their cut in pay, organized a new union, Local 109, at Patrick "P.J." McMahon's saloon at 161 Elk Street in the Ward.[42] This was a slap in the face of William J. Conners; things were about to get interesting.

On April 30th, in an effort to retaliate for the creation of a new union and to intimidate the strikers, men loyal to Fingy Conners destroyed the McMahon family saloon on Elk Street. This event was just the beginning of the violence that was about to ensue. The Fingy loyalists were smaller in number than the strikers but due to the fact that their enterprise was being threatened they struck back ferociously. Many grain scoopers faced an agonizing decision: side with the powerful Fingy Conners and continue earning smaller wages than they were accustomed to or strike with no wages and no certainty of victory. The fact that there was little in the way of a government or union safety net made the prospect even more dire. Most scoopers ultimately sided with the strikers. In the Bohen family history, the author explained the dilemma and the consequences that workers faced based on whether they sided with Conners or not. The family historian stated that, "[Timothy Bohen] lost his job in the big strike but not his dignity."[43] The history continues that Timothy "could have been rich if he would have scabbed for Fingy Conners his very close friend."[44] In the Bohen oral history, it has been retold that Fingy Conners came twice to the Bohen house at 45 Sandusky Street—just two houses away from where Fingy grew up at 51 Sandusky Street—in an effort to persuade Timothy into switching to his side with promises of riches. Timothy wouldn't budge and reiterated his support for his fellow strikers. Conversely, many of those who sided with Fingy went on later to profit handsomely as his agents with the Great Lakes Transit Corporation.

Fortunately the powerless grain scoopers had allies in the Catholic Church and in the political arena as well. Father Patrick Cronin, an Irish Catholic priest, and advocate for the downtrodden workers, wrote several articles in the years leading up to the strike in the official diocesan newspaper, the *Catholic Union and Times*, where he chastised Fingy Conners for engaging in his corrupt system. In one such article, he commented: "the diamonds he [Conners] wears are the crystallized tears of your women."[45] But Father Cronin knew that editorials wouldn't change Fingy's course of action so he decided to call a meeting with the thousand-plus scoopers at St. Bridget's Hall in the First Ward. Once the strikers assembled, Cronin delivered a passionate speech rallying the workers to stand up to Conners. As his speech was nearing an end, cheering started to emerge from the back of the hall as another church official was pushing through the crowd making way to the platform. The entire crowd rose to their feet to meet the unexpected guest; it was Bishop James Quigley.

Bishop Quigley delivered a clear, somewhat dispassionate address to the workers, but he left them with an unequivocal mandate. Specifically, the senior church leader forbade any of the strikers from working for Fingy Conners until he exited the grain business.[46] The Bishop's authority was in part derived from the groundbreaking 1891 papal encyclical *Rerum Novarum*, which for the first time officially urged Church leaders to advocate on behalf of workers' rights. Pope Leo XIII exclaimed that "the hiring of labor and the conduct of trade are concentrated in the hands of comparatively few; so that a small number of very rich men have been able to lay upon the teeming masses of the laboring poor a yoke little better than that of slavery itself."[47] Leo XIII further proclaimed that the Church could no longer be silent with regard to matters of labor and to the conditions of workers. Eight years after this proclamation, Bishop Quigley had the mandate he needed to spearhead efforts on behalf of the roughly 1,000 grain scoopers. The strikers finally had a leader who would guide them through this storm.

Despite sharing an Irish Catholic background, Bishop Quigley and Fingy Conners couldn't have been more different. Quigley was well educated and refined, while Conners was educated on the docks and unpolished. Quigley relied on persuasion and eloquence while Conners used fear and intimidation. Quigley, the former rector of St. Bridget's, became the chief negotiator and dealmaker for the strikers and he worked with a committee of lay representatives with upstanding men like Timothy Donovan, father of future hero William "Wild Bill" Donovan. Father James Lanigan, the rector of St. Bridget's Church, was also a passionate advocate on behalf of the strikers. Meanwhile, Conners employed a gang of toughs and thugs to carry out his orders.

On the political side, the Catholic strikers had what appeared to be a traditionally unlikely ally: a congressman who was both Episcopalian and Republican. The former two-term Republican congressman and future U.S. Secretary of Labor, Rowland B. Mahany, also pleaded the laborers' cause and rallied the workers.[48] Mahany grew up on Carroll Street near Chicago Street—one block north of the

Ward boundary—but because of the proximity of his homestead to the Ward and because his Irish father from County Kerry had formerly worked as a dockworker in the First Ward the locals claimed him as one of their own. Mahany attended elite schools like Hobart and Harvard, but he still had a great affection for the working class.[49] At the young age of twenty-eight, he was appointed U.S. envoy and minister to Ecuador by President Benjamin Harrison in an effort to gain the Irish-American vote in New York State during his 1892 campaign for reelection.[50] Three years later, as a result of his concern for the laboring class and despite the fact that he was a Republican, the *Catholic Union and Times* endorsed Mahany in his bid for the open congressional seat in Buffalo. More importantly, the Irish Catholics in the southern part of Buffalo—most of them Democrats—elected this distinguished and dapper gentleman to two terms in Congress representing the 32nd District.

Another motivation for Mahany's involvement on behalf of the strikers was the mutual dislike that he and Fingy Conners had for each other. Both wore battle scars from previous political contests and Fingy disdained him so much that he unleashed the editorial staff at both of his newspapers (the *Courier* and the *Enquirer*) to attack the congressman; the attacks worked and Mahany lost in his run for a third term.[51] In one of Conners' blistering editorials from the *Buffalo Courier* on May 4th, the writer explained that, "They [the strikers] are simply the tools of this man Mahany, a glib beggar, a man who lives without work, a man of no character, no standing, and no balance."[52] But Mahany, whose great oratorical skills earned him the nickname "the silver-tongued orator," would ultimately have his revenge, as he was able to use his gifts of oration to inspire the workers and the general citizens of Buffalo. Unlike previous strikes where sentiment was isolated to those in the Ward, Mahany was able to broaden awareness of the plight of the scoopers to broader segments of the populace—even the Protestant clergy joined the Catholic scoopers cause.

Meanwhile, as the grain scoopers resisted crossing the picket line, Fingy was struggling to find replacement workers to assist in unloading the boats. Conners attempted to hire local Italians and Polish immigrants to replace the stubborn Irish scoopers, but both groups declined and sided with the strikers. He eventually recruited over 1,000 scabs from outside of Buffalo and from as far away as New York City and Cincinnati, but many didn't realize they were recruited to be strikebreakers so they too defected to the side of the strikers once they arrived in Buffalo. There are even reports that the scoopers in the Ward fed and housed their would-be replacements after they declined to work for Conners.[53]

Fingy's efforts to intimidate the strikers only led to more violence such as when a group of Conners' loyalists clashed with a group of strikers at the foot of Main Street. William H. Kennedy, a nephew of one of Conners' top lieutenants,

James Kennedy, owned a saloon on the seawall and worked at one of the elevators as a timekeeper. Conners sent William Kennedy and other cronies on a mission to intimidate the strikers into ending their futile strike. The strikers had ideas of their own and one of them, John J. "Buck" Skinner, responded to the intimidation by firing shots at William Kennedy; he was a good shot and killed Kennedy. Conners was furious at his friend's death, but rather than use more force he tried a different tactic; he used his newspaper, the *Buffalo Courier*, to lambaste his critics by trying to intimidate them with words. Conners, however, was quickly losing control of the strike. The freight handlers had already joined the strike and the International Seamen's Union, which represented the crews on the ships, threatened to join as well. The strikers were emboldened after they convinced other union workers from the New York Central Railroad and men from the coal and iron industry to join the strike to assist the grain scoopers.[54] Furthermore, the strike was attracting national attention and Daniel Keefe, the president of the International Longshoremen's Association, came to Buffalo several times during the strike to assist in the negotiations on behalf of the workers. All the while, Bishop Quigley was urging the workers to maintain peace and order, which contributed to the sympathy exhibited by the wider community.

The intended effect of the strike, to halt grain shipments at the beginning of the bustling shipping season, worked perfectly. Commerce on the Great Lakes shut down and tens of millions of bushels of wheat were stuck on the freight ships; two weeks into the strike there were 3.6 million bushels of grain waiting to be unloaded on forty-three ships.[55] In Duluth alone there were over 20 million bushels waiting to be shipped to Buffalo. The entire trade route of grain from the Midwest to the East Coast was halted because of the strikers in the First Ward. If people on the East Coast had not previously heard of the grain scoopers from the First Ward of Buffalo, they did now. Finally, almost a month later, on May 23rd, the shipping companies could no longer hold out and they agreed to negotiate directly with Bishop Quigley and the new union, Local 109; the result was that William J. Conners was essentially cut out from his control of the grain-scoopers. Immediately, P.J. McMahon was named president of the new union, new officers were nominated and a new constitution was drawn up. The next day, police officers were on the docks checking the workers' union cards to make sure that they were members of McMahon's new union.

The Irish grain scoopers were satisfied with the terms: their original wage structure was reinstated, they now made about 49 cents per hour, and they were paid at their place of employment, no longer in the saloons. While the grain scoopers were content and returned to work, their strike had opened up other wounds on the waterfront. Specifically, the ore handlers, who were mostly Polish immigrants, as well as thousands of freight handlers, received no new concessions from the strike; even worse they now earned significantly less than the grain scoopers.[56] Quigley had urged the freight handlers to accept the offer, but they voted his proposal down and demanded an increase in pay.[57] After some minor skirmishes between these other dockworkers and Conners' men, major violence erupted on June 12th when Conners' henchmen shot 200 rounds of ammunition into the hatch of the *Samuel Mather*, an iron-ore carrier, where Polish workers were working in the hull. Three workers were shot, but none of them died of their injuries. A total of sixteen people were arrested for the incident and one of Fingy Conners' relatives by marriage, Dick Nugent, the husband of Fingy's niece, was arrested and sent to prison for five years for being the ringleader; Nugent operated the Nugent Hotel on Ohio Street in the same building where Fingy ran his saloon-boss operation.[58] Meanwhile, the striker Buck Skinner who killed Fingy's man, William Kennedy, received a comparatively light sentence of only eight months. Clearly the judicial system was more sympathetic to the strikers than their opponents.

While Fingy Conners lost control over the grain business in Buffalo, he had previously diversified his fortune into other activities such as newspapers, street-paving companies, poultry farming, breweries, and real estate, so the loss was inconsequential.[59] In 1904, Conners left the south side of Buffalo and wedged himself into the elite Protestant enclave when he purchased a mansion on Delaware Avenue and joined the exclusive Buffalo Club. In 1906, Fingy was selected to the powerful position of chairman of the Democratic State Committee where he was influential in the 1908 U.S. Presidential election.

In 1916, at age 59, William J. Conner's fortunes brightened once again. The Panama Act, legislation enacted by the U.S. Congress, ended the monopoly the railroad companies had on Great Lakes shipping. The railroad companies had to divest their Great Lakes shipping operations, so they urged their long-time friend Fingy Conners to consolidate their disparate lake freight lines into one company under his control. Fingy, a former cabin boy on the Lakes, quickly bought up their shipping lines and formed the Great Lakes Transit Corporation. Once again Fingy was the right man at the right time. That year, William J. Conners became Chairman of the Board of the Great Lakes Transit Corporation and one of the most powerful businessmen on the Great Lakes; the 33-vessel enterprise employed between 4,000 and 6,000 men weekly and at one point Conners claimed that he was the largest individual employer of labor in the United States.[60] Eventually he controlled a staggering 85% of the package freight on the Great Lakes.[61]

During World War I, Conners offered the entire Great Lakes Transit fleet as well as his beloved yacht, the *Mary Alice*, to the U.S. government for whatever price they offered. The war department also hired him as a consultant to figure out logistical problems they were experiencing with transporting freight to French ports.[62] After the war, Conners split his time between Buffalo and West Palm Beach, Florida where he again profited by building a toll road which went through the Florida Everglades and connected the west coast of Florida to the east coast. He also purchased 6,000 acres in the Everglades, built the Harding Memorial Bridge over the Kissimmee River, and created a massive farm which he described as "the finest farm in the South."[63] Later in life, Fingy also silenced some of his critics through his philanthropic activities such as a $1 million fund to help poor people in Buffalo, and he even leased the shuttered New York Central railcar business in East Buffalo in order to keep the 1,500 idled workers employed. When he created the board of directors for his charity in Buffalo, the newly progressive Conners stipulated that it be composed of two Catholics, two Jews, and two Protestants in order that the funds would be judiciously spent. Fingy Conners truly exemplified the American Dream: an uneducated laborer with street smarts and unbridled ambition became a nationally prominent multimillionaire. But there was an unanswered question.

For a man who grew up with so many of the grain scoopers, who had worked as a laborer himself, who shared their faith and their heritage, it is fair to ask the question of why he so ruthlessly schemed against his neighbors leading up to the Great Strike? Why did he divide the community of his birth and condone violence toward his fellow neighbors? The answer may be simply greed. Or maybe he craved power and the benefits that come with it. He certainly was a visionary in his understanding of how to consolidate the fragmented logistical business of transporting dry goods and grain. All empire builders—Vanderbilt, Carnegie, Rockefeller, Gates and Jobs—are slapped with similar labels of ruthlessness or greed, but sometimes the real motive is more difficult to understand. We may never know the real motivation for his behavior. Regardless, in his time, Conners was one of the most successful businessmen in Buffalo and he likely ranks as the most successful businessmen to ever come out of the First Ward.

Within a few years after the Great Dock Strike in 1899, labor unions in the city were growing stronger after being practically nonexistent just a decade earlier. However, certain city labor leaders were advocating a socialistic strain in their labor proclamations, and trying to organize the unions under a single umbrella called the Erie Labor Council. The Social Democrats in Buffalo espoused two major tenets: private property is immoral and the Catholic Church is on the side of the capitalists and not the workingman. Bishop Quigley, certainly a friend of labor and worker's rights, was disturbed by some of the atheistic precepts embedded in socialist thought and openly challenged their assertions. The Irish labor leaders in the Ward were not attracted to the teachings espoused by the Social Democrats, or the Socialists, as the Catholic hierarchy referred to them. Most likely Irish laborers who witnessed the work of Catholic prelates—Bishop Quigley, Father Cronin and Father Lanigan—on their behalf in 1899 would have immediately rejected the claims of Church bias toward capitalists. The German laborers on the East Side of Buffalo, however, who hadn't benefited from the work of the Church on their behalf, were attracted to the teachings of the Social Democrats. In fact, the Brewers Union, composed mostly of Germans from the East Side, was the first city union to side with the Social Democrats. Quigley had a problem with this.

Bishop Quigley felt that the socialists' teachings were hostile to the Church, so on February 23, 1902 he crafted a pastoral letter, which was read throughout all of the parishes on the East Side of Buffalo. Specifically, it condemned socialistic teachings, while at the same time protecting a worker's right to join a union. Quigley declared that, "A workingman may be a union man and a good Catholic, but he cannot be both a Social Democrat and a Catholic." This was the first time that a U.S. bishop publicly denounced the teachings of socialism as it was related to unions.[64] Shortly after the pronouncements were read at Sunday mass the strength of the Social Democrats waned and the movement never gained its momentum in Buffalo again. More importantly, Quigley emerged as the leading Catholic cleric in the U.S. on the relationship between socialism and labor unions. His efforts during the dock strike exposed him to the need for unions in order to counterbalance powerful industry leaders like Fingy Conners; and his efforts combating socialism on the East Side of Buffalo made him fluent in the Church's position on this growing movement. The involvement of a Catholic Bishop into the affairs of labor was relatively novel for this era, but it would become a model for ecclesiastical intervention into the conditions of workers over the next several decades. As a result of these experiences, on January 8, 1903, Bishop Quigley was elevated to Archbishop of Chicago, which at the time was a city at the forefront of the socialist movement.[65] Perhaps Quigley's elevation to archbishop wouldn't have happened if a courageous group of grain scoopers hadn't organized at P.J. McMahon's saloon in the First Ward.

After the strike, Rowland Mahany's prominence also rose. Shortly after the strike ended, he was named the Harbor Commissioner of Buffalo with a mandate to reform the abuses during the pre-strike days. Mahany also switched to the Democratic Party and President Woodrow Wilson named him senior attorney in the Department of Labor from 1918-1919. He was also the President's representative at the International Commission of Immigration and Emigration in Geneva, Switzerland. In 1920, he was named acting Secretary of Labor in President Warren G. Harding's administration. Out of this bloody strike, the three principal players—Conners, Quigley, and Mahany—were all elevated to even greater heights than when they started. More importantly, the grain scoopers in the First Ward had a fair wage scale and the abuses of the saloon-boss system were over forever. Interestingly, the Grain Shoveler's Union, Local 109, at 110 Louisiana Street, is the world's only union hall for grain scoopers and it is still standing today.[66]

T.V. O'Connor

First Ward grain scoopers had been involved with organized labor prior to the Great Strike of 1899. On July 17, 1882, grain scoopers in the First Ward formed the Shovelers Assembly #2052 under the charter of the Knights of Labor— this was an association but not quite a union. The list of the signers consists of entirely Irish surnames: Conners, Cavenaugh, Sheehan, O'Neil, Quinn, Clifford, O'Brian, Donovan, Mahoney, Hagerty, Crowley, Hagan, and Lewis.[67] But after the strike, the Irish-American involvement—and domination—in the local and national union movements accelerated. Between the years 1900 and 1910, Irish Americans led almost half (50 of the 110) of the affiliate unions of the American Federation of Labor.[68] The leadership of the International Longshoremen's Association—which represented stevedores and grain elevator workers along the Buffalo waterfront—was almost entirely Irish.[69] Names of local union leaders included Conners, Sullivan, Cavanagh, Donohue, and Mann. Like politics, labor involvement seemed to come naturally for the Irish. One First Warder in particular stood out and he went on to became one of the most powerful people in the labor movement in the early part of the 20th century.

Not many people from the First Ward can claim that they were close friends with three U.S. Presidents, but Thomas Ventry O'Connor could. T.V. O'Connor as he was known was born on August 9, 1871 to an Irish immigrant father who initially settled in Toronto, Ontario and then moved to Buffalo when young Thomas was four years old. Throughout his childhood, his father, who worked as a plasterer, moved the family around in Buffalo from the West Side to the First Ward to South Buffalo. As a young man, T.V. was at one time living on Ohio Street and working in various waterfront occupations such as tug fireman, ferryman, and lake sailor. By 1900, he was living with his wife Bridget Carney O'Connor at 217 Mackinaw Street in the Ward. With a formal education that ended at grammar school, T.V. always carried a book with him as he worked on the waterfront to better himself. O'Connor was described as a jovial, friendly type of person who also could be rough and tumble when needed on the docks.

T.V. O'Connor had a knack for union organizing starting with his involvement with the Tugboat Association. Later, in 1908, only nine years after the Great Strike in Buffalo, he was named the president of the International Longshoremen's Association (I.L.A.) replacing the well-known Daniel Keefe. A former tugboat worker, O'Connor steered the 90,000-member organization through twelve tumultuous years including being shot at by union gangsters in New York City on two different occasions. During the widespread three-year strike against the Lake Carriers' Association which started in 1909, he correctly urged his union members not to strike against the powerful L.C.A.; the result was that the I.L.A. was one of the last unions standing at the end of the strike. T.V. served as President of the I.L.A. until 1921. In 1920, O'Connor supported President Harding, and the Ward native was rewarded by being named Assistant Secretary of Labor in his administration. The reason that O'Connor, who was a Democrat, supported a Republican was that in his mind the Democratic Party was going to be run by Southerners who were not friendly to labor, so he felt the union interests were better served by Harding.[70]

Along the way he caught the attention of President Calvin Coolidge who appointed him to the prestigious position of Chairman of the United States Shipping Board where he served until 1933. He was also instrumental in building up the United States merchant marine. O'Connor said there were two tenets he lived by that were his secrets to success. First, "Consider the common working man as much as the man who is ten leagues ahead of him." Second, "Never forget to smile your orders as well as your thanks."[71] T.V. also served under President Hoover and it has been stated that he was friends with all three Republican presidents, quite an accomplishment for an Irish Democrat from the south side of Buffalo. T.V. O'Connor died on October 17, 1935, but not before leaving an indelible mark on the I.L.A. and the national labor movement.

CHAPTER SEVEN

NEW DOORS OPEN

[Douglas] MacArthur never was willing to forget that ["Wild Bill"] Donovan was the only American soldier who emerged from the World War I fighting in France with more medals and fame than he did.
– Historian William McGovern

ASSISTANT CHIEF MURPHY

Near the turn of the 20th century, industrial production and shipments along the Buffalo River seemed unstoppable. In 1897, *Engineering News*—a leading national magazine on trends in engineering—highlighted two innovative engineering projects from the First Ward. The first was the new Michigan Avenue Bridge. Since so many shipping vessels were journeying down the Buffalo River, a new bridge at Michigan Avenue was needed to replace the outdated swing bridge that was built in 1872. The requirements for the Michigan Avenue drawbridge necessitated some innovative features which the magazine highlighted in its August 19, 1897 issue. Specifically, this massive bridge, 150 feet in length and 22 feet wide, needed to be double hinged and had to open and close 40 to 50 times a day. It required a high-capacity boiler, with three times the normal pounds of pressure, in order to operate in the high winds that are common along the Buffalo River; and it had to be engineered so that the bridge could be elevated in 60 seconds or less (it could actually accomplish this task in as little as 45 seconds.)[1] This new, state-of-the-art bridge went a long way towards facilitating the increasing ship traffic along the river. It also offered further proof that Buffalo was on the cutting edge of technology.

Engineering News magazine also mentioned the innovative designs of the lake steamers manufactured by Union Dry Dock—the former Bidwell & Banta Company at the foot of Chicago Street. In particular, they profiled the massive ship built for the Erie Rail Line in the First Ward called the *Starucca*.[2] On August 5th, 1897, at the foot of Chicago Street on the Buffalo River, a large crowd witnessed the launch of the 346-foot long steel steam freighter, the *S.S. Starucca*. This ship—which was the biggest ever built in Buffalo and one of the strongest ships on the Great Lakes—had an impressive cargo capacity of over 4,100 tons and was fully equipped with engines built by First Ward companies: King Iron Works and Lake Erie Boiler Works. Opportunities for laborers were certainly abundant during this period.

Firemen and Police

While many First Warders continued in low-skilled positions in the grain trade or other waterfront industries, others were searching for positions with better pay and more stable hours. For the first generation, options outside low-skilled positions were limited to a handful of semi-skilled positions, saloon ownership, or possibly political office. By the late 19th century, however, a new field of opportunity arose that would propel many First Ward men and women into the middle class: civil service. These jobs, while not offering overly high wages, did offer stability in employment, more regular work hours, and they were less dangerous than low-skilled labor positions along the waterfront. For second generation men of the

Ward, positions in the police department and the fire department offered a level of financial security that their fathers would have never imagined.

As the city of Buffalo grew and as the government took over more responsibilities, a new class of government workers arose. The Irish in Buffalo who had aligned with the Democratic Party demanded a disproportionate share of these government jobs in exchange for their loyalty. The police and fire departments were two of the largest departments in the city government, and the Irish and Irish Americans gravitated toward these jobs. At around the same time, women from the Ward equally dominated the openings in the Buffalo Public Schools where they worked as teachers and administrators.

In the late 19th century Buffalo was still a predominantly German city. But by the late 1890s, leadership of the Buffalo Fire Department changed from German to Irish hands. In 1892, Bernard J. McConnell was appointed Chief of the Fire Department, and Edward P. Murphy, son of Frank Murphy (a blacksmith from 408 Fulton Street) was named the Assistant Fire Chief. In addition, John F. Malone, from 339 Michigan Avenue, was named one of the fire commissioners. As the leadership of this organization changed, so too did the hiring of the rank and file. This fact had a profound effect on many men in the First Ward. For instance, in 1890, at the First Ward Fire Engine Companies 8 and 10, nineteen of the twenty-four firemen were Irish or Irish Americans.[3] While these high numbers of Irish were to be expected in the predominately Irish First Ward, the fact that 38.2 % of the total Buffalo Fire Department was comprised of Irish and Irish Americans in 1900 is more surprising (Irish Americans only made up 20% of Buffalo's population).[4]

One of the many men who benefited from the Irish domination of the leadership at the fire department was the son of the grain scooper Timothy Bohen. On the morning of June 15, 1909, Timothy's son, Daniel J. Bohen, was given badge number 617 and assigned to Engine #29, becoming an official member of the Buffalo Fire Department. Prior to becoming a fireman Daniel was employed as a switchman for one of the railroad companies. He was assigned to the *George R. Potter* fireboat stationed in the Buffalo River next to the Erie Elevator at the foot of Louisiana Street, which was located a few blocks from his house. The crew of this fireboat consisted of a captain, a pilot, an engineer, a stoker and five firemen; Daniel was one of those firemen. The primary job of the fireboats was to put out the massive grain elevator and warehouse fires that often broke out on the bustling Buffalo waterfront.

For roughly the first fifty years of Buffalo's history, the fire department consisted of volunteers. In the early years, all male city residents were obligated to assist in fighting fires by creating a bucket line to extinguish the fire. As the city grew larger and industrial fires became more common, a full-time, paid fire department was created. On July 1ˢᵗ, 1880, the Buffalo fire department was officially inaugurated and by 1886 there were 220 fireman employed in Buffalo.[5] Buffalo was growing so fast that the number more than doubled by 1899 (488 full-time firemen were then employed).[6]

As a child and young man, Daniel, like other Warders of his time, would have witnessed some towering industrial infernos close to his home on O'Connell Avenue. Wooden grain elevators rose as high as 150-200 feet and they caught on fire easily because of the lethal combination of grain dust and static electricity. The year before Daniel was born, on August 25, 1882, there was a horrible explosion that killed five workers at Erie Elevator on Ganson Street. Four of the workers were burned to death—two of them were charred beyond recognition—and one of the workers, Timothy Driscoll, was blown out of the elevator and died from injuries from the fall.[7] Perhaps Daniel watched the Sturges Elevator burn to the ground on October 27, 1897, or the destruction by fire of the Husted Elevator on November 23, 1899.[8] These wooden behemoths were prone to fires until they were replaced by concrete and steel—more fireproof materials. On June 25, 1913, Bohen may have been called to assist in one of the most tragic fires in Buffalo's history when a massive explosion occurred at the rebuilt Husted Mill near Elk and Prenatt Streets. The spectacular event made national news as 39 people were killed and more than 80 injured from this grain dust explosion.[9] It was the greatest loss of life from a fire in Buffalo's history.

Daniel Bohen put in for a transfer on April 1, 1912 to move to the Hook and Ladder #8 on Chicago Street. This firehouse—responsible for protecting most of the First Ward residents and industrial buildings along the Buffalo River—officially opened on July 1ˢᵗ, 1897 on Chicago Street on land purchased from Frank H. Hanrahan. Many residents have stories or memories about this firehouse. At the time of Bohen's arrival, the fire pumpers were still pulled by horses, and reportedly at this particular station the beautiful white horses—Charley, Prince Pineapple and Fritz the German Boy—were local celebrities. In the Evans' family manuscript, the writer remembers that when the alarm rang, all of the children in the neighborhood would come running out to see the white horses rushing down the street with bells clanging while pulling the engine.[10] Keeping the horses fed, cleaned, fit and ready to respond to fires was part of the duties of the firemen. In the snowy winter months, the horses would pull the pumper on a sled, instead of wheels, to cut through the snow. For short distances the horse-drawn pumpers were as quick as their motorized replacements.[11] In 1912, the fire department received their first motorized vehicle. But it was not until 1921 that the horses were finally phased out. Residents remember the firemen cleaning the streets of the Ward with their fire hoses when there wasn't a fire. Children would enjoy a trip to the firehouse where they would slide down the brass pole, and the fireman would hold the ropes for the little girls who were playing jump rope.[12] This architecturally rich building, which closed in 1975, is fortunately still standing on Chicago Street.

While the daily physical demands on firemen were easier than their fathers' manual labor jobs, their work hours greatly increased. Grain scoopers and longshoremen regularly worked 12-hour days, six days a week until new legislation was passed that reduced this time commitment. Firemen at the turn of the century, however, worked almost around the clock. Historian and former firefighter Jack Supple likened the time commitment of joining the fire department in those days to joining the army.[13] For Daniel's first seven years of work as a fireman, he worked a shift called "continuous duty." This work schedule included three hours off a day for meals with your family, and only one or two days off a month. This system changed on July 1, 1916 when the Buffalo Fire Department went to a two-platoon system in which firemen worked 84-hour weeks with twelve hours on and twelve hours off with a switch every Sunday.

Another state law passed in April of 1923 stated that firemen had to have one day off for every seven days worked, in addition to the fourteen days of annual vacation that they were allowed. By 1923, the wages improved and firemen earned $1,500 a year ($19,000 in 2010 dollars). The Irish continued to dominate leadership positions in the city's firehouses. Of the 52 firehouses throughout the city of Buffalo, 25 of the chiefs had Irish surnames.[14] In the 1990s, under fellow-First Warder Mayor Jimmy Griffin, one of their own, Paul Shanks from Hamburg Street, was elevated to Buffalo Fire Commissioner. Another prominent fireman from the Ward was Edward M. Cotter of O'Connell Avenue who started the Buffalo Professional Firefighters Association Local 282. The only fireboat that patrols the Buffalo River is named in his honor. It is the oldest active fireboat in the world.

The Irish domination of the police force preceded their domination of the fire department. Prior to the Civil War, the Irish in Buffalo made up less than 2% of the government workforce, despite making up a much larger portion of the city population. One area where they were welcome was the police department. By one account, the 1859 police force in Buffalo was composed of 25 Irishmen out of 60 officers; most of these positions were filled with sons and cousins of a few prominent Irish politicians from the Ward.[15] The first superintendent of the Buffalo Police was Colonel John Byrne, a native of County Wicklow, Ireland, who served in that capacity from 1872-1879. While Colonel Byrne was not from the Ward but just north on Ellicott Street, he was an Irish Catholic. His reign marked the beginning of Irish dominance of the police force. In fact, by 1890, 50% of the police captains, 45% of the detectives, and 40% of the patrolmen were Irish or Irish Americans.

In 1890, five of the twelve police detectives at the downtown headquarters were Irish-born. Precinct 7 in the First Ward claimed that fifteen of the twenty-four patrolmen (63%) were of Irish heritage.[16] By 1910, the share of Irish in the Buffalo police force had increased to 45%.[17] These numbers are even more impressive since the Irish made up less than 20% of Buffalo's population at that time. In 1915, the Irish-born in Buffalo made up 21% of government offices, up from the paltry 2% before the Civil War.[18] Over the 140-year history of the Buffalo Police leadership, the majority of commissioners and superintendents were of Irish origin: Doyle, Byrne, Curtin, Roche, Higgins, McClellan, Cronin, Cannan, McMahon, Morin, Regan, Finney, Cunningham, Myers, Donovan. A handful of these men came from the Ward.

Both literally and figuratively, the biggest policeman to come out of the Ward came from 85 Louisiana Street. On April 23, 1906, Mike Regan became the top cop, named superintendent of the Buffalo Police Force.[19] Regan was born March 4, 1859 in Crookhaven, County Cork, Ireland and arrived in Buffalo with his family nine years later. His name has been mentioned earlier in connection with the Sheehan political shenanigans, but his record as a police superintendent was quite impressive. In 1880, the massive young man—reportedly 6'6" tall—became a police patrolman and quickly moved up the ranks to lieutenant six years later and captain five years after that. In 1901, he was remembered for successfully quelling the lynch mob that gathered to kill Leon Czolgosz, President William McKinley's assassin, at police headquarters at Franklin and Church Streets. Several years later, Regan was also involved with preventing the spread of an Italian riot in the downtown district. "Big Mike" Regan also crusaded against disorderliness in the ubiquitous saloons throughout Buffalo and especially along the waterfront. Regan retired as superintendent in 1915 and is still the second-longest serving police superintendent in the 140-year history of the Buffalo Police Department. After retiring from the police force, Mike Regan started the Regan Police Detective Agency. While he had the financial means to leave the Ward for a wealthier part of Buffalo, he continued to live in the neighborhood he considered home. He is also fondly remembered for his leadership in church and neighborhood affairs.

Regan was just the first of many First Warders who led Buffalo's police department. Austin Roche, born on Chicago Street, went on to become Buffalo Police Commissioner from 1930 to 1933.[20] Joseph DeCillis, an Italian American, lived on Miami Street and served as commissioner from 1950 to 1953. Another First Warder who became police commissioner was John B. Myers, who grew up on the Beach. Myers was a police commissioner in the mid-1980s, but he would not be the last head of the police from the Ward. Richard T. Donovan, who grew up in the Ward on Louisiana Street, served as Buffalo Police Commissioner from 1992 to 1994. It is quite remarkable that five of the police commissioners in

Buffalo's history all came from this small neighborhood. And Erie County Sheriff Tom Higgins, from Elk Street in the Valley, was the top county sheriff from 1986 to 1997.

Lawyers

The Irish also gravitated to the field of law. Perhaps it was their cultural heritage that emphasized oratorical skills as well as the written word that made them a natural fit for these professions. The Buffalo High School class of 1881 graduated three First Warders who went on to positions of prominence in Buffalo's legal community: Daniel Kenefick, William Love, and Rowland Mahany. Mahany has already been discussed in connection with the Strike of 1899. Judge Daniel J. Kenefick was born in the Ward (October 15, 1863) to Michael and Mary (O'Connell) Kenefick. Like so many in that Ward neighborhood—Fingy Conners, Donovan, Sheehan, Shea—his family traced their roots back to County Cork, Ireland. His father Michael Kenefick, a laborer from Ireland, established his home at 200 Miami Street, eventually moving his family to 226 Hamburg Street. Daniel was educated at Public School 4 in the heart of the Ward. After graduating high school in 1881, he clerked for the Crowley and Movius law firm where he studied for the Bar—passing it at age 21. Within two years, he was a law clerk for the city legal department, and by 1886, was selected the second assistant district attorney of Buffalo. On November 12, 1894, at age 31, Kenefick was named District Attorney of Buffalo by New York Governor Roswell Flower. Fellow First Warder William Sheehan was Flower's lieutenant governor at the time and may have influenced his selection.

Daniel Kenefick, the son of a Ward laborer, was in fact a Republican but it is unclear if it was out of political advantage or on principle. As district attorney, Kenefick was remembered for protecting the rights of Erie County, for his fair-mindedness, and for the fact that he did not overstep his bounds in his position.[21] Eventually he was elevated to the Superior Court of New York and then to the Supreme Court of New York where he served for nine years. After his tenure on the Supreme Court, he worked in private practice at the prestigious law firm of Kenefick, Cooke, Mitchell and Bass which traced its lineage back to Grover Cleveland's Buffalo law firm. Kenefick was the first person from the First Ward to serve on the New York State Supreme Court.

Judge Kenefick's private law career was extremely lucrative. He became so wealthy that he was able to build impressive homes for his sons on the prominent Buffalo streets of Nottingham Terrace and Meadow Road. In 1920, he was involved with the American Committee for Relief in Ireland which raised funds for relief of the Irish who suffered under the Black and Tans after World War

I. The Black and Tans—mostly former British soldiers from the First World War— were sent to Ireland in an effort to suppress the rebellion of 1920 and 1921. Instead of just focusing on their target, the Irish Republican Army, this British paramilitary group brutally terrorized ordinary Irish citizens and sometimes even burned Irish towns and villages. This was another example of the how the Irish in Buffalo—even if they hadn't lived in Ireland as was the case with Daniel Kenefick—never forgot those suffering in the land of their ancestors. Judge Kenefick also led the monumental effort in 1926-1927 to rewrite the charter of the City of Buffalo (at the time it was called the Kenefick Commission in his honor) in order to modernize city government. Most importantly, the charter separated the legislative functions of the Common Council from the executive duties of the mayor. At the time it served as a model for other municipalities, and it served as the official charter of Buffalo until a new one was drawn up in 1999. As a result Daniel is known as the "Father of the City Charter."[22] In 1934, he was awarded the University of Buffalo Chancellor Medal for being a "Great Citizen of Buffalo," and a street in South Buffalo bears his name.

Kenefick developed a friendship in high school with another First Warder, William H. Love from 146 Chicago Street. William, son of David Love, a grocer on Perry Street, was another prominent 1881 Buffalo High School graduate. After graduating from the Buffalo High School, William taught at School 29 for four years and then was quickly selected principal of School 33. By the time he left School 33 in 1890, it was largest public school in South Buffalo and one of the largest in the city.[23] In 1892, at the age of thirty, the gifted Love was selected Superintendent of Buffalo Schools which would have been groundbreaking because Roman Catholics in Buffalo were formerly excluded from this position. In fact, since 1838 the public school system was led by either German Americans or Anglo-Protestants. Love's selection was partly due to the fact that he was a competent candidate and partly because two of the three members of the selection committee were fellow Irishmen: Joseph Gavin from the Ward and Councilman James Hanrahan who owned a coal business on Perry Street. This was further proof that the Irish efforts to gain political control eventually reaped civil service positions. Love's appointment was vilified by some in the press who thought that this was due to the William Sheehan machine that still existed in Buffalo.[24] After his appointment, the Republican newspapers complained that Love obeyed Sheehan and used the office for political advancement.[25] One of the greatest successes during Love's superintendent tenure was the securing of public funds for kindergartens throughout the city.

Love maintained his friendship with fellow First Warder Daniel Kenefick and decided he too wanted to practice law. During his teaching career, he studied for the Bar each afternoon and on Saturdays and was eventually selected president of his law class. In April of 1893, Love and Kenefick, the former classmates and neighborhood chums, formed a law partnership. Their firm flourished with a diversity of work from court litigation to estates to corporate work, and both men profited handsomely. While Kenefick was active in Republican politics, Love served in various capacities for the Democratic Party in Buffalo.

In addition to Daniel Kenefick, the Ward produced another New York State Supreme Court Judge, Thomas J. O'Donnell. O'Donnell was born in 1904 in his parent's house at 151 Vandalia Street. Tommy's father, whose roots were in County Kerry, worked as a grain scooper. After graduating from Our Lady of Perpetual Help elementary school, he attended St. Joseph's Collegiate Institute. Typical of many boys in the Ward, he was active in the Mutual Rowing Club at the foot of South Street. After a short career as a lawyer, Tommy O'Donnell was elected South District councilman, becoming the youngest Buffalo councilman in history. The twenty-seven-year-old O'Donnell was even selected to the powerful position of majority leader of the council. After representing the South District, he became a judge in the Buffalo City Court and later served as a New York State Supreme Court justice from 1962 until 1975. In addition to working and raising a family, he was also chairman of Buffalo's airport advisory board, the grand knight of the Buffalo Council of the Knights of Columbus, and a trustee of St. Joseph's Collegiate Institute.[26]

John Lord O'Brian, son of John and Elizabeth (Lord) O'Brian was born on October 14, 1874 and lived at 146 Chicago Street, which was previously the home of the prominent William Love. John's father served as a justice to the police department and then entered the insurance business. The O'Brians lived in the Ward until 1883, when the senior O'Brian's prospects in the insurance business improved enough to allow them to move to 806 West Ferry and later to Cleveland Avenue. John's family did not fit the typical profile of a Ward family: they were Episcopalians and Republicans. As an aside, it is interesting to note that nowhere in John O'Brian's three-hundred-page reminisces of his life, does he mention that his early years were spent in the Ward.

Young John attended public school in the Ward and then graduated from Central High School in 1892. Following high school, he entered Harvard at the age of seventeen and during the Panic of 1893 his family lost all of their fortune and property. After Harvard, John returned to Buffalo and taught elementary school as well as adult education for four years. While teaching, he also studied law and was admitted to the Bar in July of 1898. As a Republican, O'Brian was elected to the New York State Assembly in 1907. From 1909 to 1914, he served as a U.S. Attorney for the Western District of New York. During that time, O'Brian claimed that the plain people of Buffalo thought he was highbrow because he enforced the civil service laws which were being abused in the city of Buffalo (most often by his fellow Irishmen).[27] He also, however, prosecuted industrial corporations such as the Lake Carriers' Association and the railroads.

During his term as U.S. Attorney for the Western District of New York he concentrated on anti-trust cases such as a famous Eastman Kodak case. O'Brian successfully argued that Kodak created a monopoly in the amateur photography industry between 1895 and 1910 by buying up over twenty of its competitors, dissolving them, and then transferring their assets back to Eastman Kodak, which violated the Sherman Antitrust Act. O'Brian was recognized nationally for his antitrust expertise and was eventually appointed the Assistant Attorney General of the Antitrust Division during the Herbert Hoover administration. Along the way he served as chief counsel on many important cases involving Appalachian Coal and the RCA breakup. During World War I, he led the War Emergency Division where he was responsible for enforcing the Espionage and Sedition acts. He was recognized for his balance in guarding the rights of the millions of German and Austrian Americans in the United States while at the same time protecting U.S. citizens and strategic military and political sites (in 1918 O'Brian noted that there was not one fire or explosion set by an enemy "alien").[427] Over the years O'Brian was appointed to various high-level government posts from the Theodore Roosevelt to the Harry Truman administrations. One of his most well known accomplishments occurred in 1938 with his successful defense in front of the U.S. Supreme Court of the Tennessee Valley Authority Act. Arthur Krock, a *New York Times* columnist, once described John Lord O'Brian as the "most distinguished lawyer and classical liberal of our times."[29] This was high praise for a boy who got his start on Chicago Street in the Old First Ward.

"Wild Bill" Donovan-World War I Hero

Another famous lawyer came out of the same neighborhood as O'Brian, but his fame didn't come from the courtroom; rather from the battlefields in France. His name was William J. Donovan, and he was born in the First Ward on January 1, 1883 to Timothy and Anna (Lennon) Donovan. As a result of William Donovan's eventual fame, the lives of his grandfather and father were well documented, and their biographies give us insight into the lives of other First Ward men of their time. William's grandfather, Timothy Donovan—who will be referred to as Grandfather Donovan so as not to confuse him with William's father Timothy— was a schoolteacher from the fishing village of Goleen, Ireland in County Cork. Despite his previous profession in Ireland, he worked as a grain scooper when he arrived in Buffalo. Reportedly he settled in Buffalo for two reasons: the wages were higher than in other surrounding cities and because he wanted to settle in a city where the Catholic Church was prominent.[30] Donovan was one of the fortunate

Irish immigrants to arrive in America with some money, and this enabled him to eventually purchase one of the better-constructed homes in the Ward. In fact, his brick house at 74 Michigan Street was a rarity in a neighborhood of mostly wooden, cottage-style housing stock. As a former teacher, Grandfather Donovan promoted learning among his children and made sure the house was filled with books—uncommon among working class families in the Ward during that time.

Grandfather Donovan, like many first- and second-generation Irish Americans, was an ardent supporter of Irish independence. It was even rumored that he was connected with the Fenians. It is a fact that the elder Donovan housed and supported Irish independence leaders and intellectuals who traveled and stayed in Buffalo.[31] Also, throughout the late 1800s, Grandfather Donovan assisted his fellow Irishmen by turning his homestead into a safe house for Irish refugees who would sneak into Buffalo from Canada.[32] Numerous Irish natives arrived in Buffalo illegally from Canada and were then sheltered for a short while until they became established. Grandfather Donovan was also a teetotaler and was so passionate about the issue of drinking that he was the leader of a local branch of the League of the Cross, which was dedicated to encouraging temperance among the working-class Catholic families in an effort to elevate their situation. This was the environment in which Grandfather Donovan's son Timothy—the father of William—was raised and was subsequently passed on to young William.

Timothy Donovan initially worked as a greaser for the Erie and Lackawanna Railroad.[33] As a hardworking and temperate man he rose quickly and eventually was named to the important position of yardmaster at the facilities in Black Rock. Like his father, Timothy promoted book learning to his children and abstained from alcohol, but these weren't the only traits that differentiated the Donovans from many of their neighbors. In politics, Timothy Donovan was registered a Republican—an almost unthinkable act among Irish Americans in those days. In fact, for a while he was the leader of the Republican Party in the Ward. Despite these differences, the Donovans had struggles like others in the Ward. Of the nine children in Timothy Donovan's household, the first four died of meningitis and only two survived to an old age.[34]

This left William, the fifth in birth order, as the oldest. Like many young Ward boys, Will Donovan went to St. Bridget's school, at the corner of Louisiana and Fulton Streets, for his first years and later transferred to Miss Nardin's Academy. Even as a young boy, Will had natural gifts that separated him from his peers. Will's classmates remembered him as a determined boy, and although not necessarily the brightest student, definitely one of the most tenacious.[35] In addition to possessing an abundance of natural gifts, Will was also lucky. His father was a close friend of one of the rising stars of the Catholic Church in Buffalo: Father James Quigley, who later became the local bishop (William and his brother carried Quigley's train during his solemn consecration as bishop). Quigley realized that Will was a child with special talents and he needed to be exposed to the best possible education. As a result of this relationship, Bishop Quigley used diocesan funds to pay for his studies at St. Joseph's Collegiate Institute (a prominent local Catholic high school).[36] Donovan went to Niagara University for a short while but transferred to Columbia University where he received his degree.

The handsome Bill Donovan was described as having penetrating blue eyes, and although he was only 5'8", he seemed taller to those who met him in person. Donovan grew up in a family that also promoted athletic competition so it was no surprise when he excelled as the quarterback of Columbia's football team (he also rowed on the college's varsity team). All of these traits, coupled with his charismatic personality, contributed to the perception that he was a natural leader. After undergraduate studies, he earned his law degree from Columbia University in 1908, and shortly thereafter he entered into a private legal practice in Buffalo. Teddy Roosevelt and his Rough Riders were his boyhood heroes and this probably interested him in a career in the military. Before World War I, he and a group of blue-blood Buffalonians formed Troop I—sneeringly called the "Silk-Stocking Boys" by some—which was a cavalry unit of the New York National Guard. Donovan was selected as captain of the unit, which was unusual since he was an Irish Catholic from the First Ward leading a group composed almost entirely of upper-class Protestants. Around this time, he was introduced to Ruth Rumsey, daughter of the wealthiest man in Buffalo: Dexter Rumsey. Despite the fact that Bill and Ruth came from two different worlds—the working-class First Ward and the monied Delaware Avenue elite—they married in 1914 and Bill Donovan officially entered the WASP society of Buffalo. Shortly after the U.S. entered World War I, Donovan was called to lead the 1st Battalion of the 165th infantry, also known as the "Old Fighting 69th" or just the "Fighting 69th". This unit of mostly Irish Americans from New York City—the same regiment in which dozens of First Ward men fought during the Civil War—was now, fifty years later, under Donovan's command.

There is a controversy as to how and when Donovan acquired his nickname: "Wild Bill": some say it resulted from his ferociousness on the football field at Columbia University while others attribute it to his fearlessness on the battlefield in France. Either way, Major "Wild Bill" Donovan and his men were sent to fight in several crucial campaigns in France. After proving himself in several battles he was promoted to Lieutenant Colonel where he courageously led his unit in battle at Landres-et-St. Georges during the Argonne offensive. Donovan led one of three regiments with the objective of capturing an enemy position which was well entrenched on a steep ravine surrounded by machine guns and artillery. Because of the danger of this mission, the other two supporting regiments refused to advance, but Donovan believed in following orders, so he rallied his regiment and led the advance under absolutely murderous conditions (the high command was expecting 60% casualties from this assault). Despite being hit three times during the battle by enemy fire, Donovan refused to leave the field until all of his men were administered to or removed from the battlefield.[37] It was this sort of valor that fed the legend of "Wild Bill" Donovan. When the battle was over, Donovan's regiment was devastated: 600 of his 1,000 soldiers were killed, wounded or missing in action. By war's end Donovan's regiment had suffered 644 killed in action with 3,501 casualties. In a New York City parade at the end of the war, over a million people turned out to cheer Donovan and the "Fighting 69th" regiment for their bravery. Donovan had captured the imagination of the nation and overnight became a true American hero.

As a result of his extraordinary bravery and his accomplishments in France defeating the Germans—including the elite Fourth Imperial Prussian Foot Guards—the former First Ward boy became the most decorated soldier in American history, earning the top three awards: the Medal of Honor, the Distinguished Service Cross and the Distinguished Service Medal.[38] During the war, "Wild Bill" Donovan earned more medals than even the highly distinguished Brigadier General Douglas MacArthur. Donovan had made a name for himself on the national stage, but his most important contributions to his country were still to come.

Many young men from the Ward fought on behalf of the Allied efforts in World War I, but not all of them were as lucky to survive as Donovan. Of the 18,000 Buffalonians who went to war, 851 died (or about 5% of the total). Cornelius and Earl Coughlin were sons of John J. Coughlin, an Irish immigrant who worked as a dairy inspector and later became an inspector for the Department of Health. John Coughlin arrived in the Ward as early as 1893 and raised his family at 138 Mackinaw Street and then later moved to 140 O'Connell Avenue. His oldest son, Cornelius F. Coughlin, was born on February 9, 1893 and attended Technical High School where he was a star center on the football team. For the 1910 All-High Selection for best football players in the city, the *Buffalo News* had this to say about why Cornelius Coughlin was selected as best lineman that year:

> Owing to the aggressiveness of the Tech star he is given the place. Coughlin is one good football player. He plays the kind of a game that one can't help but admire. Full of fight and grit, he is always in the game until the end and was the life of the Tech rush line. His snap-back work was about the average and on the defensive he always took care of his man. He was not outplayed once during the entire season. He was all over the field and his open field tackling was a big feature.[39]

In July 1911, after graduating from Technical High School, Cornelius found employment as a machinist at the Larkin Company—one of the largest employers of First Ward men and women during the period. After leaving the Larkin Company, Cornelius worked as a railroad fireman. In 1917, however, at the start of the American's involvement in World War I, the grey-eyed, red haired Cornelius was drafted and his days as a fireman were on hold. Cornelius was assigned to the 155th Infantry, promoted to the rank of sergeant, and embarking on what was probably a great adventure to Paris, where he served at the unit headquarters.[40] He was sent to France as part of the massive scale-up for the Meuse-Argonne Offensive in October of 1918. However, like many in that war, he didn't die from enemy fire. Rather he died from disease during the same month as the major Allied offensive, just one month before the end of the war.

There is less information on his younger brother Earl Coughlin (born in 1900), also raised in the Ward. Earl was drafted and served in the 1st Calvary, Troop G.[41] The younger Coughlin officially died July 10, 1917 from "disease" like his older brother, but unofficially he died in a training exercise with the cavalry when he fell off a horse at Fort Russell in Wyoming. Earl's death in 1917 was tragic but Cornelius' death one year later was devastating for the Coughlin family. But like many men from the First Ward who went to war, they had the chance to serve their country. The Coughlin boys, as well as 849 other men from Buffalo, paid the ultimate sacrifice by war's end.

Businessmen and Doctors

The majority of Irish Catholic immigrants who arrived in Buffalo did not possess trade or technical skills nor did they come from an entrepreneurial culture like many of their fellow German immigrants. This reality was due in large part to the fact that the Anglo-Irish controlled much of the commerce in Ireland, and most of the Irish immigrants were former fishermen and farmers, not skilled tradesmen. Natural entrepreneurs did exist like William J. Conners, who built a transshipping colossus as well as interests in newspaper, brewing and real estate. Michael Shea's entertainment empire also comes to mind as a divergence from the norm. But the fact is that most of the Irish immigrants in the First Ward worked for someone else. Not only did they lack a culture of small business ownership, but there was very little excess capital to start new businesses.

The businessmen who did emerge usually built businesses in industries that they were connected to such as shipping interests (Conners), water (J.P. Sullivan's Ice Company), or taking care of the waterfront workers, (dozens of saloon and boarding house operators). One such man was John J. Boland—born in 1875 and the son of a Great Lakes schooner captain from Elk Street—who started a vessel brokerage and chartering business on Buffalo's waterfront in 1904.[42] Three years later, Boland and his business partner, Adam E. Cornelius, started the American Steamship Company. They were referred to as pioneers in Great Lakes shipping and introduced the concept of self-unloaders to the transportation industry. Self-unloaders are shipping vessels that use a conveyor system to unload dry-bulk goods like grain, iron ore, or sand without the need for shore-side equipment or shore-side personnel.[43] This is the same technology that eventually put grain scoopers out of business. Even as the company prospered over the years, John J. Boland continued to live on South Park Avenue in the Valley rather than in a more affluent Buffalo street like his business partner Adam Cornelius. The company survived the Great Depression and prospered throughout the 1950s. It is still in existence in 2012.

Charles Diebold, Jr. was another successful businessman from the Ward. His father, Charles Diebold Sr., of French descent, and his mother, Mary, of Irish ancestry, ran a boarding house and saloon at 336 Ohio Street. This is the same saloon where Grover Cleveland famously campaigned to win the Irish vote during his mayoral campaign. Charles Jr. attended Buffalo Public School 4 in the Ward and later graduated from University of Buffalo Law School. After practicing in the firm of Coastworth & Diebold, he decided to enter the banking industry. Eventually he was elevated to president of Western Savings Bank (later called Goldome Bank). The younger Diebold was very active in community affairs serving as a trustee for the University of Buffalo, a director for the Chamber of Commerce and president of the Bar Association of Erie County.[44]

William E. Shaddock, the son of Thomas Shaddock, a native of Kilkee, Ireland and the superintendent of grain elevators for Buffalo, was born on November 17, 1879 in the Ward. After William graduated from St. Bridget's parochial school, he worked for a heating and plumbing contractor where he learned the trade. Shaddock branched out and formed his own contracting company in 1910 and eventually built a larger facility at 295 Oak Street comprising a warehouse, a showroom and a floor for engineering. Shaddock won sizeable contracts to install and maintain heating systems throughout New York State. These included heating plants in the New York Central Terminal in Buffalo and the Teaching College in Albany, New York, as well as the plumbing systems for Buffalo's City Hall and the Teaching College in Buffalo. Shaddock was active in community and church affairs and his favorite hobby was working as chairman of the board for the Parochial Schools Athletic Association.[45] He was previously mentioned for his work in the Irish independence movement with the Sinn Fein Society and his leadership with the Friendly Sons of St. Patrick.

Another businessman from the Ward was Simon Nash. Nash was born in Ireland in 1839 and was educated in the national schools before arriving in Buffalo in 1862. Like John Brinkworth and Timothy Donovan, Nash's Irish education put him at an advantage over his immigrant neighbors. Nash initially worked as a grocer in the Ward and then worked as a weighmaster for a coal company. Eventually he ran his own coal and wood business at 503 Elk Street, and was a member of St. Bridget's Parish for over 40 years. For the most part, the first generation of Irish immigrants to Buffalo were not inclined toward the natural sciences or engineering, but some did pursue medicine. One of them was Simon Nash's son, Dr. James W. Nash, who lived and practiced at 422 Elk Street in the Ward. Dr. Nash was one of several physicians who came from the Ward or took care of those in the neighborhood. Others remembered in memoirs include Dr. Edward M. Dooley at 406 Louisiana Street; Dr. Banta, grandson of the founder of the shipbuilding company Banta & Bidwell, who lived in the "White House" at Perry and Hayward; and Dr. Allen, who was a doctor in the Spanish-American War, drove a horse and buggy, and made house calls. Dr. George T. Hickelton at 322 Elk Street was the local dentist.[46] This summary of the businessmen and physicians is not exhaustive and retailers will be discussed later in the work.

As the Irish branched out beyond unskilled labor occupations many improved their financial circumstances. At the same time, they also helped silence critics of the Irish and Irish Americans who portrayed them as genetically inferior, lazy and unintelligent. By the late 19th century, the fierce discrimination against the Irish in the press slowly faded. As the Irish in Buffalo secured positions in law, business, politics, and the military, they proved to their detractors like the German-born Thomas Nast—the cartoonist from *Harpers Weekly* who regularly portrayed the Irish as ape-like in his cartoons—as well as the other racist newsmen on both sides of the Atlantic, that they were wrong. In fact, the Irish weren't genetically inferior to Anglo Americans or Germans, but simply lacked the educational and vocational opportunities in their native land, where they had been relegated to farming and fishing. Now—in some cases in just one generation—they were able to compete with the nativists as equals in the courtroom, in politics, in schools or in the world of commerce. First Ward men like Conners, Shea, Nash, Sullivan, Boland, Kenefick, O'Donnell, Shaddock, Dooley, Love, Lawley, and Donovan helped propel the Irish into the mainstream of Buffalo society.

CHAPTER EIGHT

LEISURE TIME IN THE WARD

The greatest boxer in my time was Jimmy Slattery. I know from experience. I fought him...
– Jimmy "The Cinderella Man" Braddock

Shea made his house in Buffalo the finest show stop in America.
– George M. Cohan on Michael Shea

Saloons have been a constant source of leisure for residents throughout the Ward's 170-year history. In terms of numbers, they probably peaked in the 1880s when there were an unbelievable one hundred and nineteen saloons scattered throughout the First Ward;[1] to put the number in perspective there were less than ten saloons operating in the same area in 2010. Leopold Bloom, in James Joyce's *Ulysses*, muses that a "good puzzle would be to cross Dublin without passing a pub." The same puzzle could be applied to the First Ward during the latter part of the 19th century. Saloons served a greater purpose than just a comfortable place to drink. As one expert on the Ward explained, "the irregular nature of grain scooping and other dock-based work meant that workers often utilized the saloon as a cafeteria, a hiring location where networks were forged and news was spread, a place to sleep, and a location for general conviviality."[2] Especially in the early years of the Ward, the saloon operated like an employment office where the new immigrants came to find work. In terms of social life, the saloon was the epicenter of the leisure activities of many men in this part of town.

Saloons were also popular places to pass time in the winter when work along the waterfront crawled to a halt because of the frozen lake. Another feature of the saloons was that up into the early part of the 20th century women were not allowed in saloons; thus married men would escape to a saloon as a place of refuge from the demands of their wives.[3] Even as late as 1910, Police Chief Michael Regan issued orders to crack down on saloons that allowed women into their establishments.[4] Legend has it that another reason that scoopers liked to drink, especially whiskey, was that it was the only thing that would neutralize the taste of the grain dust which was lodged in the throats of the scoopers from working all day in the mills.[5] As a result of the popularity of saloons, most saloonkeepers were generally wealthier than their patrons and were often powerful people in the Ward. In fact, Richard Max McCarthy recalls that his father told him that saloon owners were often godfathers of their patrons' children because they could "usually be counted on to give the new baby a $5 bill."[6] During the saloon-boss era, the saloonkeepers also gained enough power over their patrons—because they controlled who worked—that they could control their voting patterns as well.[7]

There were several 19th century saloons that stood out above the rest. One hotspot was Hagan's Tavern. Three Ward brothers—Peter, Henry, and John Hagan—all started their careers on the docks and then later went into separate saloon and liquor businesses. In the 1880s, Henry Hagan opened his saloon at the corner of Elk and Hamburgh Streets, and his son James later took over the operation. It was a popular place for political rallies and speeches from politicians eager to be elected and a gathering spot on Election Day, with large bonfires and celebrations.[8] It was also the home of the Blackthorn Club, founded in 1917, which has been a social club of importance for several generations of Irish

Americans. As was previously mentioned, the William J. Conners Saloon at 444 Ohio Street run by "Fingy" Conners, was home to one of the most powerful dock-labor companies on the Great Lakes. McMahon's at 161 Elk Street, where the grain scoopers formed a union to end Fingy's saloon-boss system, was also a popular hangout. Another prominent First Ward saloon was the Harbor Inn built on the triangle lot at the corner of Ohio and Chicago Streets. This saloon was built in about 1869 and was owned by Patrick Kane—a Civil War veteran and a Fenian—who ran Kane's Bar and Boarding House. A few years later Kane added a grocery store to the back of the building to cater to the needs of his boarders.[9]

Even non-drinkers patronized saloons. Timothy Donovan, father of famous First Warder General Bill Donovan, while not a drinker himself, would take young Bill to the saloon every Saturday at noon. Bill Donovan later recalled how saloons were an important part of his boyhood because he was exposed to "impassioned discussions of politics, Irish history, poetry, and any other subject that occurred to eloquent drinkers."[10] Singing songs about Ireland or love songs was also a favorite pastime in the saloons.[11] Two of Timothy Donovan's favorite saloons were the Swannie House, located at the corner of Ohio Street and Michigan Avenue, and Belgian Mary's on Michigan Avenue. Interestingly, the Swannie House is the last of the famous waterfront saloons still surviving in Buffalo.[12]

The importance of the saloon meant that the Prohibition Era from 1919 to 1933 adversely affected neighborhoods like the Ward more than other neighborhoods in Buffalo. Some saloons closed up entirely while others like Jimmy Kane's saloon adapted by selling home brews and cider.[13] Many others like Chick McCarthy's were boarded up in front, but secretly operating in the back of the saloon.[14] Some of the Irish in the Ward engaged in illegal activities like selling alcohol and operating gambling parlors, but they abstained from the more infamous activities of the Sicilians. Former District Attorney Tom Cleary, son of Roggie Lavin, justified the activities of the Irish Americans during Prohibition when describing his father's saloon and gambling parlor at 79 Fulton Street: "The Irish could morally separate what they were doing with booze and gambling from what others did in prostitution and drugs. My dad always spoke of 'an honorable man.'"[15]

Tom Cleary's father, Roggie Lavin, was one of the most colorful characters in the Ward during the 1920s and 1930s. Roger—or Roggie as he was called—was a one-time boxer, who changed his last name to Lavin from Cleary to match his famous uncle Patrick Cleary from County Kildare, who boxed with the name Paddie Lavin. During Prohibition, both uncle and nephew sold alcohol illegally throughout Buffalo, and expanded their operations to places as far as Syracuse, New York and Erie, Pennsylvania. Roggie also operated a betting parlor at 79 Fulton Street where he served illegal booze and men played cards between the horse races. The uncle and nephew team were unique because Paddie, who ran a successful rum running operation, didn't drink, and Roggie, a notorious gambling operator, didn't gamble.

As was often the case during Prohibition, competition for business sometimes escalated to violence. At one point, the Lavins infringed on another downtown operation run by a man named Kennedy. Kennedy tried to have Paddie Lavin killed; and on one attempted hit three bullets struck Paddie. The elder Lavin survived this assassination attempt, but on another day in 1929 he was not so lucky; when he went to start his car it blew up. Paddie Lavin was mourned by everyone in the Ward and treated to an elegant wake in the First Ward.[16] His nephew Roggie wielded so much power in the Ward that in 1937 he had the annual St. Patrick's Day Parade rerouted past his home on Fulton Street so his son Tom Cleary, who was ill, could watch the parade. At one time, Roggie also owned a cigar store on Hamburg Street near O'Connell Avenue which had no tobacco in the store—it was a front for his bookmaking operation. In 1954, Roggie Lavin was arrested for an alleged $50,000 a month gambling operation which stretched into Canada and down South. He pleaded guilty to a misdemeanor and paid a $250 fine. This larger-than-life figure also had a soft side and used to take neighborhood priests to the local racetrack and give them money to bet on the horses. The priests repaid the favor when they let him store his slot machines in the church basement during a raid. Other famous 20th century bookies in the First Ward included: "Bunno" McGrath, George "Ibby" Downing, "Jiggs" Lillis, "Ace" Bonner, Franny Bodkin, "Boss" McCarthy, and Frankie "Cat's" Catanzaro.

Paddie Lavin wasn't the only person with First Ward ties who was killed during Prohibition. Eugene F. Downey Jr. grew up at 485 Elk Street, the son of a patrolman from Precinct 7 with the same name. In October of 1929, the younger Downey was caught smuggling 1,000 cases of liquor from Port Colborne, Canada to Buffalo. On Christmas night in 1929, a Coast Guard patrol boat spotted Downey's boat—fittingly named the *Dodge*—with its lights off. The authorities ordered him to stop, but instead he sped up in an effort to evade them. The Coast Guard patrolmen fired and shot him in the thigh. By the time the authorities reached Downey's boat, which was tied to a dock along the Buffalo waterfront, he was critically wounded; he later died from the blood loss caused by the bullet.[17]

George "Chickie" Evans is the descendant of two prominent First Ward saloon-owning families: the Evanses and the Quinns. His paternal grandfather, Tom Evans, owned Evans Bar and Grill at 268 Ohio Street while another Evans relative, Michael Evans, ran the tavern Evans Place at 326 Ohio Street. His maternal grandfather was Michael Quinn of Quinn's tavern on Chicago Street. George's mother, Loretta Quinn, was raised in the Quinn tavern. George Evans, who was born in 1941, remembers going to the First Ward on weekends to help the Evans family with their bar on Ohio Street. Chickie Evans said the saloons in the past did not have central heat, but were heated instead with a potbelly stove. He also remembers that next to one of his family saloons there was a shed where a helper lived, and it was the helper's job to make sure the fire was stoked and that the bar was cleaned and kept up.[18] Sis Evans, the eldest daughter of the founder, ran the Evans tavern on 268 Ohio Street for several years until it was torn down in 1964.

There is a humorous Evans family story that took place during the Prohibition era. The enterprising Mike Evans, who ran Evans Place at 326 Ohio Street, owned a vacant home next to his saloon where he made moonshine. The second floor of the saloon and the abandoned dwelling were connected by a bridge-like contraption that made movement between both structures easier in order to evade suspecting dry agents. Neighborhood grain scoopers supplied Mike with the grain to make his 100-proof moonshine, which he then diluted with water to reduce it to 70 proof. One day his nephew George Evans was making moonshine on the second floor at his Uncle Mike's saloon when dry agents raided the operation. The agents rushed up the stairs and caught a glimpse of the whitish-blond haired George jumping out of the window. One of the agents yelled, "Where's the goddamn Swede gone to?" From that day on the fugitive George Evans was forever referred to as the Swede.[19] Another interesting Prohibition fact about Mike Evans and Roggie Lavin is that in the official city directories during the Prohibition period they are listed as being in the "soft drink business," which may have been a euphemism for bootlegger.

First St. Patrick's Day Parade

Michael J. Quinn, owner of Quinn's on Chicago and Miami Streets, was one of the most influential saloonkeepers in the Ward at the turn of the twentieth century. Michael "Big Fist" Quinn arrived in Buffalo from County Kerry in 1889 at the age of twenty-three. According to one of his great-grandsons, the 6'2" Michael was a natural leader and a great athlete.[20] Shortly after arriving, he immediately organized both a hurling and a Gaelic football team, which traveled across the Northeast to compete in matches. His tavern was housed in an Erie Canal-era brick building, and it was previously called the German Hotel. One of Mike Quinn's grandsons, George "Chickie" Evans, still wonders how his immigrant grandfather was able to afford to purchase this relatively expensive brick building. Chickie Evans describes the layout of the building this way: the saloon was on the first floor, the Quinn family lived on the second floor, and the third floor housed sailors during the winter months. Apparently, some of the sailors from other Great Lakes cities would come in at the end of the shipping season and would winter in Buffalo until the shipping season resumed in the spring.[21] The upper floor was also used as a boardinghouse that housed recent immigrants until they established themselves in their new city.

Mike Quinn was certainly an influential saloonkeeper, but he is most remembered for organizing the modern St. Patrick's Day parade. On the Sunday closest to St. Patrick's Day in Buffalo a visitor will find one of the largest St. Patrick's Day parades in the United States. Tens of thousands of people line Delaware Avenue, "the Park Avenue of Buffalo," for a well-orchestrated event to celebrate Irish culture and heritage. The origins for this annual tradition in Buffalo, however, can be traced directly to the First Ward. As early as 1855, there were documented St. Patrick's Day dances and demonstrations in Buffalo,[22] but it wasn't until the 20th century that an official parade was instituted. On March 17th, on a bitterly cold day in 1913, about 5,000 residents of the First Ward and surrounding areas marched in the first St. Patrick's Day parade in Buffalo. Earlier in the year, after a noon mass at St. Bridget's, Quinn and some of his friends migrated over to his tavern to discuss an issue that was bothering Mike. It was at that meeting that he told his friends that they had to do something to honor St. Patrick as well as their Irish heritage.[23] From this impromptu meeting, the seed for a St. Patrick's Day parade blossomed. While the organizers had planned for this event the previous summer, they hadn't planned for sub-zero temperatures in March.

The 5,000 members of the parade lined up at about 2:00 p.m. near the Elk Street Market and then at 2:30 p.m. the parade commenced. The paraders marched down Michigan Avenue to Elk Street to Abbott Road to Euclid Avenue and back to the market. The parade organizer and first grand marshal was obviously Mike Quinn. Behind him in line were Bishop Charles Colton and Father James Lanigan, who was pastor of St. Bridget's Church. Local political and business dignitaries were there as well including William "Fingy" Conners, William H. Fitzpatrick, Anthony McGowan and Jack White.[24] Of course, the Buffalo Fire Department was present—with Engines 8 &10 in attendance—as well as a large contingent of Buffalo police officers, which is still a tradition to this day.

For the Irish in the First Ward this was a jubilant day and a proud moment. Clearly the Irish had made great strides since their previous epoch where survival was the sacred word. Now they had prominent First Warders in the parade from all facets of life, including business, political, civil service, and religious figures. The parade symbolized that the Irish had arrived and they were going to be a force in the life of Western New York and beyond. The parade was held every year until it was suspended because of World War I in 1917 and then resumed again by Mike Quinn in 1935.

The 1935 St. Patrick's Day Parade revival was described in detail in local newspaper reports. Just like the first modern parade in 1913, the weather was cold with a fierce wind. To start the parade, the *W.S. Grattan* fireboat sounded an alarm at 2:30 p.m. Mike Quinn was once again the grand marshal and he was joined by deputy marshals Coleman J. Perkins, Robert C. Lacey, George J. Evans, Joseph J. Cooley, Thomas Merrick, Joseph J. Sullivan, Owen J. Kavanagh, James W. Mockler, Timothy Harmon, Edward J. Sullivan and Daniel J. McGirr. The marshals were dressed in high silk hats, long coats and green carnations. Two boys flanked Grand Marshall Quinn: one of the boys was dressed up as Uncle Sam and carried an Irish flag, and the other boy was dressed in green and carried an American flag.[25] In this way, the Irish organizers showed their dual loyalties to Ireland and the United States. The entire parade route was lined with Irish and American flags and banners were suspended across the street. The marchers carried an Irish banner from about 1880 and one of the best attractions was a 1858 jaunting car—a light two-wheeled carriage for a single horse—from rural Ireland that Spencer Kellogg had loaned for the event.[26] Large contingents from the Blackthorn Club, Knights of Equity, and the Ancient Order of Hibernians were present as were the firemen, police, and grain scoopers.

In 1941, the parade was moved out of the Ward to Main Street to accommodate larger crowds. Some designate 1941 as the birth year of the parade because this parade was more inclusive of the entire Buffalo community, but this isn't fair to the efforts of the men and women in the Ward back in 1913. The parade was cancelled in 1942 and 1943 because of World War II. Over the years it has hosted famous politicians such as Robert F. Kennedy, who marched in the parade with his Aran sweater in a hailstorm, and Senator Patrick Moynihan who marched in 1991. In 1981, the parade was again moved, from Main Street to Delaware Avenue because of the metro rail construction project, where it is still held today. In 1995, organizers from the Valley Community Center sought to reclaim the spirit of the original parade and organized the "Old Neighborhood" parade that retraces the original route from 1913. So now there is a second annual St. Patrick's Day parade which is held on the Saturday closest to St. Patrick's Day.

Michael Shea – The Improbable Entertainer

Another saloon owner from the Ward capitalized on the growing desire for entertainment by the middle class of Buffalo. On April 17, 1859, in the same year that the political boss William F. Sheehan was born in the First Ward, Daniel and Mary (Griffin) Shea gave birth to a boy, Michael, who would create an entertainment empire in Buffalo. It is disputed as to whether or not Michael Shea was born in the First Ward or in St. Catharines, Ontario, but sometime shortly after his birth the family definitely settled in the First Ward.[27] The young Shea attended both public and parochial schools in the Ward, and as early as age fifteen went to work on the docks as a laborer, much like the other young men in the Ward.[28] After toiling on the docks, he was hired at the Union Iron Works near his house, where he labored as a structural ironworker helping to build some of the significant railroad bridges in the United States during this era.[29] Michael was a handsome man sporting a trimmed mustache and was well liked by people who interacted with him. The first mention of young Michael Shea was in the *1879 Buffalo City Directory* where he was listed as a laborer living with his parents at 244 Katherine Street in the First Ward. In 1884, Michael or "Mickey" as he was sometimes called, opened a saloon at 535 Elk Street and continued living on Katherine Street while presumably saving money for his future endeavors. Like Fingy Conners, Michael's ownership of a saloon gave him the financial means to expand into other business ventures. Michael had grand ideas for entertaining Buffalonians. Entertainment empires like the one Shea envisioned however, were traditionally the product of people with extensive financial resources, not former dockworkers.

Shea's entry into the entertainment business started in 1892 when he opened his first music hall: Shea's Music Hall at 11 Clinton Street in the Arcade Building. Music halls, which provided entertainment for the working masses, had been popular in England for several decades, but this was one of the first music halls in the United States. At Shea's Music Hall performers from England and France appeared for weeklong engagements.[30] In 1893, a fire destroyed his building, but Michael was undeterred and started over again. Next he opened Shea's Tivoli on Washington Street next to the famous Lafayette Hotel. In 1898, Shea decided to capitalize on entertainment for the "common man" by opening the first vaudeville theatre in Buffalo, called Shea's Garden Theatre. In fact, Shea was one of the first men in the U.S. to start a vaudeville house and he is credited with helping to improve the reputation of this new form of entertainment targeted at the growing urban middle class.[31] In 1900, Shea beautified his vaudeville theater, hoping to make it one of the top vaudeville houses in the country; many who visited agreed that he accomplished his goal.[32] In addition, in an effort to improve the reputation of this new form of entertainment, he banned smoking and drinking alcoholic beverages in his theater. In 1905, the restless Shea expanded his vaudeville empire and opened Shea's Vaudeville House on Court Street with a tagline: Shea's-Devoted to the Highest Class of Exclusive Vaudeville Attractions.[33] Michael Shea was known throughout the U.S., England, and France for his efforts at promoting and helping to improve the image of vaudeville.[34]

At the age of forty, with Michael Shea at mid-life, he married Josephine Carr. Four years later, with a solid financial situation, they moved out of the Ward to the West Side of Buffalo, settling at 43 Vermont Street near Niagara Street. Shea's business ventures continued to prosper, and by 1905 he had an empire of theatres in Buffalo. Shea's genius, however, was in understanding the changing entertainment tastes of the masses, and then responding to these changes. He was always one step ahead of his competitors. This was evident when he expanded from vaudeville into motion pictures and opened Shea's Hippodrome on Main Street near Chippewa in 1914.[*] At the time it was regarded as the finest picture house between New York City and Chicago.[480] The indefatigable Mickey Shea also opened Shea's North Park Theatre on Hertel Avenue in 1920. Other theaters in his empire included the Great Lakes Theatre, the Seneca, the Century, the Community, the Park, the Bailey, and the Riviera in Tonawanda. Mr. Shea even expanded his operations internationally to Toronto, Canada where he owned two of the largest theatres in that city: Shea's Vaudeville and Shea's Hippodrome.[36]

Even in light of all of these successes, Shea still had a vision for his crowning achievement. Perhaps like Bishop Timon before him who built St. Joseph's Cathedral, Shea felt his legacy to Buffalo had to come in the form of something monumental; in his case a "cathedral" dedicated to entertainment. Soliciting the help of the prominent Chicago architects, C.W. and George L. Rapp, and with an initial budget of $1 million, Shea built and designed one of the most remarkable theatres in the United States at the time. His masterpiece, located on a prominent stretch of Main Street, was originally given the name "The Buffalo," and later called Shea's Buffalo. Shea wanted his masterpiece to rival other show houses in the major cities across the country and spared no expenses; consequently the building costs quickly escalated to $2 million. The Rapp brothers used the finest furnishing companies in Chicago and Buffalo to outfit the building including The Victor Pearlman Company, Marshall Field and Company, Wm. Hengerer Co. and Wurlitzer Company. The terra cotta exterior, crystal chandeliers, and marble staircases built in the Baroque Revival style created a look of opulence; it was meant to resemble the baroque opera houses of Europe from the 16th and 17th century.[37]

On January 16, 1926, the 4,000-seat theater opened with the kind of glitz and lights you would expect from Buffalo's greatest showman: an estimated 7,000 exterior lights were used to illuminate the theater on opening night. The theater was wildly successful and profitable for its first three years until the start of the Great Depression in 1929. During the Depression it was estimated that Mr. Shea was losing $1 million a year on his vast enterprise, but he refused to lay off employees.[38] In 1930, despite the onset of the global economic disaster, Shea and his wife moved to the most affluent neighborhood in Buffalo and settled at 675 Delaware Avenue. Despite Shea's optimism that the economy would turn around, he would never see the return of his past financial success. Michael Shea passed away on May 16, 1934 in the midst of the Depression, and his wife and daughter sold their shares in the entertainment enterprise shortly after he died.

The famous Broadway producer and fellow Irish American, George M. Cohan, once commented on Shea's success by stating that: "Shea made his house in Buffalo the finest show stop in America. He had an astonishing flair for picking what the public liked."[39] Legend has it that Michael Shea even influenced the stage careers of Eddie Cantor and Will Rogers.[40] In its first 25 years of existence, Shea's Buffalo hosted world famous performers such as Will Rogers, W. C. Fields, Mae West, Eddie Cantor, George Burns and Gracie Allen, The Marx Brothers, Bob Hope, Red Skelton, Duke Ellington, Benny Goodman, Jimmy Dorsey, Glenn Miller, and Bing Crosby. It is worth asking the question: where did Michael, who grew up in the gritty waterfront area of Buffalo and lacked a formal education past age sixteen, derive his flair for entertainment? Perhaps, drawing from his own experiences toiling on the docks and at the Union Iron Works, he simply wanted to create an oasis of beauty and happiness for his fellow workingman. Shea set the prices for shows at his theatres so that everyone could afford the price of admission and there were no reserved seats, perhaps owing to the fact that he grew up in the unpretentious First Ward.[41] In 1926, prices in his theatres started at as little as 25 cents, equivalent to about $3 in 2009. Michael Shea was certainly a genius showman in his time, and while only a few of his theatres still survive, Buffalo is richer today for what he built.

Social Clubs and Associations

Irish Americans are often characterized in general terms as a social people. Aside from gathering for politics and sports, they also joined clubs and associations with great frequency. Oftentimes these clubs had a social element to them and sometimes a networking element as well. Two of the earliest Irish clubs in Buffalo were the Friendly Sons of Patrick, which started in 1846, and the Sons of Erin, which started the following year. The Friendly Sons of Patrick, with its 130 members, consisted of older men who had more established occupations compared to those in the Sons of Erin.[42] The mission of the Friendly Sons of St. Patrick was "to aid their fellow countrymen," however, it is unclear if this meant the Irish who were suffering in Buffalo or the millions that were starving in Ireland during the famine—or perhaps both groups.[43] This group is also credited with organizing the first St. Patrick's Day Parade in Buffalo on March 17, 1848 with a march that started down Main Street and ended at St. Patrick's Church on Ellicott Street, and with an evening banquet at the Mansion House on Main and Exchange Streets.[44] First Warders were well represented in the leadership. In 1852, the president, John O'Donnell, was a boilermaker who lived at Louisiana and Fulton Streets, and one of the vice presidents, Matthew Dermody, lived at 17 Perry Street.

The Sons of Erin consisted of about 100 members who were younger, less likely to be U.S. citizens, and tended to reside along the waterfront area of Buffalo. For instance in 1852, the president of the group, Patrick Stanton, was a blacksmith living at 21 Illinois Street in the Ward. The membership list of the Sons of Erin from November 1847 shows a heavy concentration of men who lived on Ohio, Chicago, Mississippi and Illinois Streets and most of the men were laborers or sailors. Both social groups provided charitable assistance, such as funeral ceremonies for their members and support of St. Patrick's Day celebrations.[45]

In 1857, the Irish upper class formed the Mutual Protection and Equal Rights Association to agitate for better conditions for the Irish in Buffalo. At about the same time, workingmen's clubs were established in the First Ward in order to increase the naturalization of Irish immigrants and to support the Democratic opposition to monopolies and distrust of banks.[46] By the 1890s the number of Irish clubs and associations had expanded. In a *New York Times* article about the Charles Stewart Parnell scandal, the reporter lists the impressive number of Irish social organizations in Buffalo at the time. It is impossible to determine whether the members came from the West Side or the First Ward, but the membership totals in the groups are sizeable.

Irish National League	900 members
Catholic Mutual Benevolent Association	12,000
Knights of St. Columbkill	200
Sons of Erin	300
Catholic Knights	250
Black Rock Catholic Union	150
Irish-American Association	500

By the early 20th century, the Irish National League was defunct, but other groups such as the Ancient Order of Hibernians, the Friendly Sons of St. Patrick, and Knights of St. Columbkill were still thriving. By 1915, there was also a Gaelic Athletic Club, First Ward Athletic Club, the St. Bridget's Men's Club, St. Stephen's Catholic Men's Club, and the Brian Boru Club that were open to men in the First Ward.

Another important social club, the Blackthorn Club, was founded in February 1917—although it may have been in existence as early as 1915—by five men from the First Ward: James J. Hagan of 238 Hamburgh Street, Joseph F. Collins of 269 Hamburgh St., Patrick J. Quinn of 155 O'Connell Avenue, Frank J. Mahoney of 48 St. Clair Street, and Thomas Balkin of 13 Red Jacket Street. This social club—founded as a fraternal organization to provide "social intercourse among its members"—met at Hagan's Tavern at 477 Elk Street."[47] Unfortunately, the early history of the club is not well documented, but the one constant is the club's faithful tradition of prominently marching in the St. Patrick's Day Parade every year. The club has a limited membership and it has been filled with well known First Warders and South Buffalonians in the fields of politics, civil service, and commerce. One of its earliest members was James Mead, who later became a congressman and a United States senator.

In 1933, Daniel J. McGirr and James Mockler reorganized the Blackthorn Club. Prominent members during this second era were George J. "Chickie" Evans, Tom Mungovan, Sr., John Livingston, Judge John D. Hillery, Gene Korzelius, Nate Duffy, Jim and John Hagan, Vince Masterson and Jim Lillis. During the period of 1941 to 1951, the club moved its meetings from Hagan's to McGirr's at 6 South Park Avenue. The club hosted summer outings and excursions, invited prominent speakers, and raised money for the Sisters of Mercy at St. Brigid's Parish.[48] In 1951, the club held its meetings at Chick McCarthy's Avenue Grill and remained there until 1960 after which they moved to Vince Crehan's Club Como at 1779 South Park Avenue. In 1983, the Blackthorns met at Early Times Tavern (now the Blackthorn Restaurant and Pub) at 2134 Seneca Street.

One of the most popular Irish clubs in Buffalo was the Ancient Order of Hibernians, which at the turn of the 20th century had 13 divisions in Buffalo consisting of 2,500 members.[49] On May 7, 1896, the Ancient Order of Hibernians elected Buffalo's own, Captain Frank J. Killeen of the Buffalo Police Department, and son of a County Clare immigrant, as their state president of the A.O.H. Killeen grew up for a short time on Hayward Street in the Ward before his father moved the family to East Avenue. It was an honor for a Buffalonian to be elected to this position given the strength of the Irish community in New York City. There was also a Ladies Auxiliary of the A.O.H. with 1,750 members which was run by Mary Laughlin. The year 1896 was also the year that a popular Catholic fraternal organization called the Knights of Columbus started its first Buffalo branch.

Rowing

At the end of the 19th century and the early 20th century, the First Ward was dominated by big men—both in size and in personality. Men like "Big Mike" Regan, the Buffalo police chief, was 6'6" and a great athlete; "Big Fist" Mike Quinn was 6'2" and ran one of the most important saloons in the Ward and started the St. Patrick's Day Parade; Fingy Conners was a brawler on the docks who instilled fear in his associates and became one of the wealthiest men on the Great Lakes; the Sheehan brothers were both great rowers and dominated local and state politics; William Donovan, future major general and founder of the OSS, was an accomplished rower and a college football quarterback and fearless on the battlefield; Jimmy Slattery, the Light Heavyweight Champion of the World, while not tall or stocky, was the toughest guy in his neighborhood. Even Michael Shea was an accomplished baseball player and rower. This was not the era of small men.

The premier sport for young men during the 1870s-1890s, especially those from the First Ward, was rowing.[50] While baseball and football were gaining popularity, for Irish men living near the water's edge, this was the era of rowing. Rowing obviously had several practical advantages for them including proximity to the water as well as the cost of the sport. Most of the men lived within walking distance of the Buffalo River and after the acquisition costs for the boats and oars, additional costs to participate in the sport were few. First Warders joined several rowing clubs including the Hibernian Rowing Club, the Celtic Club, the Mutual Rowing Club, and the Queen City Rowing Club.

The Hibernian Rowing Club, located at the foot of Porter Avenue on the West Side, seems to have been one of the first clubs in existence with records showing its inception as early as 1869. During this year, there was the famed crew of William Jones, Cornelius Donovan, Patrick Hurley and James Nunan; the colors of this club were fittingly Irish green. During the height of the sport in the latter part of the 19th century however, details about this club are limited. It is doubtful many First Warders would have made the trek to the West Side to row, so this club probably catered to the sizeable Irish population in that part of the city.

Two years after the inauguration of the Hibernian Club, twenty-three-year-old John C. Sheehan, the future Tammany Hall boss, organized another Irish-American rowing club, the Celtic Rowing Club. The Celtic R.C. was located at the foot of South Michigan Avenue at Times Beach in the Ward. The leadership of this club also included the future State Supreme Court Judge Daniel J. Kenefick, who was secretary, and William Love, a future prominent Buffalo attorney, who was the corresponding secretary.[51] This was the first rowing organization established in the First Ward. Over the years, many accomplished men in the Ward belonged to this club, including the future Lieutenant Governor William F. Sheehan and General William Donovan. Other prominent men who rowed for them were James McCarthy, Thomas Curran, Hugh Hogan and Michael Brown. The club was still active as late as 1917 with Thomas E. Lennon from South Michigan Avenue as president and William J. Cannan as secretary.

The most exceptional rowers from the Celtic Rowing Club represented the Irish in the Ward each year in a bitter rivalry against the Queen City Club from the West Side of Buffalo. Each Fourth of July, the contest would draw thousands to the banks of the Erie Canal to watch the men race from Genesee Street to Porter Avenue. Most importantly, this contest, which was funded by the Buffalo Common Council, "brought disgrace or honor to their respective neighborhoods for a year."[52] Interestingly, in 1882, the year the Celtic R.C. crew won the local championship, William F. Sheehan pulled the stroke oar and Timothy Donovan rowed behind him. There you had a future New York State Democratic Party boss and the father of the famous General William Donovan in the same racing shell. For men of the First Ward, rowing in the late nineteenth century was often the sport that captured the admiration of others and distinguished them from their fellow man.

On a hot July day in 1881, at a barbershop at the corner of South and Hamburg Streets, the idea for the Mutual Rowing Club was conceived. The first president was James E. Sullivan, brother of the locally famous alderman John P. Sullivan, and William "Fingy" Conners served as vice president.[53] Peter P. Dalton, John McCarthy, Dennis McCarthy, John Geary and Tom Daly assisted the officers of this 55-member club. Aside from John P. Sullivan and William Conners, the club was also home to Michael Shea and two national champions: Billy Aman and Edward "Algie" McGuire. Other presidents of the club were Peter P. Dalton, Alderman John P. Sullivan, Dan Nunan, William Driscoll, Pat Cotter, William P. Sullivan, Cornelius Coughlin, John Murphy, Edward Dray and John V. Mackey.

The club was still strong into the 20th century with prominent members such as Dave Regan, Jerry Regan, Ed Stanton, Tom Noonan, Densy Daly, Bossy Daley, Captain Short, Harold Shine, John Slattery, Norman Slattery, Dan Bouquard, Jimmy Nelson, Bill O'Brien, John Quinn, John Griffin, Mike Griffin, and Denis Driscoll. There were several police officers, scoopers, and steel and iron ore workers on the membership list.[54] The clubhouse of the Mutuals, which was rebuilt in 1891 after a devastating fire, was equipped with a state-of-the-art gym for training. The Mutual Club also branched out beyond rowing and fielded handball and football teams that competed citywide. Patrick Hurley was considered the club's star runner when he won five events in 1902 at the Canisius College games.[55] The expanded club at 100 members also hosted socials and smokers for its members.

In 1906, the Lighthouse Rowing Club was established in a wood-framed building on the "Beach" in the Ward just south of the Coast Guard station. This club was only in existence for a few years but was able to win the 1908 Four-Oared Championship in Buffalo. As the number of rowing clubs expanded so too did the number of teams that competed in citywide competitions. From a July 4, 1915 program from one of these citywide contests it is clear that while rowing was the main event other activities were also popular including: a baseball game, running broad jump, a 30-yard shoe race, a 220-yard dash, a ladies' 60-yard dash, a shot put contest and climbing a greased pole. Of course, rowing events were plentiful at this summer festival including a four-oared race, an eight-oared race, a race between Ed McGuire and John Hartnett, and a race between Dave Regan of Mutual R.C. against a team of four rowers from the Mutuals.

There were also some fun contests such as the prettiest baby contest, the fattest baby contest, a fat men's race, and a clinker race between grain scoopers from various elevators. The leaders of the program included Ed. J. Stanton of Mutual R.C., Superintendent Mike Regan, Marvin Smith of West Side R.C., Willie Aman of Mutual R.C., Ed Lennon of Celtic R.C., William Barrett of Lighthouse R.C., L. Peterson of Black Rock R.C. and Bob Sullivan of West End R.C. Prizes included "good cigars" compliments of John Regan, James Cullen, James Hagan and Timothy Murphy, as well as running shoes from Dave Ruben at 372 Elk Street, shoes from A.C. Smith & Son at 366 Elk Street and a hat from Thomas Dyson at Elk and Hamburg.[56] It is interesting that in this one contest you had Mike Regan, Dave Regan, William Aman and Edward McGuire who were all famous rowers from the Ward. One could make the case that the era around 1915 was the peak of rowing in the First Ward.

Along the way, the First Ward produced two national rowing champions. The first champion was William "Billy" Aman who was born in the Ward on February 24, 1870. Billy's father, William Sr., worked for a sheepskin manufacturer near the Ohio Slip. At age seventeen, young Billy was working as a machinist and within three years, in 1890, his sterling rowing career began. Willie was described as an "awkward youth" but coach Jack Carroll of the Queen City Rowing Club saw potential in him. As a result of Coach Carroll's tutelage, within five years Billy competed in matches throughout the U.S. and won hundreds of medals along the way.

In 1907, because of his past successes, Billy was invited to compete in New York City for the World Champion Single Scull contest. Billy competed against men from all over the world, and much to the excitement of those in the Ward, he was victorious in the quarter-mile race and named world champion. In order to hold possession of the championship, the winner needed to win the cup two years in a row and that is exactly what William did when he won again in 1908. This was a remarkable feat considering that Aman was now thirty-eight-years old. With much fanfare he brought the cup back to the Mutual Rowing Club at the corner of South Street near Hamburg Street. In 1911, Billy Aman also captained the four-oared crew that won the national title for the one-mile race. His teammates were Francis "Frank" Bouquard, Dave Regan, son of the Buffalo Police Commissioner from Louisiana Street, and Jerry Regan.

The indefatigable Billy Aman finally retired from rowing at the age of forty. Despite Billy's fame, he never left the Ward but rather moved around in it. In his last thirty years of life, he lived at 264 Hamburg, 389 Fulton Street, and finally at 327 Fulton Street at the time of his death. Willie Aman died on January 22nd 1932, and he was survived by his wife Margaret, a daughter Margaret, and a son William. His obituary recalls how he was a "First Ward idol" and "hailed as the best in America."[57]

Edward "Algie" McGuire, a Buffalo police officer and member of the Mutual Rowing Club in the Ward, brought a second championship to the First Ward. In 1923, Algie McGuire shocked the rowing world with his victory in Baltimore at the National Intermediate Single Scull Championship. In this championship contest, on the choppy waters of the Patapsco River, McGuire defeated the two favorites in the mile-and-quarter scull contest.[58] Hilton Belyea, the 1922 Canadian champion, and Paul Costello, two-time Olympic gold medal winner, were favored to win the race, but "Algie" upset both of them. In describing the upset, a writer for *Time* magazine declared that, "McGuire unexpectedly diverted rowing history from its chartered course."[59] McGuire also came close to representing the U.S. Olympic team in the early 1920s, but he lost out to a fellow Irish American from Philadelphia, John "Jack" Kelly (father of the famous actress Grace Kelly). As an aside, in the 1920 and 1924 Olympics, Kelly became a triple Olympic gold-medal winner.

Rowing in the Ward started to decline in the 1920s with the popularity of the automobile and the migration of people out of the Ward. In addition, other sports like baseball became popular and interest in rowing slowly faded away. Members of the Mutual Rowing Club held their last regatta around 1924; the club finally closed in the late 1930s.

Baseball, Playgrounds, and Picnics

Several Ward memoirs mention the impact that baseball had on the neighborhood. One of the first baseball clubs in the Ward was the Travelers' Baseball and Sporting Club. This club, founded in 1864 by John Gainey, often contended for the championship crown of the city of Buffalo.[60] They played at "the Field" which was a lot bounded by Katherine, Mackinaw, Fitzgerald and Sandusky Streets. Some of their memorable players were Sandy Bannister, John and Jimmy Connolly, John "Dobber" Patton, "Goose" Gillard, Barney Jimmus, "Speck" Kane, "Monkey" Ryan, and Jack Battles.[61] They were so popular that on opening day on Sunday May 18, 1890 as many as 800 people came out to watch them play another Buffalo team—the Socials. The players on that Travelers team included guys with names like Sullivan, Kane, Mulroy, Dee, Samson, Van Allen, Gibson, and Battles.[62] The churches in the Ward also sponsored baseball teams where young men working in factories would have a chance to relax and compete against men from around the city.

William Donovan fondly recalled playing neighborhood baseball with his friends and the parish priest in the Ward, Father James Quigley. Jimmy Griffin, the future mayor of Buffalo, remembered practicing baseball every summer night with his father at Sullivan Field.[63] John Baldyga, Ward memoirist, recalled how

Joe Dudzik, the future Buffalo Councilmen, grew up pitching at Lanigan Park, and John Myers, the one-time Buffalo Police Commissioner from the Beach, was a catcher at Lanigan Park.[64] Even Michael Shea was a member of the Travelers' Baseball Club during his years in the Ward.[65]

Lanigan Park, the main playground in the Ward, stretched from Elk to Perry Streets and from Chicago to Louisiana Streets. This well-maintained park, one of the largest play areas in the city, derived its name from the well-liked rector of St. Bridget's, Fr. James A. Lanigan. In the early years, there was one section of the park for mothers and their children with a playground for the girls; an iron picket fence separated the section where the men and boys played. The men's area had sections for handball, basketball, volleyball, baseball, and swings with a slide.[66] This park also included a swimming pool and a bandstand. On Fulton Street there was even a two-story gym that was heated by a potbelly stove where the boys could go in and play basketball during the long winter months. As previously mentioned, Sullivan playground between South Park Avenue and Mackinaw Street and Sidway and Katherine Streets was another popular hangout.

Churches also served as venues for neighborhood entertainment. The annual church picnic and lawn fete at Our Lady of Perpetual Help (nicknamed Pets) was one of the most popular events of the year. In 1907, an article in the *Buffalo Express* had a caption entitled "1907 Greatest of all Picnics" and it detailed the events at the Pets picnic. The co-chairs of the event were Alderman John P. Sullivan and Police Chief Michael Regan, and it was estimated that close to 5,000 people attended the all day event. Many were excited to see the new "O'Connell Avenue" street signs that replaced the ones labeled "Sandusky Street." The other point of interest was an automobile—a novelty at that point in the Ward's history—which took people for rides around the church block. The evening highlight, however, was a tug of war between two teams: Jim Cronin, George O'Donnell, Jack Sullivan, and Mike Clifford versus Jerry Regan, Tim Meegan, Mickey Culligan and Tom O'Keefe. According to reports, the team captained by Jim Cronin "ran all over" Jerry Regan's team.[67]

A few years later, in another article about the famous Pets picnic, the writer commented on how the eating of potato cakes and buttermilk was the main event that year.[68] The potato cakes were prepared from a special recipe from Ireland—or so the legend goes—and J. P. Sullivan provided the buttermilk for free.[69] Years later, Joan Scahill, who attended Our Lady of Perpetual Help in the 1940s and 1950s, remembers how the lawn fete was "something wonderful that you looked forward to all year".[70] Other recreational events at Pets Parish included performances of short plays and minstrel shows.[516]

Hurling and Gaelic football were also played in the Ward around the turn of the twentieth century. As was previously mentioned, Mike Quinn organized hurling and football matches which were played on Sunday afternoons at the old Buffalo Creek grounds. Hurling matches were also played against teams in Detroit, Cleveland, Syracuse, Toronto, and Rochester. Mike Quinn was also recognized for his involvement in bringing a hurling match to the Pan-American Exposition in 1901. In addition, basketball is mentioned with standout players such as Vince McNamara, later a city parks commissioner, and Tom "Rocko" Griffin, the famous mayor's father, who was on the championship team, the Foley's Billiards, in 1934.[72]

There were also simpler recreational pleasures such as roller-skating on a rink built on Louisiana Street across from the Barcalo Manufacturing plant. Kids from the First Ward also went to the Masque Theatre, known by locals as the "Rat Hole", which was located at 445 South Park Avenue, for Saturday matinees. For fifteen cents admission and ten cents for a box of popcorn, the kids would watch a double feature film plus a newsreel and a cartoon. Locals claim that the place received its nickname because the place was so unbearably small. The owner Louie, who spoke with a heavy accent, would yell at the kids to be "qvieet or no Bugs Bunny"; and Whitey the Albino worked as the projectionist.[73] The older kids would sneak beers into their popcorn boxes and enjoy the show that way. For other adventuresome Ward kids, playing in the sand piles on Louisiana Street brought much joy, but it was also hazardous to your health if you fell down the sand piles and into the Ohio Basin.

Jimmy Slattery

Each generation in the Ward was bestowed with a homegrown celebrity and the generation of the 1920s was no exception. If the first generation had Fingy Conners and the second generation had "Wild Bill" Donovan, the next generation had Jimmy Slattery. While the first two Ward luminaries, Fingy Conners and William Donovan, seemed to outgrow their Ward beginnings, Jimmy never outgrew his. For this reason people still seem to mention Jimmy Slattery first when asked about First Ward idols. First Warders have mostly negative feelings about Conners because of his anti-worker sentiments in the grain scoopers strike in 1899, and then his move to the elite Protestant enclave of Delaware Avenue in Buffalo. General William Donovan became a man that many of the people in the Ward could not relate to: an Ivy-League educated Republican who married into a wealthy WASP family. Jimmy Slattery was different. Slattery, the two-time national light heavyweight boxing champion, was a man connected to his fellow First Warders even at the height of his fame. One Ward memoir remembers that Jimmy never forgot his "old gang."[74]

James Patrick Slattery was born on August 25, 1904 at 589 Fulton Street in the First Ward of Buffalo. Jimmy or "Shamus" as his family called him was the son of a city fireman named John Slattery who worked at firehouse Engine 22. One of the earliest stories about the young, lanky Jimmy Slattery deals with his accidental start as a boxer. Harp Griffin, a 210-pound neighborhood brawler, saw the young Slattery at the corner of Elk and Louisiana Streets with a box of chocolates which was Jimmy's gift for his mother on Valentine's Day.[75] Griffin, however, wanted the chocolates for himself so he stole Jimmy's chocolates out of his hand. Rather than back down, the much smaller Jimmy challenged the bully to a fight. Witnesses say that close to two hundred people from the neighborhood gathered and watched Slattery, the budding pugilist, crush his much larger opponent in about thirty minutes in front of Gene Murphy's gas station.[76] Jimmy's father recognized his son's gifts, so he set up backyard boxing matches and took him to the First Ward Athletic Club. Jimmy's meteoric career to national fame was about to begin.

In 1921, at the age of sixteen, the 128-pound Jimmy Slattery's pro career started with an impressive 35 straight wins against several boxers who were much bigger than him. It is reported that he wore green trunks for every fight of his career to honor his Irish heritage. On October 3, 1924, Slattery won a six-round decision—the fight was limited to six rounds because of Slattery's age—against Jack Delaney at Madison Square Garden in New York City. People outside of Buffalo were now taking notice of him. A few months later on February 13, 1925, again at the Garden, Slats fought the 4-to-1 favorite Jack Delaney in a regulation match. The 5'11" Slattery who danced on his toes in the ring and had one of the most effective left punches in the sport stunned the boxing world by beating Delaney again. It was this fight that put Jimmy on the world stage of boxing. After a 17-1 record the following year, Slattery put himself into contention for the National Boxing Association title. Finally, on August 30, 1927, in Hartford, Connecticut, Slats or the "Buffalo Harp" as some called him, defeated "Slapsie" Maxie Rosenbloom in 15 rounds to win the World Light Heavyweight Championship and sit alone atop of the world. From accounts in the newspapers and memoirs, residents in the First Ward went crazy when the news of his championship arrived in the Ward.[77]

Meanwhile, across the country, boxing experts, sports writers, and his fellow boxers could not contain their praise for Slattery's abilities. He was the favorite boxer of Paul Gallico, the sports editor for the *New York Daily News* and another New York sportswriter referred to Slattery as a "darling of the gods."[78] The champion James Braddock, also known as the "Cinderella Man," in a 1959 interview, proclaimed that "the greatest boxer in my time was Jimmy Slattery."[79] Braddock went on to say that "Joe Louis was a fine boxer, but Jim Slattery was far better." In 1992, *Boxing Illustrated* ranked Jimmy Slattery the seventh slickest boxer of all time behind greats such as Sugar Ray Robinson, Gene Tunney, Muhammad Ali, and Sugar Ray Leonard. Others even compared him to one of the greatest of all time: Jim Corbett. The champion Tom Loughran stated that fighting Jimmy

Slattery was like "fighting a ghost with three hands." Aside from being a darling of the press and his fellow boxers, fans loved him as well. Slats regularly fought in front of sold-out crowds in Madison Square Garden and Yankee Stadium in the Bronx. But while his boxing prowess was incomparable, on a personal level all was not well. With Slattery's increasing success came a desire for the fast life of women and alcohol. The latter would be a battle that Jimmy would face his whole life, and the demon that would eventually lead to his downfall.

While Jimmy enjoyed basking in the glory of national success, he never forgot his roots or the people in the Ward. There are countless stories of his charity and magnanimity, which ranged from buying rounds of drinks for folks in his favorite taverns to giving away his cars to people in need. When he was in town Slattery would go to one of his favorite places like Kearn's Tavern and buy everyone drinks.[80] Joe Marren, whose family roots are in the Ward and Valley, related two stories concerning Jimmy's generosity. The first one involves Joe's grandfather, who owned a candy store in the Ward. Apparently, Slattery had just purchased a new Pierce-Arrow automobile and he needed to get rid of his Cadillac. Rather than sell it, he just gave the Cadillac away to Joe's grandfather with no strings attached. The other story involves Marren's father, who suffered from polio. Slats encouraged Joe's father to work out for free with him at his gym to help strengthen his limbs.[81] There are other stories of his donating a new altar for his church, buying books for an elementary school, and even dropping money out of his car during the Depression for children to grab. Some referred to him as a sucker for a good sob story and he regularly gave money for medical operations, shoes, coal for heating homes, and funeral expenses.[82] One First Ward memoirist referred to him as a "good Samaritan with a heart of gold."[83] However, between his charitable acts and his high living, Jimmy managed to squander away $400,000 in earnings, which would be equivalent to over $5.3 million in 2009 dollars. By 1931, Slats was broke and his slow descent began.

There is a general consensus that if Jimmy had trained harder and stayed away from alcohol that he could have become a legend for the ages. The stories of his drunkenness are legendary. One of Jimmy's close associates refuted the rumors and claimed that Jimmy refrained from drinking around the time of his fights and that his drinking really started after his career was over. However, too many other accounts dispute this claim. After losing the title to Tom Loughran, Slattery tried a comeback in 1930 and was in contention to win a second title if he could defeat Buffalo's West Side Italian legend Lou Scozza. In front of a sold-out crowd at Broadway Auditorium in Buffalo on February 10, 1930 that is exactly what Slats did. For a brief time, he was once again on top of the world with his New York State World Light Heavyweight title. Unfortunately, in that fight Slats took a left punch from Scozza to the throat that left him hoarse for the rest of his life.

Hoarseness, however, was not his only worry. His struggle with alcohol persisted and soon took its toll on his boxing. Slattery lost his title only four months after regaining it when he lost to Maxie Rosenbloom at Offermann Stadium in Buffalo. Apparently, Slats partied at the Palais Royale on Main Street in his hometown until 2:30 a.m. the night before the fight. Two busboys, Al and Leo DiGuilio, had to help him into a taxi.[84] Slats retired from boxing in 1934 and his troubles with alcohol and the law accelerated. In fact, in June 1935, he was put on probation for charges related to drinking and a month later he crashed his car as a result of booze. His legal problems mounted with new charges ranging from robbery to assaulting a police officer.[85] Through the Great Depression years Slattery was arrested at least ten times for crimes that involved either alcohol or fighting or both.

In 1942, Jimmy suffered from pulmonary tuberculosis, which was the same disease that killed his father and brother. Jimmy was lucky to have friends who paid for his recuperation in Arizona and assisted him in obtaining a city job in the Buffalo Parks Department where he tended to flower beds at Delaware Park. Slats was now a long way from the chanting crowds that filled Madison Square Garden to see him fight. In 1946, former heavyweight champion Jimmy Braddock came to Buffalo to host a fundraiser to assist Slattery with his medical bills. Jimmy's troubles didn't end there. His marriage eventually fell apart and he was forced to sell his house, but he still couldn't break his love for Scotch which he consumed regularly at the House O'Quinn on Chippewa Street. Finally, one night in late August of 1960, Slats collapsed at House O'Quinn and was taken to his flat which was close by; the next morning his lifeless body was found on the floor of his boarding house on Franklin Street. Slattery was so poor that he was buried in an unmarked grave in Holy Cross Cemetery, and a life which read like a Shakespearean tragedy was now complete. Despite his downfall, a fellow First Warder, Mayor Jimmy Griffin, retold how Slattery was an idol in the Ward in the 1930s and 1940s. Griffin remembered how those in the Ward loved the way he fought, drank, and took care of the less fortunate.[86]

Slattery's trouble with alcohol was far from unique when it came to other Irish immigrants and their descendants in Buffalo. We know that in the 1840s and 1850s Bishop Timon wrote and preached exhortations encouraging the Irish to imbibe less alcohol at wakes and the St. Patrick's Day parades which had the reputation of being alcohol-fuelled engagements. Timon even brought Father Mathew, the famous temperance preacher from Ireland, to Buffalo to preach to the faithful about abstaining. One local historian has detailed the family problems including family dissolution and premature death that resulted from alcohol abuse by Irish immigrants in the mid-19th century.[87] The first person executed after Buffalo's incorporation as a city was Irish immigrant Michael

Kelly who in 1835 stabbed his wife under the influence of alcohol. Two of the most famous Buffalo executions—both carried out by Grover Cleveland—involved two other Irishmen, Patrick Morrissey and John Gaffney, both of whom were drunk when they committed their crimes. A central theme of Buffalo Bishop Stephen Ryan's reign from the late 1860s to the early 1890s was intemperance among his flock. Ryan preached about the evils of alcohol throughout his diocese and claimed that morality, virtue, and religious duty were all easier when someone abstained.[88] In fact, when Bishop Ryan administered the sacrament of confirmation, he made the boys pledge to avoid alcohol until manhood.[89] Alcoholism in the Ward was a problem which remained private and not openly discussed over the years.

Mayor Jimmy Griffin in an interview about Slattery had this to say: "Jimmy liked to drink. Let's face it. We all do. I like to drink. There's no shame in that." Griffin went on to say, "What he [Slattery] did with his life, he enjoyed himself. That's the way I'll remember the guy. Down in the First Ward, people didn't have a hell of a lot. They worked hard down there, and they played hard. Still do."[90] While most people could handle their alcohol, people like Slattery who couldn't suffered dearly. Despite his demons with alcohol, Jimmy Slattery will always be remembered as Buffalo's first authentic athletic celebrity.[91]

First Warders can claim another boxing champion as their own—Bobby Scanlon. Scanlon came close to the greatness reached by Jimmy Slattery, but never reached it. Robert Emmett Scanlon was born in 1936, one of six children of a couple who split up in his teenage years. Bobby lived at Perry and Hayward Streets in the Ward and attended St. Bridget's elementary school. After his parents split up, he was sent to Father Baker's Orphanage in Lackawanna because his mother couldn't take care of all the children. It is reported that he was picked on because he was a small kid, just 5'5", so he learned how to box and became the champion of the orphanage by age fourteen. After working for the Baltimore and Ohio Railroad as a laborer, the handsome but shy Scanlon met a former boxer who taught him the art of the sport. After winning fifteen of his first sixteen amateur fights, "Irish" Bobby Scanlon brought home the Golden Glove bantamweight championship.[92] Scanlon's pro career began in 1954 and his future looked bright as he won his first twenty-nine professional boxing matches. One of Scanlon's sisters remembers the now confident and successful Bobby driving his powder-blue Thunderbird through the First Ward. Bobby was popular and very well liked by the fans in Buffalo, and he received the same reception from the Irish when he moved to San Francisco.

While he was on the West Coast he defeated two ex-lightweight champions: Wallace Bud Smith and Lauro Salas. Scanlon's career however was slowed by various physical ailments such as double vision. Scanlon came home from San Francisco to fight Jackie Donnelly, another First Warder, for the lightweight championship of New York State, which Scanlon won in a controversial 12-round match. One boxer who knew Bobby well claimed that if Scanlon had trained harder and more regularly he could have become the Lightweight Champion of the World. In 1966, at age thirty, Bobby Scanlon was forced to retire. Sadly, on June 23, 1975, after a decade of struggling to find a career after boxing, he died in a horrific fire at the Hotel Lackawanna.

A few First Warders claim another world champion boxer—Jimmy Goodrich—as their own. Goodrich, who's real name was James Moran, was born in Scranton, Pennsylvania but his boxing career took off after moving to Buffalo in 1917 and fighting under manager Paul "Red" Carr. Carr managed him from 1917 to 1923 and then again from 1928 to 1930. For several years he did live in the Ward. The 1920 *Buffalo City Directory* lists Goodrich as a laborer living at 133 Tennessee Street. The following year he worked as a clerk and by 1923 he was no longer listed in the city directory as living in the Ward. In 1925, a five-month tournament was held in New York City to choose the next world lightweight champion. Jimmy Goodrich beat the Chilean fighter Stanley Loayza to win the world championship. Although he lost the title five months later, he continued to box top world contenders for the next five years of his career. After 182 professional matches he could also make the bold claim that he was never knocked out.[93] In 1928, he was managing a boxing gymnasium on Main Street in Buffalo and living on Franklin Street. He owned several businesses around Western New York and spent his retirement in Buffalo and Angola, New York. In 2010, he was inducted into the Buffalo Sports Hall of Fame.

In addition to Slattery and Scanlon there is another locally-grown boxing great who was a product of the Ward: "Irish" Jackie Donnelly. As was mentioned previously, he lost to Bobby Scanlon in a controversial match in 1960. John J. Donnelly was born in the Ward on December 22, 1934, just two years before Scanlon. Jackie attended St. Bridget's elementary school and started boxing at the young age of nine. After attending McKinley High School, he entered the Air Force in 1952 at age seventeen. While in the Air Force, Donnelly won the U.S. Air Force Bantamweight Championship and the All-Service Bantamweight title. After his discharge from the Air Force, Donnelly entered the ranks of the pros in 1958. Donnelly dominated during his three years as a pro, racking up a 32-2 record. His first loss was to Bobby Scanlon, who beat him in the twelfth round in the Lightweight Championship in 1960. The controversy surrounding this match resulted from an after-the-bell punch that Scanlon landed on Donnelly and dropped him to the floor. Despite the foul, Donnelly fought on until the end. In 1961, Jackie retired and tried a comeback in 1963, but then decided to retire for good. After his boxing career Donnelly worked for thirty-seven years as an ironworker. Always a fan of boxing, Jackie opened his own gym to coach amateur boxers in his spare time. He still lives in the First Ward in the house he was born in on Tennessee Street.

There were other First Warders who didn't necessarily achieve national recognition, but boxed to make extra money or because they loved the sport. One of these men was Charles Comerford. Comerford, a prizefighter, fought with the name of Dummy Burns and was unique in the ring because he was deaf from a childhood swimming accident. When he wasn't boxing Charles worked at the grain elevators as a scooper and raised a family of ten children on St. Clair Street in the Ward. Dummy fought twenty-five bouts from 1911 to 1925 throughout New York State, Ohio, Pennsylvania, and Minnesota where he accumulated a record of 11 wins, 7 losses, and 7 draws with eight knockouts.

From saloons to rowing to boxing to baseball, First Warders found relief from their demanding jobs along the waterfront in sport and socializing. Several achieved fame beyond their hometown of Buffalo.

CHAPTER NINE

WOMEN, SCHOOLS, AND HOMES

*There was practically no man of Irish descent of stature in Buffalo from 1875
to 1940, who was not taught by the Sisters of Mercy. They educated practically
all the Irish immigrants for generations at St. Brigid's, St. Stephens and Holy
Family churches. They took these kids and taught them about the finer things of
life—and their own Irish values, the songs and poetry. They gave them a sense
of identity, of belonging, because the fact was that they had no position in the
community. They inculcated in us—at a very early age—a sense of the poetry
of life and the true values which accompany life.*
– Peter Crotty, Erie County Democratic Chairman

Like many histories prior to the 20th century, men have dominated this one.
Information on the lives of women in the First Ward from the mid-to-late 19th
century is limited due to the fact that their lives revolved around domestic roles:
motherhood and taking care of the house. Ward women in those years did not
have opportunities in athletics or politics and only had limited opportunities in
commerce. Consequently, in the 19th century there were few references to them
in newspapers and periodicals. Women did, however, have a considerable impact
on child rearing, household maintenance, and adding culture and respectability to
the community.

In terms of their role in household maintenance, one biographer of the famous
Ward resident General William Donovan explained the roles of women in this way.
He claimed that the housewives kept "their homes scrubbed clean and tidy even if
they could afford to hang only muslin or net curtains at their windows."[1] But they
did much more than keep a tidy home. The Donovan biographer also claimed that
the mothers were the disciplinarians in both the family and the neighborhood, and
consequently juvenile mischief was limited.[2] In the First Ward Crowley memoir
the author claimed that, as in Ireland, the mother was "the boss of the family."[3]
Supreme Court Justice Walter J. Mahoney from Buffalo recalled that "there was
a terrific bond between Irish mothers and their sons, and the former were the
strict disciplinarians. You might be able to 'get around' Father but not Mother."[4]

John Baldyga also remembers how women were the disciplinarians in the family. One historian argued that when Irish men arrived in America their familial role was diminished while the women's role rose, and as a result women held far greater authoritarian roles than they did in Ireland.[5] Women's roles in the household increased partly because there was a relatively high desertion rate by Irish men in the 19th century, and also because new opportunities were open to Irish women in America (white-collar jobs like teaching and nursing) which weren't available to them in their native country.

And it wasn't just Irish mothers who ran households. Rose Procknal, who was a Polish immigrant, raised fifteen children in the Ward by being a strict disciplinarian. Her granddaughter Pat Regan, who grew up in the Ward on Hamburg Street, explains that her grandmother was a stern disciplinarian and there was never any fighting allowed among her children because Grandma Procknal knew if she let her guard down even once there would have been bedlam in the house.[6] Eddie Stack from the Ward remembers it differently. He claimed that the father was the "undisputed head and the patriarchal monarch." You referred to him as "the mister" or as "himself", as in "the mister got home late," but his opinion seemed to be in the minority.[7] Aside from being strict disciplinarians, women also brought respectability to the community through a strict adherence to their Catholic faith. Commenting on the role of First Ward women, Professor William Jenkins wrote:

> While men were slow to lose their status as purely nominal Catholics, Irish women became, alongside the clergy, the practical backbone of parish life as prime receivers of the new devotional and family-centered ideology from the 1850s on. They were instrumental in fashioning new senses of Catholic respectability that would become integrated into everyday family lives.[8]

Domestic Servants

With regard to work, before they settled down to have children, Irish immigrant women in Buffalo often worked as servants for wealthier Americans. The high point for domestic servants in Buffalo was from roughly 1860 to 1925. Almost all of the wealthy Buffalonians, many of whom lived in mansions on Delaware Avenue, had domestic servants, most of whom were newly landed immigrants from Ireland or Germany. In 1860, former President Millard Fillmore had four servants, all born in Ireland, listed at his residence: Ann Lawler, Julia Lawler, John Dooley, and John Nash.[9] The president lived with his wife and a son, so there were more servants than there were residents of his house. While most of the domestic servants were female, German and Irish men were also employed to assist the wealthy industrialists. Usually the servants were single, ranging in age from their teens to their thirties, but occasionally servants were married with children and the whole family would live in the servants' quarters in the mansion. This was the case at the mansion of John Ganson, the president of New York and Erie Bank, where two of his servants were married with two children under the age of four.

In fact, according to the New York State Census in 1855, "recently arrived Irish females" in Buffalo worked overwhelmingly as domestic servants. While many of their fellow Irishwomen living in East Coast cities worked in factories, those in Buffalo were equally compensated for a less onerous workday. Of the "recently arrived girls" who were aged fifteen to nineteen, over 70% worked as servants in contrast to the native-born Buffalo girls of whom only 15.6% worked as servants. Even 40% of the ten to fourteen-year-old Irish new arrivals worked as servants compared to only 5.6% of the native-born girls of this age.[10] Once the women were assimilated to the local environs, the percentage of women working as servants dropped off pretty significantly. In fact, after five years of living in Buffalo only 32% of the fifteen to nineteen year old Irish girls worked as servants. By age twenty-one, 50% of Irish immigrants were married, and those working as domestic servants dropped off significantly. By age twenty-six, only 12% of Irish women worked as domestic servants.[11]

The exception to these trends were single Irish women in their forties to sixties who were either widowed or had never been married. Many of them worked as domestic servants. Middle-aged Irish women in Buffalo were unmarried at a much higher rate than other ethnic groups. Between the ages of forty-one to sixty, Irish women were listed as married only 53% of the time in 1855 compared to 78% of the Buffalo German women of the same age. It is impossible to tell how many of these middle-aged Irish women were single because of death, divorce or desertion.[12] Men also worked as servants, but they usually had different roles in the house. Within the role of "servants" there were various subspecialties such as general house servants, cooks, nurses, laundresses, butlers, coachmen, maids, nannies, gardeners, and chauffeurs.

One of the interesting results of the Irish girls working in the finest homes in Buffalo is that they were part of a domestic culture that many of the Irish men working on the docks were not exposed to.[13] Irish men in the First Ward in the 19th century, who lived in a much more insular environment, would have had a different framework of other cultures and events in the city compared to the Irish women who worked as servants. This exposure would have been exported to the Ward and presumably helped the enculturation of the Irish. In addition, Irish servant girls benefited materially with a "private room, board, and Christmas bonus, and gifts of discarded clothing and other personal items from employers."[14]

While many Irish women in the Ward worked as domestic servants, other occupations were open to them including helpers, bookbinders, and clerical positions at the nearby Larkin Soap factory. In a 1920 study in Buffalo, the author claimed that Irish women did a better job of moving up the job ladder than their Irish male counterparts. In fact, Irish women immigrants even did a better job than native white American women when it came to career advancement.[15] Irish women in Buffalo also had higher rates of job longevity, education, and skill level than their Irish male counterparts.[16] A small minority entered religious life and spent their lives working at hospitals and schools throughout Buffalo. A few were even busy working as midwives delivering the thousands of newly arrived babies. This was during the days when babies were delivered in a house, not in a hospital. John Baldyga mentions two women in particular who delivered a lot of babies in the neighborhood: Mrs. Kulczyk from Fulton Street and Mrs. Shuler from Hamburg Street.[17]

Other women ran boardinghouses for the multitude of single dockworkers and sailors throughout the Ward. In 1860, out of forty-eight boarding houses in Buffalo—many of which were located in and around the First Ward—women ran thirty-two of them.[18] Widows such as Mary Calivan at 50 Ohio Street, Jane Ferguson at Elk and Michigan Streets, Susan Stephens at 24 Chicago Street, and Minerva Brownwell at 22 Chicago Street all supported themselves by running boardinghouses in the Ward. Some women were entrepreneurial in other ways, such as Mrs. Hutchinson who lived on Elk Street near Michigan Avenue. Legend has it that one day some sailors asked Mrs. Hutchinson where they could get their shirts washed and ironed. She offered to do their laundry herself. Word spread to other sailors about her services and she started receiving bed linens from freighters and passenger boats such as the *Cleveland & Buffalo*. Soon Mrs. Hutchinson's business was washing all of the laundry on the waterfront.[19]

In the 20th century, some women, such as Kit Clohessy on Elk Street, were still managing boardinghouses, but other women were running the ubiquitous delicatessens, general stores, and grocery stores found throughout the Ward. Ma Carr owned a well-known candy kitchen and soda bar on Elk Street (South Park Avenue). It was a popular hangout for people of all ages during the 1930s, 1940s, and early 1950s, and particularly for teenagers who had a place to dance in the back of her shop. Mary Kennedy was another enterprising woman who ran a tavern called Kennedy's (now Cooks Bar and Grill) on Katherine Street. During the 1940s and 1950s, Stella Goslinski had a grocery store at Kentucky Street and O'Connell Avenue which catered to the workers at the Barcalo Manufacturing plant, and Mary Dalton ran Dalton's Store at 148 South Street near Hamburg Street. Tricia Needham operated a store called Tricia's at O'Connell Avenue and Hamburg Street, and Nunie Neth oversaw a delicatessen at Alabama and Mackinaw Streets from the 1950s to the early 1980s.

Rose (Wilczak) Procknal was originally from Poznan, Poland and settled in Maryland with her husband and seven children. Labor troubles broke out at her husband's place of employment, so they decided to move to the First Ward in Buffalo where the labor situation was more peaceful at the time. Unfortunately, Rose's husband suffered from asthma or black lung disease from his years as a coal miner, and did not have steady employment for many years of their marriage. After their arrival in the Ward, they added to their family and were soon raising fifteen children, so Rose needed to supplement the family's income. Her granddaughter, Pat Regan, describes her grandmother, who spoke Polish better than English, as "a strong woman in body and in will."[20] While raising a family of seventeen people, she decided to open a tavern (Procknals) at Katherine Street and O'Connell Avenue. Operating the tavern was a family affair where one daughter sang Irish tunes on Saturday nights, the other children cleaned the bar, and Rose cooked—she even acted as the bouncer from time to time. The enterprising Rose served free spaghetti dinners Wednesday nights to the local neighbors as long as they drank beer during their stay. Rose later sold the tavern and opened up a deli on the opposite corner. Hardworking women like Rose Procknal were often the backbone for struggling families in the Ward. Pat Regan's memories of her grandmother, Rose Procknal, were pretty typical of the sentiment others had for the women in the neighborhood:

> My grandmother was a very strong woman without a bashful bone in her body. She believed in following the rules, hard work, and taking responsibility for yourself. She not only expected this from her own family, but from anyone she came in contact with. She never complained about hard work or initiative.[21]

Cooking was another time-consuming female task. For the first- and second-generation residents, the Elk Street Market, situated at the western edge of the Ward, was their destination for food and even occasionally for entertainment. The Elk Street Market opened in 1850 and was the primary market for fruits, vegetables, animals, and other everyday staples. Farmers and food merchants, many from the rural areas of Western New York, would set up their carts in this open-air market and display their wares. Saturday night shopping at the Elk Street Market was a popular activity for residents of the First Ward. In addition to food merchants, residents also met men who sold patent medicine, gadget vendors, street musicians, and even beggars.[22]

The farmer's market on Elk Street was not the only place for the first generation to obtain food. Some of the Ward residents, immigrants from rural areas of Ireland, also raised their own animals such as chickens, geese, ducks, pigs, and even cows.[23] These animals were either sold or consumed by the owners. In an 1857 newspaper, Patrick O'Sweeny from Elk and Chicago Streets took out an ad looking for his two milch cows which went missing from the area.[24] Congressman Richard "Max" McCarthy once recalled how his grandmother used to take the family cow down to graze near the Ohio Basin.[25] He also recalled that his father Ignatius took care of 100 chickens in his Kentucky Street backyard.[26] The Crowley manuscript describes how as late as 1872, ancestor Hannah Crowley of 19 Tennessee Street kept "a couple of cows" in a shed in the backyard for supplemental income. Mrs. Crowley walked house to house throughout the Ward selling her cows' milk.[27] Incidentally, she originally wanted to live on the West Side of Buffalo, but cows were not permitted there so she settled in the Ward, which had more lax bylaws.[28] Another memoir claims that the area at the corner of O'Connell Avenue and Hamburg Street was named Dalton's Pond after Mr. Dalton, who had a pig and chicken farm at that location.[29] Not far away at 265 Katherine Street, Rose Procknal kept chickens in her yard as well. Ice fishing was also a popular pastime to supplement the family's food supply. One resident remembers stories of how her Uncle Mike Comerford used to fish each winter on the frozen lake in order to raise some extra money. Each fall Uncle Mike would make new shoes for his dog to enable him to walk on the frozen Lake Erie.[30]

In terms of what food was served in households, there are various memories. In the early years meat was definitely a rarity because of its high cost. Residents of the Beach definitely consumed Lake Erie fish because it was abundant and close and they sold their surplus to others in the Ward. One resident in the 20th century recalls that creamed cod on Fridays was a specialty. Corned beef and cabbage, a meal unknown to Irish natives, became a popular meal in the First Ward because of its relative affordability. One resident recalled that everyone bought their corned beef from Joe Waite's butcher shop, which was remembered for the sawdust scattered on the floor of the shop.[31]

Teachers

The profession of teaching was available to many second- and third-generation Irish women. For single and married women, the teaching jobs that were available to them were in the public schools; parochial schools were usually staffed by religious brothers, priests or nuns. These moderately well paying jobs helped supplement the family's financial situation. Thanks to local politicians who had responsibilities for appointing teachers, Irish Ward women flooded the profession. Education was also one of the few occupations available that allowed women an opportunity to obtain leadership roles as principals and administrators.

In the reform era of the 1890s, there were many newspaper stories decrying the fact that education and politics were intertwined. During that period, teaching positions were part of the patronage jobs that were doled out by politicians, and the Irish politicians were particularly adept at seizing them for their daughters, wives, and friends. Concerned citizens complained that these political appointees were often not qualified because they themselves did not even have high school diplomas. It was even claimed that an inordinate number of Irish saloonkeepers' daughters were appointed to teaching positions.[32] Eventually rules were instituted requiring teachers to take an exam and the superintendent of the Buffalo Public Schools, not politicians, chose candidates from a list. Teachers were also given contracts that had to be renewed each year based on performance. Even with these changes, by 1908 American-born daughters of Irish parents made up over 26% of all Buffalo city teachers (a much higher percentage than the overall Irish-American population of the city).[33]

Despite the perception that all Catholic children in the Ward went to parochial schools, many families could not afford to send their children to Catholic schools or they chose not to for other reasons. There were some well-known public schools that were available to these children including Schools 3, 4, 30, 34, Central High School and South Park High School. School 3 was built in 1831 at the corner of Perry and Illinois Streets in what was then the First Ward, and it was the third school built in Buffalo. This school, originally a tuition-supported school, was eventually incorporated into the Buffalo public school system. In 1851, a beautiful three-story brick building replaced the wooden structure. As the area became more industrialized, enrollment declined and this school was closed.[34]

School 4, an elementary school built in the Ward in 1835, was located on Louisiana and Elk Streets. The fact that there was a school in this part of town in 1835 is evidence that there was a sizable community in the Ward by this time. The wooden-clad building was known as the "Little Red Schoolhouse." The location of the school was prone to flooding and during a particularly devastating flood the school was swept away and had to be rebuilt. A new school was built of brick and was enlarged several times (1850, 1856, and 1881) to accommodate the growing number of students.[35] The school was completely replaced in 1925. A review of the surnames of the principals at School 4 exemplifies the transfer of leadership from native-born Americans (Sackett, Smith, Pratt, and Barker) to those from Ireland or their descendants (McDonough, Kennedy, Maddigan, Coveney, Duly and Donahue). The change in principals over the years was not just related to ethnicity, but also to gender. All eight of its last principals were women, which was proof that women dominated public schools south of the city.[36]

School 30, created in the 1860s, resided in a home—less than a mile from the Ohio Street toll bridge—donated by the wealthy industrialist and farmer George Washington Tifft. The superintendent of schools in 1865 claimed that the school was located at "the bleakest spot" in Erie County.[37] In 1860, the school, which had one teacher, Eliza McGowan, had an average attendance of about twenty-six students a day. The attendance rate at School 30 was 76% compared to an 89% attendance rate citywide, probably due to the fact that some of these children had to work to support their families.[38] By 1869, the enrollment rose to 175 during the large immigration of Irish into the Ward. The school was eventually moved near the Elk Street swing bridge because the physical conditions at the original school were less than ideal (it was built on sand and there were frequent Lake Erie floods).[39] The new building, completed in 1890, had six classrooms, natural lighting, steam heat, and three lavatories. By 1890, all of the teachers were Irish, including the principal, Anna Donovan, and 62% of the students were Irish.[40] In 1902, Anna Donovan was still the principal and the teachers were all single women: Miss Margaret T. O'Brien, Miss Margaret Quinn, Miss Kathryn Moore, Miss Ellen Boland, Miss Mary T. Cotter, and Miss Mary R. Bohen. After roughly seventy years of service, the school was demolished in the 1930s.

Another well-known First Ward school, School 34, was located at the intersection of O'Connell Avenue and Hamburg Street. The building, which was dedicated during the Civil War on January 13, 1865, was considered the finest and most expensive public school built in Buffalo at the time.[41] The school was expanded in 1895 and, shortly after, the eleven coal stoves that heated the building were replaced with steam heaters and electricity was also added. A review of the school's principals throughout its history shows that leadership of the school passed from WASP names to Irish ones shortly after the Civil War. By the late 1800s, all the successive principals were Irish including Charles Kennedy, John J. McGee, William J. Candee, and Anna M. Donovan.[42] The school was closed in 1976 after 112 years of service to the Ward.

In terms of high schools, there was not a dedicated high school located in the First Ward throughout the 19th century. The residents of this area of Buffalo who were lucky enough to attend high school usually went to Central High School, located at the corner of Franklin and Court Streets, which closed in 1914. South Park High School, located in South Buffalo, opened in 1915, and became the new destination for public high school students from the First Ward. South Park High School was not however an exclusively Irish student body. In fact, a review of the 1927 South Park High School Dial yearbook, shows an almost even split between German and Irish surnames among the 140 students in the senior class at South Park High School. Even the leadership was split with a German principal, Robert T. Bapst, and an Irish assistant principal, Francis P. Regan. Out of seventy-six faculty members, about thirty-three had Irish surnames and the rest were either German or English. In terms of gender, of the seventy-six faculty members at South Park High School fifty-seven of them were women.[43] Thus by the late 1920s, secondary teaching was dominated by women at this South Buffalo high school.

St. Bridget's (Brigid's) Elementary School

There were also those who did attend Catholic schools. The oldest school in the First Ward, St. Bridget's, first opened in 1858 and witnessed explosive growth in enrollment. In 1878, there were 917 children attending St. Bridget's school with 551 females and 366 males learning catechism, reading, writing, geography, arithmetic, algebra, bookkeeping, and Biblical history.[44] The higher enrollment ratio of girls to boys was due to the fact that many young men were already working in their early teens. Attending grade school was often a luxury for boys in the Ward from the mid-1800s until the turn of the 20th century. Attending high school was even more rare. Former Congressman Richard McCarthy provided the statistics of his father Ignatius D. McCarthy's 4th grade class at Our Lady of Perpetual Help in the early 1900s. Out of eighty-four boys at Pets school, only seventeen graduated from 9th grade and only three finished high school. To put it simply, less than 20% of the boys finished the 9th grade and less than 5% of the boys in the Ward during this period finished high school. The rest dropped out in order to work and support their families.[45]

A quick survey of the heads of households in the First Ward from the 1940 New York State Census shows a similar level of educational achievement with many men only finishing the 8th grade. Fireman Daniel Bohen (born 1883) of 45 O'Connell Avenue only finished 8th grade, but this was an improvement from his father Timothy (born 1850) who could neither read nor write. Meanwhile Daniel's son, Joseph Bohen (born 1917), also from 45 O'Connell Avenue, not only finished high school but also attended college for two years. Joseph eventually became an executive with the US Postal Service in Buffalo. This survey of three generations from the same household was fairly typical. The Irish were finally progressing in the realm of education. Thomas D'Arcy McGee, the 19th century defender of the Irish and proponent of advancement through education, would have been proud.

Father John Nash, a student at St. Bridget's from 1874-1877, remembered the rigor of the academic program that the nuns instilled. Nash recalled how in addition to reading, writing and arithmetic, the students memorized famous passages such as Longfellow's "Psalm of Life," Tennyson's "In Memoriam," Julius Caesar's "Speech of Marc Anthony," and Hamlet's soliloquy, "To be or not to be."[46] They also became proficient in proper grammar with a thorough understanding of *Brown's English Grammar* and its twenty-six rules of syntax. In addition to a rigorous academic curriculum, the Mercy nuns taught the students about Irish history, poetry, and the saints.

On September 11, 1898, a new building was constructed to house St. Bridget's school, which replaced the "dark and dingy" 1870 school.[47] The design and materials of the new school exemplified how far the Irish in the Ward had progressed since classes were taught in a horse barn in 1858:

> It was built of golden brown Pompeian brick with tasteful terracotta and brown stone trimmings. Classic in every outline it embodies every requirement for the comfort and accommodation of its pupils. Both staircases are built of highly polished wood, elegant in design. The rest of the interior is of Georgia Pine. The building, solid in construction, is practically fireproof.[48]

By 1900, St. Bridget's school was staffed by about nineteen Sisters of Mercy who taught the students the standard elementary school curriculum. For some of the more proficient students they offered an additional two-year academic curriculum. It has been noted that many of the Buffalo diocesan priests during the latter part of the 19th century and early 20th century passed through the halls of St. Bridget's.[49] But the school did not just train future priests. Peter Crotty, the one-time Democratic Party Chairman for Erie County, remembered:

> There was practically no man of Irish descent of stature in Buffalo from 1875 to 1940, who was not taught by the Sisters of Mercy. They educated practically all the Irish immigrants for generations at St. Brigid's, St. Stephens and Holy Family churches. They took these kids and taught them about the finer things of life—and their own Irish values, the songs and poetry. They gave them a sense of identity, of belonging, because the fact was that they had no position in the community. They inculcated in us—at a very early age—a sense of the poetry of life and the true values which accompany life.[50]

Two of the most remembered Sisters of Mercy from St. Bridget's were Sister Mary Bernadine Hagan, who instructed the boys of the First Communion classes, and Sister Mary Patricia McMahon who taught the older boys in the school.[51] Other sisters who left memorable impressions from the late 19th century included Sister Mary Scholastica Corbett, Sister Mary Boland, Sister Mary Antonio Holmes, Sister Martha Cocleagh, and Sister Mary Aloysius McCammon.[52] By 1910, the Sisters of Mercy were operating ten schools in Buffalo, many in the South Buffalo area, and they were educating 8,000 children around Western New York.[53] These sisters, however, weren't the only ones educating Ward children. Our Lady of Perpetual Help elementary school, opened in 1908, catered to the children in the central part of the Ward. Within a few years they were educating about 900 children a year in a sixteen-room school building. But unlike the other Catholic schools in the Ward, the Allegany Franciscan nuns ran this school. As a result of changing demographics, the school closed in the late 1960s, but not until the Allegany Franciscans left their imprint on many First Ward boys and girls.

There were a few Catholic high schools that the men and women from the Ward attended: St. Joseph's Collegiate, Canisius High School, Mount Mercy High School, Bishop Timon High School, and Bishop Quigley High School. For boys, St. Joseph's Collegiate, originally located at 1 Delaware Avenue in downtown Buffalo, was the main destination for first- and second-generation boys. This school opened in 1861 and was staffed by six members of the Christian Brothers order from New York City and Montreal. Men such as the former pastor of St. Bridget's, James E. Quigley, General William J. Donovan, John C. and William "Blue-Eyed Billy" Sheehan, Comptroller Joseph Gavin, and Supreme Court Judge Tom O'Donnell were just a few well known men from the Ward who made the trek downtown to go to high school. The opening of Canisius High School provided an alternative to St. Joseph's Collegiate Institute. In the fall of 1877, four of the brightest students at St. Bridget's school (Joseph Garen, Michael Kane, William Candee, and John Nash) marched up to enroll in this Jesuit-run high school on Washington Street. Out of the four star students from the Ward in this class, three of them became accomplished priests and the other became the principal of School 34.[54]

For over a hundred years there had never been a Catholic high school for boys or girls in the boundaries of the First Ward. If girls went to a parochial high school, most went to Mount Mercy Academy in South Buffalo which opened in 1905. Things changed, however, in August of 1946 when the Diocese of Buffalo created a girls high school named Bishop Quigley High School in honor of the former rector of St. Brigid's. The temporary location for this new school, which was run by the Mercy Sisters, was on the third floor of St. Brigid's elementary school at Fulton and Louisiana Streets. The school attracted young women from the Ward as well as from twenty-two parishes all over Buffalo where girls were promised a solid Mercy education for tuition of only $50 per year.[55] The girls immediately started a school newspaper, a drama club, and a French club, and by the third year the girls were playing on baseball and basketball teams at Lanigan Community House.[56] There were plenty of social activities such as dances, roller-skating, and a prom.

The first year enrollment at Bishop Quigley High School was seventy girls and the school quickly expanded, which necessitated a separate building instead of the co-sharing arrangement with St. Brigids. In 1953, Bishop Joseph Burke presided over the groundbreaking ceremony on a $300,000 three-story brick building equipped with nine classrooms, a library, a cafeteria, and a gym for the girls' high school. The new school opened to students two years later.[57] By 1954, there was an impressive total of 258 students enrolled and all were educated with the "Christian Social Living" principles taught by the Sisters. Due to various reasons, however, the high school closed eight years later, and then the students from St.

Brigid's elementary school were moved into the building that had housed the high school.

The same year that Quigley High School opened, a boys high school opened in the Ward. In 1946, seventy boys started at newly created Bishop Timon High School which resided on the second floor of Our Lady of Perpetual Help school. This was just a temporary arrangement, however, since the school was awaiting a new building to be built in South Buffalo. When the building was completed in the fall of 1949, Bishop Timon High School moved out of the Ward to McKinley Parkway in South Buffalo where it resides today.

Homes in the Ward

Prior to the 20th century, home ownership by Irish Ward residents was fairly limited. In fact, in 1880, only 27.3% of the Irish residents owned their own home.[58] Twenty years later, out of the 757 dwellings in the Ward, 183 were owned outright, 187 were mortgaged, and the rest were rented by the occupants.[59] Things were improving, but still less than 50% of families owned their own house at the turn of the 20th century. The second Bishop of Buffalo, Stephen Ryan, advocated for home ownership as a means to improve the situation of the Irish. He recognized the thrift of the German and Polish immigrants in Buffalo when it came to saving for a home, but this was not the case for many Irish immigrants who rented or lived in crowded boardinghouses.[60] Therefore, in 1884, Bishop Ryan helped establish the Irish-American Savings and Loan Association, which allowed Irish Americans to pool their money together in order to create loans and mortgages for their members. Members made weekly contributions into these savings deposit accounts, and then financing was made available to other Irish Americans who previously would have been shut out of home ownership. In 1897, the Irish-American SLA advertised that they made loans and mortgages for as little as $130 and up to $10,000.[61] Irish-American home ownership rates improved as a result of the association.

Without this savings and loan association, it is uncertain how immigrants would have amassed enough money to purchase their homes since mortgages were not readily available to the working class. If you could get a mortgage, it often required a 50% down payment, and with the meager wages accrued from working on the waterfront the ability to save large sums of money would have been improbable. Sometimes the previous owner would hold the title until all payments were made. This was the case with Mike Quinn's saloon on Chicago Street. Quinn did not receive the title for his saloon, which was held by the previous owners of the German Hotel, until he made his last payment to them. Michael and Hannah Crowley bought a lot on Tennessee Street in 1872 for $1,400 from William Glenny, a wealthy merchant from Main Street. The Crowleys gave Glenny $700 for a down payment and then paid him the remaining $700 over the course of three years.[62] Sometimes family members would pool their money together to help a relative pay for their home.

The facts about Timothy Bohen's home on Sandusky Street were typical of others in the Ward. The central part of the First Ward, around Pets Parish, was developed in earnest in the 1860s and 1870s. It was during this time that Irish laborers were able to purchase their own homes from the wealthier Buffalonians who owned large tracts of land in the central part of the First Ward. On March 23, 1863, in the midst of the Civil War, the Buffalo Common Council issued a ruling that Sandusky Street (later O'Connell Avenue) be opened between Louisiana Street to the Buffalo Creek Reservation. Within ten years of this resolution, streets such as Sandusky, Tennessee, Kentucky, and Louisiana Streets were settled by former County Cork residents with surnames like Driscoll, Mahoney, McCarthy, and O'Brien. Around this time, on December 15, 1873, Timothy Bohen purchased a cottage at 45 Sandusky Street for $540 from John L. Kimberly, owner of a cider and vinegar manufacturing plant on Chicago Street. Kimberly, however, lived at 682 Seventh Street on the wealthier West Side of Buffalo; like other well-established merchants and industrialists in Buffalo he probably owned 45 Sandusky Street as a rental property or held it for land speculation purposes. In this same year there were only about six dwellings on Sandusky Street, which increased over the years to around 100 homes. Years later when Timothy's son Daniel died, a writer for the *Courier-Express* claimed that the Bohen home was "a neighborhood landmark, one of the first homesteads built on the street."[63] During the 1870s to the 1890s, streets like Sandusky exploded with growth, but it took until 1890 for the Buffalo Common Council to finally approve funds to pave the street and run a water pipe down it. This exemplified how the Ward was often not the first priority of the city leaders.

Like many men, Timothy converted an existing cottage into a house. Over the years, he put more additions onto the existing structure with the result that he eventually had a two-family house with a small cottage in the back. Throughout the years, Bohen rented out one flat in his house as well as the cottage in the rear of his house in order to supplement his income. The need for additional income to make ends meet was particularly important for grain scoopers who were unemployed for four months of the year in the winter. The cottage was torn down around 1913, but the two-family structure still remains. Pictures of the house from the early 20th century show rough-sawn clapboards on the outside of the structure which remind one of the crude structures from the frontier towns in the western United States. The size of the house is typical for doubles in the Ward: a two-story building, 2,440 square feet of living area, with two bathrooms and six bedrooms. The wooden clapboard has now been covered over with green aluminum siding.

In terms of geography, Timothy's house on Sandusky Street was in the midst of an industrial beehive. Situated one block from the Ohio Basin, his home was close to three lumber yards: the J.R. Smith yard, the John Ganson yard and the Dart Planing Mill. The Dudley and Company Refinery was located one block to the north and just another block north of that were the tracks for the New York, Lackawanna & Western R.R. Company. One block south of Timothy's house was the New York Lake Erie and Western R.R. Company tracks. But there were also neighborhood institutions such as Police Precinct 7 and Public School 4, both just three blocks away. For leisure time there was a popular saloon located at the corner of Sandusky and Kentucky Streets, just one block from his house. To the east of Timothy's house were several blocks of residential streets but he was clearly on the immediate edge of the bustling Buffalo industrial hub. Author Roger Dooley describes the sensual experience of living in such a neighborhood with "continuous puffs and wails and subdued roars from railroad and harbor, the warm, malty First Ward smell."[64] Others also mention the malty smell prevalent in the air. In one memoir the author vividly describes the environment in the Ward:

> Always discernable in the Ward was the strong, malty smell from the nearby grain elevators and mills. This pungent scent, floating through countless kitchen windows was as much a part of the First Ward streets as their horse-troughs and their carbon arc lights. Also familiar to the Ward was the sounds of the blowing whistle of a departing lake steamer, the clang of railroad engines, the rattle of a distant trolley, the sound of horses' hoofs hauling loads of lumber, scrap-iron or beer barrels or the rumbling of the farmers' wagons over the cobblestones on their way to the Elk Street Market.[65]

Not all residents built their own homes. On occasion First Warders physically moved their homes from one location in the Ward to another. One way to do this was via barges up the Buffalo River.[66] One resident knows for a fact that a house on Mackinaw Street was moved there from the Beach.[67] The home next to the Local 109 union hall on Louisiana Street was another example of a house that was moved from the Beach. First Warders were also possessive of their homes—or maybe just practical. They often sold their homes to other family members when it was time for them to leave. Jim Shine recalls that three sets of his relatives (the Newmans, the Smiths, and the Shines) passed down the same house on the Beach over three generations.[68] When his family moved to Tennessee Street, they continued the tradition of passing that house down through the family as well. The Bohen family homestead stayed in the family for over 75 years through three generations, and Joan Scahill claims that her family home at 146 South

Street was passed down by family members for 100 years from the 1850s until the 1950s. Multi-generational homesteads were not uncommon, and sometimes were the norm.

So what did a typical home or the surrounding environment look like? In the mid-to-late 19th century, many of the homes were somewhat crude and looked more like cottages. This was especially true in some areas like the Beach. In photos of a house from the 1920s it appears that the wood steps and wooden siding have crudely-cut edges. Some general impressions can be gained from the well-researched Roger Dooley novels about the First Ward. According to Dooley the color of the exterior of homes in the First Ward was often painted with "sober colors." The exterior was layered with dirt and grime as well.[69] The blackened exterior was a result of the pollution from the railroads and the numerous waterfront factories that were scattered about. In addition, the soil was very sandy so that homes had no basements, but were built instead on sturdy stone pillars.[70]

William Donovan's biographer writes, "...each of the cottages along the dirt streets was surrounded by a white picket fence, a kitchen garden, and flowers blooming around the doorway."[71] In addition to blooming flowers, one author mentions how nature's gift to the First Ward was the lofty poplars that lined the streets and provided wonderful shade in the summer.[72] Congressman Richard "Max" McCarthy described the homes in Hakertown, in the heart of the Ward, like this: "...wood frame houses, most of which had little picket fences, gates and tiny front yards set back from wooden sidewalks and dirt streets."[73] The dirt road claim was only partially true because some streets like Perry Street were made of cobblestone. It is true that even in 1888, the only road paved in the First Ward was the section of Ohio Street from Michigan Avenue to the Ohio Basin. In contrast almost all of the West Side of Buffalo and the wealthier areas around Delaware Avenue, Richmond, and Elmwood were paved at that time.[74]

The streets were kept clean from a combination of the efforts of fire hoses when fireman had free time and from a regular street cleaner. The street cleaner apparatus was comprised of a drum with bristles on it pulled by mules that helped remove dirt from the streets.[75] This period also pre-dated street signals to direct traffic. One memoirist describes how the intersection at Elk and Louisiana Streets was the busiest intersection in the neighborhood because you had horse-drawn wagons, streetcars, Model T cars, and the Buffalo-Lackawanna and Erie rail cars all competing for space. The solution was a traffic cop standing in the middle of the street with sign that read, "stop" on one side and "go" on the other, flipping the sign to direct traffic.[76] Many of the sidewalks were made of wood and resembled boardwalks like the ones at Miami and Mackinaw Streets.[77] John Crowley, who was born in the late 1890s, recalls that because the area of Hakertown near the

Buffalo River was marshy, wooden sidewalks were built about two feet above the ground, which enabled children to play under them.

Prior to electric lights, gas lamps were the dominant light source and there was someone who was paid to ride a bicycle to each lamp every night in the Ward. With the aid of a pole with a lighted flame, he would relight each gas globe.[78] Another person was responsible for maintaining the globes and fixing the heating element. While electric streetlights appeared in some areas of the Ward, it took decades to make a complete switch from gas lamps. A new, modern street lighting system was wired in the First Ward in June 1925.

As for the interior of the homes, even after the turn of the 20th century, an indoor bathroom was considered a luxury in the First Ward.[79] While the exterior may have been drab, Dooley claims that the interior of First Ward homes often looked like other middle-class homes throughout the city.[80] The task of warming the homes in the winter was hard work because you had to haul the coal into the house, clean the ashes out, and start the fire—a difficult task on cold mornings.[81] As Tom Dixon explained, houses would have a shoot that ran into your basement— if you were lucky enough to have a basement—where the coal would be dumped for storage. It was the job of the youngest kid in the household to restoke the stove at about 2 a.m. each night.[82] For 25 cents you bought a bushel of coal from Weaver's Ice and Coal yard on Miami Street, or in later years you had coal delivered to your house by the Floyd family. If you didn't have much money you would walk down the tracks of the Erie Railroad hoping that the fireman on the train had "accidentally" tossed a couple of shovel loads of coal over the side for you to collect.[83] If you had wood delivered to your house instead of coal, you were considered "high-hat."[84]

There were two choices for lighting in your house. One way was with a kerosene lamp and the other, if you were wealthier, was a gas lamp. Regardless of your choice you went to Clohessy's Store to buy the supplies.[85] There was also a neighborhood iceman who went door to door with his cart to drop off blocks of ice to keep your icebox cold.[86] The woman of the house would put a card in the window, which told the iceman how many pounds of ice to drop off (25 lb., 50 lb., etc). Another resident remembered that if you were not regular in draining the drip pan under the icebox you would be left with a real mess.[87] Even by the 1870s most of the Ward still lacked a central water system and there were few private wells.[88] Therefore, as Congressman McCarthy explained, his grandmother would have to leave the Ward and walk all the way to Main Street and Terrace in order to get clean water for the house. This demanding yet essential chore would have been typical for women in the Ward in the 19th century.

CHAPTER TEN

THE CATHOLIC CHURCH: INSTITUTION IN THE WARD

The church and its teachings pervaded their whole life; it formed their moral outlook.

– Margaret Ann Kilgallon, Ward memoirist

For first generation Ward residents, the Catholic Church was not almighty and certainly not all-powerful. Buffalo's vast network of Catholic institutions did not exist until the end of Bishop Timon's reign, and the sacramental life and regular devotions until his arrival were scarce for some worshippers and nonexistent for others. Subsequent generations in the Ward, however, were fully immersed in the life of the Catholic faith. In one First Ward manuscript the writer proclaimed, "the church and its teachings pervaded their whole life; it formed their moral outlook."[1] Furthermore, church attendance every Sunday and enrollment in a Catholic elementary school were basic expectations.[2] The Irish, German, Italian, and Polish Catholics of the Ward lived the life of the institutional church with Sunday mass, weekly confession, summer festivals, St. Patrick's Day, May Procession, Christmas pageants, and the whole calendar of religious holidays.[629] Residents were immersed in the entire Catholic parish cycle of events: baptism, First Communion, parochial school, confirmation, marriage, devotions, parish sports teams, summer festivals, and then funerals.

By the late 19th century, "the parish would become key to Catholics' understanding of their social worlds and lifestyles," as one Ward expert claimed.[4] Professor William Jenkins added that religion for First Ward Irish immigrants was not simply a badge of ethnic identity, but an institutional force."[5] Sister Helen Parot, a Mercy sister of Polish heritage who grew up in the Ward, commented that the religious in this era served in the important capacity of social workers. People turned to them for all of their needs—taking care of the sick, serving the poor, and educating their children.[6] Congressman Richard McCarthy claimed that the clergy were not just concerned with the parishioners' spiritual welfare, but also their economic welfare, social advancement, and education. On one occasion, the congressman asked his father if the clergy was influential in the Old First Ward. The senior McCarthy looked at him, laughed, and replied, "They were ALL powerful."[7] Ward resident Eddie Stack described how confessions on Saturday and Mass on Sunday were part of the weekly routine.[8] While the influence of the church on the lives of residents was primarily a positive force, sometimes it seemed to border on tyranny. An example is evident in the March 1937 St. Brigid's parish bulletin, where the pastor listed each parishioner next to their yearly donation to the church. Parishioners who had not contributed anything to the parish were also included on the list for everyone to witness. That might have been fair enough, but to add insult to those who hadn't contributed, a statement was typed on the top of the bulletin that read:

> The following list contains the names of those who are supposed to be supporters of our church. As a matter of fact, it contains the names of some who are decidedly not supporters of the church. The continued blanks after their names tell the tale of their disloyalty. Month after month and year after year some of these have failed to pay their assessment or to take any interest whatsoever in their parish. They are the dead wood with which our parish is encumbered. Have they no sense of honor, no feeling of shame? Must we continue to regard them as a liability to the parish? Let them question their conscience occasionally in regard to this matter, for it is a matter of conscience![9]

As time went on, residents' lives became more and more intertwined with their parish. In addition to weekly worship services, most were educated at the parish school, played on the parish baseball team, and socialized with others from the immediate community. One of the strongest parishes in the Ward—if not in the city of Buffalo—was St. Bridget's (St. Brigid's). As the first church in the Ward it was considered the spiritual home' for Ward residents throughout the mid-to-late 1800s, and held a lofty position throughout the entire diocese. As has been mentioned, dozens of prominent priests, lawyers, businessmen, and physicians graduated from St. Bridget's elementary school, many of whom made an impact in Buffalo and beyond. Up until World War II, St. Brigid's was also the most affluent parish in the Ward—many doctors and lawyers were members.

There were several memorable pastors of St. Bridget's who made tremendous contributions to the local community. Father William Gleason—who baptized, confirmed, married, and buried thousands of First Ward residents during his 24-year tenure—left an indelible mark. He was succeeded by the future Bishop of Buffalo, James E. Quigley, who only served for a year, but made a lasting bond with the parishioners, remodeled the rectory, and drew up plans for a new school.[10] The talented Father James A. Lanigan—who was the top administrator of the diocese after Bishop Steven Ryan's death—took over the reins of St. Bridget's parish after Father Quigley was elevated to replace Bishop Ryan. The fact that a future bishop and the top administrator of the diocese were appointed to lead St. Bridget's is evidence of the important standing that this parish had in the diocese at the turn of the 20th century.

Fr. James Lanigan, born in Nova Scotia and educated in Montreal, was ordained to the priesthood in Buffalo by the second Bishop of Buffalo in 1869. He served as an assistant at St. Bridget's shortly after his ordination and then returned decades later to become pastor. This beloved priest was sort of a Renaissance man as he was an eloquent pulpit preacher, a linguist, an accomplished musician, and an artist. The Sisters of Mercy, with whom he closely worked, remembered him as a talented pastor, and "one of the most accomplished and devoted priests in the United States."[11] At his death, the diocesan newspaper related a few of his accomplishments: he was dedicated to educating children as his first ambition; he added Greek and Latin to the grammar school curriculum; he organized a student choir that was second to none; and he instituted the ringing of the curfew bell to protect children in the neighborhood.[12] Father Lanigan was also responsible for significantly enlarging the school at St. Bridget's to accommodate roughly 1,000 students. In one First Ward manuscript, the writer remembered the financial struggles the church experienced which led to "tear-choked pleas" from Father Lanigan that if more money was not donated the ornate marble altar would have to be sent back to Europe.[13] Whether this was true or not we don't know, but the donations kept flowing and the parish kept prospering.

Father Luke Sharkey was another notable pastor of St. Brigid's who served from 1920-1939, after Father Daniel O'Brien's leadership. Father Sharkey was responsible for updating the church with a beautiful set of stations-of-the-cross, new windows, and an elaborate main altar. As previously mentioned, sometime in the early 1920s, during his leadership, the name of St. Bridget's was officially changed to the more authentically Irish name St. Brigid's.[14] However, it was also during his tenure that St. Brigid's started to experience major changes, weakening its status as the spiritual home of the Ward. Scores of people left the First Ward for South Buffalo and the previously overcrowded mother church of the Ward started to decline. In fact, in 1927 St. Brigid's lost more parishioners than any other parish in the diocese.[15] The year Sharkey left, the Commodore Perry Projects were under construction, and the spiritually and historically important parish was about to change forever.

In one of the histories of the Mercy Sisters, written in 1958, the author gives an update on St. Brigid's in that year. According to the sister, the parish which used to be filled with Irish parishioners was now populated by those of Polish and Italian backgrounds. In fact, Italian children from the Dante Project were leaving their home parish of St. Joseph's Cathedral to attend St. Brigid's school. The Mercy historian lamented that the school and the sisters' convent were both desperately in need of repairs and renovations. One positive trend she noted was that while the enrollment at St. Brigid's parish and school had been declining as people moved away from the area, the number of families at the nearby Perry Projects was helping enrollment.[16] One of these St. Brigid's students from the Perry Projects was James Ambrose Johnson Jr.—later known as Rick James—who was the famous funk musician of 1980s fame.[17] The Mercy historian claimed that the academic rigor at St. Brigid's remained lofty as was evidenced by the fact that two boys, Michael Coffey and Francis O'Connor, both came in second place for the annual diocesan scholarship in 1955 and 1956 respectively against hundreds of other students.[18]

St. Stephen's Parish

In about 1874, businesses that were engaged in the burgeoning iron and steel industries started to move into the Ward and surrounding area. This development led to even more workers moving into the already overcrowded Ward, so some were forced to settle further down Elk Street toward South Buffalo.[19] St. Bridget's was already overcrowded so Bishop Stephen Ryan decided to build a new church for the residents in this area and named the church after his patron saint, St. Stephen.[20] This area down Elk Street and its surrounding area was technically outside the Ward boundaries at the time. There is still a lively debate today about whether this neighborhood, which gained the nickname the "Valley" in the 1960s, is part of the Ward. The former Erie County Sheriff Thomas Higgins, who is a native of this area, is passionate that it is. He acknowledges that the Valley (so named because the area was surrounded by bridges and viaducts and the only way out was over a bridge) technically lies outside the First Ward's former political boundaries, but the spirit of the people was the same as those from the Ward.[21] The reason that the Valley neighborhood has been included in this book and not other nearby areas like the Hydraulics is that there was a strong link between the Ward and the Valley. Many of the initial settlers of the Valley were from the Ward, many of the sisters from St. Bridget's convent staffed both schools, the assistant pastor at St. Bridget's started the new parish at St. Stephen's, and many of the Valley residents worked for businesses inside the Ward boundaries. The bonds between the two communities were deep. The purists, however, are correct—for most of Buffalo's incorporation this area was not technically part of the First Ward.

Father Eugene McDermott, the assistant pastor at St. Bridget's, was put in charge of establishing St. Stephen's parish, and the cornerstone was laid on September 4, 1875. Father McDermott initially constructed a plain, brick building with a simple rectory. But within just a few years this once sparsely settled area was also overcrowded and so too was the new church. Therefore, Father McDermott worked with the congregation to erect an impressive stone building which "would be a credit to the congregation and an ornament to that part of the city."[22] The architect Frederick Hampel designed a pillar-less interior, which was one of the best examples of this construction technique at the time. The larger and statelier church was finally completed in 1888. The original design had two large spires, but because of structural weakness these were torn down sometime after 1932.

In late summer of 1882, Father Eugene McDermott secured some Mercy sisters from the convent at St. Bridget's to start a school at St. Stephen's parish for about a hundred students. Sisters Mary Clare Loftus and Mary Liguori Brown were the first two teachers at the school. Assisting them later were Sisters Mary Antonio Holmes, Mary Francis Dolan, Mary Agatha Grant, and Mary Evangelist Gainey.[23] For ten years, the nuns who staffed St. Stephen's school made the arduous 1.5 mile walk back and forth from their St. Bridget's convent—many times in the middle of winter with the brutal lake winds in their faces—in order to teach the students in this community. In 1894, the growing student body exceeded the initial school building capacity, so the congregation erected an imposing three-story brick school at the corner of Elk Street and Euclid Avenue.[24]

A few years earlier, Father McDermott had raised enough money to build a new rectory for the priests, but he realized that the Sisters of Mercy's need for a convent at St. Stephen's was a more pressing need and he gave the money to them instead.[25] McDermott was remembered as "a great-hearted priest, ever ready to sympathize with the needy poor, ever ready to help the distressed."[26] During difficult financial times like labor strikes he would buy fifteen or sixteen carloads of coal at wholesale rates and distribute it to the poor.[27] The smiling Father McDermott was remembered for encouraging the students in his school to be dedicated to their studies. With his death in 1898, Father H.M. Leddy replaced him and was responsible for handling the large debt that was accumulated during the two-decade long building boom. Leddy Street in the Valley is named for this popular priest who was remembered for his gentleness and for the fact that he was temperate in word and in action.[28] In June 1913, a tragedy struck St. Stephen's parish when the Husted Mills plant, on Elk Street plant, had a terrible explosion. This disaster—mostly likely caused by spontaneous combustion—killed thirty-three people and injured another eighty workers and residents from the parish. The sister of pastor Father Barrett claimed that she saw more death following the explosion than she had seen as a survivor of the sinking of the Titanic four years before. While this claim was certainly hyperbole, the destruction was nonetheless devastating for such a close-knit community.[29] In fact, the nearby explosion was so powerful that it shattered the west transept window of the church titled "St. Stephen Addressing the Council." A second tragedy struck St. Stephen's parish on December 27, 1948 when a horrific rectory fire killed Father Martin Fell, the pastor of St. Stephens, and his assistant Father John Peel.[30] Both were remembered for bringing much comfort to the parishioners who suffered the loss of loved ones during World War II.[31]

By the 1950s, the Polish and Ukrainian immigrants were moving into the neighborhood and the parish demographics quickly changed. In 1952, one Mercy sister fondly recalled the Polish residents' loyalty to their heritage. She commented on the expense and time that Polish parents spent in sewing native costumes for their children who participated in a parish Jubilee celebration.[32] By 1958, a sizable Irish-American contingency remained, but the majority of parishioners were now Polish.[33] Extensive changes were made to the church in the 1960s and 1970s to conform to the Vatican II liturgical changes. Notable parishioners of this parish included Bishop Joseph Burke, Sheriff Tom Higgins, Jimmy Slattery (part of his childhood was in the Ward and part in the Valley), Peter Crotty, and Jack Shimski of Harvey Place who originally coined the term "the Valley" in the 1960s.

St. Stephen's Parish also produced many priests and religious sisters over its history. By 1975, the 100-year anniversary of St. Stephens, the parish had produced one bishop, Joseph A. Burke, and at least twenty-two priests including Austin Crotty, John J. McMahon, Michael Lillis, OFM, Cornelius Shea, Daniel O'Connell, Edward Fitzhenry, Harold Blake, OFM, David Herlihy, Dennis Shea, Henry Romanowski, Leonard Racki and Charles Zadora. The parish also produced at least twelve sisters, nine of whom were Mercy Sisters including Mary Veronica Kinsella, Mary Alicia Barry, Mary Marcella, Mary Josita Crotty, Mary Johanna, Mary Rosara, Mary Catherine Durkin, and Mary Alma McGrath.

One of the most successful of these religious was Sister Mary Mechtilde O'Connor, who was the founder and administrator of Kenmore Mercy Hospital.[34] She was born on April 15, 1886 and given the name Anne Margaret O'Connor. Her parents Mr. and Mrs. John O'Connor ran a grocery store on Smith Street and were leaders at St. Stephen's Church. Both Anne and her sister, Sister Mary Florence, RSM, joined the Mercy Sisters after attending St. Stephen's elementary school. Sr. Mechtilde went to Central High School and Buffalo State Normal School and then did some studies at Canisius College and Catholic University in Washington, D.C.[35]

After professing vows, O'Connor became an elementary school teacher and later a principal at several Mercy schools in Western New York including St. John Evangelist, St. Martin's, St. Teresa's, and St. Thomas Aquinas School. In 1930, at age forty-four, Mary Mechtilde, after a successful career in education, accepted a new challenge: running St. Jerome's Hospital in Batavia, New York. As an effective administrator in Batavia, she was later made the administrator at the flagship Sisters of Mercy hospital: Mercy Hospital in South Buffalo. During her tenure at Mercy she oversaw the construction of three more wings at this important South Buffalo institution. All of these experiences prepared her for her biggest challenge: the construction of a new hospital in Kenmore, New York. In 1948, she spearheaded the fundraising and planning efforts for this new 100-bed hospital. After it opened in 1951, she served as the hospital administrator until 1977. A writer from the *Courier-Express* described the keys to her success: "her courage, determination and business skills guided the hospital through its difficult early years."[36] Even into her late 80s, she was still guiding the hospital through numerous expansions and building projects.

Fortunately, her work over the years did not go unnoticed. Sr. Mechtilde was honored by the National Jewish Hospital and Research Center in Denver, Colorado for her concern for the needy. Locally she won the Judge John D. Hillery Memorial Scholarship Award. Bishop James McNulty presented her with the "Pro Ecclesiae et Pontifice" medal from Pope Paul VI for "her magnificent contribution to our society as an educator and administrator."[37] The grocer's daughter from Smith Street was also the first woman to receive the Canisius College President's Medal for her work in the classroom and with the sick. The Town of Tonawanda Republican Committee gave her the Public Service award— she was the first non-politician to receive it—as the "Most Distinguished Citizen in the Town of Tonawanda." She was also a fellow of the American College of Hospital Administrators. In the lobby of Kenmore Mercy there is a plaque with her picture commemorating her service at the hospital from 1951 to 1977. In a different era, it is quite possible that the talented Sister Mary Mechtilde may have served as a successful CEO of a Buffalo corporation.

Our Lady of Perpetual Help Parish

At the end of the 19ᵗʰ century, St. Bridget's and St. Stephen's parishes were both overflowing with congregants. It was decided that a new parish was needed in the geographical center of the Ward to handle the growing Catholic community. The first services of this new parish, called Our Lady of Perpetual Help—later referred to as Pets by the locals—were held in the "Club House" at 100 Louisiana Street on July 11, 1897. Father Richard C. O'Connell used Mrs. Glavin's Saloon—later Bill Travis's Delicatessen—as the temporary rectory when he first settled in the Ward.[38] Father O'Connell then purchased property at the corner of Sandusky and Alabama Streets to build the new church.

On November 21, 1897, thousands turned out to watch Bishop James Quigley lay the cornerstone of O.L.P.H. followed by a parade down Sandusky Street. A local newspaper account commented that, "it was a great day for that portion of the city, for it meant the realizing of hope, the consummation of a long sustained effort among the people of that section of the city to secure a suitable place of worship."[39] The Gothic-style church made of Medina sandstone, built over three years at a cost of $65,000, was dedicated on March 21, 1900. The stained glass windows—made in Innsbruck, Austria—are the most beautiful feature in the church. O.L.P.H. parish also included a 16-room school built in 1909 and run by the Franciscan Sisters of Allegany. The sisters also lived in a convent next to the church.

After a fruitful decade ministering to the residents of the Ward, the founding pastor, Father Richard O'Connell, died on February 8, 1907. The local residents had such affection for Father O'Connell, who was remembered for his great demeanor and good preaching, that they requested that Sandusky Street be changed to O'Connell Avenue in his honor. This request was honored the year he passed away, and it is the only street that has been officially changed in the First Ward excluding the honorary designations for certain streets such as Gene McCarthy Way or Jimmy Slattery Way.

Aside from Father O'Connell, the famous newspaperman Jack O'Brian fondly remembered one of the assistants at Pets named Father Francis "Sol" Growney. He recalled that Father Growney used to wear green cashmere sweaters while driving around in a green Pontiac convertible with his Grand Slam golf clubs hanging out of the car. Father Growney was tied for the best score at South Park Golf Club with a 29 for nine holes. He also was a respectable actor who used to work with Katharine Cornell before he became a priest. It was Father Growney who taught Jack O'Brian about theater, which was invaluable to him in his career as an entertainment writer.[40]

Msgr. John Nash, Reverend Joseph A. Burke, and Msgr. John P. Boland

By the end of the nineteenth century, the Catholic institutions in the First Ward and Valley started to produce their own priests and sisters; many went on to make a profound impact on the diocese of Buffalo and beyond. John Nash, John Boland, and Joseph Burke, all of them taught by the Sisters of Mercy, were three who made the most significant contributions. Together, these three dominated the building of the Irish parish system in South Buffalo and were involved with land procurement for parishes, fundraising for church buildings, managing the Catholic hospital network, establishing parochial schools, and delving into local and state labor issues.

John Joseph Nash, born one month after the end of the Civil War on May 18, 1865, was the son of Simon Nash from Killadysart, County Clare and Catherine Mahoney, whose family came from County Cork. This is the same Simon Nash mentioned earlier who established a successful coal distribution business. Simon followed his brother Richard, a lake sailor, to Buffalo around 1860. At one time, Simon worked as a grocer and then later as a weighmaster at a coal dealer on Elk Street. He and his wife Catherine were married at St. Bridget's Church on January 3, 1864 and settled at 230 Hamburg Street. Their eldest son, John, was educated by the Mercy Sisters at St. Bridget's where he was identified as a bright student, and was asked in 1877 to give an address at a school program to the Vicar General of the Diocese. Interestingly John himself would serve in this same important capacity for the diocese of Buffalo years later. After excelling at St. Bridget's and then at Canisius High School, Nash, at the young age of seventeen, entered the seminary and was sent to the prestigious Catholic University of Innsbruck in Austria—he was only the second Buffalonian ever sent there, even more remarkable because he came from the working-class First Ward. His fellow St. Bridget's classmate, Joseph Garen, also a star student, was sent to the Propaganda College in Rome to study to become a priest, which supports the fact that in that era the best and brightest were often encouraged to enter the religious life.

Ordained a priest in April 1888 in Freising, Bavaria, Nash returned to Buffalo and became pastor of a rural church in Dayton, New York for four years. In 1902, Bishop James Quigley tasked Father Nash with creating a new parish in the southern part of the city, and with the help of about fifty men and women in the South Park district of Buffalo, John Nash founded Holy Family Parish. The original church was established in a renovated barn because funds were lacking to build a proper church.[41] Eventually, a prominent church as well as a school were built on South Park Avenue, and the former St. Bridget's student chose the Sisters of Mercy to staff it. Nash also assisted the Sisters of Mercy in establishing their first hospital on Tifft Street in the old William J. Conners' home. Nash was a very capable administrator of this important parish, and he was remembered as a strict disciplinarian. He was known to walk South Park Avenue where he strictly enforced a 7:00 p.m. curfew for boys who might be wandering about.

In 1934, this son of a coal dealer was elevated by Pope Pius XI to the title of Prothonotary Apostolic, which was the highest designation given to a priest below the title of bishop—Father Nelson Baker was the only other one who held the title at that time.[42] In 1937, John J. Nash was elevated to the administrator of the Buffalo diocese, and presided over the diocese for six months as Buffalo waited for Rome to appoint a new bishop; eventually Bishop John Duffy from Syracuse, New York was selected. Witnessing the expansion of even more Irish into South Buffalo, the forward thinking Father Nash purchased land on Ridgewood Road to establish a future parish: St. Ambrose Church was established in 1949.[43] Nash never forgot his Irish roots and served as the Erie County Chaplain for the Ancient Order of Hibernians. Throughout his years as a priest, Father Nash was also the de facto chaplain for the Sisters of Mercy, where he tirelessly presided over solemn masses, funerals, and dedications related to the Sisters and their work. This larger than life character was also down to earth and loved to relax with a cigar and enjoyed listening to episodes of the Lone Ranger on the radio.[44]

In the winter of 1953, at the age of eight-eight, Father John Nash, who had served eight bishops, including his former altar boy, Joseph Burke, passed away. In his eulogy, Bishop Joseph Burke praised John Nash for being "a learned theologian, a unique spiritual leader, and as an enthusiastic promoter of the religious education of the youth committed to his care."[45] The bishop also reminded the congregation about Msgr. Nash's financial generosity for aiding students who pursued higher education after graduating from Holy Family School. Burke added that the "whole diocese is indebted to him for his numerous contributions to the welfare of our citizenry..."[46] A Sisters of Mercy historian stated, "his name is written indelibly on the hearts of his people, not because of the honors conferred upon him, but because he was the living exemplification of the virtuous priest."[47] In his will John Nash left his assets to causes he cared about: $3,000 for high school tuition assistance for students of Holy Family Church, $1,000 to the St. Vincent DePaul Society, and $500 to furnish an annual Thanksgiving dinner for his beloved Sisters of Mercy.[48] There is a plaque in the vestibule of Holy Family Church in honor of the founder of this important South Buffalo parish.

Success can sometimes be measured by the impact one has on those under his charge. This was the case with Father John Nash whose altar boy eventually rose to an even higher position in the diocese than he did. Joseph Aloysius Burke, son of Joseph S. Burke, an Irish immigrant who worked as a boilermaker, and Amelia Howard Burke, of Welsh and Irish descent, was born on August 27, 1886 and was raised on Abbott Corners Road (later South Park Avenue) in the Valley. Burke's father eventually left his job as a boilermaker to open a saloon and boarding house on Indiana Street in the Ward. In the 1890s, the elder Burke witnessed the migration of people to South Buffalo so he moved the family and opened a new saloon and hotel at 575 Abbott Corners Road. Bishop James Quigley baptized the young Joseph Burke at St. Joseph's Cathedral, and he was educated by the Mercy Sisters first at St. Bridget's and later at St. Stephen's school.[49] On his World War I draft card, the future bishop was described as short in height, medium build, with gray eyes and black hair.[50] It was said that his first desire to become a priest occurred at six years old. After his studies at Canisius High School and Canisius College he entered the priesthood and studied at the University of Innsbruck in Austria, following in the footsteps of his former pastor, Msgr. Nash. Father Burke served as an army chaplain on the French and Belgian Front during World War I when he was part of the 91st Division, also called the "Wild West Division."[51]

Msgr. Burke was elevated to auxiliary Bishop of Buffalo in 1943, and, in a touching tribute, John Nash exclaimed, "The old pastor bows submissively to his auxiliary bishop assuring him no yoke could be sweeter, no burden more light, while from a heart overflowing with gladness he thanks God who permitted him to live to see this day."[52] On April 30, 1952, Auxiliary Bishop Burke was elevated as the ninth Bishop of Buffalo. During his ten-year reign he was particularly dedicated to the foreign missions, the Holy Name Society, the Puerto Rican immigrants in Buffalo, the building of St. John Vianney Seminary, and to displaced persons. The son of a laborer from the First Ward, he was also a natural advocate for labor. Unfortunately, in October of 1962, during the first week of the Vatican II Council, the Bishop passed away from a sudden heart attack.

Father John P. Boland, another native priest from the Ward, born April 27, 1888 only one year after his neighbor Joseph Burke, was nationally known for his involvement in labor and social justice causes. John Boland lived at 299 Elk Street and attended St. Bridget's primary school. His vocation to the priesthood eventually took him to Rome, Italy where he received three doctoral degrees. After returning from Europe, the tall, medium-build, blue-eyed priest was made the assistant pastor of St. Joseph's Cathedral in downtown Buffalo. Later, he returned to the Ward where he was appointed assistant pastor of St. Bridget's around 1915. Father Boland's fluency in Italian from his studies in Rome assisted him in additional ministerial responsibilities with the growing Italian community. Boland wrote two books in Italian: "Workingman's Prayer Book" and "The Workingman's Catechism." In addition, he founded St. Anthony's (Italian) Church in Lackawanna, New York. In 1920, he served as director of Catholic hospitals for Buffalo, where he was responsible for the building of Mercy Hospital in South Buffalo. In 1926, both Father Boland and Father Nash laid the cornerstone and made the dedication for this new 200-bed hospital.[53] In 1934, after his stint as director of hospitals, Msgr. Boland was appointed by President Franklin D. Roosevelt to chair the National Labor Board district office.[54]

As his expertise in labor relations grew, he was appointed the first Chairman of the New York State Labor Relations Board in 1937 where he served for five years. In 1939, he created the Diocesan Labor School in Buffalo. Boland, who grew up among the working class, was sympathetic to their plight. Trained in Rome, he was also armed with the church's pronouncements in favor of organizing trade unions. With both of these experiences, he advocated on behalf of the worker's right to organize. Boland railed against business owners who were not in favor of collective bargaining, but he was also opposed to the communist radicals and racketeering elements in the labor movement. He believed that the government's involvement in labor should be restricted to a mediator in disputes. Thus, Boland forged a middle ground that was in keeping with his First Ward roots: protective of the workingman's right to organize but opposed to the communists' desire for government's active involvement in the labor movement.[55]

In 1942, Father Boland became pastor of St. Thomas Aquinas School in South Buffalo, and at the same time served in the War Relief Services in Europe, the Middle East, and Japan during World War II. In 1948, Msgr. Boland was recognized for his efforts in this cause. Boland was stationed in London during the last days of the war and was active in assisting Dutch people who were interned in the German labor camps in 1945. The government of the Netherlands gave him the "Order of Orange and Nassau" award for this relief work as director of the Dutch-Belgian districts for the National Catholic Conference.[56] Meanwhile, the Italian government recognized him for his relief efforts for Italians, and he was commended with the Grand Order of SS Mauretias and Lawrence award.[57] Father Boland also served as a labor relations consultant to General Douglas MacArthur in Japan in 1947. The indefatigable Father Boland finished his illustrious career as pastor of St. Thomas Aquinas in South Buffalo during the 1950s. Both he and his former neighbor, Bishop Joseph Burke, celebrated the Sisters of Mercy centenary anniversary mass on February 11, 1958.[58] Boland's remarkable career, which included ministries with Buffalo's Italian community, the labor movement, War Relief Services, and his beloved Sisters of Mercy came to an end with his death in 1968. All three of these men—Nash, Burke, and Boland—left a deep and lasting impact on the Diocese of Buffalo.

Priests and Sisters from the Ward

There were other notable priests and nuns from the First Ward and the Valley. Vincent Donovan, the brother of William "Wild Bill" Donovan, became a successful Dominican friar. Like his famous brother, he grew up on Michigan Street and then attended Nardin Academy and St. Joseph's Collegiate Institute. A lifelong teacher, he taught at Providence College and the Dominican University in Rome, Italy. Donovan's teaching specialty was Gregorian chant, and he was a proponent of the teachings of St. Thomas Aquinas. He founded the Catholic Thought Association of America and also served as a chaplain at Sing Sing prison. Another accomplished priest was Father Harold Blake, son of a carpenter, who was born in 1900 and raised at 2 Harvey Street. Father Blake became a Franciscan friar and immediately after ordination taught at the Franciscan seminary in Callicoon, New York. In 1940, until his death in 1973, he held the important position of Superior of the Franciscan Friars at various priories in Patterson, New Jersey; Boston; Fairlawn, New Jersey; and Providence, Rhode Island.

Other priests and sisters from the Ward, while not achieving the fame and recognition of Nash, Burke and Boland, were integral in building up the church in Buffalo. The Patrick and Catherine Roche family from the Ward raised two children (Edward and Catherine) who dedicated their lives to the church in their native city. Patrick J. Roche, was the son of James Roche and Anne Maddock from County Wexford, Ireland. James and Anne Roche brought their family to Buffalo near the start of the Civil War. By 1860, the Roche family was settled at the corner of Louisiana and Perry Streets where James worked as a joiner. Their son Patrick, who was born in Ireland and raised in the Ward, worked as a fireman and an engineer. In 1881 he married Catherine Brinkworth, daughter of the earlier mentioned John Brinkworth, and they settled at 290 Perry Street raising seven children. Two of their children, Edward and Catherine, attended St. Bridget's school where the seeds of their vocations were planted. Catherine Roche, born in 1901, attended St. Bridget's school for a while, and eventually graduated from Mt. Mercy Academy. She taught for a few years at St. Stephen's elementary school in the Valley before entering the Sisters of Mercy in 1923 where she received the name Sister Edmunda. Throughout the period from the 1920s to the 1940s she taught at various schools throughout Western New York. In the 1950s to 1960s she served as principal at St. James in Jamestown, New York and then at St. Bonaventure in West Seneca, New York. After dedicating over half of a century to teaching hundreds of students and running several Catholic schools, Sister Edmunda came to rest. Her fellow sisters remember her as having a quiet sense of humor and "a special gift to elicit a smile and a good laugh when it was most needed."[59]

Her brother Edward L. Roche attended St. Bridget's elementary school until he was eleven years old, and then the family moved to Holy Family Parish. He attended Canisius High School, Canisius College, and St. Bonaventure where he was ordained a priest of the Diocese of Buffalo on March 7, 1925. For his first assignment he was named an assistant pastor at St. Joseph's New Cathedral and at one time served at St. Brigid's. In 1949, he was named pastor of Our Mother of Good Counsel in Blasdell, New York. During his tenure there he built a new elementary school and a new church, which was fully paid for in just a few years. There is plaque on the back wall of the vestibule in his honor. In 1959, he was named a domestic prelate with the title Right Reverend Monsignor by Pope John XXIII.[60] Edward and Catherine Roche were typical of many others who sacrificed much in order to raise up the prospects of those in their community.

Another honor for the Roche family would come many years later when Father William J. Roche, nephew of Edward and Edmunda, was chosen as the grand marshal of the 1998 Buffalo St. Patrick's Day Parade on Delaware Avenue. This role often goes to a prominent politician, bishop, or other important community figure, so it was an honor for it to go to a parish priest. While Father William Roche was not born in the Ward, his roots were in the Ward, and in 1964 he became the temporary administrator of Our Lady of Perpetual Help in the Ward.

The author of one Ward manuscript remembers other First Warders who made a contribution to the church including Father Donnelly, Father Harmon (the pastor of Mother of Good Council Church), Father Sullivan (pastor of St. Bonaventure Church) and Father Juvenal Ellis (teacher at Bishop Timon High School.)[61] Other Ward-born clergy included Fathers Donny Fitzgerald, Billy Fitzpatrick, Larry Milby, Danny Grosso, Billy Frankhauser, Tom Conway, Donny Devine, Joe Coughlin, Lee Mays and Art Sullivan.[62] Just as many women became religious sisters. Sister Marie Bernard of the Mercy Sisters, one of Rose Procknal's fifteen children, entered the Sisters of Mercy, as did Joan Sherry from St. Brigid's parish.[63] Some streets in the Ward produced more religious than others. From Kentucky Street, there was Mary Ann Michaels, who took the name Sister Mary Nadine; Mary Ann Hoare, who took the name Sister Madonna; and Sister Helen Parot who joined the Sisters of Mercy. On the same street, Patricia Redmond became an Allegany Franciscan sister. Several blocks away, the Hens family, who lived across the street from Pets on O'Connell Avenue, raised four girls who entered into the religious life: two became Mercy Sisters and two became Sisters of the Divine Child. Barbara Hahn, also from O'Connell Avenue, entered the Allegany Franciscans. Father Don Fitzgerald's sister, Sister Mary Celine, also became a religious sister.

The Ward, which in its early years had been so dependent on priests and sisters from outside of the community, was now producing religious leaders of its own who provided leadership in the parochial schools, hospitals, and parishes throughout Western New York. Their multitude of contributions to the welfare of others was just another sign that First Warders had arrived. Bishop John Timon would have been proud.

The Harbor Inn, one of the oldest
waterfront saloons, built in 1869
and demolished in 2003.

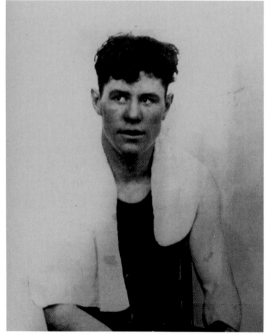

The handsome Jimmy Slattery,
became the Light Heavyweight
Champion of the World.

Michael Shea, during the height of his entertainment empire.

Michael Shea's magnificent theater on Main Street in Buffalo.

Algie McGuire (in the center with a white hat) stands with his fans in front of the Mutual Rowing Club. From left to right: Irving Barrett, Mike Daley, Leo Sullivan, Ed Dray, Huskey Lampsher, Vic Sullivan, Algie McGuire, Bill Meegan, Jim Nelson, Joe Cullen, Dan Bouquard, Denis Driscoll, John Sullivan, Tim Meegan.

Graduates of the class of 1946 at St. Brigid's school.

The Mercy Sisters at St. Bridget's school educated thousands of Ward children.

The bustling Elk Street Market where residents purchased food and dry goods.

44

Father James Lanigan advocated
for the workers in the Great
Strike of 1899. Lanigan Park and
Fieldhouse are named after him.

45

Father Richard C. O'Connell
founded Our Lady of Perpetual Help
parish. After his death, Sandusky
Street was changed to O'Connell
Avenue in his honor.

World War I national hero, Colonel William J. Donovan.

(Collection of Buffalo and Erie County Historical Society, used by permission)

Father John Boland was a national church expert on labor issues.

The retail scene on Elk Street was vibrant throughout most of the Ward's history.

(Collection of Buffalo and Erie County Historical Society, used by permission)

An iconic picture of school children, Louisiana Street near South Street in the Ward.

(Collection of Buffalo and Erie County Historical Society, used by permission)

Ma Carr, one of many women entrepreneurs in the Ward, ran a popular soda bar on South Park Avenue.

In 1959, the *Tewksbury* freighter broke from its moorings, floated down the river, and destroyed the Michigan Avenue bridge. (From the coll. of Lower Lakes Marine Historical Society)

One of several 19th century Lake Erie storms that demolished the Beach community.
(From the coll. of Lower Lakes Marine Historical Society)

The Ohio Basin was gradually filled in with city garbage. Eventually, in the 1950s, it was completely filled in with the remnants of Frank Lloyd Wright's Larkin Building. It was later turned into Father Conway Park. (From the coll. of Lower Lakes Marine Historical Society)

First Ward lawyer George "Chickie" Evans (center) with Jim Mockler (left) and John Horan (right).

First Warders from Louisiana, St. Clair and Kentucky Streets gathered to go on a summer outing in July 1925. Some of the families represented include the Regans, Manns, Sullivans, Gibsons, O'Briens, Donovans, Granvilles, Houlihans, McBrides, Diggins and Leahys.

The 8'7" John "Red" Carroll (center) was the fourth tallest man in the world.

Mayor Jimmy Griffin was the longest serving mayor of Buffalo. Many of his efforts were directed towards improving the First Ward and downtown Buffalo. (Collection of Buffalo and Erie County Historical Society, used by permission)

Gene McCarthy serving a beer at his famous tavern on Hamburg Street.

Ed Carney was secretary of Local 109, the only grain scoopers union in the world.

Ray Lawley served for many years as the Erie County Republican Chairman.

First Warder Thomas Connors was one of thousands of waterfront workers in Buffalo.

Mayor Jimmy Griffin (center) with Paul Snyder, (left) Larry Quinn (behind), and Ed Rutkowski (right) at a development project. (Collection of Buffalo and Erie County Historical Society, used by permission)

In the First Ward there was a unique intersection between the residential and industrial.

This aerial photo of the Ward shows Elevator Alley (A), Father Conway Park (B), the Buffalo River (C), City Ship Canal (D), and Commodore Perry Projects (E).

(From the coll. of Lower Lakes Marine Historical Society)

In 2003, for the last time scoopers manually shovel grain out of the hull of a freighter.

Scooper President Fred Brill (center) with Mike McCarthy (left) and Bob Matevia, Jr. (right) on the last day of a 160 year tradition of scooping.

For several decades, First Ward resident Peggy Overdorf has been a leading advocate for the Valley and the First Ward.

A tugboat carries the ice boom along Elevator Alley.

PART III

THE WARD TRANSFORMED

CHAPTER ELEVEN

PEOPLE LEAVING, PEOPLE ARRIVING

A maze of crooked streets, railway tracks, viaducts and ramshackle buildings. Glimmering yellow lights flashing dully through the fogs that sweep up from the harbour. Swarms of children, gossiping women. Men with dinner pails and odorous pipes. Stunted trees lining the sidewalks. Dingy churches and halls, blackened by the smoke of years. Dingy houses and dingy schools. That is Buffalo's old First Ward...
– Willis Wilber, writer for the *Buffalo Times*

From the turn of the 20th century through the Great Depression, life in the First Ward was marked by change. Some things, however, did remain constant. Irish immigrants were still arriving in the Ward, but at a much slower rate than during the 19th century. Moreover, waterfront industries were booming which meant that employment prospects were bright. But some Ward residents were growing tired of the pollution, noise, and health hazards that came with living in overcrowded industrial neighborhoods. They longed for homes in a pastoral setting, which would offer newer amenities and larger yards. Advances in transportation, like a new streetcar line down Seneca Street, and later the automobile, allowed these residents of the First Ward to migrate into newer housing developments in South Buffalo. As some of these Irish moved out of the Ward, other ethnic groups were eager to take their place.

It is a common misconception that the First Ward and the Irish are synonymous. When the devastating tidal wave hit the Ward and the "Flats" area in 1844, the demographic mix of those who perished was a balance of Anglo-American and German surnames with only a sprinkling of Irish surnames. By the 1880s—what would be the peak of the Irish era—the population of the First Ward was mostly Irish, but still mixed: 70% Irish, 10% German, 4% American, 6% English, and 3% Scottish and others.[1] On any given street most people were Irish, but there could be a smattering of Dutch, Danish, English, Scottish, and American laborers and skilled workers.[2]

A second misconception is that most of the First Ward Irish in Buffalo were descendants of famine immigrants. While some families arrived in the Ward immediately after the Irish Famine, many First Ward families descended from immigrants who arrived in the United States after 1860. In fact, Irish immigrants were steadily streaming into the Ward in the late 19th century and even into the early part of the 20th century. During this period—fifty years after the Great Famine—jobs were still more plentiful in Buffalo than they were in most parts of Ireland. Extended family members not only settled in the same city, but they often found homes in the same neighborhood. In May of 1898, twenty-five years after Timothy Bohen landed, "Big Dan" Bohen—a cousin of Timothy—and his family arrived in the Ward from Goleen, County Cork in the very southern tip of Ireland. They settled on Vandalia Street around the corner from Timothy. The Evans family from County Kerry had a similar migration pattern. In 1885, Thomas Evans came over the Atlantic and settled in the Ward in order to work as a laborer. Over the next forty years, he recruited five of his brothers from Ireland along with several nieces and nephews to settle in the Ward. Another brother, George Evans, who remained in Ireland, was forced to watch six of his twelve children follow the extended family to their new home in the Ward.[3]

This stream of new Irish immigrants to Buffalo and the Ward lasted until the 1920s. From the 1870s until 1910, there were consistently about 11,000 people living in Buffalo who were born in Ireland. By 1910 this number dropped to only 9,000 and it continued to decline in subsequent years.[4] According to the 1910 U.S. Federal Census, the number of Irish (defined as first or second generation) in the Ward had indeed decreased for the first time. The new ethnic mix was now 50% Irish, 7.8% German, 16.4% American, 3.4% English, 5.2% Scottish, 7.5% Canadian, and 9.7% other European. But these numbers are misleading since the third-generation Irish were counted under the "American" category, making the total number of Irish Americans actually higher than the reported 50%.[5] In addition, many of the "Canadians" were also of Irish ancestry, so the percentage of Ward residents with an Irish background was probably closer to 60 or 70%. While the Irish migration to the First Ward slowed, the overall population of the Ward actually continued to expand during this period. By 1910, the Ward was home to 17,947 residents. Throughout the 19th century, until the turn of the 20th century, the Germans were the second largest ethnic group in the Ward, to be replaced in a short time by the Poles.

It was not just ethnicity, but also religion and parish affiliation that shaped the Ward. By the early part of the 20th century, the Ward was overwhelmingly Roman Catholic. The four Roman Catholic parishes of note were Our Lady of Perpetual Help (O'Connell and Alabama Streets), St. Bridget's (Fulton and Louisiana), St. Stephen's (Elk near Smith Street) and St. Valentine's at 434 Elk Street. There was also a small Protestant community that was prominent in the mid-to-late 19th century. Their two churches were St. Mark's (founded in 1856), a Methodist/Episcopalian congregation located at Elk near Hamburg Street, and St. Thomas (founded in 1876), an Episcopalian congregation located at 404 Elk Street. John Lord O'Brian and Congressman Rowland Mahany were two famous Episcopalians who came out of the First Ward.

By the middle part of the 20th century, Roman Catholic residents were less likely to be defined by their parish. With the rise of the automobile culture, people were less confined to their parish neighborhood and recreational activities like baseball assisted in assimilating people from different parishes as well as residents from different ethnic backgrounds. During this period, children also ventured out of the Ward to attend Central High School, St. Joseph's Collegiate Institute, and Canisius High School, where they met and mingled with people from different Buffalo neighborhoods.

West Side and South Buffalo Migration

The geography of the First Ward—with natural boundaries such as the Buffalo River and man-made divisions such as canals and railroad tracks—isolated it from the rest of the city. Partly because of these boundaries, and partly because of the insular nature of the Irish who lived within the boundaries, many people in the 19th century moved around within the Ward. But hardly anyone moved out.[6] One local historian suggests the reason why: "The tightly knit, ethnocentric bonds of Irish nationality and Catholicism provided a supportive and comforting environment for this highly vulnerable immigrant community."[7] During most of the 19th century many Buffalonians, including business owners, newspaper editorial staffs, and even sometimes their fellow Catholics, the Germans, were less than sympathetic to the plight of the Irish. As a result, a strong bond emerged between Irish immigrants and the Catholic Church, the Democratic Party, and Irish social societies in Buffalo. Often this support network provided jobs, economic assistance, and spiritual comfort. To leave this nurturing environment—the Ward—was to risk alienation from the group and consequently the benefits associated with group membership. This helps to explain much of the loyalty among the Irish and their fellow First Warders and conversely their distrust of outsiders: Yankee Protestants, Germans, Italians, Poles, and African Americans.

By the 1880s, however, as industrialization in the Ward accelerated, some upwardly mobile residents decided to leave the Ward for greener pastures.[8] Contrary to some local lore, the destination for the first migration of the Irish from the Ward was not South Buffalo, but rather the West Side of Buffalo. The West Side offered above-average housing stock around Holy Angels Parish, where new residents would find established Irish Catholic populations on Niagara Street, Fargo Avenue, and Prospect Avenue. The West Side, like the Ward, provided the comforts of being surrounded by people of a similar background, without the negative consequences of living in an area enveloped by industry. Those who left the Ward for the West Side, however, were viewed as defectors. One Ward memoir captures the widespread sentiment toward these transplants:

> The real "high-toned" Irish lived on the other side of Main Street and they were conscious of their position. They were proud, not with the remote, taken-for-granted superiority of those families on Delaware Avenue, but with a fierce Irish pride that was sometimes resented but nonetheless recognized by most of those who shared their ancestry.[9]

One noted Irish-American judge from the West Side told a story of courting a girl from the Ward. The judge recalls his friend warning him to "watch out" because he couldn't vouch for the reception that he would receive from the First

Ward Irish boys.[10] Despite this animosity many of those with the economic means to do so eventually moved out of the Ward to the West Side or the Delaware Avenue area of Buffalo. A partial list of those who left during the latter part of the 19th century includes Rowland Mahany, John Lord O'Brian, Michael Shea, William Donovan, William Love, Daniel Kenefick, and William J. Conners.

The West Side migration—which happened in earnest from the 1870s to the 1890s—paled in comparison to the second exodus of First Warders, who decamped for South Buffalo. "South Buffalo" is the name given to the area south of the First Ward and up to the boundaries of the city of Lackawanna and the town of West Seneca. The major thoroughfares in South Buffalo include Seneca Street, Abbott Road, McKinley Parkway, Potters Road, and South Park Avenue. This area also includes two beautiful Frederick Law Olmsted-designed parks: Cazenovia Park and South Park. There were two primary reasons that people migrated out of the Ward to South Buffalo in the late 1890s: the advent of the Seneca streetcar and the Lackawanna Iron and Steel Company. In 1896, the Seneca streetcar began service into the farmlands of South Buffalo, enabling people to live in a more pastoral setting and commute to work via a trolley car. The second development occurred in April of 1899, when the Lackawanna Iron and Steel Company announced it was constructing a massive steel mill on the waterfront south of the First Ward. Of the two developments, the steel mill in Lackawanna was even more significant than the streetcar. By 1904, as a result of newly created jobs in the mills, almost 7,000 people had relocated to the new neighborhoods in the South Park area to be closer to their place of employment.[11] While not all of these transplants came from the First Ward, there was a sizable contingency that did.

William H. Fitzpatrick, a one-time milk dealer who owned a farm at Seneca Street and Bailey Avenue, envisioned the migration of the Irish out of the First Ward. He became the prominent homebuilder in South Buffalo, erecting houses on former farms and orchards. The enterprising Fitzpatrick built many of the homes in the Butler Park area of South Buffalo as well as homes on Geary, Stevenson, Ryan, and the Seneca Parkside area.[12] With a new streetcar, new housing, and a new employer, all signs pointed to an Irish exodus out of the industrial Ward into the more bucolic South Buffalo area. The enterprising William J. Conners, who initially left the Ward for Tifft Street in South Buffalo, became another prominent developer of homes in South Buffalo. But it was not just land developers who witnessed this tidal wave of migration out of the Ward. Bishop James Quigley was also monitoring this substantial southerly migration of his flock. In response he quickly set about responding to the needs of these transplants. One year after the Seneca streetcar opened, in April of 1897, Quigley established St. Teresa's Parish on Seneca Street, just a few miles from the Ward.[13] Five years later, witnessing the ongoing exodus, he authorized former First Warder Father John Nash to purchase the William J. Conners estate at Tifft Street and South Park Avenue to create Holy Family Parish. This would mark the beginning of the explosion of Catholic institutions in South Buffalo.

The Sisters of Mercy, whose first settlement in Buffalo was in the Ward, also quickly reacted to this migration to South Buffalo. In 1902, their superior, Reverend Mother Mary Dolores, purchased the Rufus P. Choate estate at Red Jacket Parkway and Abbott Road, across from Cazenovia Park, to build a new motherhouse for the Sisters of Mercy.[14] On September 24, 1904, the Mercy Sisters also opened a new hospital, Mercy Hospital on Tifft Street, near the newly created Holy Family Church on the Conners' estate. In the same year, on May 24th, the Mercy Sisters opened their motherhouse at 1475 Abbott Road. Three years later, the sisters also staffed a six-room school located at St. Teresa's Parish. Some Buffalonians thought the school was unnecessary because it was out "in the wilderness of South Buffalo." They were proven wrong by fall of that same year when the Sisters had enrolled one hundred and thirty-five students.[15] A girl's high school on Abbott Road, Mercy Academy, was opened in 1904, and another elementary school at Holy Family was established in 1908. The Catholic Church had not abandoned the Ward—they built Our Lady of Perpetual Help in the Ward after this southward migration—but the foundations and infrastructure were now in place for the anticipated resettlement of the Irish into South Buffalo. At this point, there was no stopping this migration.

Like those who left for the West Side one generation earlier, South Buffalo transplants were also teased by their former Ward neighbors. In one of Roger Dooley's novels about the Ward, one of the characters states that he would not move to "the country" or South Buffalo as it was called because it was a "remote wilderness that could never rival the incomparable convenience, liveliness and familiarity of the First Ward."[16] First Warders referred to those who moved to South Buffalo as "lace-curtain Irish" or "bean-eaters" because they were so poor after paying their expensive mortgages that they couldn't afford to buy meat.[17] They also referred to McKinley Parkway as "the Delaware Avenue of South Buffalo."[18]

Despite this migration out of the Ward into South Buffalo, many First Warders continued to stay even if they had the economic resources to leave. Professor William Jenkins from York University in Toronto researched the phenomenon of why so many Irish families remained in the Ward, generation after generation. Jenkins compared the First Ward to another Irish blue-collar community in Toronto that dissolved much more quickly. He found that one reason some stayed in the First Ward was that the Ward had been geographically cut off from the rest of the city for so long that a very solid and supportive network had developed and this network of natives discouraged moving out. Certainly the proximity of the Ward to waterfront jobs and the short commute to work also made the Ward a desirable place to live. The fact that the Irish in the First Ward controlled an entire political ward was another factor in the durability of this Irish settlement. In contrast, the Toronto Irish immigrants never dominated a political ward, so remaining in their community of origin was less advantageous to them than their counterparts in Buffalo.[19] Jenkins claims that the First Ward is one of the oldest and most enduring blue-collar, Irish Catholic neighborhoods in the United States.[20] This is remarkable considering the multitude of Irish settlements throughout the Northeastern and Midwestern United States.

During this period of change, another group in the Ward was actually forced to move from their neighborhood. The Beachers—the seventy-year-old community of Irish and Portuguese fishermen and mill workers along the seawall strip—were forced from their land in 1917. At the turn of the 20th century, city politicians and the business leaders made proposals to reclaim the seawall community in order to convert it into land for commercial purposes and a 1903 article in the *Buffalo Times* predicted the imminent end of the Beachers' community.[21] One city plan proposed to clear out the residents and their cottages in order to sell the land to the railroads, ensuring that each of these railroad companies could have equal access to the waterfront. Part of this plan also included creating space for pleasure grounds, bathing areas, and excursion docks.[22]

A more ambitious plan proposed creating a grand boulevard, lined with waterfront businesses on the land where the squatters had been living. But none of these schemes accounted for the interests of the approximately 1,000 non-tax paying residents who lived on that land. Although some members of the Common Council were able to forestall this mass eviction of the Beachers, in the end the commercial interests won out. The city of Buffalo took their case for ownership of the land along the seawall strip to the State Supreme Court and won. Around 1917, during Mayor Louis Fuhrmann's tenure, the residents were officially evicted in order to make way for a railroad project.[23] During the court case, the city took photos of the Beach cottages and in the photos often the Beachers themselves posed next to their home (see photo #4). Perhaps for many of the Beachers it was the first—and maybe the only—picture ever taken of them. More interestingly, did the residents realize as they posed for the camera that they would shortly be evicted to make room for a railroad? While many residents were forced to leave immediately after government orders, it would take another 35 years to remove the most stubborn Beachers who had refused to leave. To add insult to the numerous families that were forced from their homes, the main artery running along this land was later named Fuhrmann Boulevard.

Another group of residents left the Ward and Buffalo altogether. The economic depression in the 1880s forced some First Warders to leave Western New York for better job prospects elsewhere. In addition, the fact that many laborers were unemployed for the four months a year that Lake Erie was frozen caused some to look for opportunities in western locales like San Francisco where one could work all year long.[24] In fact, during the period from the 1860s to 1900, the "persistence rate" for the Irish in Buffalo was only 32%, which means that only 32% of Irish families were still in Buffalo after any ten year period of time.[25] Obviously the high mortality rate of the early generations of settlers helps to explain this low number.

Economic Boom and Roaring Twenties

The period after World War I was the high point of Buffalo's waterfront economy.[26] Grain elevators were scattered up and down the Buffalo River. The railroads had seventeen terminals and tracks throughout the city. Coal and ore docks were bustling with business. Ford had established an assembly plant on Fuhrmann Boulevard that was producing close to 2 million cars a year. The grain trade reached its peak in the 1920s with grain shipments at around 200 million bushels each year, continuing throughout World War II. During the 1920s and 1930s Buffalo also became the largest flour-milling city in the country, surpassing Minneapolis.[27] All of these waterfront industries needed workers. As the Irish moved out of the Ward or into different occupations, there were plenty of other immigrant groups that were happy to take their place.

During this same period architectural innovations were occurring in the Ward that would impact construction techniques throughout the world. In 1907, the American Elevator was built using an innovative technique: reinforced concrete. Now more durable grain elevators could be built in as little as ten days. European architects were enamored with these massive new structures in the Ward that were taller than any buildings on their continent.[28] In 1915, John Rammacher built the largest grain elevator in the world: the Concrete Central. The Concrete Elevator measured a quarter-of-a-mile long. It had 250 silos, stored over four million bushels of grain annually, and employed over 1,000 workers.[29] Prospects were so bright that the massive Lake and Rail Elevator was expanded four times between the 1920s and 1930s.

It wasn't just the economy that was flourishing during the 1920s, but also First Warders themselves. In 1926, Michael Shea erected his cathedral to entertainment, Shea's Buffalo Theatre, which opened in June. That same year, the Conners family merged the *Buffalo Courier* and *Express* to create one of Buffalo's leading newspapers, *The Buffalo Courier Express*. One year later Jimmy Slattery won the NBA light heavyweight title by defeating Maxie Rosenbloom, and William J. Donovan was elevated by President Coolidge to assistant attorney general in charge of the Justice Department's Antitrust Division. The future looked very bright for residents of the Ward.

Italians and Poles Invade

Congressman Richard Max McCarthy's father, Ignatius, grew up in the Ward around the turn of the 20th century. He once told his son that he "couldn't mention a dozen non-Irish families" in the Ward.[30] Ignatius McCarthy lived in the heart of Pets parish, which was solidly Irish at that time. But the Ward was larger than Pets. People from other ethnicities were settling north and east of this area, while still living within the Ward boundaries. From the beginning there had always been a fairly sizable German community residing in the Ward, but it appears that the more dominant Irish culture subsumed most vestiges of German culture. German families in the Ward included the Overdorfs, Heidingers, Hoffstetters, Schollards, Minstermans, Deichmans, Guises, Kaisers, Snyders, Eggloffs, Moeschs, Hahns, Jacobsons, Hackemers, Neffs, Diehls, Laettners, Mueckls, Sumbrums, and Frankhausers.[31] Throughout the 19th century, there are not many documented problems between the Irish and the Germans in the Ward—or with any of the other nationalities like the Scottish and English—who were intermingled in the various neighborhoods within the Ward. But in the late 19th century this would start to change when another Catholic immigrant group, the Italians, started to move just north of the Ward on Swan Street.

For the most part the Italians who settled in Buffalo were poor and unskilled. It is certain that the Irish viewed them as competition for the desirable waterfront jobs. The Irish, as well as many other Buffalonians, viewed the Italians as "foreigners." Local newspapers used derogatory words like "criminals" to describe this newest immigrant group.[32] The fact that the Italians were fellow Catholics didn't seem to lessen the animosity between these two groups. In 1894, the *New York Times* reported that a race riot broke out in Buffalo between the Irish and Italians after four Irishman refused to pay for a tab in a saloon in the Italian section of the city. By the time the fight was over, there were two hundred men on each side armed with guns, knives, and bricks. Fortunately no one was killed but many were injured, and Irish pride was wounded upon reading in the newspaper report that the Italians had won the fight.[33]

One day early in May 1907, the Italians in the downtown corridor requested a permit to have a religious march in their Canal District neighborhood. Buffalo Police Chief Michael Regan, a resident of the Ward, granted this request, anticipating that they would confine their celebration to this area. The Italians, however, were upset about being segregated in their neighborhood and decided to expand the parade down Main Street closer to the central business district. Police officers, many of whom were Irish, and several non-Italian citizens who were in the area on this particular day reacted swiftly in driving the Italians back to their "ghetto." While there were only a few injuries and a handful of arrests, the newspapers claimed that it was the biggest riot in the city's history.[34] Shortly after this event, Chief Regan was quoted as saying, "I think the Italians are a dangerous class because they break the law."[35] It is likely that this sentiment trickled down to many First Ward Irish police officers under his command.

Tensions between the Italians and Irish also revolved around politics and religion. Specifically, the Italians resented the control the Irish had over both institutions. Irish priests ministered at many of the Italian parishes and they dominated the leadership of the Church in Buffalo. Thus Italians viewed the Church as an Irish-American institution.[36] The same was true in the political realm. The Irish had a stranglehold on the leadership of the Democratic Party, which they were unwilling to share with Italians. In fact, from the turn of the 20th century until the campaign of Democratic candidate Al Smith for president in 1928, Italians in Buffalo aligned themselves with the Republican Party.[37]

Even decades later, during the 1940s, some Ward residents recall that there were still tensions between the two groups. One resident claimed that during this period it was taboo for Italians to cross back and forth over the South Park and Seneca Street bridges because an altercation might arise.[38] Another resident reported that Italians also did not dare to cross the Louisiana Street Bridge for fear a fight might break out. Still another First Ward denizen recalls a time when the Irish in the Ward looked at the Italians as lower on the pecking order than African Americans. Some Irish First Warders would not even let Italian children play with their children in their homes. One writer described this situation:

> Another divider in the Ward was the Louisiana Street Bridge, which separated the Irish and the Italians. Down on Seneca, Scott, and Myrtle Avenue were to be found the crowded Italian tenements. And woe be it to any young Italian boy who ventured into the Ward to take out a young Irish girl. He would be met by a group of the local boys and "taught a lesson.[39]

By the 1930s and 1940s, however, mixing between Italians and Irish became more common. Mike "Cat's" Catanzaro, who grew up in the Ward in the 1940s and 1950s, had an Italian father, Bruno Catanzaro, and an Irish mother, Ann Cunningham, who were married at St. Brigid's on August 4, 1937. According to Mike Catanzaro's family history, his grandfather, Michael J. Catanzaro, was the first Italian resident of the First Ward. Grandfather Catanzaro worked for the Lehigh Valley Railroad and lost his leg in a railroad accident in Pennsylvania. Lehigh Valley R.R. transferred him to their Buffalo office and gave him compensation for his accident. He used this money in 1910 to buy a house on 422 Louisiana Street, near St. Brigid's Church. Apparently Catanzaro ended up in the Ward because he could not find a house in the overcrowded St. Lucy's Parish off of Swan Street, north of the Ward.

After Catanzaro settled on Louisiana Street, other Italian families settled in the this area of St. Brigid's Parish: the Previtys, Copollas, Cortos, Grassos, Perrones, Santoras, DeJacs, Mirandas, Shipannis, Camanos, Sorrentinos, DiChristophers, Vastolas, and LaFarros. Then families like the DeMarcos, Britzzalaros, Cataenos, Cannazis, Cultraras, Polos, Concheiros, Moscas, Stasios, and Marinos started to settle in Pets Parish as well.[40] In 1937, according to the St. Brigid's enrollment directory, there were 27 Italian members of the church out of 858 adult parishioners. Almost half of these families lived on Fulton Street, with many others living on Louisiana Street. In 1943, out of the 1,000 adult parishioners in Pets parish, there were only twelve Italians. In a history of the Mercy Sisters, the author claims that St. Brigid's parish—which was predominantly Irish for much of its history—was filled with Polish and Italians by 1958.[41] By the middle of the 20th century, it had become more commonplace to see Irish and Italians intermingling. While the northern and eastern boundaries of the Ward were changing, the geographical heart of the Ward, Our Lady of Perpetual Heart Parish, remained predominantly Irish throughout most of the 20th century.

During the period of 1885 to 1895, a new Catholic immigrant group, the Poles, started arriving in Buffalo—settling mostly on the East Side of the city. By 1900 the Poles reached 60,000 residents citywide, with a small minority settling on the northern streets of the Ward like Perry Street and South Park Avenue.[42] The First Ward Irish, always suspicious of outsiders, did not spare this new immigrant group their distrust. There is even one account of a potential riot when a few newly arrived Polish families tried to go to Mass at St. Bridget's.[43]

Tom Krzeminski, a former Ward resident of Polish descent from Miami Street, claimed that even in the 1950s—fifty years after their arrival—the Poles and Irish essentially socialized among themselves. Krzeminski's gang consisted of other Poles from the north side of South Park Avenue and "one token Irish guy." Around 1920, Krzeminski's maternal grandfather, John Ryszka, landed in the Ward on Miami Street near Public School 4. Ryszka chose the Ward as his home because he worked nearby at the National Analine Chemical Company. John Ryszka's brother, Frank, who settled in the Ward on Perry Street around 1910, was a sort of godfather for the Poles who moved to this area. When a newly arrived Polish immigrant needed money to get established in the Ward they went to Frank, who had a safe filled with cash in the basement of his saloon and residence at 578 Perry Street. One of the conditions of borrowing the money was that you had to rent one of his many apartments in the area. This arrangement allowed

Frank to profit handsomely. Frank Ryszka also expanded his Polish empire when he opened Ryszka's Hall, which was the popular place for Polish communion and confirmation parties. In addition to a saloon and party hall, this Polish family also operated a grocery store.

By 1920 there were 180 Polish families living in the Ward between Louisiana and Red Jacket Streets: enough for them to form their own Catholic parish.[44] On August 10th of that year, a group of Polish immigrants met at Frank Ryszka's house to make plans for the creation of a Polish church in the Ward called St. Valentine's.[45] Father Ladislaus Brejski performed a solemn mass in front a small group at Ryszka's house. Shortly after this event, land was acquired at Elk and Alabama Streets in order to build a church and a school. While they waited for the contractor to finish the church, these Poles held church services in the parish hall at Saint Thomas Episcopal Church instead of the nearby Catholic parishes of St. Brigid's or Our Lady of Perpetual Help. Shortly before the church was completed in 1923, the number of Polish families in the parish reached 450 (not all of the parishioners actually lived in the Ward) and 625 children were enrolled in St. Valentine's school.[46] After the leadership of Fr. Brejski, other prominent pastors of St. Valentine's included Fr. Stephen Szczepanski, Fr. Casimir Tomiak, Father Anthony Krawczyk, and Fr. Henry Stachewicz.[47] Since its opening in 1920, St. Valentine's School was staffed by the Felician Sisters, who educated hundreds of Polish children in the Ward.

Throughout the 20th century, St. Val's continued to serve the needs of the Polish families in the Ward; but as Poles continued to expand down Elk Street into the Valley, they increasingly joined St. Stephen's and eventually became the dominant ethnic group of this Valley parish. While Poles primarily lived north of Elk Street and in the Valley, there was a scattering on every street in the Ward by the early 1940s. One Irish resident who grew up in the Ward during the 1940s could only remember one Polish American in the central part of the First Ward: Julia Solarczyk, who ran Julia's Tavern on Hamburg Street, which later became Gene McCarthy's. By 1943, out of the 1,000 adult parishioners at Pets parish, there were 104 Poles, or close to 10% of the parish census, scattered on streets such as O'Connell, Mackinaw, Vandalia, and Vincennes.[48] Mary Comerford, a second-generation Irish woman from St. Clair Street, married Karl Dyczek from Poland in 1952. She claims that by the 1950s her husband's Polish ethnicity was not an issue at all.[49] Examples of Polish families included the Kolodziejs, Nowadlys, Lukomskis, Drewiegas, Dziedzics, Schutas, Procknals, Nagowskis, Kanias, Mazureks, Simonicks, Yushiws, Szcygiels, Pelows, Dzjolgas, Burkowskis, Bienkos, Smolinskis, Zasadas, Bankos, Wronas, Gasuiks, Swiateks, Ratchuks, Swiateks, Burvids, Aztecs, Kalvinowskis, and Szaras.[50] After the turn of the 20th century there was also a sizable Hungarian population that moved into the Ward to work at the Union Furnace with surnames such as Tutuska and Soto.[51]

Great Depression

While the Irish in the Ward were trying to accommodate their new Italian and Polish neighbors, an even greater challenge arose during this period: the Great Depression. While most Ward residents did not live extravagantly during the economic boom times of the 1920s, they certainly paid an economic price for those who did. By 1932, just three years after the start of the greatest economic catastrophe to affect the nation, close to 33% of the able-bodied males in Erie County could not find a full-time job.[52] While there are no specific figures on unemployment in the Ward, the fact that many residents were laborers and working in the manufacturing sector—two areas most impacted by the Depression— indicates that unemployment was probably at least 33%. There were, however, a few bright spots regarding employment. In later years, Jimmy Griffin recalled that the grain mills were still hiring during the Depression, so there was work for scoopers and others who worked in the mills. Indeed Buffalo's milling business was extremely busy during the 1930s as it overtook Minneapolis as the grain-milling capital of the United States.[53]

Others remember that things were so challenging that some grain scoopers and construction workers were forced to supplement their income in the winter through activities such as ice fishing and working as day laborers. During this period the abundant supply of fish from Lake Erie was in great demand by residents of the Ward. After a long day of ice fishing, men would sell their fish from Jerry Foley's Boat Livery—a rustic fish-house on the water's edge at the foot of Michigan Avenue.[54] Other grain scoopers like Charles Comerford supplemented their income by working as day laborers, employed by the city during the winter months while grain business remained idle. On winter days during the Depression, dozens of men would arrive each day at the steps of City Hall in downtown Buffalo, hoping to be picked for day jobs like shoveling railroad crossings or sidewalks. Jimmy Cleary from Kentucky Street in the Ward was the man responsible for picking the day laborers. He took good care of many fellow residents from the Ward like Charles Comerford.[55]

Times were tougher for some than for others. For residents with civil servant jobs, like fireman Dan Bohen, work was steady and paychecks were regular. Others, such as Leo Guise, benefited from national work programs like the Works Progress Administration (WPA). Guise worked as a scooper and supplemented his income during the Depression working on a WPA project building a service road alongside modern-day Fuhrmann Boulevard.[56] Other First Warders built the wall along South Street in the Ward, erected to prevent flooding along the Buffalo River. Still others were involved in the government project to widen and dredge the Buffalo River, which was re-coursed to be 25 feet deep, 215 feet wide and 2,000 feet long.[57]

Circumstances were so bleak for some residents however, that when the City of Buffalo created a trash dump along Fuhrmann Boulevard in the First Ward, some city residents became trash pickers. Needy families would pick trash at the dump for copper, lead, iron or anything worth selling for a few dollars.[58] Eventually these desperate families and individuals created living structures such as lean-tos, huts, and shacks near the dump to be closer to their means of survival.[59] One Ward resident remembers how these people were very content and civilized in the midst of their poverty.[60] Eventually the City of Buffalo stepped in and evicted the residents of the dump because of sanitation issues. Hundreds of people lived in makeshift shacks in another area nicknamed "Hobo Jungle" which sprang up near the foot of Smith Street. As the trains would slow down over the Buffalo River, the vagrants could hop on and off the trains. Eventually the Buffalo Police would also disband the residents of Hobo Jungle.[61]

During the Depression, people entertained themselves with simple pleasures and resisted government handouts. Jimmy Griffin, the four-term mayor of Buffalo who grew up in the Ward during the Depression, proudly boasted, "even though times were tough, they [First Ward residents] paid their taxes and over-subscribed to every charity."[62] Griffin describes life in the Ward during the Depression: "Nobody had phones, cars, television sets in those days. There were no safety nets and what welfare there was, it was called relief. Down in the Ward, a lot of kids wore the uniform of the depression— patches on their pants."[63] Another resident claimed that the Irish "tried to do things on their own and wanted to be independent"—government handouts would only be considered as a last resort.[64] In addition, those who had extra resources shared with those who did not. Mary Dyczek remembers her father Charles Comerford telling the family not to turn away anyone who came to the door looking for food. She recalls hobos coming to their door looking to trade work for food, and her father and mother would give them food for nothing in exchange.

Gene McCarthy, the former owner of McCarthy's Tavern on Hamburg Street, once said: "We didn't know whether we were rich or poor because we never had a yardstick to measure wealth and poverty. All we knew was that we helped one another."[65] Eddie Stack, who grew up in the Ward between World War I and World War II, remembers the poverty in terms of how many people in your house had to use the same bath water to clean themselves. He joked, "At our house, we were fairly well-off, only three of us used the same water. Believe me, some had it tougher."[66] Stack also remembers his family cutting their Proctor & Gamble bar soap into three pieces to make it last longer. When it got really small it was put into a wire cage where it was shaken in the water to make suds and stretch it out.[67] Dyczek remembers how her mother would buy bushels of fruit from the Elk Street Market and then canned all summer to provide food in the winter. Dyczek also recalls how her mother was constantly sewing in order to repair clothes so they could be used as hand-me-downs for the younger children; her mother would even sew leftover scraps together to make blankets.[68]

Just four months after the Great Depression commenced, on January 7, 1930, Willis Wilber from the *Buffalo Times* described the physical characteristics of the Ward in one of his columns:

> A maze of crooked streets, railway tracks, viaducts and ramshackle buildings. Glimmering yellow lights flashing dully through the fogs that sweep up from the harbour. Swarms of children, gossiping women. Men with dinner pails and odorous pipes. Stunted trees lining the sidewalks. Dingy churches and halls, blackened by the smoke of years. Dingy houses and dingy schools. That is Buffalo's old First Ward...

Wilber's description of the First Ward between the Wars might sum up the physical characteristics of the Ward, but it does not capture the spirit of its people. Even photographs from this period capture residential streets with well-manicured lawns, tall trees, and smiling residents.

Toward the end of the Depression, an effort was spearheaded to bolster the commercial district of the Ward. A proposal was circulated to change the name of Elk Street, the main artery of commercial activity in the Ward, to South Park Avenue. The reason for the proposed name change is that the mass migration of residents south of the city to South Buffalo and Lackawanna created a need for a main artery to connect them to downtown Buffalo.[69] Residents from Lackawanna would have a confusing journey over four streets to get downtown. It was thus proposed to take part of Ohio Street in the Ward along with parts of Elk Street and rename it South Park Avenue, which would then connect to the existing South Park running through South Buffalo and Lackawanna. This would assure significant traffic through the Ward's commercial center if the residents accepted the proposal. Three First Ward groups analyzed the proposal and advocated on behalf of the Ward residents: the William J. Gleason Republican Club, the Pioneer Civic Association, and the Blackthorn Club. Finally, in May of 1939, at a meeting at the Blackthorn Club, James Hagan, a Blackthorn, announced that the group accepted the name change because it would "eventually result in a bigger and better South Buffalo unified by one main thoroughfare."[70] Other representatives from the other organizations that were responsible for the name change included George Hanny, Jr., Andrew Jacobson, John Horni, Michael E. Regan, Franck Schreck, Raymond O'Connell, and Joseph J. Sullivan. Thus most of Elk Street in the Ward became South Park Avenue.

Commodore Perry Projects

On July 1, 1940, just as the Great Depression was winding down, a contentious housing project was completed in the First Ward. This 21-acre project would dismantle the bustling neighborhood near St. Brigid's and eventually change the demographics of the Ward. The Commodore Perry Projects were created during the last years of the Great Depression from federal and city efforts to provide housing for low-income residents in Buffalo. The city purchased single-family homes between Fulton and Elk Sts. near Alabama Street in order to build the Commodore Perry Tower and later the Perry Extension project—which consisted of one and two-story buildings. In order to create this low-income housing project, the government destroyed entire blocks of residential housing including 295 dwellings that government officials referred to as "slums." As a result hundreds of families were displaced, some of whom had lived in this area for generations. This building project also led to the destruction of the oldest home in the area: the 1820 home of the famous shipbuilder Jacob Banta from Bidwell & Banta.[71] Many of these displaced families tried to settle into other parts of the Ward. Finding this difficult, however, the majority of them moved further out of the Ward to South Buffalo. The strong enclave of residents living around the once-thriving, eighty-year-old St. Bridget's Parish was changed forever. Mike Catanzaro said this housing project displaced both sides of his family (the Catanzaros and Cunninghams). Fortunately, they were able to resettle into the area around Our Lady of Perpetual Help parish. Others, however, were forced out of the Ward altogether.

A group of concerned First Ward residents created the Pioneer Civic Association in 1939 to protect the interests of the Ward during this time of change. Their primary focus was the Commodore Perry Projects, but they also tackled the issues dealing with filling in the Ohio Basin and the proposed St. Lawrence Seaway Project.[72] The group lost their battle concerning the Perry Projects. After it was built, however, they waged war with the Buffalo Housing Authority, demanding that it address problems arising from this housing project. This organization, led by Hugh R. Shreenan and Michael E. Regan, was incensed that former First Ward residents who were displaced by the project—and who were initially promised a chance to live in the new housing project—were later shut out because of income level requirements. Specifically, many of the local workers in the grain elevators and mills had incomes that, while modest by most accounts, surpassed the project's maximum income limits. The Pioneer Civic Association fought this issue and advocated that former First Ward residents should be given priority when applying for admission into the Commodore Perry Projects.[73] They also urged the Housing Authority not to create a separate playground on the grounds of the project because they did not want to create a community within a community. Instead they wanted the residents to share in the recreational services in the First Ward environs.

At first the demographics of the projects consisted mainly of Irish-American and Italian-American residents. After federal desegregation court cases in the 1950s, however, federal and city housing projects were required to integrate African Americans and whites. During the racially charged 1960s, African Americans moved into the projects at an increased rate. In 1958, Mable Betty Johnson's family was one of the first African-American families to move into the projects. One of her sons, a young boy of ten at the time, went on to become the famous funk musician: Rick James. In James's autobiography, he claims that other black families starting moving into the neighborhood around 1961.[74] The demographics of the immediate neighborhood then started to change quickly. By 1966, the Commodore Perry Towers were 19% African American, and the Perry Extension projects, across the street, were 58% African American.[75]

As the years went by, African Americans and Hispanics increasingly occupied the 772 units in the Perry Projects. As a result tensions grew between these new ethnic groups on the northern edge of the Ward and the Irish and Polish residents living south of the project. In fact, Rick James claimed that his family experienced fierce racism, and that "they were the most racist white folks I had ever encountered."[76] In one *Courier Express* article First Warders claimed that even though the Perry Projects were technically in the Ward boundary, many of the residents who lived south of South Park Avenue did not regard this as the Ward anymore.[77] These two disparate groups, African Americans on one side of South Park Avenue, and mostly Irish and Poles on the other side, shared very little in common. Occasionally they would run into each other at the shops on South Park, but they worshipped in different churches and worked in different occupations.[78] By the 1980s the population in the Perry Projects was about 2,500 residents versus 1,500 residents in the homes in the old Ward boundaries. This change in demographics bore significant political and social ramifications for the Ward.

The main cause of distrust between African Americans and Irish revolved around economic competition. Tensions between these two groups extended as far back as 1846 when there was a New York State referendum to give African Americans the right to vote. Voters in the First Ward voted 87% against the measure, the highest percentage of any of the wards in Buffalo.[79] Other issues that fueled the mutual distrust included the riot between the two groups during the Civil War years when African Americans were brought in as strikebreakers for the Irish dockworkers. The First Ward Irish overwhelmingly voted for Senator Stephen Douglas instead of the anti-slavery candidate Abraham Lincoln.

Incidents surrounding the Draft Riots in July 1863 in Buffalo pitted Irish against African Americans, adding to their dislike of each other.[80]

The Irish felt somewhat justified in their views of African Americans. Prior to the Civil War, the Catholic clergy and press in Buffalo did not think that jeopardizing the Union to end slavery was justified.[81] Irish resentment towards African Americans continued throughout much of the 19th century and even flared up when Fingy Conners brought in African Americans to replace the striking Irish grain scoopers in 1899. Niles Carpenter, a prominent sociologist from the University at Buffalo, pinpointed the cause of the modern race tensions to 1916 when African Americans from the Southern states were brought into Buffalo to act as strikebreakers against the striking longshoremen.[82] In the 1920s, Buffalo factory owners recruited even more southern African Americans to work in their factories, which added to the list of ethnic groups competing with the Irish for unskilled labor jobs. Unfortunately, the conflicts between these two groups would continue through much of the 20th century.

By the 1960s and 1970s, the Irish, Italian, and Polish children who populated St. Brigid's School were increasingly replaced by African Americans and Hispanics. Around 1957, the first African American student enrolled in St. Brigid's School.[83] Shortly after, Mercy Sister Mary Pierce noted that while the census at St. Brigid's Parish and school had been declining as the Irish moved away from the area, the number of families at the nearby Perry Projects helped bolster the school enrollment.[84] In 1977, about a third of the teachers at St. Brigid's and almost half of the children were African Americans.

By the 1980s, masses at St. Brigid's were also said in Spanish, which was the language of one of the new immigrant groups entering the Ward. Unfortunately, the school, which educated thousands of First Warders throughout its more than a century of existence, closed for good in 1984. In the early part of the 20th century, many Irish and Germans left the Ward for different neighborhoods in Buffalo. But the Ward did not die, it simply adapted to the changing demographics.

CHAPTER TWELVE

THE WARD REMEMBERED

*The First Ward was not a political division or even a
neighborhood but a way of life, a state of mind.*
– Roger Dooley, author of *House of Shanahan*

I was born in the Ward and I will die in the Ward.
– Sam McCarthy, tavern owner

Documented personal memories of life in the First Ward in the 19th century are
relatively scarce. Fortunately, this was not the case in the 20th century. Several
sources of information about the period from the 1920s to the 1940s—including
John Baldyga's "Recollections" and stories from *Buffalo News* reporters like Ray
Hill and Anthony Cardinale—captured the remembrances of people who grew
up in the period before, during, and after World War II. Fond memories: that was
a common characterization of their years in this unique neighborhood. However,
nostalgic reminiscences sometimes masked the hardships that many endured.

Joan (Graham) Scahill compared growing up in the First Ward in the 1940s
and 1950s to "... growing up in a small town. Everyone knew everyone else and all

of their business (or tried hard to know it). It was great to walk down the street and wave 'Hello' to people sitting on their porches."[1] For some former Warders, the industrial commotion of the Ward was a reason to move to South Buffalo, but Scahill had a different opinion:

> We didn't know how unique it was to look out our front window [on South Street] and see lake freighters being pulled by a Great Lakes tug or food delivered by the *Peggy* boat. If we looked out our back window, we might see a train. Some nights we went to sleep listening to a limestone boat being unloaded. In the middle of the night my whole bedroom might light up as a spotlight on a freighter navigated the hairpin turns along the Buffalo Creek.[2]

Scahill has fond memories of attending Our Lady of Perpetual Help School as well as Bishop Quigley High School. One of her best memories of high school was acting in a play about Ireland called "Follow Your Heart" with the boys from Timon High School. One of the Timon boys in the play, John "Red" Carroll, later became famous in the Guinness Book of Records as the fourth tallest man in the world. He is listed at 8'7" tall, but some claim he was closer to 9'.

Joan's brother, Jim Graham, grew up in the Ward in the 1940s and recalled that "the First Ward was as down to earth as it gets, with the Irish working class people that lived there. No uppity people allowed."[3] The Graham siblings grew up in a house built in 1830 on the "other side of the tracks" in the Ward, on the edge of the Buffalo River (originally the Buffalo Creek), and thus they were called "crick rats." You were not allowed to use the word "creek," it was "crick" according to Jim Graham. There is a debate as to whether the "crick rat" nickname for these particular residents from the Ward came from the Buffalo Creek Railroad that ran through the neighborhood or from the Buffalo Creek (River) nearby.

Graham fondly remembers going as a young boy to a small delicatessen on South Street called Maurice O'Brien's where the kids could buy a cigarette for a penny or two. For a nickel, O'Brien would even write you a forged note if you desired to skip school. Graham also remembers a field at the corner of South and Vandalia Streets where people gathered every November in the 1940s and 1950s for a particularly special event: Election Day. As the residents eagerly waited the election results, they would build an enormous bonfire from wood that came from many sources throughout the neighborhood. The list included—but was not limit-ed to—cooper doors from the grain railcars, debris scavenged from the neighbor-hood, porch steps, Maurice O'Brien's old garage, fences, and wooden walkways.[4] Celebrations on election night were a hundred-year-old tradition in the Ward and evidence that politics played an important part in the lives of its residents.

Graham recalls two hangouts for teenagers during the mid-20th century: J.K. Whitey's at Alabama and Mackinaw Streets, where they served great BBQ burgers and had a jukebox, and Nick's on Hayward and South Park Avenue, where they also had a jukebox and more importantly, where Jim met his wife.[5] Nick's was owned by Greek immigrant Nick Pappas who not only served delicious cheeseburgers, but also bailed out many neighborhood boys when they were arrested for disorderly conduct or fighting.[6]

Jim remembers that jobs were plentiful in the Ward during the 1940s and 1950s, and even if you were underage you could still get a job in the mills or working on the railroads. He also remembers that in those days civil service jobs did not pay as much as they do now, and if you worked as a fireman or police officer you almost always needed a second job to supplement your income.[7] Jim Graham was born in the Ward in 1938 and moved out in 1959 after he got married, but he still has fond memories of his years there.

The raconteur James Graham had some other humorous memories of this era. He remembers how people used to let their dogs out in the Ward without a leash, and consequently there were lots of puppies roaming around in the Ward and an unsuspecting kid had to watch his step when playing in the fields. Graham recalls how the Sisters at Our Lady of Perpetual Help were strict disciplinarians and fondly remembers one sister who would often call out one of the students: Teddy "Ozzie" Overdorf. The sister would yell, "Theodore, take your glasses off and come up here!" and Teddy would be shaking knowing that another beating from the sister was imminent.[8] Eddie Stack recalled similar punishments from some of the sisters at his school. Stack remembered the double insult of "being hit frequently, apparently for nothing, by Sister Lawrence and not being able to complain about it to your parents 'because then you'd really get it.'"[9]

Jim McGeever, who lived at 64 O'Connell Avenue, enthusiastically exclaimed, "I cannot imagine growing up anywhere else. There was so much to do and everyone was your friend." He added that the families that were in your part of the neighborhood became part of your family, almost like aunts and uncles, and all of the kids would go from house to house as if it was their own.[10] Sister Helen Parot grew up in the Ward from the 1930s until the early 1950s, and she remembers how wonderful it was in its heyday. She fondly recalls how the ethnically diverse merchants—Jewish, Polish, Italian and Irish—owned shops along South Park Avenue which catered to your every need. These sorts of sentiments about the old neighborhood seem to be the norm from interviews and memoirs from this era. Sam McCarthy, the owner of a tavern at the corner of O'Connell Avenue and Kentucky Street, once proudly declared, "I was born in the Ward and I'll die in the Ward."[11] Many others in the Ward had such a sentiment.

Eddie Stack nostalgically remembered the social events in the Ward during this period. After the holy day of St. Patrick's Day, wakes and funerals were the next big social events in the neighborhood. According to Stack, "You just wouldn't dare send your mother or father to be buried from a funeral parlor. It would be in bad taste."[12] Instead, as was typical of the Irish—since at least the 1840s—neighbors would come to the home and celebrate the life of the deceased with drinks and a feast. Another Ward resident remembers that there was a group of "professional" pallbearers in the Ward and they never missed a wake or funeral. It wasn't just the dead that received respect. Eddie Stack also fondly remembers that if you were sick the neighbors would visit with homemade chicken noodle soup.

Bert Guise-Hyde, whose family arrived in the Ward from Alsace in the 1880s, grew up in the 1940s and 1950s on Kentucky Street and smiles when she recollects growing up in the Ward. Unlike some who left the Ward because of the industrial commotion of the place, Bert Hyde declared that her "amazement of watching the tugs move around in the Buffalo River never ceased."[13] She also conveyed the tight-knit nature of the residents when she described the annual Ward event called "Clean-up, Fix-up, Paint-up now". At this spring cleanup, everyone in the Ward pitched in to clean up the neighborhood. The young people went to the seniors' houses and did any kind of cleaning and painting that might have been needed after a long and destructive Buffalo winter. Someone would also volunteer for the undesirable task of cleaning out the storm sewers at the corners of the streets so there wouldn't be spring flooding.

In a *Buffalo Courier Express* article, Helen O'Donnell Patton recalled how much she missed growing up in the Ward. Patton nostalgically recalled how, "Sometimes when I go back there now I walk with my eyes closed and remember the way it used to be, all the shops and stores that are closed now. But most of all I remember the people. We were very close. When anyone died there was always a big Irish wake, with everyone pitching in with a big meal, hams and homemade bread and all. It was a regular party, and I saw many of them."[14]

Tom Krzeminski was born in 1941 and lived in the Ward from the 1940s until the early 1960s. Both his paternal and maternal (the Ryszkas) families were of Polish descent and lived in the Ward by the early part of the 20th century. Like his Irish neighbors, Krzeminski remembers the Ward in a mostly positive light. The Krzeminskis lived a typical life with their father Stanley working as a laborer at Maritime Milling. Like many others in the neighborhood, Stanley had to walk to work because he never owned a car. Tom fondly remembers going to school at St. Valentine's School, playing football with his friends, and hanging out at Nick's or the Canteen Ice Cream shop. He also remembers Jack Mazurek, who was one year ahead of him at St. Valentine's, and whose bakery on South Park Avenue has been a staple in the Ward for decades. Krzeminski recalls the days of hanging out as a teenager with his gang, which in those days was led by Sonny Dudek, the biggest guy in the group. His gang, however, wasn't like the one from the script of *West Side Story* that fought with knives. These kids just hung out together roaming the neighborhood.

Proud Ward residents wrote poems and songs to capture their feelings of their unique neighborhood. One of the most commonly recited expressions is: "I am proud as a lord because I was born in the Ward". One resident summed up his feelings in this poem:

Where are the friends of yesterday?
Gone like the leaves of fall.
Gone from the place that once was gay
I miss them one and all.
Down in the old Neighborhood.

Though we were humble
Though dollars were few
Still we were happy.
What good times we knew.

Where are the boys and the gals?
Neighborly neighbors and pals.
Gee, but I wish we could all meet again
Down in the old Neighborhood.

Frank Dunbar, another Ward resident, expressed his memories in this poem:

Wet streets
And everything is ripe
Elk wines and liquors
Old Elk Street is a sight

Wet and cold streets
Everything's asleep
Down old Elk Street
To Joe Weight's
And the A&P
To Boulanger
And Szary's
To watch them build the Commodore Perry

Wet and cold and hot streets
You know where to go
I rent a room from Boulanger

I winter in Buffalo:
Each day the sky is paler
Then one day the spring thaw
And freedom for the Great Lakes sailor
The life I love most of all

Wet and dry and cold and hot streets
Mazurek's pie
H&O oats
The river lined with green and red tug boats
But quiet streets now
With more than most of it gone
Even changed Old Elk Street's name
And the years keep rolling along
But once there was a Hagan's
A Friendly Inn
And a Swannie House
And once we went homesteading
On the river's mouth.

Another Ward resident remembers that crime and theft were practically non-existent in the First Ward, but pranks were plentiful.[15] Throughout the 20th century, in fact, the Ward was a safe place to raise a family. Katherine Nehin Harris was raised on Chicago Street and she remembers it was perfectly safe as a young girl to walk at 10:30 p.m. from Louisiana Street by the Buffalo River to her home.[16] According to one police officer active in the 1960s at Precinct 7 on Louisiana Street, during his career there were mostly minor crimes—although some unfortunate domestic disputes—in the heart of the First Ward.[17] Even in 1981, a *Courier-Express* reporter claimed that the First Ward had the lowest crime rate of any neighborhood in the city.[18] One of the residents explained it this way:

> That's because if you live here and you are going to pull a burglary you go somewhere else to do it. If you pull something here you are going to be found out—everyone is related to everyone else somehow or another. We take care of our own affairs. You steal from one of your own, and you gonna get your head broken.[19]

Occasionally the local residents didn't even call the cops if they caught a robber. Instead they handed out their own justice by roughing up the criminal.[20] Another former resident fondly remembered that the only "trouble" in the neighborhood came from a group called the McCarthy Gang, but they weren't really a gang in the modern sense. Instead, it was a group of six or seven guys that enjoyed roaming around the Ward and engaging in pranks like turning off the electricity at your house.[21]

Commercial District and Retailers

A visitor to the First Ward in the 21st century would find it hard to conceive that the Ward once had a vibrant commercial district. Instead the stranger would witness countless vacant storefronts along much of South Park Avenue. During the 1930s to the 1950s however, this area was a bustling beehive of activity lined with numerous retailers. Residents could get whatever they needed on South Park Avenue—formerly called Elk Street—from shoe repair to a haircut to ice cream sundaes. Popular places on this strip included Healey's Deli, Butler Coffee and Tea, Bo Redmond Delivery, Sullivan's Cigar, Sam the tailor, Costanzo's Shoe Repair, Frank the barber, Marine Bank, Dublin Restaurant—a popular restaurant and meeting place, and Lo Jacano's Drug Store, where one could enjoy a sparkling soda or a banana split.[22] The preceding list exemplifies that while Irish merchants were still prominent in the retail trade, Italian merchants now joined them. One South Buffalo resident remembers his father driving him down to South Park Avenue in the mid-1950s where he saw so many people shopping in this busy retail district that it was nearly impossible to find a parking spot.

The South Park Avenue (Elk Street) strip wasn't the only thriving commercial area. There was another lively district on Chicago and Ohio Streets, which included O'Neil's Saloon, Dick Nugent's, the Mackinaw Hotel, Driscoll's Store, Raymond's Saloon, the Irish A.C. Club, Tom Evans' Saloon, and Chick Evan's Saloon. Other retailers in the Ward included Ma Carr's Ice Cream Parlor, Grand Drugs, Nick's Restaurant, Loblaws, A&P, Danahy Faxon's, Joe Waite's Meats, Sinclair Oil, Dalton's, Maurice O'Brien's, Doman's, Overdorf's, Debbie Keefe's, Sullivan's, Bozzie's, Ernie Stone's, and Stanley the Butcher.[23]

The Elk Street Market, which opened in 1850, was the primary place to shop for vegetables, fruits, meat and live animals such as chickens, ducks, geese, pigeons, and rabbits until it closed in 1939.[24] A handful of grocery stores sprang up to fill the void and they included Coppola's near Chicago Street and Lamy's near Elk Street.[25] Joe Waite's Butcher shop was one of the places where one went for cold cuts or meat for the pot.[26] Delis and corner stores were a prominent feature in the Ward during the mid-20th century and they were even more popular destinations than supermarkets. O'Brien's Deli at Fulton and Alabama Streets, owned by Jimmy Griffin's uncle Harold O'Brien, was one that St. Brigid's neighborhood residents remember. Danny Haggerty's Store, located at the corner of O'Connell Avenue and Tennessee Street, was a popular destination for those in the Pets neighborhood. Danny and his wife Nellie had a deli case, shelves stocked with dry goods, and a coal-fired stove in the center of his store to cook and bake.

In addition to providing food and dry goods, these corner stores had a second function: a social hangout. One of the best examples of this was Bill Travis's Deli— previously known as Glavin's Tavern—at O'Connell Avenue and Vincennes Street. From its opening in 1947 until it closed in 1990, it was simply referred to as "the Store" or "Bill's" and it served as a hub of social gathering for many people, including many retirees, in the Pets neighborhood. At Travis's Deli you could pick up bread, milk, newspapers, penny candy, and then discuss neighborhood events or politics. One South Buffalo visitor remembers going with his First Ward-born father in the 1950s to both Haggerty's and Travis's where his father would reconnect with old neighborhood friends.[27] In good weather, the legendary Bill Travis would sit in a chair in front of the store and hold court with his regulars about a range of topics. As was the case with other Ward retailers, there was a deep bond between the storeowner and his patrons. In fact, at Travis's shop, the patrons would make their own change from the register, sweep the sidewalks, stock the shelves, and if they were short on cash, make an IOU for what they owed.[28] Another resident remembered that you brought the items you wanted to a seated Bill Travis and he quickly calculated how much you owed and told you to place the money in the register. This same customer remembers, however, that if you asked for anything from the deli case—which required Bill to get up from his chair—you could receive a short remark of displeasure. For forty-three years Bill worked at the store, seven days a week, closing only two days over that entire period. Unfortunately a diagnosis of cancer forced him to close this memorable institution in 1990. Similarly, most of the other corner stores have closed and a little bit of the character of the Ward has disappeared as well.

Waterfront and Recreational Memories

Memories of the waterfront also abound from this period. The Buffalo River was indeed a memorable sight teeming with commercial vessels that competed with other boats in order to load and unload their cargo. Passenger vessels were common on the river as well. One such boat was the *Seeandbee*, which was operated by the C&B Transit Company, and brought passengers from Buffalo to Cleveland and back again, landing at the docks near the jack-knife bridge on Michigan Avenue in the First Ward. The C&B Company claimed that their *Seeandbee* ship was the largest steamer on inland waters in the world —it measured 500 feet long by 96 feet wide. At the time, it was also the costliest to build. In 1926, for $5.50 you could leave Buffalo at 9 p.m. on a summer night and arrive in Cleveland at 7 a.m. the next morning after sleeping in one of the ship's 510 luxurious rooms. Four daily steamers operated between the cities with diversions to Cedar Point and Put-in-Bay for an additional $1 added to the base fare. According to one local memoir, enterprising Ward boys earned a nickel carrying the tourists' luggage off the boat.[29] Numerous other tourists from throughout the United States arrived on ships which docked in the Ward on their way to other destinations such as Niagara Falls. The tourists would make their way to Main Street and take a streetcar to the Falls. While not all First Ward residents could afford to travel on luxurious accommodations like the *Seeandbee*, they found other ways to enjoy the lake as well. Trips to Crystal Beach, Ontario on the *Canadiana* and the *Americana* boats, for instance, were common memories of many residents. Eddie Stack remembered daylong Sunday picnics at Crystal Beach feasting on a basket full of sandwiches and salads, which sustained you for both lunch and dinner. Stack also recalled the exhausted feeling you had on the return trip from the sunburn and hard play during the day.[30] Other residents took the *Canadiana* to the Crystal Beach Ballroom in Canada and were entertained by the Harold Austin Orchestra until the ship arrived back in Buffalo at midnight.[31] First Warders also traveled to Canada on the *Erie Beach* boat, which took them across the lake to Erie Beach. This beach boasted the world's largest outdoor swimming pool and a massive dance pavilion.[32] In August of 1940, 1,500 Ward residents, mostly waterfront workers and their families, enjoyed a five-hour cruise on Lake Erie aboard the steamer *Greater Buffalo*.[33] This excursion served as a community bonding event and offered residents an opportunity to discuss some of the important issues they were encountering such as the Commodore Perry Projects.

For those who could not make the journey to Canada for summer fun there was a destination closer to home: Times Beach. This recreational spot was located along Lake Erie near South Michigan Street and equipped with a boat harbor and swimming beach. Geraldine Butler's father, Leo Grandy, used to take her and her siblings there to swim on hot summer days.[34] In addition to swimming and boating, residents also engaged in spear fishing and duck hunting at Times Beach.[35] This beach, which was created as a WPA project in the 1930s, was eventually closed because of pollution in the area.[36] Swimming in the summertime was mentioned by many in their reminiscences of growing up in the Ward. General Bill Donovan remembered swimming at the foot of Michigan Avenue, while others remember crossing the Ohio Street Bridge and walking down to Lake Erie for a swim near the modern-day Freezer Queen plant. John Baldyga claimed that the Tifft Beach was a popular swimming hole with a bathing house and clean sand. Others remember swimming in the Buffalo River, the Ohio Basin, sections of the abandoned canal, or anywhere else to cool off during the hot summer months.

By the 1920s, sports and recreation were integral in the daily lives of residents. In addition to rowing organizations such as the Celtic Rowing Club and the

Mutual Rowing Club, baseball was also a favorite pastime, with hundreds showing up to watch games at Gaelic Field where various First Ward teams would compete. The baseball teams had names like First Ward, Standards, Wildons, Tiger A. C., and Perpetual Help.[37] The central park in the Ward—and one of the largest play areas in the city—was Lanigan Park. This well-maintained playground stretched north and south between Elk Street and Fulton Street and west and east between Louisiana Street and Chicago Street. The park derived its name from the well-liked former rector of St. Bridget's, Fr. James A. Lanigan, who was instrumental in leading the workers in the Great Strike in 1899. In the early years, one section of the park was reserved for mothers and their children and this area contained a girl's playground as well. An iron-picket fence separated this area from the portion where men and boys could play. The men's area included handball, basketball, and volleyball courts, baseball diamonds, and swings with a slide.[38] The park also included a swimming pool and a bandstand. On Fulton Street there was a two-story gym that was heated by a potbelly stove, where the boys played basketball during the long winter months. Sullivan Playground, located between South Park Avenue and Mackinaw near Katherine Street, was another favorite for the locals. Jimmy Griffin mentions this area as the place where his father would take him every day to hit baseballs.[39]

Other recreational activities included roller-skating at a rink on Louisiana Street across from the Barcalo Manufacturing plant.[40] Children and young adults from the First Ward went to the Masque Theatre—also known as the Rat Hole—to watch matinees on Saturdays. The theatre received this less than flattering name because it was located in such a cramped space. Other adventuresome kids had simpler pleasures like playing in the sand piles on Louisiana Street, which could be hazardous to your health if you fell down the piles into the Ohio Basin. In the winter, at the foot of Hamburg Street, a crater in a limestone pile would freeze with water, creating a natural ice-skating rink for kids to enjoy. The Ward residents were certainly a creative and easily amused group of people.

For the adults, especially the men, the saloons were still the top destination for relaxation after a long day of work. Similar to their purpose in the 19th century, saloons also offered a place for socializing and job networking and were the venues where political careers and major Ward events were conceived. The saloon-boss labor system had been hatched in Fingy Conners' saloon on Ohio Street, the grain scoopers union was organized in E.J. McMahon's, Mrs. Glavin's saloon had been the temporary rectory for Our Lady of Perpetual Help, and the St. Patrick's Day parade was planned in Mike Quinn's Tavern. In the 20th century, Jimmy Griffin's mayoral run was launched in Kennedy's Tavern and Councilman Andrew Morrissey's candidacy sprang from Tutuska's Tavern. The Blackthorns also met regularly in a saloon.

Saloons were vital institutions in the Ward and some of the well-known ones from this period included Crotty's on Louisiana Street, Conway's on O'Connell Avenue and Kentucky, Kennedy's on Katherine Street, McCarthy's, Kane's, and Goodrich's.[41] Many grain scoopers in the 1940s and 1950s went to Dick Cotter's on Louisiana and St. Clair Streets across from the Scoopers Union Hall. Jimmy Flood's Bar at 301 Louisiana Street was a popular bar in the 1950s and 1960s, and it was purportedly one of Jimmy Griffin's preferred hangouts. Jack Montondo, a retired police officer and bartender at Flood's, claimed, "Flood's was the original Cheers Bar—it was a popular hangout where everyone knew your name."[42] Mike Catanzaro's father, Bruno, was also a popular bartender at Flood's. Then there was Boulangers—also known as the "Dirty Diaper"—on South Park Avenue, which derived its name because women frequented it and some would change their babies' diapers on the bar.[43] Other famous taverns during the 1950s included The Friendly Inn, Maloney's, Kanias, Paskuly's, the Per Lou, Walter's, Julia's, Hagan's, Adolph's, Roberts, Larry McCarthy's, Tutuska's, Swannie House, Harbor Inn, Cook's, Frank Hahn's, Whitey's, and Kennedy's.[44]

Toward the end of the 20th century, there were significantly fewer saloons in the First Ward than in previous years. The brothers Sam and Gene McCarthy owned two of the most popular saloons in their day. Sam McCarthy's saloon, located at O'Connell Avenue and Kentucky Street, was opened in 1958 by Sam and his brother Gene. The building in which Sam opened his saloon had been a continuous saloon since the 19th century and had undergone several name changes over the years, such as Conway's and Walter's. *Buffalo News* reporter Ray Hill claimed it had been the senior corner saloon in the Ward for decades until it closed in 1986.[45] With an International Longshoremen's Association banner draped on McCarthy's wall, numerous grain scoopers and mill workers patronized the saloon during their one-hour lunch break, in the evenings after work, and on Saturday afternoons. Offering inexpensive meals like a thick roast beef sandwich and a bottle of beer for $1.45, McCarthy's kept the regulars coming back.[46] As a young man Jimmy Griffin became President of the Sam McCarthy Social Club and launched his nascent political career from the saloon—culminating in his historic sixteen-year stint as mayor of Buffalo. Another significant saloon during this era was the Harbor Inn, which had roots back to 1869. From 1975 until it closed for good in 1995, Edward and Julie Malloy and their four children ran the famous institution serving food and drinks to sailors, scoopers, and folks from all over the city.

At the end of the 20th century, Gene McCarthy, Sam's younger brother, operated his saloon a few blocks away at 73 Hamburg Street. For decades it was arguably the most well known First Ward tavern and one Buffalonian even referred to it as the "unofficial headquarters of the Ward." Eugene (Gene) McCarthy, a former employee at the Pillsbury grain elevator, and his wife Mary McCarthy, had started their tavern on Hamburg Street, just five blocks from his brother's tavern, in 1964. The couple worked well together as Gene tended the bar upfront while Mary McCarthy ran the back dining room from 8 a.m. until late in the evening 364 days a year (they only closed for Christmas Day). Mary explained that they stayed open so much because their tavern was more of "a meeting house" and there were many elderly residents who were alone and whose social life revolved around coming to McCarthy's to visit with friends.[47] To distinguish their establishment from other rowdy saloons, the McCarthys hung a sign behind the bar, which stated, "This is a high-class place-act respectable." Mary McCarthy always forbade swearing in her establishment, and it is a rule that was always enforced. One writer in 1990 described the tavern this way: "McCarthy's overflows with Irish pride...Shamrocks hang from the ceiling. Photos of Notre Dame's 1988 national champion football team and the Edward J. Cotter fireboat square off against each other on the walls."[48] During the Shamrock Run and St. Patrick's Day festivities it is impossible to get a seat in this tavern, and there is a steady crowd during the weekdays and Saturdays as well.

World War II

Residents of the Ward hobbled through the Great Depression, and were then thrust into the mobilization to defeat Germany and Japan in the Second World War. Many heroes emerged from the Ward, but the most prominent First Ward native in this conflict was the same hero from World War I: William J. Donovan. In between the wars, "Wild Bill" served in various political positions and was a partner in a successful Wall Street law firm where he reportedly became a millionaire. In 1922, as the U.S. Attorney for Western New York, he was responsible for enforcing the Prohibition laws, which he did faithfully (in fact, some speculate that his overzealous enforcement efforts may have cost him a chance at higher political office). It is rumored that Herbert Hoover offered Donovan the position of Vice President on his ticket in 1928, but he turned it down, hoping for the Attorney General slot. However, at that time there was too much animosity toward a Catholic enforcing U.S. laws, so Hoover couldn't offer Bill Donovan his desired position. In 1932, Donovan unsuccessfully ran as the Republican candidate for governor of New York and was once considered a possible Republican presidential candidate. But for various reasons higher political office would elude Donovan for the rest of his life.

"Wild Bill" Donovan and President Franklin Delano Roosevelt, former classmates at Columbia University, were close personal friends despite their different political affiliations. When hostilities began in Europe preceding the U.S.

entry into World War II, Roosevelt called on Donovan to assist him. Donovan's first assignments involved diplomatic missions to assess the evolving crisis and he met with leaders such as Winston Churchill and King George VI. At the start of war between England and Germany, Ambassador Joseph P. Kennedy's assessment was that the English were finished and would capitulate to the more powerful Germans. Donovan's assessment was much more optimistic and he urged Roosevelt to provide resources to assist England. Roosevelt trusted Donovan's opinion more than Kennedy's and as a result the U.S. started sending material aid to the British through the Lend-Lease program. Upon his return to the U.S., Donovan also urged Roosevelt to prepare for a global war.[49]

After Donovan's information-gathering European mission, the crippled Roosevelt had even grander plans for the former boy from Michigan Street whom he once referred to as "my secret legs."[50] Prior to the U.S. involvement in the war, the United States had an ineffective and fragmented foreign intelligence network, so Roosevelt tasked Donovan with centralizing these disparate organizations. On July 11, 1941, Bill Donovan was named the Coordinator of Information for the U.S. Government. One year later, on June 13, 1942, Roosevelt appointed Donovan as director of the newly created Office of Strategic Services (OSS)—a centralized intelligence agency, which aided the U.S. during the Second World War. Donovan propelled the U.S. intelligence agency from outdated tactics into the 20th century and hired the best and brightest from across the country; he reportedly claimed that his ideal candidate was someone with a PhD who could win a bar fight.[51]

Donovan's organization provided valuable information for the Allied Forces during the Second World War and in 1944 he was promoted to the rank of Major General in the U.S. Army for his efforts. While Roosevelt admired Donovan greatly, his Vice President, Harry S. Truman, strongly disliked Donovan. At the end of the war, after Roosevelt's death in 1945, President Truman dismissed Donovan and dissolved the OSS. One year later, Truman re-established the department under the name of the Central Intelligence Group, but did not appoint Donovan, the likely candidate, as director. Despite this egregious snub, Donovan is still considered the "Father of American Intelligence" and his portrait hangs first in the gallery of CIA directors at CIA headquarters in Virginia. After his directorship of the OSS ended, Donovan was asked to assist during the Nuremberg Trials, and he later served as an ambassador to Thailand.

William J. Donovan was clearly the most remarkable person to come out of the First Ward in terms of his impact on national and international affairs. His accomplishments for his country rank up there with other native Buffalonians including Presidents Millard Fillmore and Grover Cleveland. The United States recognized Donovan for his indefatigable efforts by honoring him with the four highest decorations that the nation confers: the Congressional Medal of Honor, the

Distinguished Service Cross, the Distinguished Service Medal, and the National Security Medal.[52] Judge Salvatore Martoche, a Bill Donovan expert, claims that, "Buffalo never produced such a colorful figure on the national or international stage [as Bill Donovan]."[53] Sir William Stephenson, known as "Intrepid", was a British Intelligence director who worked closely with William Donovan during World War II. Stephenson boldly claimed that William Donovan "was one of the significant men of our century." At the end of the war, Admiral Wilhelm Canaris, the German Intelligence chief during World War II, stated that of all of the Allied leaders he wished to meet he would choose William Donovan.[54] More importantly, Donovan biographer Richard Dunlop claimed that Adolf Hitler "feared and hated him [Donovan] more than he did any other American."[55] In 1959, after William Donovan passed away, President Dwight Eisenhower declared that the young man from the First Ward was "the Last Hero".[56]

The Ward produced another hero during the Second World War; however, unlike Donovan, this hero was not a native-born son of the Ward. Fr. Thomas M. Conway, born on April 5, 1908 in Waterbury, Connecticut, was the oldest child of two Irish immigrants. After attending Niagara University, he discerned that he had a calling to the priesthood for the Catholic Diocese of Buffalo and was ordained a priest on May 16, 1934. After various assignments throughout the diocese, he ended up at St. Brigid's in the Ward where members of the parish fondly remembered him as a "priest in touch with and sympathetic to the blue-collar realities of his parishioners."[57] Conway was also remembered as a "man's man" and as a man who loved to sail on Lake Erie in his small boat, which was parked alongside the rectory in the Ward.[58] His halcyon days sailing along Lake Erie would soon end, like those of others in the Ward, when the Japanese bombed Pearl Harbor in 1941.

On September 17, 1942, Fr. Conway enlisted in the U.S. Navy to serve as a chaplain. After serving at various naval bases on the East Coast, on August 24, 1944, Father Conway was assigned to the cruiser USS *Indianapolis*, which swiftly sailed to fight in the Pacific Campaign against the Japanese. The USS *Indianapolis* was engaged during the infamous Battle of Okinawa and a kamikaze bomb claimed the life of nine sailors on board; Father Conway, at his own expense, used his leave to fly to various parts of the country to comfort the families of these fallen men. He returned to the *Indianapolis* and resumed his duties of ministering to both Catholics and non-Catholics alike, all of whom were unaware of the impending disaster awaiting this naval cruiser.

On July 30, 1945, just a month before the end of the war, a Japanese submarine struck the *Indianapolis* with two torpedoes shortly after midnight. The ship sunk in just fourteen minutes. Of the 1,196 crewmen on board, 300 of them went down with the ship while the other 900 were left floating in the debris strewn, shark-infested waters of the Pacific. Numerous sailors later recalled the actions of Fr. Conway during those harrowing days. For three days, this thirty-seven-year-old priest from the Ward assisted the frightened sailors in many ways: he brought back sailors who had floated away from the group, he prayed with the sailors to calm their fears, he heard their confessions, he performed last rites, and he consoled sailors who had lost hope. Many remembered the constant encouragement he gave the scared, exhausted sailors as well as the confidence he inspired that their rescue was imminent. Unfortunately, after three days floating in the ocean, and only one day before the remaining sailors were rescued, Father Conway died from exhaustion and drowned like 600 of his fellow sailors.

Of the nearly 1,200 sailors on-board the USS *Indianapolis* only 316 survived, and it is still remembered as the second worst disaster in U.S. naval history after Pearl Harbor. The causes of death were numerous: starvation, dehydration, shark attacks, salt poisoning, and hypothermia. As a result of delirium some men even killed their fellow sailors and themselves. It was a horrific experience for all who endured it. Shortly before Fr. Conway left for his U.S Navy duty he recorded a tape for a close friend. On the tape the assistant rector of St. Brigid's told his friend: "So, don't miss me. I'll be back. Remember me in your prayers and I'll remember you." Despite Thomas Conway's optimism, he never returned to sail his boat that waited for him alongside the rectory in the First Ward.

Ward residents contributed to the war effort in the Second World War much as they had in the Civil War and the First World War. Some, like James R. Hagan, son of the founder of the Blackthorn Club, who was killed in 1944 in France, made the ultimate sacrifice. Stanley Siergiej from 228 Hamburg Street in the Ward was the very first American soldier to enter Liege, Belgium after the Allies had taken it from the Germans. Stanley was even interviewed by a news reporter for this accomplishment, but seven months later he was killed in the German offensive. Two of Stanley's brothers also fought in the Pacific campaign, and fortunately both of them returned home alive. Bert Hyde's uncle, Joseph Buckley from Mackinaw Street, was killed at the Battle of Iwo Jima. Jerry Reilly, a star baseball pitcher from South Park High School who was raised both on Perry Street and O'Connell Avenue, perished with the five famous Sullivan brothers on the USS *Juneau* on November 13, 1942. Jim Shine related the sad tale of his great-uncle, John J. Connors, who was from the Beach area of the Ward. Connors was killed in Germany just four days before Hitler committed suicide and less than two weeks before the end of the war in Europe. Connors' mother thought that John was safe because the letter informing her of his death only arrived a full month after the war was over.

All four of Mr. and Mrs. Walter Astyk's boys from Smith Street fought in World War II. One of them, Denner Astyk, was injured in France, and another,

Vincent, was killed when his ship was torpedoed in 1944. Francis McGuire, 26, from O'Connell Avenue, was killed on July 7, 1944 in the horrific Battle of Saipan. In a departure from past wars, the dead in this conflict were not just male residents of the Ward. In February 1944, Lieutenant Jean Herko, from 580 South Park Avenue—one of the first flight nurses who enlisted during the war—died in a plane crash in Italy.

Some men were fortunate only to be maimed or injured during the war. Vincent Lore from 98 Louisiana Street was wounded twice in France and received the Purple Heart for his service. Mrs. Amanda Burshtynski of 469 South Park Avenue had to cope with the injuries to her son, Walter, and her son-in-law, Royal Dunmyer, in the campaign in France. Tommy Sullivan from the Ward left for the war as a healthy young man, but he came back from combat with one less leg and arm. As a result of his injuries, and because he couldn't quite "fly straight" anymore, Tommy earned the life-long nickname "Tailspin." Thomas Scanlon from Sidway Avenue was wounded by an exploding mortar shell and was awarded the Purple Heart for his heroics in France in 1944. Frank and Peter Nowicki of Fulton Street were both casualties in the European campaign in 1944. Leo Kirinowicz from Alabama Street was wounded in the Metz Campaign in France and received the Purple Heart for his efforts in silencing two German machine gun nests in that battle. As the partial list above makes clear, the war touched many people from all of the neighborhoods and ethnic enclaves throughout the Ward.

Continued Hardships But One Triumph

This period not only included the tragedy of the war, but also the unique hardships that many First Warders faced. Stable employment was still elusive to many workers in industries tied to the waterfront. Tom Krzeminski remembers that when his father Stanley struggled to find work, he did what other Poles did at the time: he visited "Big Joe" Dudzick's tavern at 770 Seneca Street. After a short discussion with Dudzick, the 6'11" politician and barkeeper, Stanley Krzeminski returned home and told his wife he needed $100 in cash. Stanley returned to Big Joe's saloon, gave him the money, and three days later, Stanley Krzeminski had a job at H-O Oats. This was how things were done in those days.[59] Tom Krzeminski's family suffered another hardship when their house burned to the ground in 1954 after a fire in a next-door neighbor's shed leaped to their house. The homes and cottages were so close together in the Ward that fires often spread very quickly with devastating results. As a result of the fire, his family had to move next door into a smaller, two-bedroom home and the 6'3" Tom had to sleep in the same bed with his brother Steve until he was twenty-one.

Industrial accidents were fewer than in the previous generations, but still equally tragic. On December 18, 1950, on a snowy 23-degree day, twelve men left at 6:00 a.m. from Buffalo across Lake Erie to Dunkirk, New York. The winds were fair at only 14 miles an hour, but for some unknown reason the tugboat *Sachem* sank near Dunkirk. Two years later the boat was recovered and deemed seaworthy and no definitive cause of the accident could be ascertained. One of the most credible theories is that a seiche or a lake tidal wave may have hit the boat and capsized it.[60] All twelve of the crew onboard, including a few First Ward men like Thomas Shine, perished in the wreck.[61]

Dave Mann, one of ten children, remembers the hardship when his father died from appendicitis in 1944 at the young age of thirty-nine. As a result, Dave Mann's mother went to work and his two older brothers, sixteen and seventeen years old, were forced to drop out of school in order to support the family.[62] People in the Ward found a way to survive through hard work and much sacrifice. Jim Graham's father had a good job as an engineer for the Buffalo Municipal Housing Authority, but even with that Jim and his siblings only received one gift at Christmas. Money was scarce for many First Warders and the industrial nature of the neighborhood was still fraught with dangers for young and old. In March 1949, eleven-year-old Richard Guise, brother of Bert Guise-Hyde, and his friend Richard Trala were searching for baby pigeons along the abandoned docks on the Buffalo River. Guise slipped and fell into the murky river near Louisiana and Ohio Streets and drowned just a few feet from shore. This tragedy occurred only four weeks after the Corbran family at 124 Smith Street lost their twelve-year-old son, Thomas Joseph, who was playing on a pipe pontoon at the foot of Katherine Street. The young Corbran slipped and drowned in the unforgiving Buffalo River.

In the early 1950s, the First Warders finally triumphed over one industrial nuisance: the Ohio Basin. The Basin had been a public hazard since the 1850s when the Hamburg Canal was decommissioned, causing foul water to pool up in the Basin. The Ohio Basin was also a possible source of the deadly cholera epidemics that plagued the First Ward throughout the mid-19th century. Apparently, the odor from the stagnant water was particularly noxious in the summer months. Mayor James Griffin recalled that the name given to the Basin in his youth was the "Scummy Basin." In addition to the foul smell, the Ohio Basin was particularly dangerous for children who liked to play near it during the winter and summer months. The Evans family memoir related the tragic story of how they lost their four-year-old relative, Timmy Evans, to drowning in the Ohio Basin. On January 4, 1949, the Basin claimed two other young boys. Seven-year-old Frederick Fox and ten-year-old St. Brigid student Raymond Sturm both drowned after falling through the ice on the Basin. Numerous other children drowned or were injured at the site of the Basin over the years, and the public repeatedly called for its closure, but the Fox and Sturm tragedies pushed the limits of the local residents' patience.

For close to 100 years, despite numerous health hazards, the industrial interests at the Ohio Basin prevailed over the interests of the residents. The local residents were no match for powerful companies like Banner Flour Mill, Mann Bros Linseed Company, Laidlaw Lumber, and Niagara Sand Company. These businesses argued that they needed to keep the Ohio Basin open so lake freighters could load and unload their goods.[63] Like businesses prior to them, they were worried that a closure of the basin would eliminate their access to the Buffalo River and consequently Lake Erie. In the early 1950s, local residents, with the help of local politicians and the tragic deaths of Fox and Sturm, finally won the 100 year-old fight. The Ohio Basin was finally filled in with the remnants of the famed Frank Lloyd Wright-designed Larkin Building.

Jack O'Brian

In Jack O'Brian's obituary published in the *New York Times* on November 8, 2000, the writer knighted him as the "Columnist of the Entertainment World."[64] The author of the obituary described Jack as "a newspaper columnist who brought a breezy, peppery style to writing about television and Broadway gossip."[65] However, this famous First Ward resident was more than just a famous gossip columnist. He was also an accomplished reporter and an ardent anti-communist during the 1950s. During the "Red Scare," O'Brian's gossip columns evolved into political diatribes against people in the entertainment world who had liberal political sympathies. His column—which excoriated suspected Hollywood Communists—carried extra weight because of his friendship with Roy Cohn and J. Edgar Hoover. One person even claims that O'Brian's newspaper columns contributed to the suicide of the famous CBS reporter, Don Hollenbeck.

John Dennis Patrick O'Brian was born on August 16, 1914 to Charles J. O'Brian and Josephine Loretta Kelleher. Like other famous First Ward men, he was quickly introduced to a life of hard work in occupations along the waterfront of Buffalo. After attending Our Lady of Perpetual Help school, just a few blocks from his home at 198 O'Connell Avenue, John "Jack" O'Brian dropped out of school at age 13, never to return to formal education. Later in life O'Brian joked that "he was too busy getting an education to go to school."[66] Like others in the Ward, his first job was at the Larkin Soap Company where he worked as a messenger boy. After that stint he worked in hundreds of day labor construction jobs, as a sailor and even as a gravedigger. O'Brian recalled one memorable job he held where he loaded one-hundred and two-hundred pound bags of limestone into railcars for 10 hours a day.[67] Jack explained that "from the time I was a lad, I don't remember a job I ever held—except journalism—that didn't involve sweat and muscle, and pick and shovel."⁶⁸ Many First Warders could relate to this statement.

Work was not the only challenge in Jack O'Brian's life. His family situation was tumultuous as well. He was the son of an alcoholic New York Central railroad conductor and he suffered the tragedy of his mother's death when he was a teenager. O'Brian described his early life in the following way: 'I was pretty much on my own, a teenager out of work more than not. I didn't even know I was homeless—I just knew I often for months was dead broke and I actually fainted three times, at least, from hunger.'⁶⁹ Both of O'Brian's grandfathers were saloon owners in the Ward, so he was no stranger to the inside of a tavern.⁷⁰ To numb his pain, Jack frequented saloons in the Ward and some incorrectly think that this earned him the nickname "Kegga" O'Brian, but more about that later. O'Brian saw himself as a "barstool Irishman, and friend of First Ward cops and saloon waiters."⁷¹ Jack was described by one of his daughters as "stocky and strong as a bull—he had put a couple of men in the hospital."⁷² These rough formative years in the Ward definitely influenced his later life as a feisty and brawling columnist.

At age seventeen, Jack's writing career began at the *South Buffalo News* and the *Catholic Union and Times*. After a short time he was asked to write for the Bugle, a newspaper that wrote about famous Buffalo divorces. At first, it was this particular gossip journalism in which he excelled, and it would later be his springboard to fame. In 1939, after working for the *Buffalo Times*, he moved to New York City to work for the *New York World-Telegram*. After only a year in New York, he moved back to Buffalo to write for the Conners family at the *Courier-Express* until 1943. In that same year, he was nominated for a Pulitzer Prize for a story in which he uncovered a large-scale fraud with food rationing coupons during World War II. His story led to the conviction and confessions of forty-seven people and the closing of several clubs, saloons, and restaurants.⁷³ At age twenty-nine, Jack left the Ward for the last time and relocated to New York City to work at the *Associated Press* headquarters where he wrote drama, movie, and radio reviews.⁷⁴ O'Brian quickly reached fame as 1,400 newspapers across the country carried his column called "Broadway." The outspoken O'Brian even hosted a radio program at that time. But the young man from the docks and saloons of the Ward was not content covering Broadway plays and actors. The former day laborer from the Ward envisioned a larger role for himself as "the voice of the common folk, champion of decency, and fighter against soft-on-Communism liberals.⁷⁵

In 1950, he started a column in the Hearst *New York Journal-American* called "On the Air" which ran uninterrupted for over fourteen years. O'Brian became one of the nation's leading critics of televisions shows, actors, and news reporters. He was extremely critical of many popular entertainers including Steve Allen, Ed Sullivan, Danny Kaye, Jackie Gleason, and Mike Wallace and only approved of a few such as Perry Como and Walter Cronkite.[76] O'Brian had many detractors who loathed his vitriolic style, and even he acknowledged his bad behavior when he exclaimed, "I don't blame people who hate my guts."[77] In 1958, the famous TV personality Steve Allen exclaimed that O'Brian "is the only TV critic in the nation who is rude, inaccurate, unchristian and vengeful."[78] Steve Allen described O'Brian as the "neighborhood bully," "shockingly vulgar," "[exhibiting] emotional immaturity," and with "the sensitivity of a mastodon when it comes to the feelings of others." Allen even reminded his readers that O'Brian and Jackie Gleason almost came to blows in a restaurant in New York City. Perhaps the qualities attributed to Jack O'Brian by Steve Allen were the result of O'Brian's difficult family circumstances and upbringing. Certainly O'Brian's development in tough environs and in occupations along the waterfront combined with his difficult family circumstances influenced his critical and biting writing style.

O'Brian wasn't only a successful gossip writer; he was also an accomplished reporter. In addition to uncovering the food rationing scandal, he was also influential in exposing the shocking scandal on the NBC quiz show called *Twenty-One*. One of his newspaper columns in 1958 claimed that the NBC show was rigged, which led to a Congressional hearing regarding his accusations. In fact, his claims were correct and the contestant in question, Charles Van Doren, admitted in the Congressional hearings that the show was fixed. But O'Brian's legacy isn't associated with his journalistic excellence—rather with his controversial anti-communist columns and even more controversial support of the Wisconsin Senator Joe McCarthy and his chief counsel Roy Cohn.

In a recent book by Loren Ghiglione entitled *CBS's Don Hollenbeck: An Honest Reporter in the Age of McCarthysim*, the author details the facts around Jack O'Brian's upbringing in the Ward and how it shaped his opinions during the "Age of Senator McCarthy." In the book, Loren Ghiglione makes the claim that O'Brian's anti-communism can be attributed to "the columnist's conservative, anti-intellectual, working class roots [in the First Ward]."[79] O'Brian once admitted that he was not an intellectual but he had "the popular mind."[80] Regardless of where O'Brian's opinions originated—in the Ward or somewhere else—O'Brian made it his mission to expose reporters, actors, and other entertainers if he suspected that they had communist sympathies. Three of the targets in his columns were Edward R. Murrow, Barry Gray, and Don Hollenbeck.[81] O'Brian even tried to physically harm broadcaster Barry Gray one evening on the streets of New York City, but he was restrained by his wife.

But it was the CBS reporter Don Hollenbeck, renowned for his reporting during the McCarthy hearings, who was the main target of Jack's ire. O'Brian repeatedly wrote in his columns that Hollenbeck was soft on Communism and hard on Senator McCarthy. This unrelenting barrage of public criticism from

O'Brian had its effect on Hollenbeck, who was already suffering from depression, alcoholism, and several failed relationships. Hollenbeck became obsessed with the frequent attacks and was in fear of losing the last thing in his life: his job at CBS.[82] One day, in the summer of 1954, Hollenbeck could not handle the taunts from the O'Brian assaults anymore, so he ended his pain by turning on all of the gas burners in his apartment until he went to sleep.

Following Hollenbeck's suicide, his fellow CBS reporters stepped up their attacks on O'Brian. Walter Cronkite described O'Brian as a "McCarthyite Red-baiter who had the distinction, as far as we at CBS News were concerned, of having hounded to a suicide's grave one of our most distinguished reporters." Cronkite added, "O'Brian was a very bad man."[83] CBS reporter Mike Wallace continued, "He [O'Brian] was a really bad guy. He was a mean son of a bitch, a mean-spirited man."[84] While it may be true that O'Brian contributed to Hollenbeck's death, it must be stated that Hollenbeck suffered from the twin demons of alcoholism and depression, so it is not fair to entirely blame O'Brian for this tragedy. Regardless, after the suicide, O'Brian continued his attacks on others that he felt were traitors to his country, and he never regretted his actions regarding Hollenbeck. For a guy who had learned the art of survival in the First Ward, the relentless counterattacks that Jack O'Brian received from his detractors couldn't penetrate his thick skin.

While O'Brian penned most of his famous columns in Manhattan, it was his years in the Ward that formed his style. His opponents described him as gritty, anti-intellectual, and pugnacious. His feisty, tough-guy personality was similar to that of other First Ward men such as "Fingy" Conners, the Sheehan brothers, and later, the famous mayor of Buffalo, Jimmy Griffin. In fact, O'Brian was like a skilled boxer who could use words to get under his opponent's skin and then destroy them. In a sense, the inflammatory rhetoric in O'Brian's columns was similar to the provocative opinions of modern-day TV personalities like Bill O'Reilly or Jon Stewart.

Jack's unlikely rise from the saloons of the Ward to his friendships with powerful men of his day like Roy Cohn and J. Edgar Hoover was quite remarkable. O'Brian self-admittedly was not an intellectual giant, but he was endowed with the understanding that you succeed from hard work, determination, and sometimes a touch of ruthlessness mixed in. On November 5, 2000 in Manhattan, at the age of eighty-six—four years after his beloved wife Yvonne passed on— Jack O'Brian finally came to rest. O'Brian's two daughters, Kate and Bridget, and four grandchildren survived him. His story is still relatively unknown to many Buffalonians.

Nicknames

The name of Jack "Kegga" O'Brian brings us to a lighter topic. One of the most distinguishing traits of the Ward is that almost every resident receives a nickname at some point in their life. There are various theories on why nicknames are commonplace in the Ward, but it appears that it was a necessity. Specifically, there were so many people with the same last name and some were even burdened with the unthinkable dilemma of having both the same first and last name. Therefore, there had to be a system to distinguish each of them and creating nicknames was it. For instance, there were three different Daniel Bohens on O'Connell Avenue in the 1920s, so a nickname was often the only distinguishing mark. The nicknames often arose from a peculiar physical characteristic or a memorable event, and some stuck for life while others evolved over time. Nicknames were such a part of someone's identity that as one Ward resident claimed, it often wasn't until you read the person's obituary that you knew their real name.[85]

In a letter in 1974 to a columnist from the *Courier-Express*, news columnist Jack "Kegga" O'Brian corrected those that thought he received his nickname because he liked to frequent the local taverns in the Ward. Instead Jack O'Brian explained that his mother's maiden name was Kelleher and when he was about one-year-old, living at 198 O'Connell Avenue, he used to call his maternal grandmother "Gramma Kegga" because he couldn't quite say Kelleher."[86] O'Brian also explained how nicknames had a way of evolving over time as was the case with one of his brothers. His brother James was originally nicknamed "Jim", but their father felt the Gaelic version "Shamus" was more appropriate. Over time "Shamus" became "Shimeo" and eventually "Schimmel."[87] His other brother Joseph Henry O'Brian couldn't be nicknamed "Joe" because that was his mother's name and their uncle was already "Henry," so he received "Harry", but that wasn't sufficient for his pals so they called him "Harpo."[88] Jack O'Brian's father, whose name was Charles, was called "Charlie," "Chazz," and "Cuckoo," which described how his father acted when he fought.[89]

Congressman Richard McCarthy remembered "Silver Sleeves" Patty O'Reilly, who received his name from his habit of wiping his running nose on his sleeve. Another person was nicknamed "Head of a Bishop" because as an infant it was said his head resembled a bishop. Other nicknames McCarthy remembered were "Bumble Foot" McGloin, "Diapers" Flannery, "Kisses and Pickles" Riordan, "Potatoes" McGovern and "Handsome" Jerry O'Rafferty.[90] According to his son, George "Chickie" Evans, the well-known First Ward lawyer and politician, received his nickname from his inability as a child to pronounce the word "chicken." George's son, George, as well as his grandson now share his nickname.[91] (For a partial list of First Ward nicknames go to Appendix B.)

CHAPTER THIRTEEN

THE WARD STUMBLES, GETS BACK UP

The St. Lawrence Seaway...symbolizes the accomplishments which are possible when two nations cooperate in peaceful endeavor. I am delighted that our nation is associated with our Canadian partner in this monumental development and use of the international waters of the St. Lawrence River.
– President Dwight D. Eisenhower, 1958

A thriving First Ward was dependent on a thriving Buffalo, which was dependent on its strategic location on the eastern end of Lake Erie. For 100 years this symbiotic relationship worked very well for all parties. Even when the railroads appeared in the 1850s, and it appeared that the Erie Canal would become obsolete, Buffalo and the Ward adapted to the new reality and continued to thrive. At that time there was also competition for grain transshipments through New Orleans via the Mississippi River, but the Midwestern farmers decided that Buffalo was the preferred destination because of its proximity to the major grain markets of New York City, Boston, Philadelphia, and Baltimore.[1] In 1932, the expansion of the Welland Canal in Canada, which improved marine shipping between Lake Erie and Lake Ontario, threatened Buffalo's strategic location again; but it was a short lived threat because during World War II U.S. shippers were forced to ship domestically for security reasons, so Buffalo was preferred over Montreal and thousands of jobs in the First Ward were saved.[2] When the national highway system was implemented in the 1950s, it allowed trucks to bypass Buffalo, but industry leaders and politicians found ways to keep adapting and growing, and the Ward continued to thrive. The announcement, however, by the Canadian and American governments in 1954 that it would build a canal system to connect the Atlantic Ocean to the Great Lakes via the St. Lawrence River—which would essentially allow shippers to bypass Buffalo—was a development that would profoundly effect the economy of Buffalo and the First Ward for decades to come. In fact, the Ward would never be the same.

Plans for the expansion of the St. Lawrence Seaway to handle oceangoing freighters had been proposed as early as 1895, but powerful railroad interests and East Coast ports in the U.S. continually blocked them. From 1934 to1952, Congress defeated eight different bills concerning the St. Lawrence Seaway project because of effective industry lobbying efforts.[3] As early as 1940, the Pioneer Civic Association—made up of residents in the First Ward who realized the negative consequences for the Ward if the Seaway was built—rallied supporters to defeat the plans being pushed by the Canadian government.[4] According to a 1955 *Time* magazine article, the project sponsors envisioned a "man-made Mediterranean, on which seagoing ships can sail westward 2,300 miles into America's heartland."[5] Concerned First Warders realized that ships could come in from the Atlantic and go down the St. Lawrence Seaway, past Quebec and Montreal onto Lake Ontario, through the Welland Canal and then onto Lake Erie without ever having to stop in Buffalo. Buffalo's strategic position as the "choke-point" for moving goods from the Great Lakes to the East Coast, its economic *raison d'être* and the key to its prosperity for over 100 years, would essentially be eliminated.

Supporters promised that this would be a positive development for everyone involved. The project promised that the price of shipping goods to the Atlantic from the Midwest would drop from $13 a ton to $1.70 a ton, so consumers and factories would benefit, and it was thought that Great Lakes cities would benefit as well. One writer exclaimed that: "Such lakefront cities as Chicago, Cleveland, Duluth, Buffalo, Toronto and Hamilton will become genuine deepwater ports, 500 miles closer to Europe by seaway than at present."[6] Finally, after much pressure from the Canadian government and declarations that they would build it alone without the support of the U.S. Government, in 1954 Congress assented and signed a bill allowing for construction of the St. Lawrence Seaway project. Within a year, 15,000 workers were busy dredging the St. Lawrence River, building canals to bypass the International Rapids along the New York and Ontario borders, and expanding the Welland Canal to handle ocean freighters. The concerned Ward citizens from the Pioneer Civic Association were right to be worried.

In 1957, two years before the St. Lawrence Seaway opened, Buffalo hosted a "World Port Celebration" from September 21-30 in order to highlight the glories of the past 125 years since Buffalo's founding and to generate excitement for its future importance as a world port; the souvenir program for the celebration even reminded the reader, in case they were not aware, that "Buffalo is the first major U.S. port on the St. Lawrence Seaway."[7] Despite the optimism of the celebration and the reminders of Buffalo's proud heritage as a powerful port city, things were about to change. After much fanfare, with President Dwight Eisenhower and Queen Elizabeth cutting the ceremonial ribbon, the St. Lawrence Seaway opened on June 26, 1959 and shippers throughout the Great Lakes, who obviously hadn't had time to read Buffalo's World Port Celebration brochure, immediately started bypassing Buffalo. Oceangoing ships sailed from Great Lakes' ports like Duluth and Chicago out to the Atlantic without even stopping for a cup of coffee in Buffalo. Buffalo was about to suffer economically from this new route to the Atlantic, and the First Ward was going to be devastated.

Tewksbury Disaster

The First Ward, located right next to Lake Erie, had a particularly intimate history with the violent lake storms that continually pummeled Buffalo. The 1844 seiche (tidal wave) was certainly the most devastating in terms of loss of life (78 fatalities), but other storms inflicted significant damage as well. On January 22, 1874, a January thaw caused water to accumulate at a pontoon bridge that had been created the year before at Ohio Street. The dammed water eventually burst through the makeshift bridge and rushed down toward Michigan Street. On its way, it broke seven boats off their moorings near Chicago Street (the *J.G Masten*, the *Sam Flint*, the *James D. Sawyer*, the *James C. Harrison*, the *Thomas P. Sheldon*, the *Benjamin F. Bruce*, and the *Erastus D. Corning*), which all raced down the Buffalo River to see how much damage they could do to the grain elevators. By the time the stampede was over, a tower at the Plimpton Elevator collapsed, two of the iron abutments holding up the Niagara Elevator had fallen, three supports holding up the City Elevator crashed down, and 500 feet of freight sheds along the shore of the river were crushed. Fortunately, the Michigan Street jack-knife bridge was able to stop the onslaught. All told, over $100,000 ($1.8 million in 2010 dollars) of damage was done to the area around the First Ward.[8] (In the next century a similar event would occur, but the results for the Michigan Street Bridge wouldn't be so favorable.)

Ten years later, on December 15, 1884, another winter storm with 64-mph winds destroyed a large number of the seawall cottages occupied by fishermen and their families.[9] The waves from Lake Erie were so powerful they even broke down parts of the seawall itself and huge lumber piles were scattered for hundreds of feet.[10] Raging floods on May 20, 1894 caused the Buffalo River to overflow and several square miles in the Ward and in South Buffalo were flooded. During this storm, an unexpected tide inflicted a heavy loss of property, and a vast area of the southern part of the city of Buffalo was accessible only by boat.[11] In fact, a review of the Common Council proceedings in 1908, which mentions the May 1894 storm, stated that floods in the First and Thirteenth Ward were a yearly occurrence; in the First Ward the problem area tended to be east of Hamburg Street.[12]

Next there was the massive 1907 Great Gale storm on January 19 and 20, which caused over $3 million in property losses with hurricane winds (84-mph gusts) that caused devastation all the way from the Erie Basin to Tifft Farm. The epicenter of this storm was the foot of Michigan Street. Two massive lake freighters, the *Herbert Smith* and the *Nottingham*, were actually lifted out of the water by the winds and beached at Michigan Street, a stunning sight for all who witnessed it.[13] Two other smaller ships simply sank near the foot of Michigan Street. The winds caused a rush of water down the Buffalo River, with the water rising six to eight feet in some spots. These waters swelled the Ohio Basin, which then flooded basements and caused general flooding throughout that section of the Ward. A large brick wall 60 feet high by 40 feet long, which enclosed the Mutual Transportation Company's elevator at the foot of Ganson Street, collapsed from the wind and crushed the freight sheds below it. The Precinct 7 police station on Louisiana Street was devastated with five feet of water in its basement, and John P. Sullivan's Ice House disappeared near the Buffalo Creek railroad bridge.[14] It seemed that every generation of Ward residents was used to severe, damaging storms, but the one that took place in 1959, the same year as the opening of the St. Lawrence Seaway, left an indelible memory for all who witnessed it.

On January 21, 1959, Buffalo was experiencing an unseasonably warm and rainy day. As a result of the warm temperatures, at about 10 p.m. an ice dam on Cazenovia Creek—near the Cazenovia Street Bridge in South Buffalo— gave way and unleashed a wall of water carrying hundreds of large chunks of ice downstream.[15] Three-foot thick ice boulders as large as 25 by 35 feet smashed holes into home basements, upended cars, and wiped out utility poles and trees.[16] The immediate impact from the ice dam breaking was significant flooding in South Buffalo, but the most costly damage was saved for the First Ward. As the water rushed downstream toward the Buffalo River in the Ward, the violent current of water broke the moorings of a 500-foot long corn freighter, the *MacGilvray Shiras*. This ship rushed downstream and subsequently broke the moorings of the grain freighter *Michael K. Tewksbury*, parked at the foot of St. Clair Street. Eyewitnesses say they had never witnessed anything like it as the two unaided "ghost ships" navigated the winding, curving Buffalo River, which is a difficult task in pristine conditions with a captain on the bridge and tugs guiding the ship.

As the 525-foot long freighter, the *Tewksbury*, propelled by gale force winds, raced toward the Michigan Street Bridge, the bridge operators were purportedly enjoying a drink in the Swannie House unaware of the events unfolding on this stormy night.[17] They were finally alerted to the impending disaster and rushed to raise the bridge before it was hit, but they arrived too late. The *Tewksbury* crashed into the Michigan Street Bridge with a deafening roar which witness Charles Halloran described as a "sickening, scratching crash like an auto accident magnified a million times."[18] The *Tewksbury's* collision with the bridge left a pile of mangled steel and weakened the 130-foot bridge tower, which collapsed the next morning. More importantly, the freighter was wedged under the bridge, creating a dam that flooded an eighteen-block area of the Ward.[19] City officials were worried that all of the bridges connecting South Buffalo to the city would be washed away unless the floodwaters receded.

While the storm caused only a few human injuries and no deaths, it turned out to be the most expensive Great Lakes accident in history.[20] Property damages were estimated at $1 million dollars and the damage to the twenty-year-old Michigan Avenue Bridge was over $5 million. The *Buffalo News* claimed that "all told Jan. 21, 1959 will go down as one of the worst dates in the area's long history of weather disasters," and "it was the worst flood disaster on record in the metropolitan Buffalo area."[21] For residents of the Ward, it was one more calamity.

Consequences of St. Lawrence Seaway

The storm came and went and the Ward cleaned itself up, but the nightmare of the St. Lawrence Seaway was beginning to set in. Within three years of the Seaway opening, the shipbuilding and marine supply industries, which existed in the First Ward even longer than grain storage and transshipment, quickly closed up. Banta and Bidwell, at the foot of Chicago Street, which went through numerous transformations over its hundred and thirty year history, including name changes (Mason & Bidwell, the Union Dry-dock Company in 1870, Buffalo Dry Dock Company in 1896, and American Shipbuilding Company in 1918), shut its doors in 1962.

Throughout the years, despite an evolution in boat styles—sailing vessels, steamers, and steel freighters—Banta & Bidwell remained one of the most prominent shipbuilding operations on the Great Lakes. Many Buffalonians who lived in the 20th century would be familiar with the famous *Canadiana* and the *Americana* (the Crystal Beach boats), which were manufactured by the Buffalo Dry Dock Company off Chicago Street.[22] After providing employment for thousands of families in the Ward for its long history, shipbuilding at the foot of Chicago Street simply vanished. Skilled riveters like Bud Guise and Leo "Sonny" Guise were both out of work and had to find new occupations.

Companies related to repairing and supplying ships also abruptly left the Ward and the waterfront. Other smaller manufacturers and distributors of boat supplies such as motors and boilers also closed up from a lack of business. Grain shipments didn't abruptly end in 1959—that would take a few more years—but they started to show signs of a decline. Now instead of expanding grain elevators in Buffalo, new ones were being built along the St. Lawrence Seaway in places like Montreal. The hope in 1955 "that Great Lakes Cities expect to get their money back fast when the seaway dream is a thriving reality" faded quickly in Buffalo.[23]

The St. Lawrence Seaway was devastating to the grain transshipment and storage business in Buffalo, but some ships continued to arrive because of Buffalo's artificially low shipping rates, which were set by the International Commerce Commission in the 1950s as a concession for lost business when the New York State Barge Canal closed.[24] However, in 1965, the International Commerce Commission eliminated these discounted shipping rates. Now the Midwest grain shippers had absolutely no reason to ship through Buffalo; they could simply ship via truck or rail around Buffalo. The results were immediate and painful. The Marine A Elevator in the Ward closed in 1966, the Eastern States Elevator was shuttered the same year, and the Connecting Terminal and Concrete-Central closed in 1967. Cargill closed down their Electric, Superior, and the Pool Elevators shortly after that, and H-O Oats cereal plant and the GLF/Agway Elevator complex were closed in the 1970s. Pillsbury shut down the historically important Great Northern Elevator in 1981.[25]

During the 1960s, it wasn't just port industries connected to the First Ward that were leaving. Some companies decided to leave because of lower taxes and fewer union regulations in states outside of New York. The Barcalo Manufacturing Company, for example, left the Ward when the company was sold and its manufacturing was relocated to the sunnier locale of Rocky Mount, North Carolina in 1965. The company was founded in 1896 and had a massive presence off Louisiana Street with a complex of five interconnected buildings. Barcalo specialized in metal bed frames and cribs and was a key national player in this market; they also made a wide variety of other products including a complete line of drop forged hand tools. The company would eventually become known throughout the U.S. in the 1940s for their invention of a unique reclining chair, the Barcalounger, which spawned a new industry of reclining chairs.

Barcalo was also an important company for another important reason. Labor historians claim that Barcalo Manufacturing was the site of the first coffee break at a U.S. company. Company records and newspaper clippings claim that in 1902 the management at Barcalo agreed to grant ten to fifteen minute mid-morning and mid-afternoon coffee breaks for its employees.[26] Shortly thereafter, other companies across the country started introducing their own coffee breaks, but it was not until 1952, that the term *the coffee break* became official. By 1964, the UAW and the Big Three automakers had agreed to stop the machines in order to let their workers enjoy a fifteen-minute coffee break. While others think the first coffee break occurred at another Buffalo institution, the Larkin Company in 1901, most coffee and labor historians agree that the coffee break was initiated at the Barcalo Lounge Company in the First Ward.

As companies left the Ward, they left a wake of unemployed people and devastated families. But lost jobs weren't the only thing they left behind. Several companies left extensive environmental damage to the Buffalo River and its water-shed. Businesses involved with petroleum, lumber, and chemicals used the river for transportation, as a source of water, a place to dump wastewater, and sometimes to dispose of waste products.[27] Over a hundred and fifty years of pollution took its toll on the wildlife and fish native to the area; even as early as the 1930s there was little dissolved oxygen to support schools of fish.[28] Few of the area's natural animal, fish, bird and plant species that existed prior to Dart's elevator in the 1840s still inhabited the Buffalo River watershed in the mid-20th century.[29] The only silver lining of the factory closings in the Ward was the significant reductions in the environmental damage to this area.

First Ward resident Rich Szczygiel remembers playing along Katherine Street in the 1950s at a place nicknamed "The Rockies" by the locals from the mounds of slag that were dumped there years before. He insists that there must have been chemicals dumped with the slag as well because a bluish-green ooze would occasionally emerge from the pile and the kids would often attempt to set it on fire. Szczygiel also remembered when the Buffalo River at the foot of Katherine Street actually caught on fire in the late 1950s.[30] One resident of the Ward recalls that some residents in the mid-20th century would regularly throw bags of trash into the Buffalo River. However, trash from residents was a minor issue when compared to the damage industries did to the Buffalo River and the plants, animals and fish that depended on it.

Starting in the 1960s federal, state, and local organizations implemented new anti-pollution regulations and resources were employed to clean up the river and sites along its path. Concerned citizens in the Ward also became increasingly interested in the environmental quality of their neighborhood and started taking action. One such initiative occurred in 1972 when the City of Buffalo purchased an area just south of the Buffalo River opposite Katherine Street with the intention of creating a landfill. This large parcel of land was once a large dairy farm owned by George Washington Tifft, and it was later transformed into a coal and iron ore transshipment center.[31] Ward and Valley residents led by Anthony Pierzchala urged the city to abandon the landfill plans and instead create a nature preserve. The citizens persevered and, in 1976, the Tifft Nature Preserve was created on this former industrial site just south of the Ward. This 264-acre park is a sanctuary for wildlife, plants and fish, and also a place for recreation with five miles of hiking and snowshoeing trails. Administered by the Buffalo Museum of Science, this natural oasis in the middle of Buffalo's industrial corridor represents a commitment to environmental and conservation education in the heart of the city.[32] In recognition to Tony Pierzchala's efforts the two ponds and lake at Tifft Nature Preserve were named for his three daughters.

The 1960s also brought an end to the political identity of the First Ward. On January 1, 1968, the City of Buffalo officially ended the system of dividing the city into wards and replaced them with districts, which had completely different boundaries. No other people in the city were so intertwined with their political ward as those in the First. This political boundary, which initially had given the early Irish immigrants a voice in the city's decision-making and later provided a means to patronage jobs and a middle-class income for many residents, had sadly come to an end. Almost as important to the patronage jobs and a voice in government was the sense of identity, history, and pride that the designation "First Ward" brought to the residents of the area. So in April 1967, a dinner dance was held on South Park Avenue at Club Como to mark the end of the ward system and to commemorate the previous successes of those from the First Ward. The two dignitaries and hosts at the event were David J. Moran, the current First Ward supervisor, and Andrew J. Morrissey, the previous supervisor. Mr. Morrissey gave a speech that touched on the impact that men from the Ward had had on the city of Buffalo: he discussed the successes that Ward men had achieved in building up the city in pre-Civil War days; he recounted the First Ward's involvement in the Fenian invasion and how many of the men who fought in the battle decided to stay in the Ward after the failed attempt; and he listed numerous prominent citizens of Buffalo that sprang from the Ward such as William "Blue-Eyed Billy" Sheehan, Michael "Mickey" Shea, Bishop Joseph Burke, Msgr. John Boland and Charles R. Diebold Sr.[33] An era in the Ward's history had ended and now this community along the Buffalo River was referred to as the "Old First Ward."

The Ward Gets Back Up: Jimmy Griffin

By the 1980s the Ward had drastically changed from its pre-St. Lawrence Seaway days. The majority of the manufacturers and waterfront industries had closed or were significantly downsized; and the grain scooping industry was doing a fraction of the business it enjoyed during the heyday; the hustle and bustle along the Buffalo River, which was a constant since the 1840s, was noticeably diminished. In 1981, First Ward resident John Baldyga lamented what the First Ward had become:

> It is not a pretty sight or scene. The river is silent, not a ripple in it. No ships plying this waterway as before. The towering elevators, Concrete and Superior, [are] silent. No ships docking there anymore. The only movement, around the elevators now is the pigeons flying in mass formation or scurrying from one elevator to the other, decorating them for sure with their droppings.[34]

The Ward was once again in need of some reason to hope as it had one hundred and thirty years earlier when things looked bleak. In the late 1840s it was an outsider, Bishop John Timon, who arrived to lift Ward residents out of their misery; but this time they got one of their own. Jimmy Griffin's story, like so many before him from the First Ward, begins in humble circumstances. Griffin was born on June 29, 1929, four months before the start of the Great Depression, an event that significantly shaped his views on self-reliance. His father, Tom, worked hard as a hardware clerk for Beals, McCarthy and Rogers in the Ward, and in Jimmy's words, "my dad never made much money, but he'd take us to Sullivan playground on Sidway Street between South Park and Mackinaw every day and hit flies."[35] The Griffin family home was at 602 South Park Avenue near Hamburg Street, and as a boy, when not playing baseball, Jimmy hauled bags of potatoes at the Elk Street Market. While attending St. Brigid's elementary school, he worked part-time at McMahon's store and hauled Budweiser kegs at the Elk Street Market during the summers.[36] Jimmy dropped out of high school to work on the waterfront, returned to complete his diploma and then fought in the Korean War in the 82nd Airborne as a paratrooper. At one time he worked for Maritime Milling at Hopkins and Tifft Streets as a laborer and even scooped grain from railcars.[37] Eventually he fell in love with and married a First Ward woman, Margie McMahon, from Tennessee Street. His biography essentially mirrors other prominent men from the Ward: he worked in the mills, worked for the railroads, and operated a saloon: Hagan's Tavern.

In an article about First Ward legend and prizefighter Jimmy Slattery, Griffin shared his four heroes in life: his father ["Rocco" Griffin], Harry S. Truman, Warren Spahn, and Jimmy Slattery.[38] Of Harry S. Truman, Griffin said "he made a lot of tough decisions and wasn't afraid to. He did what he thought was right."[39] Griffin also mentioned that if he could meet one famous person in history he would have liked to meet St. Paul because "he was a warrior. He knew how to sway people who listened to him."[40] Griffin also shared some of his philosophy on life in the Ward when he was describing Slattery: "They loved Slattery for the way he fought, drank, and took care of the less fortunate."[41] Winning, fighting, and leading were three things that his heroes exhibited and Griffin did too.

In 1961, the scrappy former tavern owner won a seat in the Buffalo Common Council representing the Ellicott District, and five years later won higher office in the New York State Senate. Griffin had great political instincts, a knack for connecting with people, and a gift for remembering names and faces. Griffin, however, lacked one important ingredient for establishing a base to run for higher office: the ability to give jobs to loyal deputies. The feisty Griffin sparred with Peter Crotty and Joe Crangle, two of the leading Democratic leaders in Buffalo, and therefore they "starved him out of any political patronage jobs."[42]

The upstart Griffin befriended Jimmy McMahon, who held a powerful position at the Bethlehem Steel Company, and through McMahon's assistance, Griffin was able to get forty to fifty First Ward friends jobs at the steel mill. Jimmy Griffin now had the base of supporters he needed to run a successful citywide campaign.[43]

In 1977, after meeting with his top advisors at Kennedy's Tavern on Katherine Street in the Ward, Griffin was convinced he had to run for mayor of Buffalo, a feat that no Irish Catholic had yet accomplished. However, the Democratic leadership in Buffalo had decided on an African-American candidate, Arthur Eve, so it appeared Griffin would have to wait a little longer. But the former infantry platoon leader thought *he* should lead Buffalo, so he ran on the Conservative Party line instead. In a heated campaign, Griffin carried the Irish vote in South Buffalo and also convinced a sizable group of Poles on the East Side, many of whom were Democrats, that their interests were best served by him and not Arthur Eve. In a three-way race, Griffin beat the favored Democratic candidate Arthur Eve and then proceeded to win four consecutive mayoral terms; his sixteen years as Buffalo's mayor stands as a local record.

Jimmy's common sense management philosophy as mayor was most likely shaped by his upbringing in the Ward. Griffin once said:

> I campaigned on very simple ideas. Everybody said, "You've got a simple solution to everything." Well, that's the way life is. You can't make it complex. If the people in a neighborhood say that they want a stop sign, that stop sign goes up. I don't wait for surveys. If I think there should be more policemen on the streets, I don't wait for FBI statistics. I believe in the simple way of doing things. More than experts, we need people with common sense in government.[44]

An example of this management style was best remembered in his famous decree during the Blizzard of 1985 when he urged Buffalonians to: "Stay home. Enjoy the family. Watch Channel 7, and get a six-pack." Griffin's gut-instinct leadership served him well in many areas, but some of Buffalo's problems were more complex and required input from other elected officials and community leaders; Griffin often refused to include them in the decision-making and historians will have to judge whether that hurt or helped the city.

Griffin created many admirers as well as detractors throughout his years as mayor. The Irish from South Buffalo and the First Ward mostly loved him. In fact, after his first term 65% of the citizens of Buffalo felt that he was doing a good or excellent job in handling the city.[45] His administration and staff were loaded with his trusted advisors from the Irish section of the city, both from the First Ward and South Buffalo, such as his long-time friend John "Scanoots" Scanlon, Dave and James Comerford, Rick Donovan, Donald "Bughead" Smith, Stan "Boots"

Buczkowski, George "Ortsie" Gould, John B. Myers and Danny Bohen. However, while many of the Irish loved him, there was a definite tension between Jimmy and the African-American leaders of Buffalo.

The First Ward, which had been badly battered by lost industries in the 1960s and 1970s, benefited from the Griffin administration's renewed focus on this section of the city. In fact, from 1978 to 1990, the Griffin administration was busy giving out homeowner block grant loans worth $1.26 million in the First Ward. Other city funds that went to the Ward included $276,239 for free paint and rehabilitation loans and over $585,000 in commercial loans. With the help of the Housing Trust Fund, the city also built ten new homes in the area.[46] Griffin did not forget where he came from or those who helped him get to Buffalo's top elected office. Yet, despite Griffin's revitalization efforts, he couldn't slow the closing of nearby plants and mills, which were the lifeblood of jobs for those in the Ward. Pillsbury closed the Great Northern Elevator in 1981, and two years later the closing of the Bethlehem Steel plant dealt a devastating blow to the region. This was followed by the closing of Republic Steel a year later. All three of these businesses employed thousands of Western New Yorkers and hundreds from the First Ward.

Even with the plant closings and lost jobs, there was still a real sense of hope in the Ward during the Griffin years. In 1990, a Buffalo journalist from *Business First* predicted that as a result of the business development occurring in the downtown area, the Ward "stands on the verge of economic rebirth."[47] Developer Carl Paladino was another optimist and in 1987, despite the high unemployment in the Ward, he developed a 17,000 square foot retail plaza at Louisiana Street and South Park Avenue to address the limited retail opportunities in the Ward. Evidence that the Ward was stabilizing during the Griffin years was seen in the parish enrollments. Our Lady of Perpetual Help (Pets) and St. Valentines were still growing in terms of the number of families. Pets grew from 250 families in 1982 to 340 in 1990, and St. Valentines increased from 200 families in 1985 to 250 in 1990.[48]

However, while there was optimism and energy in the Ward, another part of the city wasn't so lucky. The East Side of Buffalo, with its predominantly African-American population, deteriorated rapidly during the 1970s and 1980s. Much of this decline was due to the closing of manufacturing plants and the loss of countless jobs in the blue-collar East Side. But some of Griffin's opponents blamed him and cited the deterioration of race relations in Buffalo under his tenure as one of his failures. It is true that Griffin continually sparred with Councilman James Pitts, one of the city's leading African-American leaders; Griffin even challenged him to a fistfight after a nasty argument. The Griffin administration was also criticized for its minority-hiring track record, and the poor allocation of neighborhood revitalization funds to James Pitts's Ellicott district.[49] At the start of his third term as Mayor of Buffalo, the feisty Griffin even purged African Americans from the top spots in his administration and replaced them with two Puerto Ricans.[50]

The mayor from the Ward refused to close City Hall on Martin Luther King's birthday because he felt the city workers already had too many days off.[51] Griffin was personally opposed to the forced busing that was imposed by Judge John Curtin in 1981 and he took the matter to court, but Curtin's decision was upheld. Griffin also petitioned the federal courts to end the minority hiring quotas in the public schools. One African-American social worker was quoted in 1981 as saying: "He's [Griffin] not perceived as being sympathetic to the black community. But I don't think anybody hates him or anything like that."[52] Perhaps his animosity toward African Americans, which was shared by others who grew up in the Ward, stemmed from the century-long distrust between the two groups.

Griffin accomplished much during his tenure as mayor despite the declining population, loss of Buffalo's manufacturing base, and lower tax revenue. Major projects included the gentrification of the Theatre District on Main Street and the restoration of the historic Market Arcade building. Many voters thought his greatest accomplishment was on the waterfront where he led the development of housing and commercial buildings on the Erie Basin Marina. Griffin also led the effort to bring a Triple-A baseball team back to the city with the hopes of eventually bringing a major league team. To accomplish this, he spearheaded efforts to secure funds to build Pilot Field, arguably the finest minor league baseball stadium in the country in 1988. During his tenure, a metro rail line was built from downtown to the University at Buffalo on Main Street, and over 1,000 affordable homes were constructed. Griffin, a product of the Great Depression, also believed in fiscal discipline and was able to pay off the city's $19 million deficit after only five years in office.

Griffin has been described as a feisty, "dukes-up" Irishman. In his 1978 inaugural address Griffin exclaimed, "I promise I won't let you down." For many Buffalonians, especially those in South Buffalo and for those with downtown interests, Griffin did not disappoint. Griffin's legacy with downtown Buffalo, the waterfront, the baseball stadium, the Theatre District, mass transit, and thousands of affordable houses has and will benefit generations of Buffalonians to come. At Griffin's farewell party in 1993, the Buffalo developer Frank Ciminelli said, "Here's a guy who broke his neck for this city, and people just don't realize it. There were deals I never would have touched if it wasn't for him. It was always 'Aw c'mon Frank. The city needs it.'"[53] As one *Buffalo News* columnist stated after Jimmy's death, "[Jimmy Griffin] might rank as the most dominant political figure of modern Buffalo."[54]

But members of Griffin's administration weren't the only people looking out for the First Ward and the Valley. The late 1960s and early 1970s were a period of upheaval for the Ward and its surroundings. As industries closed up after the opening of the St. Lawrence Seaway, more residents were underemployed or unemployed and crime became more prevalent. In 1968, the Valley Community Center was started on South Park Avenue to improve the social well-being of its residents. Concerned citizens were interested in stemming the violence and vandalism that was occurring in the neighborhood and they wanted to create recreational activities for the young people in the area. One of the founders was Rev. Hugh G. Carmichael III, an Episcopalian priest in a mostly Roman Catholic neighborhood. Under his leadership, the center thrived and made a positive contribution to the neighborhood during most of the 1970s. Father Carmichael was tragically killed in an automobile accident in 1988, and the Valley Community Center was named in his honor. Another volunteer from the center, Geraldine Butler, has faithfully served the community for over 35 years, and the senior citizens center in the Valley is named in her honor.

In the early 1970s, Our Lady of Perpetual Help elementary school was closed and local residents—who had relied on the school's gym for basketball games, Friday night dances, socials, and card parties—were left out in the cold. Recreational activities for the youth were limited because the parks in the area were run-down and children were forced to play in dangerous places like neighborhood warehouses. Then, in 1974, a mishap on a playground was turned into an opportunity. One afternoon, Bert Hyde, a First Ward resident, took her daughter to a playground on Sidway Street where her daughter fell through the platform on a slide at a playground—which had just been inspected by the City of Buffalo. She and other concerned citizens met with Ellicott Councilman George Arthur who urged them to march down to the Common Council and request money in order to create a community organization to benefit their community. The determined Bert Hyde and others did just that, and they secured funds to create a new community organization. The Old First Ward Community Association was created with the mandate of providing recreational and social activities for the youth and for the senior citizens in the neighborhood. The founders included Bert Hyde, Peggy Szczygiel, Mike Overdorf, Robert and Bobbi Crawford, Betty Guise, Tom Nunan, Sr., Tom Keefe, Esther Casey, John Needham, Kathy Ford, Sue Felshow, Ruth Barren, Mary Smerka and their new organization was started in School 34. The organizers are still most thankful for the assistance of Councilman George Arthur who they fondly remember as a "real friend of the First Ward."[55]

The founders created activities for the kids like bus trips to cultural activities, floor hockey in the school's gym, and even cooking classes. The group later moved into the basement of Pets school after the pastor, Fr. Claude Bicheler, deeded it to the Old First Ward Association.[56] In 1979, Jay Duderwick, a project manager from the city's Office of Neighborhood Revitalization, credited the local residents for creating a friendly community center, made possible through funds they raised themselves. He also noted that the neighborhood around Pets parish had the lowest crime rates in the city thanks to the fact that on any given day 150 to 200 residents were playing in the community center.[57] After some serious economic setbacks suffered during the 1950s to the 1980s, the Ward was stabilizing thanks to efforts by local citizens and politicians, but its future was still unclear.

CHAPTER FOURTEEN

THE REBIRTH OF THE
FIRST WARD

Prior to the 1830s, the First Ward was a swampy plot of uninhabited land with a silt-filled creek running through it. Throughout the 19th and 20th centuries, however, the same area was transformed into an industrial powerhouse complete with towering grain elevators, lumber mills, iron ore processing facilities, ship-builders, railroad terminals, all sustaining a vibrant neighborhood community. Now, with most of the industry gone, what will become of this neighborhood adjacent to downtown Buffalo? For those still residing in the Ward, it is their home. To many Buffalonians with roots in the Ward it is a nostalgic area where their ancestors once lived and worked. Some of these same Buffalonians are supporting initiatives to improve the quality of life in the neighborhood, and to share the area's rich history with people throughout Western New York and beyond.

Several people have sought to capitalize on the nostalgic and historical aspects of the Ward. During the gloomy economic years of the late 1970s—after many Buffalonians had forgotten about the First Ward—one man had an idea for showcasing this once booming area. In March of 1979, Mike Malaney, the Executive Director of the Old First Ward Community Center, spearheaded the Shamrock Run, a five-mile running road race. The event organizers estimated that they would have only a handful of runners for their first run. They were shocked when close to 400 runners turned up for the inaugural race. Subsequently, the Shamrock Run is held every year during the first weekend of March, and many recognize it as the first official road race of the season in Buffalo—only the hardiest Buffalonians show-up to run in the race against the bitter weather off Lake Erie during March. Over the thirty years that it has been held the number of participants continued to grow. By 2010, the number of runners increased to over 5,000. Thousands more show up to cheer on the runners and celebrate the beginning of spring. The impact of the event, which raises funds for the Old First Ward Community Center, is more than financial. One First Ward resident claimed that the Shamrock Run was the turning point that put the First Ward on the map again.[1] This race has introduced thousands of Western New Yorkers, some of whom had never been to the Ward before, to this unique area of Buffalo. Many First Ward descendants from South Buffalo and the southern suburbs of Buffalo continue to enjoy running through neighborhoods where their grandparents and great-grandparents used to live and work.

While the Shamrock Run attracts people to the Ward at the end of winter, the Buffalo River Fest draws thousands of people to this area in the summer. The Buffalo River Fest actually sprang out of another community event called The Rally in the Valley, which was held from 1980 to the late 1990s. This event celebrated the successful efforts to tear down the Ralston Purina Mill in March of 1980. A fire in 1972 destroyed the mill at Elk and Smith Streets, and despite numerous protests from local residents to tear down the rat-infested building, it was not until Mayor James Griffin was elected— and a neighborhood boycott of Ralston Purina products led by South Councilman James Keane was threatened— that money was secured from the company to demolish the building.[2]

As time went on, the organizers of the Rally decided to create an event that would attract more people from outside the neighborhood and draw people from all over the Buffalo area. In 2001, they changed the name of the event to Buffalo River Fest and moved the location to Father Conway Park, only one block away from the Buffalo River. The two-day event is filled with activities such as a boat regatta where participants make their own watercraft and are awarded generous prizes for the "Most Creative Seaworthy Vessel." There is also live music, softball games, food, drink, historical lectures, tours, memorabilia, and photos for all to enjoy.

Another annual event that emphasizes the heritage of the Ward is the "Old Neighborhood" St. Patrick's Day Parade. In 1994, Peg Overdorf—with a group of other Ward backers such as Mike "Ozzie" Overdorf, Laurie Overdorf, Mike Mulqueen, Joey Griffin, John Nostrant, and Sharon Boulanger—started the "Old Neighborhood" St. Patrick's Day Parade. The idea came to the organizers after reading John Baldyga's memoir in which he detailed the original 1913 parade through the First Ward. Unfortunately, most people who attend the current St. Patrick's Day parade on Delaware Avenue have no idea that the parade was originally conceived and celebrated in the First Ward. Because of logistical limitations, the "Old Neighborhood" parade does not trace the exact streets of the 1913 parade but it does closely capture the spirit of the original parade. When asked why this St. Patrick's Day Parade is different from the one on Delaware Avenue, organizer Peggy Overdorf explained that, "The people can identify and connect more. They can imagine what it was like at the turn of the century with their ancestors marching down the same streets, celebrating in the same way."[3]

The First Ward parade is held on Saturday so as not to interfere with the Delaware Avenue parade that takes place on the Sunday closest to St. Patrick's Day. This parade originally had about twenty marching units when it began; it now has 60 units, which is about half the number in the larger Delaware Avenue parade.[4] The parade contains floats, Irish step-dancers, and family marching units. The local Irish labor heritage is also celebrated by the fact that the Police Emerald Society leads the parade, and local firemen and members of the unions follow them. One way the organizers raise funds for the event is to sell flags with local family names to decorate the poles along the parade route. For $70 people can purchase a banner with their family surname on it and the price has not prevented over 500 families from paying for one.

Numerous political and civic leaders are working on improving the quality of life in the First Ward and its environs. One of the best known is Margaret "Peg" Overdorf, the Executive Director of the Valley Community Center, and a passionate advocate for both the "Old Ward" and the Valley. Peg Overdorf still lives on Mackinaw Street near Tennessee Street in the heart of the Ward in the same house in which she was born. Peggy's ancestry, like others in the Ward, is a blend of Irish and German. Her mother's family, the O'Rourkes, came from County Cavan in Ireland, and her father's family, the Overdorfs, was one of the first German families residing in the Ward in the late 1800s.

Peg Overdorf is championing several initiatives, which she hopes will transform the Ward and the Valley. Her first vision—already in progress—is to improve waterfront access with parks and a pedestrian trail that will ultimately connect the Erie Basin Marina all the way to Smith Street in the Ward. In addition, she is involved with two new parks that were being built in the Ward in 2010. The first one, Mutual Riverfront Park— located at the end of Hamburg Street on the Buffalo River—is already under construction by the New York Power Authority. As part of the agreement with the Power Authority, the leaders of the Ward agreed to locate the ice boom—an apparatus of connected steel pontoons put into Lake Erie in the winter to reduce the spring ice flow down the Niagara River—in their neighborhood, while the Authority agreed to help beautify the area and build a one-acre park at the foot of Hamburg Street. This park will have public access areas, a boathouse for canoes and kayaks, and will be home to the Waterfront Memories and More Museum.

On June 11, 2010, there was a ribbon cutting for a second park, currently called River Fest Park, which was built further up Ohio Street near the Michigan Street Bridge, on land that was purchased through a Margaret Wendt Foundation grant. This two-acre park located on the banks of the Buffalo River, hosts the annual River Fest festivities and is open to the public year-round. New York State Assemblyman Mark Schroeder was a key player in securing the funds to build the park, which includes a beautiful green space, a boardwalk, boats slips, a pavilion, and a proposed clubhouse. Eventually a new heritage trail, which will run through these two new parks, will connect the Erie Basin Marina to Hamburg Street. This bike path/walking trail will offer convenient access to the Buffalo River and points of interest in the Ward, and include interpretive signage reminding visitors of the rich First Ward history.

Another element of Peggy Overdorf's vision is to create market-rate housing along the Buffalo River in the Old First Ward, to be located at points such as the intersection of Hamburg and South Streets. There is already a great demand to be near the water for recreational activities like boating, kayaking, and fishing. Moreover, the Ward's proximity to downtown and the sports stadiums make it a hidden gem for those who want to live near these attractions. To improve the quality of housing, leaders in the Ward vigilantly alert city officials about vacant and dilapidated homes in order to prevent blight, reduce the risks of arson, limit criminal activity, and help stabilize property values. A recent group of Urban Planning students from York University in Toronto remarked that "there weren't boarded up buildings in this section of town" compared to the West Side and East Side of Buffalo, which they had also visited on their trip.[5] The Old First Ward Association is another organization helping to promote the Ward as a place to live or locate a business. The group stresses the three most important assets of the First Ward: availability, affordability, and accessibility. The Ward has plenty of *available* commercial buildings and parking lots; commercial and residential real estate is *affordable*; and the community is *accessible* to downtown, railroads, the water and highways.[6]

According to Peggy Overdorf, New York State Assemblymen Mark Schroeder is the politician who has done the most to improve the First Ward. Although Schroeder grew up in South Buffalo, his family homestead is at 14 Kentucky Street in the Ward. Schroeder's great-grandfather, Mark "Doc" Cronin, was a co-founder of Local 17 Hoisting Engineers, and his other First Ward great-grandfather, Patrick Quinn, was the youngest police captain at Precinct 7.[7] According to his friend Peggy Overdorf, Schroeder has a vision for the Buffalo River similar to Congressman Brian Higgins' vision for the Outer Harbor of Buffalo.[8]

The area also has its first museum: Waterfront Memories and More. Originally housed in a building at the corner of Smith and Elk Streets—the former Helen Beaman Center—the museum is home to a treasure trove of First Ward, Valley, and waterfront memories. The museum contains wonderful pictures, artifacts, books, newspaper clippings, and yearbooks related to this area. Peggy May-Szczygiel, Bert Guise-Hyde, and Joan Graham-Scahill manage the museum and host visitors on Tuesdays and Saturdays throughout the year. The museum receives a steady stream of visitors from all over Western New York who are interested in learning more about the neighborhood where they or their ancestors grew up. As interest in genealogy increases, so too will the value of this center. In June 2012, the museum moved into a new building on Hamburg Street in the heart of the First Ward.

Another museum that is currently in the planning stages is called the Heritage Discovery Center, which will be a multi-themed historical museum. This museum will be located on the 35-acre Buffalo Color site on Lee Street between Elk Street and South Park Avenue, a site that the railway society purchased for $490,000 in 2010. When this site is remediated of pollution, there will be a railroad and a steel plant museum filled with artifacts related to these important Western New York industries. The key feature of the museum will be a four-story exhibition hall, which will be home for several old railcars. The museum organizers plan to board train rides on the tracks adjacent to the building with destinations such as Niagara Falls, Jamestown, Medina, and even Cleveland.[9]

Lifelong Ward resident Bert Hyde, whose family arrived in the Ward from Alsace, France in the 1880s, smiles when she thinks of how everything is finally coming together in the Ward. There is the new lake boulevard that will make it much easier to get to and from Lake Erie to the Ward; there is the new park at the foot of Hamburg Street; another park developed along Ohio Street; bike paths and a heritage trail to connect the First Ward to downtown Buffalo; and the Buffalo River is gradually being cleaned up and converted into a recreational destination.[10]

Businesses and Industry Today

Not all businesses and industries closed down or left the First Ward. In fact, some have even thrived in recent years. One of these companies is Rigidized Metals, a textured metal shop, which opened in the Ward on July 8, 1940 at 689 Ohio Street. Two years prior to opening his shop, founder Richard S. Smith developed a unique embossing process for steel. Smith developed a process to emboss three-dimensional patterns onto rolled steel, which enhanced the attractiveness of the steel, and made it more rigid and much stronger. In a 1957 magazine advertisement, the company boasted that their modern textured metals increase strength in all directions without adding weight. Uses for their products were numerous: planes, cars, buses, trains, appliances, gas pumps, counter tops, TV sets, elevators, and hospital equipment. During World War II, fifteen women, many from the neighborhood, proudly assisted in the war effort by making steel products for the U.S. Navy. Three generations later, under the leadership of Richard Smith III, Rigidized Metals is still a thriving business in the Ward and a world leader in the production of deep-textured, three-dimensional metals used in architectural, industrial, and transportation applications.

Rigidized Metals is also a model community-minded organization, supporting numerous First Ward events such as River Fest, the Shamrock Run, and other First Ward and Valley events. To add artistic beauty to the industrial Ward, Rigidized installed an impressive metal sculpture called "Energy Weave" on their company grounds in January 2009; Mr. Smith felt that the Ward could use some art. Commuters on the new waterfront parkway can now view this unique metal sculpture glistening in the sunlight as they drive by the company headquarters.

In 2010, other businesses in the Ward included the Buffalo Mercantile Center, located in the massive former Barcalo Manufacturing complex. On Ganson Street, flour milling is still represented by two of the industry giants: Archer Daniels Midland (ADM) and General Mills. The General Mills plant, located on South Michigan Avenue, has since 1941 been the largest producer of Cheerios cereal—the most popular brand of cereal in the United States. It is also the source of the pleasant smell of toasted oats that often permeates downtown Buffalo. Other businesses in the Ward include Burnett, St. Mary's Cement, LaFarge, and J.H. Dodman Meats on Michigan Avenue. Katherine Street is home to Irish Propane, National Tractor Trailer School, Safety-Kleen, and BIDCO-Buffalo Industrial Diving. Another iconic business in the Ward that is still operating is Bouquard's Boat Rental located at the end of Tifft Street along Fuhrmann Boulevard. Bouquard's has been in business since 1907 when Ward resident Eugene Bouquard established a rowboat rental business for muskie fishermen on Lake Erie. Over the years, the business expanded with motorboat rentals and moorings for sailboats. Thousands of Buffalonians have been able to enjoy Lake Erie and its abundant fishing thanks to this multi-generational family business.

Another Western New York treasure with Ward roots is Heintz and Weber, a food products manufacturer that opened a four-story manufacturing plant on Louisiana Street in the First Ward in the late 1930s. This plant—which was known locally as the "pickle plant"—was the leading supplier of mustard and pickles to over 300 mom-and-pop delis in Western New York.[11] For seventy years the company was a steady employer in the Ward, processing 80 products, including ten different varieties of pickles, sauerkraut and its premier product, Weber's Horseradish Mustard. Fortunately, this successful business still operates in Buffalo, but in 2002, the company built a new processing plant in South Buffalo just outside of the Ward.

The Ward's Legacy

There were many First Ward citizens and events throughout the years that left an impact on Buffalo and sometimes even on the nation. Due to various circumstances, some of these people and historical events have been forgotten. Not only were people forgotten, but so too were prominent buildings and institutions that were established in the Ward. Fortunately, efforts are under way to both remind people of the rich Ward heritage and to stop the physical neglect of these important buildings.

In many minds, the grain scoopers are one of the symbols most closely associated with the Ward. In 1998, the number of scoopers had fallen to just 55 men from an estimated high of 1,500 during the peak of the industry at the turn of the 20th century. In 1998, the number of days of work for the scoopers also declined to only 38 days a year, and their wages, which had not risen in fifteen years, were a paltry $10,000 per man.[12] A year later, one hundred years after the Great Strike of 1899, there was only a single grain ship arriving in the Ward and it served only three elevators. In February 2003, one hundred and sixty years since Dart's steam-powered elevator was inaugurated, a momentous event occurred: the First Ward scoopers unloaded their last hull of a grain ship when they emptied the contents of the *Kinsman Independent*, bound for the General Mills plant. With technological advances, most freighters are now fully automated (self-unloaders) and do not require scoopers to clear the remaining grain from the hull of their ships. Sadly, the scoopers services are no longer needed.

Fred Brill, a fourth-generation grain scooper, was the last president of Local 109—the world's only grain scoopers union. His great-grandfather, of German ancestry and a resident of the Beach, was scooping in the 1880s and actually died in the hull of one of the grain ships in 1890 of either a heart attack or an accident. Fred Brill's great-grandmother was widowed with several children, and Fred's grandfather eventually joined the scoopers as well. Brill's father scooped from 1941 until 1977, and then Fred himself scooped from the early 1970s until 2003. It is fitting that Fred Brill—who obviously had scooping in his blood—was the last one to hoist the shovel before the pulleys were taken down from the *Kinsman Independent* on that sad day in February of 2003. The industry that had provided steady jobs for multiple generations of mostly Irish Americans for over 160 years had vanished. A significant part of the Ward also disappeared because its identity was so intertwined with grain and scooping. It would be fitting that a monument be dedicated to the thousands of men from the First Ward who toiled in dangerous conditions so that millions throughout the United States and across Europe could have bread and breakfast cereals on their tables.

In the Ward, grain milling, the sister activity to grain shipping, is also a shadow of its former self. During the heyday in the 1920s, there were eight large flour millers: Washburn Crosby, Pillsbury, Russell-Miller, H-O Oats, Husted, Spencer-Kellogg, Thorton & Chester, George Urban, and J.A. Walter. Scattered around the Ward and the Buffalo River, there were also at least five feed mills: Park & Pollard, Mapl-Flake, Maritime, Ralston Purina, and the Grange League Federation

(GLF).[13] In 2010, there were only two grain mills left: Archer Daniels Midland (ADM) and General Mills. Throughout most of the 20th century, Buffalo was one of the chief grain storage and milling centers in the United States and the world, but the industry is now just a vestige of its former self. The hundreds of jobs along the waterfront shoveling coal and unloading lumber are gone and the number of railroad company employees in the area has also significantly diminished.

One of the other great industrial legacies of the First Ward is the towering grain elevators that line the Buffalo River. Although there are hundreds of grain elevators still standing throughout the Midwestern United States, Canada, and Europe, the greatest collection survives in the First Ward in Buffalo, New York. At one point in the 1920s, Buffalo had 34 elevators, mostly concentrated in the Ward and along the Buffalo River.[14] Most of the massive, indestructible grain elevators still line the banks of the Buffalo River, but almost all of them are dormant and deteriorating. For instance, the impressive Marine Leg "A" Elevator, which formerly stored millions of bushels of grain during the season, is now nothing more than a quasi trash dump. Fortunately, as has been the case with other architectural treasures, Buffalo's poor local economy prevented the destruction of most of these treasures because there was not money to properly tear them down. The historically significant H-O Oats Mill, however, was torn down to build a Seneca Indian casino currently held up in federal court.

Another reason that more of the elevators were not torn down was due to the work of former University at Buffalo professor Reyner Banham, author of *A Concrete Atlantis*, which documents the architectural significance of these Buffalo treasures. Professor Banham, with the help of the Industrial Heritage Committee and the Preservation Coalition of Erie County, was able to convince the National Park Service to come to Buffalo to document the elevators, which were in danger of being demolished. The elevators were photographed, measured, researched, and documented by the Historic American Engineering Record.[15] These groups were also able to obtain city landmark status for the Great Northern Elevator, and they spearheaded efforts to put the Concrete Central on the National Registry of Historic Places.[16]

At one point there were preliminary plans to re-use one of the elevators for ethanol processing, but this plan was scrapped because of public opposition and changing market dynamics in the ethanol market. Other proposals to convert some of these towering elevators into hotels and apartments seem destined to materialize only far in the future. One proposal is to turn one of them into a grain elevator museum. Buffalo historian Mark Goldman has proposed that Buffalo create an "Island of Art and Industry" with the dormant grain elevators near the Ohio Street Bridge. He believes that some of the majestic elevators should be painted or draped in canvas or even transformed into giant outdoor movie screens.

In addition, Goldman proposes illuminating the Ohio Street Bridge, emphasizing important heritage sites, and creating recreational venues throughout the area. Goldman said that the Elevator District is "a place where art and nature come together with beautiful sunsets, birds and water, and then you present movies against that incredible industrial architecture..."[17] He also suggests installing sculptures and lighting on the land from the Island down to the Outer Harbor.

Efforts are underway to try and save some of the historic commercial buildings in the Ward. As in other Rust Belt cities, developers have converted old warehouses into loft apartments and commercial offices. The Elk Street Market—formerly the main supply of food for so many people in the Ward and other parts of Buffalo—was converted into high-end loft apartments in 2002. These apartments command high rents and have low vacancy rates, a positive sign for the area. After demolition plans were presented to tear down the historic E. & B. Holmes complex on Chicago Street in 2006, Clinton Brown, a local architect, stepped in to save the building. After initial efforts to stabilize the building, Brown plans to restore it and create 24 lofts in this historic structure, at an estimated cost of $6.6 million.[18] The middle building in the complex—which dates back to 1859 as the Chicago Iron Works—is one of the oldest standing structures in Buffalo and certainly deserves preservation.

The rich religious heritage of the First Ward is also a shadow of its former self. St. Brigid's, the former mother church of the First Ward, which opened in 1858, suffered a massive fire on July 4, 1968. Fortunately the building was salvageable. But the church leadership witnessed the flight of parishioners from the city to the suburbs during this period and decided the church was no longer needed. Sadly, it was torn down the following year. The community continued to hold church services in a chapel in the school building from 1968 to 1987, and a new chapel was even built in 1984.[19] In the 1980s, the parish changed its mission to focus on the poor Spanish-speaking immigrants who lived in the neighborhood. Facilities were set up to serve two hot meals daily to poor children in the community; a food co-op was established to sell food at cost for the poor residents; and a Head Start program was created to assist children in speaking English. In 1987, the Diocese decided to officially close the parish of St. Brigid's entirely and merge it with the nearby parish of St. Columba. Father David Gallivan, whose maternal family roots stem from the Ward and the Valley, was fittingly the last priest to live in the St. Brigid's rectory.[20]

The St. Brigid's parish that was created by Bishop Timon in 1858 and contributed so much to the First Ward, especially its Irish residents, has vanished. For over one hundred years, the church and school molded countless businessmen, politicians, teachers, and religious leaders in Buffalo. Fortunately, across the street from the site of St. Brigid's Church, the Mercy sisters recently built a comprehensive outpatient clinic for adults and children in the community, so at least the site continues to provide material benefit to the people in the area. As for Bishop Timon himself, the prelate who had such a great affection for the downtrodden Irish in the Ward and did so much to try and ease their discomforts, he was remembered in the naming of the first men's Catholic high school in South Buffalo: Bishop Timon High School. Timon's name also adorns an apartment building for senior citizens on Delaware Avenue and a street in Buffalo. His masterpiece, St. Joseph's Cathedral, has been restored and has been an inspiring house of worship for over 150 years. Another giant in the local church, Monsignor John Nash—one of the chief builders of the church in South Buffalo—has his name attached to one of the largest Knights of Columbus branches in South Buffalo.

The once flourishing Sisters of Mercy, a community of nuns who started their Buffalo foundation in the First Ward in 1858, continues to decline in the Buffalo area. At its height, the community grew to over 300 members working throughout the Diocese of Buffalo. In their heyday in 1942, the sisters were a force throughout the diocese with one hundred and fifty-five of the sisters educating 6,429 grammar school students;[21] nineteen sisters were dedicated to teaching students piano, violin and vocal music; twenty-four sisters were running two high schools; and thirty-nine staffed Mercy Hospital, which treated thousands of people every year.[22] The sisters are still active in various ministries in Buffalo, especially in South Buffalo, but like most religious orders the number of new entrants has significantly decreased from their peak years. By the late 1960s, the sisterhood peaked with 450 sisters in the Buffalo diocese. Through no fault of their own, their activities in the First Ward, from whence they sprang, are almost non-existent today. Today, there are at least three Mercy sisters who came from the Ward and are active in ministry: Sr. Joan Sherry, Sr. Marie Bernard Procknal, and Sr. Eugenia Vastola. There are currently no Roman Catholic schools operating in the First Ward or the Valley: St. Brigid's, Our Lady of Perpetual Help, St. Stephen's, and Bishop Quigley are all closed.

In 1979, St. Valentine's school, which had educated hundreds of Polish children, also closed due to declining enrollment. As Polish families moved out of the neighborhood, Hispanic families moved in, and the church started offering Spanish masses. Meanwhile, the parish census, which was as large as 450 families in 1923, had fallen to just 160 by 2000. Built by the Polish residents in the Ward, St. Valentine's Church was closed by the Diocese of Buffalo in 2007. Local developer Carl Paladino purchased the church building and the school in June 2009 for a mere $75,000 with plans to repair and develop the property, which is located near another two-story building he owns at South Park Avenue and Alabama Street. Paladino stated that the area will be difficult to develop, but it has potential because "it's in the shadow of downtown."[23] Meanwhile, Our Lady of Perpetual

Help Church (Pets) continues as the bedrock of the neighborhood and should remain so for many years after surviving the diocesan consolidation plan in 2009.

The main church in the Valley, St. Stephen's, which produced so many priests and religious sisters, has gone through many changes over the years. The name of the parish changed to St. Jude Shrine in 1991, but in 1995 the name reverted back to St. Stephen's. In 2007, a new Catholic parish was created at this site from a merger of St. Valentine's, St. Patrick's, St. Rita's, and St. Stephen's and the name chosen for the new parish was St. Clare. The parish still serves as the Shrine of St. Jude for the diocese.

After the Great Strike of 1899, the grain scoopers of Buffalo conducted only two more minor strikes in the 20th century: in 1948 and in the early 1970s.[24] Three of the central figures in the Strike of 1899 have been formally recognized with plaques, parks, and building namings in Buffalo. Father James Lanigan, a central figure in organizing the strikers at St. Brigid's, is the namesake of a park off South Park Avenue in the Ward and of Lanigan Field House, a community center run by the Buffalo Parks Department at 150 Fulton Street. Bishop James Quigley High School, named for another leader, was located off Fulton Street until it closed in 1962.

The city of Buffalo recognized William J. "Fingy" Conners, the third major figure in the labor struggle of 1899, in the historical signage at the terminus of the Erie Canal in downtown Buffalo. The signage, with a caption: "Cabin boy: self-made millionaire," includes a picture and small write-up about the unlikely industrialist. A plaque on Ohio Street where he ran his infamous saloon-boss operation would also be fitting. Several of Conners' local businesses are now defunct: Great Lakes Transit Corporation, one of the most successful Great Lakes shipping companies, ceased operations after World War II, and Magnus Brewery closed in 1956. The *Courier-Express* newspaper, once one of the premier newspapers in the country, ceased operations on September 18, 1982. There were many factors that contributed to its demise including the declining Buffalo population and a dispute with the unions, leaving Buffalo with one newspaper, the *Buffalo News*.

Before William J. Conners died in 1929, he oversaw the construction of a beautiful headquarters for his *Courier-Express* newspaper at the corner of Main and Goodell Streets in downtown Buffalo, but never saw it completed a year later. This five-story, Art-Deco building of granite and terra cotta has served as the headquarters for the Catholic Diocese of Buffalo since 1983. It is an important piece of architecture in Buffalo, known for its Medieval and Celtic decorative motifs.[25] Fingy Conners established the William J. Conners Foundation with $1 million dollars to assist the poor and needy, but it is unclear when his foundation ceased operations. William J. Conners III, Fingy's grandson and one-time publisher of the *Courier-Express* newspaper, also set up a charitable foundation (The William J. Conners and Barbara Conners Foundation), which has contributed funding to local causes such as Gilda House, located in the former Conners' mansion. One hundred years later, Fingy's fortune is still helping Buffalo.

A monument to the First Ward men who fought for the Union in the Civil War has also finally been erected. In 2002, almost 140 years after the efforts of the 155th regiment during the 1864 Virginia Campaign, a monument was erected on the waterfront in the heart of the Naval Park in Buffalo. A committee chaired by Gary N. Costello hired Henry J. Schmidt to sculpt a two-sided granite monument in honor of the Irish volunteers, many from the Ward, who fought and died during the Virginia Campaign and helped bring the Civil War to an end. The Fenian invasion of 1866 is well known today in Ireland, but remains a chapter of local history largely unknown to many Buffalonians. Fortunately, thanks to efforts by New York State Senator Timothy M. Kennedy and others a permanent memorial to commemorate this audacious invasion of Canada was finally dedicated on March 16, 2012. A prominent commemoration ceremony or reenactment would certainly be in order in 2016 to mark the 150th anniversary of the invasion.

General William Donovan was remembered in 1962, just three years after his death, when New York State named a prominent government building in his honor in downtown Buffalo, just blocks from where he grew up. Unfortunately this building was closed in 2006. In 2010, there was an effort to keep the Donovan name alive by naming the new $137 million federal courthouse at Niagara Square in Buffalo in his honor. If this effort fails, some significant tribute to this larger-than-life First Ward figure seems necessary. For General William Donovan's portrait hangs first among the directors of the Central Intelligence Agency at its headquarters in Langley, Virginia.

Another World War II hero from the First Ward has also been remembered posthumously. Fr. Thomas Conway received the Purple Heart for his tireless efforts in providing comfort for the hundreds of sailors who were stranded in the Pacific Ocean during the USS *Indianapolis* tragedy. Unfortunately, Fr. Conway would never see his medal or meet the 5,000 people who attended a dedication ceremony in 1954 at a park named in his honor in Buffalo. Father Conway Park, the site of the former Ohio Basin, is the largest park in Buffalo's First Ward. Fr. Conway was further honored in his adopted hometown when on May 20, 2006 Bishop Edward Kmiec dedicated a bronze statue of the heroic priest at the Buffalo and Erie County Naval and Military Park, located along his beloved Lake Erie. Father Thomas Conway has now received his recognition and his name will be remembered for years to come.

As for the legion of politicians that the Ward produced throughout the years, William "Blue-Eyed Billy" Sheehan probably had the most influence of them all on politics in the Ward, New York State, and the nation. Still he is largely unknown in his hometown. Sheehan's machine politics were often vilified at the time, rightly so. But many hundreds, if not thousands, of people have him to thank for improving their lot in life. His prominent memorial, built by McDonnell & Sons, in Holy Cross Cemetery in Lackawanna, is the last vestige of this important political figure. Billy's older brother, John C. Sheehan, who left Buffalo after an embezzling scandal, has rightfully been forgotten, but his short leadership of New York City's Tammany Hall deserves some local recognition—a marker or plaque in front of the old Sheehan's homestead on Elk Street (South Park Avenue) would be an appropriate recognition for these two former Buffalo River ferrymen.

Jimmy Griffin served a remarkable sixteen years as mayor of Buffalo. The indefatigable Griffin was still engaged in politics after he finished his fourth term in 1993. In 1996, he initiated a campaign to run for the Democratic nomination for President of the United States; his opponent was the popular incumbent William Jefferson Clinton. He ran on a platform of reducing the size of the federal government and cutting waste and fraud in federal programs. Jimmy never made it beyond New Hampshire and finished in eighth place in that contest. Griffin made another comeback in 2003 when he won the Buffalo Common Council seat for the South District; however, his best years as a politician were behind him. This former mill worker from the First Ward and one-time U.S. Presidential candidate finally came to rest after a bout with a rare neurological disease in 2008. Over 1,100 Buffalonians attended the mayor's funeral, and thousands more came to pay tribute at his wake. Most of the remembrances of the feisty boy from South Park Avenue in the Ward were positive. Even some of his political enemies made flattering comments about his accomplishments as mayor. Whether one loved him or hated him, Buffalo will probably never again see an elected official like Jimmy Griffin. On June 30, 2009, Jimmy Griffin was remembered by the city in a ceremony to thank him for his efforts at spearheading the baseball stadium project in the 1980s. The plaza outside Coca-Cola Stadium, home of the Buffalo Bisons, is now named Jimmy Griffin Plaza, and a plaque in the plaza commemorates him. Efforts are also underway to erect an $80,000 statue of Griffin in the plaza.

Jack O'Brian's legacy has been somewhat tarnished posthumously. In a 2008 book, *CBS's Don Hollenbeck: An Honest Reporter in the Age of McCarthyism*, the author Loren Ghiglione vilifies O'Brian, the former laborer and famed 1950s journalist. Ghiglione pins most of CBS' Don Hollenbeck's suicide squarely on O'Brian and blames O'Brian's newspaper columns for stoking the anti-communist hysteria throughout the McCarthy years. O'Brian was also referenced several times in George Clooney's 2005 award winning film *Good Night, and Good Luck*. When a First Ward historian was asked recently why there is very little recognition or mention of Jack O'Brian's success, he replied, "O'Brian was a very bad man."

While this may be true, his meteoric rise in journalism from such an unlikely background was quite an accomplishment. The other famous O'Brian, John Lord O'Brian and no relation to Jack, who only lived in the Ward as a young boy, has been remembered with his name fixed to the building that houses the University at Buffalo's Law School (O'Brian Hall).

In 1960, Jimmy Slattery—the 1930 Light Heavyweight Champion of the World— was buried in an unmarked grave before a small group of mourners. For decades after his heroics in the ring, Slattery was mostly forgotten in Buffalo. Then in 1976, thanks to members of Buffalo Veteran Boxers Association Ring 44, a headstone for his gravesite was purchased to honor Slattery. At the ceremony, led by President of Ring 44 Jimmy Harkins, Msgr. Franklin Kelleher, Joe Gimbrone, and Joe Muscato, Slattery finally received the recognition he deserved.[26] In 1997, thirty-seven years after his death, a play called *Jimmytown* was written about Slattery and performed by the Buffalo Ensemble Theatre Company to enthusiastic crowds throughout Buffalo. On June 11, 2006, Jimmy Slattery made history when he became the first Buffalonian inducted into the International Boxing Hall of Fame. Two months later, a ceremony and a fight were held to commemorate Slattery at the Valley Community Center and not long after, a sign was erected at the corner of Bolton Place and South Park Avenue to commemorate "Jimmy Slattery Place"—where in 1925 Jimmy purchased a house for his mother with his boxing winnings. Jimmy Goodrich, another prizefighter who lived in the Ward for several years and won the 1925 Lightweight Championship, was inducted into the Buffalo Sports Hall of Fame in November 2010 for his achievements in boxing.

Michael Shea's "Wonder Theatre," his masterpiece entertainment palace on Main Street, escaped demolition in the 1970s. The City of Buffalo took ownership of the property in November 1974, and a non-profit organization, the Friends of the Buffalo Theater, was immediately formed to preserve the theatre from almost certain destruction. In 1975, the theatre was designated on the National Register of Historic Places, which ensured its survival. Various groups managed the theater from 1978 until 2000 with varied success. During the 1990s, the stage and dressing area were expanded in order to handle larger shows. In the 2000s, the iconic "Shea's Buffalo" sign was repaired, new seats and draperies were added to the theatre and the terra cotta façade was restored.[27]

Additional renovations at Shea's Theatre began again in 2011 with a $10 million dollar campaign that included a $1.75 million newly restored ceiling; $2.25 million for the main theatre renovations, including new chandeliers and restoration of the proscenium arch; $500,000 to replace the brass doors at Pearl and Main Streets; an elevator tower off Pearl Street; and additional meeting space.[28] Shea's is a thriving theatre hosting sold-out Broadway shows throughout the year. Michael Shea would be proud to know that his dream of entertaining

Buffalonians of all walks of life will continue to be realized well into the 21st century. Two of Shea's other theatres are still surviving as well: the Riviera in North Tonawanda and the North Park on Hertel Avenue. This one-time saloon owner from the Ward and laborer at the Union Furnace will be remembered for generations to come.

As for saloons, there are very few left in the Ward. Descendants of John Brinkworth, the long-serving saloon owner from Perry Street, are still active in the bar business in Buffalo with popular saloons such as Brinks, Colter Bay, and the Blue Monk. The family also opened WJ Morrissey on Mississippi Street, located only a few blocks from the original saloon that John Brinkworth opened in 1868.

In the spring of 2006, Gene and Mary McCarthy decided to sell their iconic tavern on Hamburg Street, which essentially ended the McCarthy saloon dynasty in the Ward. The owners sold the tavern to Gerhardt Yaskow, a young man of Polish, German and Ukrainian ancestry, who has instilled new life into this important tavern. Mike Quinn's saloon on Chicago Street changed names over the years from Kitty O'Malley's to McBride's in recent years. Unfortunately, the saloon was demolished on March 10, 2008 after two devastating January storms that year ripped off the roof and collapsed one of the walls. Now, there remains a pile of bricks on this historically rich site. In 2003, the First Ward lost another historic saloon. The Harbor Inn at Chicago and Ohio Streets, an institution since 1869 and one of the last remaining taverns from the saloon-boss era, was torn down.

The St. Patrick's Day Parade, first organized at Mike Quinn's saloon in the Ward in 1913, is stronger today than ever. In about 1940, the St. Patrick's Day parade was moved from the Ward to Main Street in order to accommodate the larger crowds. The parade was cancelled in 1942 and 1943 because of World War II. In 1981, it was moved to Delaware Avenue because of metro rail construction on Main Street. The parade has grown from more than just an all-Irish gathering to a diverse crowd of all ethnicities, becoming one of the largest annual events in Buffalo. The "Old Neighborhood" Parade, which goes through the Ward and the Valley, also continues to expand each year.

Rowing has recently made a dramatic comeback in the Old First Ward area. In August 2010, the Buffalo Scholastic Rowing Association officially opened its temporary canvas boathouse along Ohio Street near the current Department of Environmental Conservation boat launch site. The organizers looked at forty-five sites before selecting this one in the Old First Ward. Carl Paladino, owner of the site, spent between $50,000 to $100,000 of his own money to clear the site for the first new rowing club in Buffalo in over seventy years.[29] Members of the Buffalo Niagara Riverkeeper, Ellicott Development, and the Scholastic Rowing Association also constructed a floating dock on the Buffalo River to accommodate the rowers. This rowing club is the launching pad for the Buffalo Seminary,

Canisius High School, and Bishop Timon-St. Jude High School rowing teams. Witnesses report that it is encouraging to see sculls on the Buffalo River again after the long absence of the First Ward rowing club: the Mutuals. The Scholastic Rowing Association claims the Buffalo River has advantages over the Black Rock Channel because the water is smoother and more sheltered.[30] On June 19, 2010, the club organized the first regatta on the Buffalo River since 1924.[31]

One of the last social clubs in the Ward, the Blackthorn Club, is still thriving and its members meet regularly at the appropriately named Blackthorn Tavern on Seneca Street in South Buffalo. The venerable organization received some national press a few years ago when then *Meet the Press* host Tim Russert mentioned the club in a book about his father. Onlookers at the annual St. Patrick's Day Parade continue to see the Blackthorns proudly marching in the front of the parade in their black hats, dress coats, and walking sticks.

There are the countless, unremembered Irish immigrants who survived the journey across the Atlantic in order to toil on the waterfront of Buffalo. Over a pint of Guinness, Lawrence Shine, an Irish immigrant and esteemed lecturer at Buffalo State College, and Rob Ferguson, an engineer, sketched an idea about a famine memorial. With the help of prominent Buffalonians like Sheriff Tom Higgins, the memorial was built and dedicated in August of 1997. This memorial—fittingly situated at the waterfront where so many Irish immigrants worked—is a poignant reminder of the tragic circumstances from which so many hungry and impoverished Irish emigrated from their homeland. It offers a beautiful spot to relax and reflect.

For over 100 years, Buffalo had been a welcoming and generous city for Irish independence leaders to come and garner support and funds for various causes in Ireland. Some rebels like Thomas D'Arcy McGee of the "Young Ireland" movement made Buffalo home for several years, while other leaders from the Fenians to the Land Leaguers to the Sinn Fein frequently visited. In recent years, Buffalo and the Ward have not been a top destination for prominent Irish politicians and activists to visit; however, on March 15, 2008, Gerry Adams, president of the political wing of Sinn Fein, came to Buffalo after an invitation from U.S. Congressman Brian Higgins to speak to the community. In his speech at the Irish Center in South Buffalo, he urged the participants not to "forget your Irishness" and he thanked the Irish of Buffalo for their support over the years for the Irish cause of freedom; he also urged them to continue the fight until Ireland was truly united.[32] In addition, Adams reminded the audience that 150 years before, on March 17th, 1858, the Irish Republican Brotherhood (the Fenians) was founded. He added that the Fenians in 1866 did fail in their attempt to take Canada, but "they made a go of it." This towering 20th century Irish political figure marched that year with Congressman Brian Higgins in the "Old Neighborhood" Parade in the Ward, not the Delaware Avenue parade.

The notorious Beach or Seawall community, although officially disbanded in 1917, was still home to stubborn squatters for many years thereafter. The Beach community lost its last resident in 1953 when George Donovan passed away; his home was on the beach near South Michigan Avenue.[33] Donovan, a cousin of "Wild Bill" Donovan, was born in 1899 and served in both World War I and II. His home was torn down in 1953 just two weeks after his death, and the Beach community which had survived for over 120 years was gone. Some monument to this hidden but vital community should be considered to remember its residents.

Around 2000, the transformation of Buffalo's Outer Harbor, partially located in the Old First Ward, began. In 1998, then freshman New York State Assemblyman Brian Higgins was able to secure $1 million dollars from the Speaker of the New York State Assembly to revamp a decrepit parcel of land just south of the Ward. With the money, Higgins quickly enacted a plan for a park, a fishing pier, a boardwalk, and a beach. The park is called Gallagher Beach after the former NFTA president Raymond Gallagher. While it was a modest beginning, it proved to be a catalyst for other waterfront projects such as the Outer Harbor Parkway. Most importantly, Higgins was able to show that the waterfront did not need a grand plan, but rather a series of small steps to improve access and create recreational spaces. As a U.S. Congressman, Higgins oversaw the creation of an $80 million parkway along the waterfront that has reconnected the First Ward to downtown Buffalo and to the Southtowns. The new parkway replaces the confusing, maze-like Fuhrmann Boulevard and should assist the development of recreational and commercial uses for the abandoned waterfront area.

There are also environmental success stories in the Ward. One of these is Times Beach, an area along Lake Erie that was a U.S. Army Corp of Engineering dumpsite for sediments dredged from the lake. In 1991, the City of Buffalo declared the area a nature preserve and since then the aquatic and wildlife species have flourished. Strategically located off Lake Erie, this 50-acre retreat is a prime bird migrating area where more than 220 species of birds have been observed.[34] First Warders and other Buffalonians can now enjoy it.

Efforts are also underway to clean up the historic Buffalo River. In recent years, bank stabilization and dredging have been instituted to help renew the river.[35] Some of these efforts have led to both a return of birds and fish species and to safer recreational activities along the river such as kayaking and canoeing. Buffalo Niagara Riverkeeper, an organization that seeks to protect Buffalo's waterways, has plans for more remediation of the Buffalo River past Hamburg Street toward South Buffalo. As a result of the reduction in pollution, the Buffalo River is once again a passageway to spawning areas for Great Lakes fish and a nursery for larval and young fish.[36]

In 2009, $16 million was allocated to help clean up the 55-acre site that Buffalo Color, a dye manufacturer, utilized for over 100 years.[37] Unfortunately, the land and the river adjacent to the plant are heavily contaminated. In addition to this effort, there is a Buffalo River Restoration Project that calls for remediation of certain sections of the river. According to the project leaders, the two sections of the Buffalo River that are the most polluted are the section from Katherine Street to South Park Avenue (near Lee Street), and the section along the City Ship Canal.[38] The U.S. Environmental Protection Agency, the Buffalo Niagara Riverkeeper, the New York State Department of Environmental Conservation, and the U.S. Army Corps of Engineers are working together to tackle the pollution problems of the river. Their efforts, which started in the spring of 2011, focus on remediating contaminated sediments, restoring wildlife habitats, improving public access, and improving water quality.[39]

The vast industrial and maritime opportunities that existed along the waterfront in Buffalo during the 19th and 20th century are drastically diminished, resulting in a changing demographic. In 2007, the population of the Old First Ward was about 1,963 people, even though the area includes slightly more landmass than the original boundaries of the First Ward. This number stands in striking contrast to the peak population of about 17,000 First Ward residents in 1910.[40] Recent censuses continue to show a more diverse ethnic mix in the Old First Ward including growing African American and Hispanic populations now living alongside an aging Irish and Polish population. There is good reason to hope that there is a strong foundation in place to support a strong residential community that can enjoy a healthier quality of life than that which existed during the Ward's industrial heyday.

Conclusion

Today, in its streets and saloons, you will still hear debates over the physical boundaries of the Ward—whether or not such and such a street belonged to the First Ward. But the First Ward was more than a geographical area in the city of Buffalo. One Ward resident, Thomas Connors, explained that the "boundaries of the First Ward were more spiritual than they were geographical."[41] Another descendant of the Ward, the prominent novelist Roger Dooley, suggested that the Ward was not a place or geographical area but "a way of life, a state of mind."[42] Finally, one news reporter claimed that, "sentimentally, it [the Ward] extended much farther out Elk St., and took in St. Stephen's and parts of St. Patrick's parishes, including the "Valley," a group of homes situated between two viaducts."[43]

Whatever its essence or boundaries, there are certainly other interesting neighborhoods in Buffalo. None, however, have endured with such continuity for as long as the Old First Ward. For most of its 170-year history, this working-class neighborhood was home to mostly Irish Catholic immigrants, providing these vulnerable residents and their descendant a supportive network. As a result of their geographical isolation and disadvantaged economic situation, these residents came together to raise the prospects of the entire group. Noble and ignoble politicians used their power and influence to hand out civil service jobs to improve the conditions of their constituents. Priests and sisters lovingly dedicated their lives to educating the children and caring for the sick and poor. Leaders in the labor movement struggled mightily to protect the interests of the workers while the occasional celebrity athlete, such as Jimmy Slattery, generously shared his wealth with those in need. The fierce loyalty of First Warders caused them to shun those who turned against the group for their own benefit, such as Fingy Conners during the Great Strike of 1899. Sometimes their isolationism caused them to mistrust outsiders and their strong desire to improve their lot led some to turn a blind eye to abuses in the political and civil service realm. But they always shared a collective will to move the community and its members forward.

No one knows what the Ward will look like in thirty years. We do know that its past has been inspiring. Irish, German, Italian, and Polish immigrants arrived in the Old First Ward with very little. They were thrown into backbreaking jobs along the waterfront, forced to work for poor wages and unforgiving bosses. With the help of each other, their extended and immediate families, the Catholic Church, labor organizations, and homegrown political leaders, these poor immigrants managed to improve their lot and that of their children. They survived horrific lake storms, towering elevator fires, cholera outbreaks, labor unrest and violence, the unsuccessful Fenian invasion, heavy losses in the Civil War and both World Wars, and the devastating effects of the St. Lawrence Seaway project. Still this same group of men and women produced a future Archbishop, the founder of the OSS, two world champion boxers, two champion rowers, an entertainment genius, a legion of savvy politicians, and the longest serving mayor of Buffalo. These downtrodden immigrants asked for little, received even less, but contributed greatly to our city and our nation.

On that crisp autumn day in Buffalo in 1842, along the banks of the Buffalo Creek, did Joseph Dart ever envision the history that would enfold in the First Ward as a result of the technological revolution brought about his grain elevator? The story of the Old First Ward is not finished; it remains to be written by the next generation.

APPENDICES

APPENDICES

Appendix A — First Ward Relatives of the Author Mentioned in this Book

John Brinkworth - *Great-great-great-grandfather*
Daniel Driscoll - *Great-great-great-grandfather*
Julie Driscoll - *Great-great-great-grandmother*
Timothy Bohen - *Great-great-grandfather*
Mary Driscoll Bohen - *Great-great-grandmother*
Daniel Bohen - *Great-grandfather*
Mollie Roche Bohen - *Great-grandmother*
Joe Bohen - *Grandfather*
Cornelius Coughlin - *Great-great-uncle*
Earl Coughlin - *Great-great-uncle*
James Roche - *Great-great-great-grandfather*
Patrick Roche - *Great-great-grandfather*
Sister Edmunda Roche - *Great-great-aunt*
Father Ed Roche - *Great-great-uncle*
Father Bill Roche - *Distant cousin*

Appendix B — Nicknames

Margaret "Butsy" Allman
"Muckle" Allman
William "Willy" Andrews
Ken "Spook" Ashburn
"Sharper" Ashe
Ignatius "Iggy" Banko
"Gimp" Bannister
"Twister" Bannister
John "Butch" Barrett
Pat "Buddy" Barrett
Eddie "Adolf" Barron
"Scoop" Barry
Donny "Don-O" Barry
"Cuckoo" Baynes
Roy "Rubber Leg's" Bays

Al "Elmer" Benzow
Ronnie "Bibs" Bieber
Jackie "Boner" Bienko
Jimmy "Binks" Bienko
Ken "Bertha" Bienko
Darren "Casper" Black
Donald "Peanut" Black
Jackie "Blackie" Black
James "Tita" Black
Joe "Jo-Jo" Black
Jimmy "Nutsy" Bodkin
"Swickey" Boeckel
"Putty" Bohen
Francis "Fry" Bohen
"Rubber Nose" Boland

"Ace" Bonner

Francis "Bud" Bonnes

"Chili" Bouquard

"Red" Bouquard

Bobby & Jimmy "Bogey" Bouquard

Cyril "Ziggy" Bouquard

Dick "Dicker" Bouquard

John "Angelo" Bouquard

John "Eggsy" Bouquard

Dickie "Bo" Bowe

Bobby "Egg Head" Brady

"K-O" Brennan

Bobby "Boobs" Brill

Freddy "Hoss" Brill

Jack "Swab's" Brill

Mickey "Twig" Brill

Mike "Pidge" Brill

"Sailor" Brinkworth

Brian "Fritter" Brittzzalro

"Pooch" Buckley

Stan "Bootsie" Buczkowski

"Duffy" Buggers

Tom "Bud" Bulger

"Turkey Leg's" Burke

John "Duke" Burke

Mike "Pickles" Burke

Ray "Bushelhead" Burke

Eddie "Kutcher Burke" Burkowski

Gene "Sonny Burke" Burkowski

Joe & Donny "Burke" Burkowski

Tony "Chief" Burvid

Bill "Windy" Byrnes

George "Byrnsie" Byrns

"Twitters" Cadigan

Gerry "Critter" Caetano

Joe "Mika" Callahan

Ray "Skip" Canazzi

"Ma & Dope" Carr

Jimmy "Jimbo" Carr

Winifred "Winnie" Carr

Jereimiah "Jerry" Carroll

John "Red" Carroll

"Pussy" Carroll

Michelle "Mimi" Cassidy

Mike "Ky-Bo" Cassidy

Bobby-Mike "Cats" Catanzaro

Bruno-Jimmy "Cats/Simon" Catanzaro

Frankie "Cat's" Catanzaro

Tony & Mickey "Cat's" Catanzaro

Bill "Weepers" Cavanaugh

Steve "Tucker" Cavanaugh

Steve "Wick's" Cavannaugh

"Hi-Lo" Cavern

Kathleen "Red" Chilcott

Jack "Chickie" Chillicott, Sr./Jr

"Spirits" Clark

Bill "Willy Lavin" Cleary

Edward "Ginger" Cleary

"Little Ginger" Cleary

Roger "Rogie Lavin" Cleary

Bill "B" Coad

"Cooney" Colern

Charlie "Cha's" Comerford

Ed "Buzzy" Comerford

Mike "Mickey" Comerford

Charles "Dummy Burn's" Comerford, Sr

David "Cheesey" Concheiro

William "Fingy" Conners

"Crowbar" Connors

Dave "Buddy" Connors

Frank "Unk" Connors

Henry "Corky" Connors

Jimmy "Flab/Bull" Connors

John "2 Cent" Connors

Tommy "T" Connors

Tony "Paul Revere" Connors

"Rosey" Conway

"Rosie" Conway

Billy "Coach" Conway

Jimmy "Buck/Snake" Conway

G. William "Bill" Coppola

Tommy "Corky" Corcoran

"Red Knee" Cotter

Jim "Chaw" Coughlin

Dick "Scratch" Courtney

Bobby "Star's" Crawford

Jim "Tart" Crotty

Joe "Froey" Cultrara

"Sham" Cummings

Ed "Ebbie" Cummings

Dan "Diver" Cunningham

Eddie "Snake" Cunningham

Dickie "Skitch" Czekai

"Gas Pipe" Daley

"Bean's" Danahy

Jimmy "Scratch" Danieu

Pat "Pete" Danieu, Jr

"Dewey" Daugherty

Jim "Ding Dong" Daugherty

Patrick "Poochie" Daugherty

Andy "Clyde" Deichman

Jackie "D" Dejac

Donny "Ducky" Diehl

Murray "Sonny" Diehl

"Preacher" Diggins

Mike "Milt" Diggins

"Swing" Diggens

Louie "Stogie" Dingleday

Phil "Curley" Dissek

"Stitch's" Dodgers

Paul "Demo" Dominick

Jackie "Irish Jackie" Donnelly

Danny "Donuts" Donovan

Dickie "Erk" Donovan

Jim "Big Jimmy" Donovan

Gen. Bill "Wild Bill" Donovan

Mary "Big Mare" Donovan

"Hunky" Dorries

"Ibby" Downey

Joe "Nick" Downey

Jack "Beaver/Bucky" Downing

"Lemon" Doyle

Franny "Pickles" Drewiega

"Bright Eyes" Driscoll

"GA" Driscoll

Dennis "Gah" Driscoll

Florence "Flurry" Driscoll

Jack "Sam" Driscoll

Stan "Sonny Boy" Dudek

"Rubber Nose" Duggan

Frank "Sheep's Head" Dziedzic

John "Spike" Dzjolga

Vince "Beany" Edbauer

Jack "Spider" Eggloff

Louis "Louie" Eggloff

"Chicken" Ellis

George "Ace" Ellis

Tommy "T-Bone" Ellis

Victor "Vicky" Essex

"Chickie" Evans

"Goosie" Evans

John "Goosie" Evans

"Whitey" Everett

"Sheep" Evoy

Dennis "Bunky" Evoy

Tommy "Butchie" Evoy

Tom "Duke" Farry

Tommy "Big Tom" Feeney

William "Mickey" Feeney

Bobby "Biby" Felschow

Hank "Fel" Felschow

Henry "Bootie" Felschow

Jimmy "Flip" Felschow

Norman "Nafa" Felschow

Ray-Jerry-Jackie "Foo-Foo" Felschow

Robert "Boulder" Felschow, Sr

Don "Irish" Ferron

Tommy "Hank" Finucane

"Berry" Fitzgerald

"Kegsy" Fitzgerald

Edmund "Emmy" Fitzgerald

Francis "Lump" Fitzgerald

"Hacker" Fitzgerald

Paul "Fitz/Beansie" Fitzgerald

"Shorty" Fitzgerald

Mike "Beaver" Fitzpatrick

Florence "Flossy" Flanigan

Steven "Tony" Flanigan

Jackie "Flash" Flood

John "Pi-Jo" Flood

Mike "Hook Nose" Floo

Pat "Floody" Flood

Jimmy "Bucket's" Flood, Jr.

Jim "Dusty" Flood, Sr

Laverne "Sonny" Fluker

Yavonne "Vonny" Fluker

Dickie "Angel/Scuff" Foran

Gail "Weiner" Francis

James "Chickenshit" Francis

Freddy "Popeye" Frankhauser

Jerry "Mousey" Gaikowski

Gary "Bugger's" Galente

Donny "Bozo" Gales

"Putsie" Gallagher

Jimmy "Gigy" Gallagher

"Putsie "Gallagher

"Abe" Galvin

Eddie "Gaz" Gasuik

"Gee" Gavin

"Huck" Geary

Harold "Jappo" George

Red "Bumper" Gervics

Tony "Blinky" Gervics

Jackie "Pig" Gilberts

Harold "Honey" Girdlestone

"Buffalo" Gleason

Charles "Buffalo" Gleason

Bruce "Moe" Gould

George "Ortsie" Gould

"Mole" Graham

Bill "Mole" Graham

Bob "Waldo" Graham

Ed "Noodles" Graham

Jimmy "Otto" Graham

Mary "Peach" Graham

"Noodles" Graham

Pat "Potatoes" Graham

"Snarly Puss" Graham

Tom "Ducer" Graham

Vincent "Pape" Graham

Bobby "Ole" Grande

Gerry "Bootsie" Grandy

Dan "Granny" Granville

John "Yoxie" Granville

Jimmy "Mayor" Griffin

Jimmy "Pop" Griffin

Joey "Hammer" Griffin

Mary "Susie" Griffin

Tommy "Rocco" Griffin Sr./Jr.

Tommy "Griff" Griffin

Eddie "Kip" Griffiths

Bob "Cap" Guillow

Evelyn "Sis" Guise

Walter "Beaver" Guise

Walter "Gussie" Guise

William "Whitey" Guise

Leo "Sonny" Guise, Jr.

"Niecey" Hackemer

John "Boxy" Hackemer

Charles "Dolly" Hahn

"Dolly" Hahn

Frankie "Button's/Dutch" Hahn

Gary "Hershey" Hahn

George "Yika" Hahn

Henry "Puddin" Hahn

Joe "Shorty" Hahn

Kevin "Capt" Harmon

Joe "Beaver" Harrigan

Ed "Brownie" Harris

Bill "Willy" Hartnett

Dickie "Ace" Hassett

Frank "Bear" Hassett

Jackie "Ace" Hassett

Jereimiah "Jerry" Hassett

Jerry "Abe" Hassett

Jim "Happy" Hassett

Jimmy "Jaw's" Hassett

Joe " Jo-Jo" Hassett

Lorraine "Lolli" Hassett

Donald "Ducko" Hayes

Dave "Hazen the Raisin"Hazen

Herbert "Salty" Heering

Mary Ann "Dinker's" Heidinger

Paul "Paul T" Heidinger

"Dutchy" Helms

"La" Hennigan

Tommy "Tommy-Joe" Hennigan

Jackie "Jace" Higgins

Mike "Monkey" Higgins

Paul "Hig's" Higgins

Tom "Slim" Higgins

"Puddin Head" Hoare

Donny "Tucker" Hoare

Patrick "Fish" Hoare

Ritchie "Duck" Hoare

Timmy "Shecky" Hoare

Ann "Huff" Hoffstetter

Mary "Muddles" Hoffstetter

Robert "Ollie" Hoffstetter

Tom "Chinky" Hoffstetter

Mike "Boo-Boo" Holleran

"Happy" Hoolihan

"Ball" Horace

Dan "Butchie" Horrigan

George "Doc" Howell

Bertha "Bert Guise" Hyde

Jim "Boey" Hynes

John "Dutch" Irish

"Yuckle" Jacobson

Harry "Bongo" Jacobson

"Ray" Lawley James

Dennis "Jazz" Jasen

"Heinz" Jennings

"Oysters" Joyce

Billy "Buddy" Kaiser

"Dwarf" Kane

Eddie "Kaz" Kania

Frank "Butch" Kania

Jim "Debbie" Keefe

"Torch" Kelly

"Sonny" Kemp

Theresa "Sissy" Kemp

Charlie "Goosie" Kenefick

Don "Stinky" Kenefick

"Bing" Kennedy

Jack "Spider" Kennedy

Patrick "PJ" Kennedy

Jack "Butchie" Kennefick

Eddie "Captain" Knight

Jackie "Knoxie" Knox

Maureen "Moe" Knox

Patricia "Queenie" Kobus

Charlie "Whitey" Kolodziej

Ed "Sam" Kolodziej, Sr. & Jr.

"Lefty" Kulzak

John "Ju-Ju" Kurdziel

Sta "Hound-Dog" Kurdziel

George "Big George" Laettner

Ed "Little Egg's" Lannon

Jerry "La" Lannon

Pat "Bronco" Lannon

Billy "Swede" Larson

Robert "Louie" LaRusch

Harry "Budso" Lauber

Tommy "Tomso" Lauber

Harry "Goose" Lauber, Sr.

Bill "Bounce" Lawler

James "I.O." Leary, Sr.

Bill "Moose" Leight

Bobby "Unk" Leight

Jimmy "Red" Lickfield

Wayne "Butchie" Lickfield

"Jigg's" Lillis

"Jigg's" Lillis

Michael "Jimmy" Lillis

"Sis" Lonerghan

Danny "Lump" Lukomski

"Apples" Lynch

"Willy" Billy Lynch

Francis "Curly" Lyons

Bill "Big Billy" Mackey

Noreen "Twiggy" Madigan

Slyvester "Jud" Madigan

"Blackie" Mahoney

Billy "Flash" Mahoney

"Wig Wig" Makowski

Charlie "Capt" Manley, Sr.

David "Spic" Mann

Donald "Mikey" Mann

Ed "Eddie-Boy" Mann

James "Dinny" Mann

John "Scud" Mann

Patrick "Paddy" Mann

William "Tuffy" Mann

Alice "Bubbles" Marsh

Charlie "Spike" Marsh

"Minuch" Martin

Tom "Shakey" Masterson

Phil "Flip" Mazur

Jack "Baker Boy" Mazurek

Billy "Mac" McAndrews

"Sauce" McBride

Tom "Fried Cakes" McBride

Will "Daddum's" McBride

"Chicky" McCarthy

Art "Johnny" McCarthy

Donny "Mac" McCarthy

Henry "Hank" McCarthy

Joe "Big Joe" McCarthy

Joe "Boss" McCarthy

John "Midge" McCarthy

"Midge" McCarthy

Mike "Mac" McCarthy

Samuel "Sammy" McCarthy

William "Genie" McCarthy

Jerry "Moo" McDonald

Michael "Mickey" McDonald

Mike "Magoot's" McElligott

"Dirty Shirt" McGee

Eddie "Hootsie" McGowan

Frank "Dino" McGowan

Mike "Hippo" McGrath

"Elgie" McGuire

Eddie "EJ" McGuire

Richard "Joll's" McGuire

Jimmy "Nipper" McHale

"Onions" McIrney

Larry "Tex" McLaughlin

Florence "Babe" McLauglin

Tim "Yazee" McLauglin

"Big Bud" McMahon

"Little Bud" McMahon

"Red" McMahon

"Stretch" McMahon

John "Tosh" McNamara

Raymond "Ray Mac" McNamara

Steve "Steveo" McNamara

Ray & Jack "Mick" McNaughton

Eddie "Snooky" McNeight

Mary "Bunny" McNeight

"Pecker Head" McNerny

"Muck" Meany

Tim "Timmer" Meegan

Florence "Toot's" Michaels

Tommy "Mooner" Michaels

Mike "Bunno" McGrath, Sr.

Harry "Milo" Miller

Eddie "Butchie" Milligan

Jack "Dutch" Milligan

Jimmy "Moe" Milligan

Billy "Bullet" Minsterman

Joe "Luke" Minsterman

Vince "D-D" Miranda

"Gooky" Moesch

August "Gussie" Moesch

John "High School Harry/Red" Montondo

Tony "Moe" Morlock

Collette "Sugar" Mosca

Eddie "Oscar/Neck" Mosca

Freddy "Hot Fudge" Mosca

Joe "Muck" Mueckl

"KO" Mullen

Bill "Moon" Mullen

"Curly" Mullins

"Hickory" Mullins

"K-O" Mullins

Jimmy "Moon" Mullins

Kathleen "Chatty" Mullins

Jerry "Moose" Murawski

"Beans" Murphy

Jimmy "Mur" Murray

Ed "Cesar" Myers

Jack "Jacko" Myers

John "Commissioner" Myers

Kathryn "Doo" Myers

Charles "Butchie" Naffky

Frank "Nugget's" Nagowski

Dave "Goose" Needham

Jack "Sash" Needham

Jimmy "Needles" Needham

Pat "Unk Fester" Needham

Florence "Nunny" Neff

Larry "Spic" Neff

Myron "One Arm Bandit" Neff

"Spit's" Neville

Tommy "Noot's" Noonan

John & Jerry "Noey" Nostrant

"Hosenose" Nowadly

Joe "Snidely" Nowadly

Walter "Loge" Nowadly

Jack "Kegga" O'Brian

"Harp" O'Brien

Ray "Tippy Toe's" O'Brien

Don "Mooch" O'Connor

"Flip" O'Connor

Gene "Weiner's" O'Connor

Eddie "Weanie" O'Donnell

George "Red Eye" O'Donnell, Sr.

"Red Eye" O'Donnel

"Ice" O'Grady

Bob "Hump" O'Leary

Jack "Little Emmett" O'Leary

Jackie "Big Jackie" O'Leary

Aileen "Hook" O'Neill

Dan "Ray/Phantom" O'Neill

Irv-Teddy-Mike-Gene "Ozzie" Overdorf

Wally "Sonny/Pecky" Parrot

Bill "Will Eye" Patton

Betty "Fuzzy" Pelow

Bob "Butchie" Pelow

"Acre's" Pendergast

"Tap's" Pendergast

"Sambo" Perkins

Tom "Cy" Perkins

John "Jinx" Perrone

"Chisel Chin" Piatko

Frank "Butchie" Piotrowski

Paul "Bone's" Pitcher

Marty "Murph" Polo

Dave "Spook" Powers

Ed "Junior" Powers

Ritchie "Wolf" Powers

Ralph "JT" Powers, Jr.

Bill "Berry Nose" Powers, Sr.

Andy "Archie" Procknal

Dick "Prock" Procknal

Frank "Bozo" Procknal

Johnny "Yonko" Procknal

Mike "Mugsy" Procknal

Richard "Murph" Procknal

"Buttsy" Quinn

Jimmy "Twister" Quinn

Joe "Hi-Lo" Quinn

Lavern "Vern" Ragolin

"Pickles" Ransford

Bob "No Ass"/"Rance" Ransford

Joe "Scully" Ransford

Peter "Petey" Ratchuk

"Pig Iron" Redden

Tom "Tucker" Reddington

"Bo" Redmond

"Raisin" Redmond

Eddie "Ed-Boy" Redmond

Dave "Chum" Regan

Dick "Rocky" Regan

Jackie "Yixie" Regan

Teddy "Silver Fox" Regan

Timmy "Mouse" Regan

Tommy "Mother" Regan

Pat "Ortie" Richards

"Pork Chop's" Ring

"Tootsy" Rinker

Billy "Diapers" Riordan

Dan "Peanuts" Riordan

Eddie "Pinky" Roberts

Dick "Dickle's" Robinson

Tom "Cooney" Robinson

Mike "Forty" Rogers

Bobby "Rivets" Ryan

Dickie "Smiley" Samaelish

Frank "Moosey" Santora

Pat "Sarge" Sargent

"Irish" Bobby Scanlon

Jimmy "Murph" Scanlon

John "Scanoots" Scanlon

Mike "Mickey" Scanlon

Joe "Left My Heart" Schaeffer

Dennis "Ducky" Schollard

Joe "Yogie" Schollard

Cernas "Niecey" Schuta

Joe "Kanee" Schuta

Kenny "Buddha" Schuta

Lynch Gene "Scrooge" Schuta

"Rooster" Shanahan

Eddie "Slugsie" Shaner

Stewart "Stu/Stuie" Shanks

John "Bruno" Shaw

John "Normie" Shea

Edward "Pork" Sheehan

Jimmy "Cigar" Sheehan

"Pork" Sheehan

William "Blue-Eyed Billy" Sheehan

"Ducky" Shine

"Red" Shine

Ed "Chester" Shine

John "Pete" Shine

Tommy & Jackie "Spook" Shine

Hugh "Dewey" Shreehnan

Jimmy "Dino" Simmons

Bob "Ripper" Simonick

Eugene "Butch" Simonick

Mike "Choo-ch" Simonick

Paul "Kielbasa" Simonick

John "Jamaican" Skinner

Julia "Pumpkin" Skinner

Dickie "Bunny Ears" Slattery

Jimmy "Slats" Slattery

Jack "Slice" Sleshinger

Frank "Moose" Slomba

Art "Jr." Smith

Danny "Socko" Smith

Dennis "Shine" Smith

Don "Bughead" Smith

Eddie "Carl" Smith

Jimmy "Jim-Boy" Smith

Joe "Champagne Joe" Smith

Welton "Tennessee" Smith

"Butch" Smolinski

Ed "Pie" Snyder

Paul "Snip" Snyder

Robert "Ra Ra" Snyder

Eddie "Pelican" Stack

Albert "Peanuts" Stasio

Clarissa "Mickey" Stasio

William "Bubble's" Stasio

Albert "Crazy Al" Stelmach

Pat & Mike "Stitty" Stitt

George "Rooster" Stranahan, Sr./Jr.

Dan "Suke" Suchan

"Busy" Sullivan

Daniel "Bizzy" Sullivan

Eddie "Wingy Ding" Sullivan

Joe "Popcorn" Sullivan

Joe "Slow Joe" Sullivan

John "Socks" Sullivan

Mike "Silky" Sullivan

Paul "Sully" Sullivan

"Snooky" Sullivan

"Tailspin" Sullivan

Tommy "Tailspin" Sullivan

William "Willow/Zev" Sullivan

Bobby "Doodle Bug" Sumbrum

Jim "Buck" Sumbrum

Justin "Buzzy" Sumbrum

Joe "Sid" Suto

Joe "Fuzzy" Swiatek

Eleanor "Porky" Szaras

Jimmy "Tunie" Szaras

Joe "Zeke" Szczygiel

Tom "Cosmo" Szczygiel

John "Sud's" Szewczyk

Eugene "Pie Face" Taylor

Tom "Rube" Thompson

Tom "Rube" Thompson

"Tee-O" Travis

Bill "Poop" Travis

Bud "Nucka" Travis

B. John "Brownie" Tutuska

Dave "The Barber" Tutuska

Joe "Fuzzy" Tututska

"Butch" Vastola

Carmen "Mickey" Vastola

Jack "Squash" Walsh

Mary Alice " Red" Walsh

Pauly "Mombo" Walsh

Red "The Barber" Walsh

Eddie "Weasel" Warren

Jimmy "Fritzy" Watson

"Foxy" Weir

"Minnow" Whalen

Jerry "Big Jerry" Whalen

John "Capt" Whalen

JK "Joe" Whitey

Francis "Duke" Wiemar

"Monk" Woods

Stan "Stogie" Wojtowich

"Jigg's" Wright

Henry "Big Hank" Wrona

Elizabeth "Bootsie" Yuskiw

Kenny "Schnuazer" Zabawa

Ronnie "609" Zamer

Walter "Ollie" Zasada

Appendix C — *Remembering Some of our First Ward Born Clergy*

Father Gene Bagen

Father Hugh Boyle

Father Tom Conway

Father Joe Coughlin

Father Donny Devine

Father Juvenal Ellis

Father Donny Fitzgerald

Father Billy Fitzpatrick

Father Billy Frankhauser

Father Earl Gardner

Father Danny Grosso

Father Paul Herbert, U.S.A.F.

Father Lee Mays

Father Larry Milby

Father Art Sullivan

Appendix D — *Some of our Favorite Bartenders*

Bruno Catanzaro

Hi-Lo Cavern

Eddie Barron

Dick Cotter

Bart Crotty

Mary Donovan

Joe Boulanger

Jimmy Foran, Sr.

Jimmy Flood, Sr. & Jr.

Abe Galvin

Joe – Jimmy – Tommy Griffin

Frank Hahn

Ray Hassett

Paul Heidinger

Jimmy Hoare, Sr.

Eddie Kania

Mary Kennedy

Andy Kull

Billy Lewis

Genie – Boss – Sammy McCarthy

Pat McGinty

Mike McGrath

John Montondo

John Nostrant

Jinx Pirone

Billy Reardon

Joe Shaver

Frank Slomba

Joe Smith

Joe Szczgiel

Ma Tutuska

Joe Whitey

Thank God for the Priest's and the Bartender's –
they both served us very well!

INDEX

PHOTO CREDITS

A special thanks to the following people who provided photos or assisted in the photo selection process for this book:

Paul Pasquarello, Cynthia Van Ness, Dan Dilandro, Jack Mèssmer, Joan Scahill, Barb Sullivan, Bert Hyde, Peggy Szczygiel, Kathy Best, Jack Montondo, Gene Witkowski, Jim Shine, Tim Bohen, Kimberly Blessing, Bob Martin, Amy Doyle, and Colleen Bohen.

1. Collection of Buffalo and Erie County Historical Society, used by permission. Photos: the front cover photo, 7, 35, 46, 48, 49, 57, and 62.

2. Coll. Of Lower Lakes Marine Historical Society Photos: 2, 6, 8, 9, 10, 11, 12, 51, 52, 53, and 64.

3. Waterfront Memories and More Museum Photos: 29, 30, 34, 37, 40, 50, 54, 55, 56, and the chapters 10, 11 and 12 photos.

4. Library of Congress. Photos: 36 and the chapter 4 photo.

5. Massachusetts Commander Military Order of the Loyal Legion and the U.S. Army Military History Institute (MOLLUS) Photo: 16.

6. Courtesy of Buffalo State Archives & Special Collections (photos by Paul Pasquarello). Photos: 58, 59, 61, and 63.

7. Gene Witkowski Photos: 65 and 66.

ENDNOTES

In order to put in more photos, the endnotes and bibliography for this book can be found on my website: www.oldfirstward.com. Please visit the website for additional information on the First Ward.

To learn more about the First Ward, the Valley and Buffalo's waterfront, please visit Waterfront Memories and More Museum at 41 Hamburg Street, Buffalo, New York.

Inquires should be addressed to Timothy Bohen at tim@oldfirstward.com

ACKNOWLEDGEMENTS

There are so many people I have to thank and I apologize in advance for those who I may miss. I must thank Philip Nyhuis, my editor, who helped make my dry writing style palatable. Thanks for your encouragement and countless suggestions! Thanks to my wife Kimberly who has offered me unlimited support and ideas throughout this five-year journey—without her this project never would have been completed. Kimberly: "I promise we will finally have our Saturdays together again."

Thanks to my "girlfriends" at Waterfront Memories and More who provided the vast majority of content in this book, as well as their countless hours of proofreading for historical accuracy: Bertha (Bert) Guise-Hyde, Joan Graham-Scahill, Peggy May-Szczygiel, and Sue Lafko-Matteson. Thanks to Mike Catanzaro who filled in so many gaps in my story and contributed so many stories and lists of people. This story would have been incomplete without you. I owe a great deal of gratitude to Paul Pasquarello who generously contributed many of the photos in this book. And to my father, Tim Bohen, Sr., who read every chapter multiple times, gave me valuable advice, stories, and encouragement throughout these many years. This was a heck of a long project just to find out the correct spelling of our last name.

Many thanks to the following people who provided so many valuable stories and resources which made this project possible:

Collen Bohen, Peggy Redmond, Dan Redmond, Elizabeth Oldfield, Mary Alma Johnson Duggan, William Jenkins, Fred Brill, Judge John O'Donnell, Bernie O'Donnell, Jack Supple, Joe Bieron, Dan Starr, Sister Helen Parot, RSM, Sister Shelia Marie Walsh, Tom Krzeminski, Tom Higgins, Mary Dyczek, Jim Graham, Jim Shine, Donna Shine, Bill Murphy, Mary Murphy, Julie Cleary, Richard Szczygiel, Dan J. McCue, Jack Montondo, Dave Mann, Peggy Overdorf, Ed Patton, Jim McGeever, John Nash, Pat Regan, Frank Kowsky, Betsy Bohen, Brian Bohen, Kate Bohen, Barbara Sullivan, Donny Thompson, Joe Marren, David Bertuca, Tom Dixon, Ron Cozzi, Jerry Malloy, Kathy Best, Bill Lawley, Sr., Richard Donovan, Kathy Marren, Gene Overdorf, Jack Montondo, Mark Schroeder, Dennis Dargavel, Jack Messmer, Kathy Kelley, Geraldine Butler, Msgr. David Gallivan, Robert Blessing, Cynthia Van Ness, Joe Tomasulo, Gene Witkowski, and George "Chickie" Evans.

ABOUT THIS BOOK

Against the Grain tells the story of a group of mostly Irish immigrants who toiled in the hulls of grain ships and in other waterfront industries in an area called the First Ward of Buffalo, New York. The First Ward was a geographically isolated area of Buffalo primarily inhabited by settlers from the south and west of Ireland, but was also home to enough Germans, Poles, and Italians to make life even more interesting. This economically deprived area produced an abundance of historically important people including Fingy Conners, the largest private employer on the Great Lakes; Michael Shea, Buffalo's greatest entertainment showman; "Wild Bill" Donovan, the founding father of what became the CIA; John Sheehan, one-time Tammany Hall boss; Jimmy Slattery, the Light Heavyweight Champion of the World; and Jimmy Griffin, the longest serving mayor in Buffalo history. The stories of other lesser-known but equally important Ward residents such as Mike Quinn, Jack White, Algie McGuire, Roggie Lavin, Father Thomas Conway, the McCarthy brothers, and even Rick James are also told. Readers will also learn about historical events that Ward residents were thrust into such as the Tidal Wave of 1844, the Fenian Raid, violent railroad strikes, the Great Strike of 1899, the Tewksbury Disaster, and the opening of the St. Lawrence Seaway—the ultimate cause of the demise of Buffalo's waterfront economy.

ABOUT THE AUTHOR

Timothy Bohen is a business professional and amateur historian who lives in the city of Buffalo with his wife Kimberly. Various members of his paternal family (the Bohens, Driscolls, Roches, Brinkworths, and Coughlins) lived in the First Ward of Buffalo from 1849 to 1949.